YUKARI TAKINAMI

I WISH I COULD SAY "THANK YOU"

FAN FARE · PONENT MON

INDEX

CHAPTER 1

NO ONE LOOKS LIKE MOM

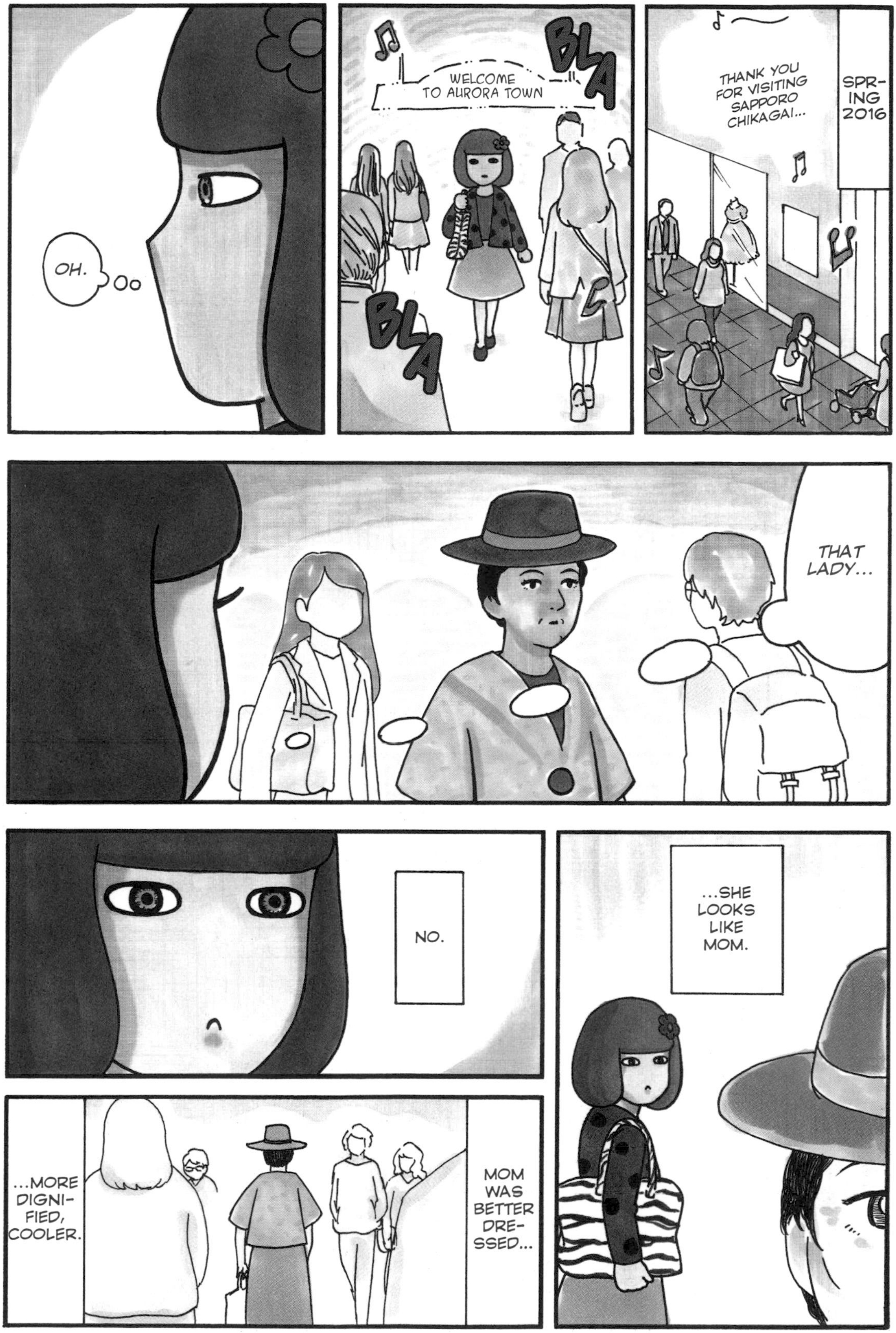
SPR-ING 2016
THANK YOU FOR VISITING SAPPORO CHIKAGAI...
BLA
WELCOME TO AURORA TOWN
BLA
OH.
THAT LADY...
...SHE LOOKS LIKE MOM.
NO.
MOM WAS BETTER DRE-SSED...
...MORE DIGNI-FIED, COOLER.

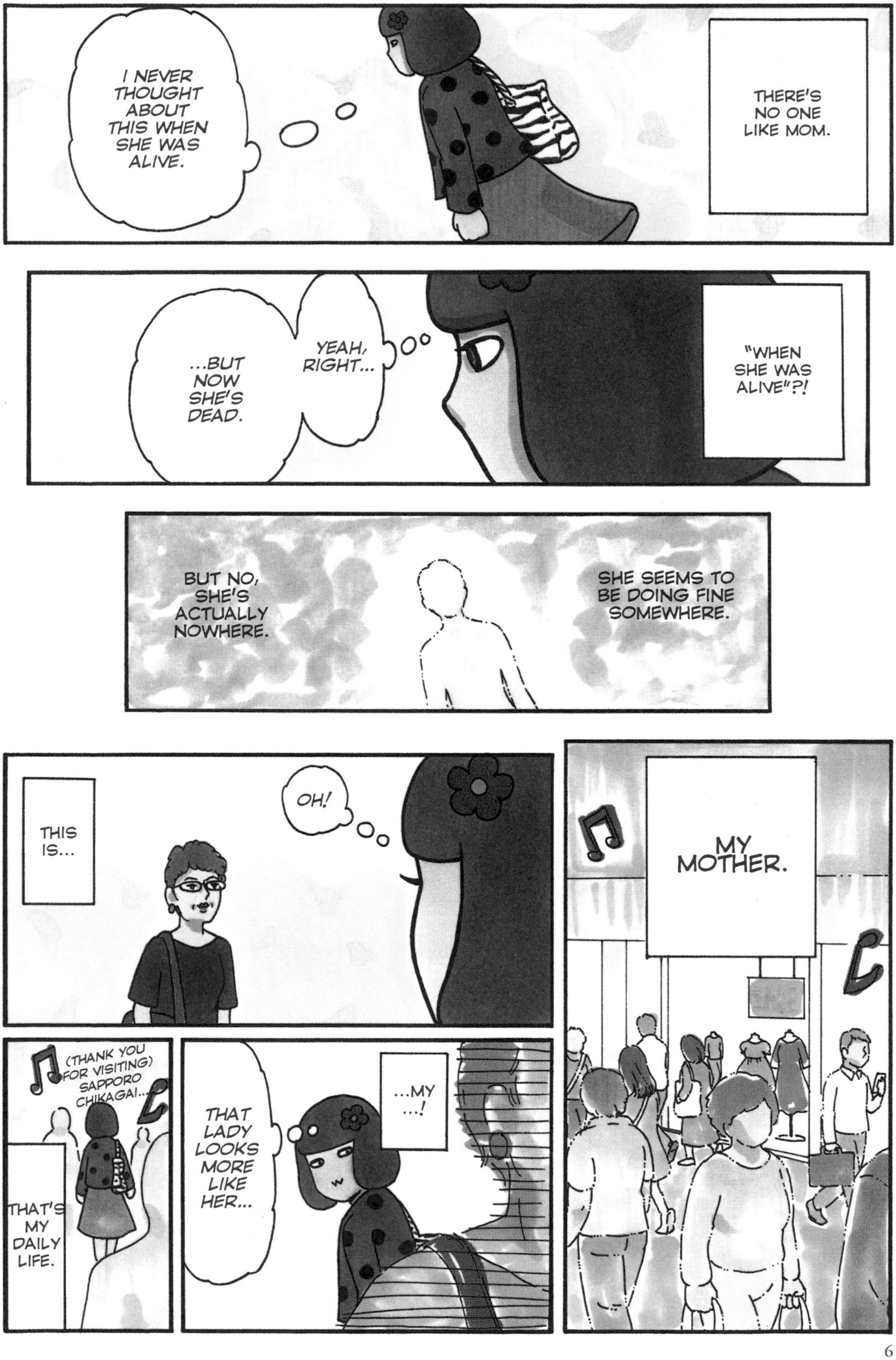
THERE'S NO ONE LIKE MOM.
I NEVER THOUGHT ABOUT THIS WHEN SHE WAS ALIVE.
"WHEN SHE WAS ALIVE"?!
YEAH, RIGHT...
...BUT NOW SHE'S DEAD.
SHE SEEMS TO BE DOING FINE SOMEWHERE.
BUT NO, SHE'S ACTUALLY NOWHERE.
MY MOTHER.
OH!
THIS IS...
...MY ...!
THAT LADY LOOKS MORE LIKE HER...
(THANK YOU FOR VISITING) SAPPORO CHIKAGAI...
THAT'S MY DAILY LIFE.

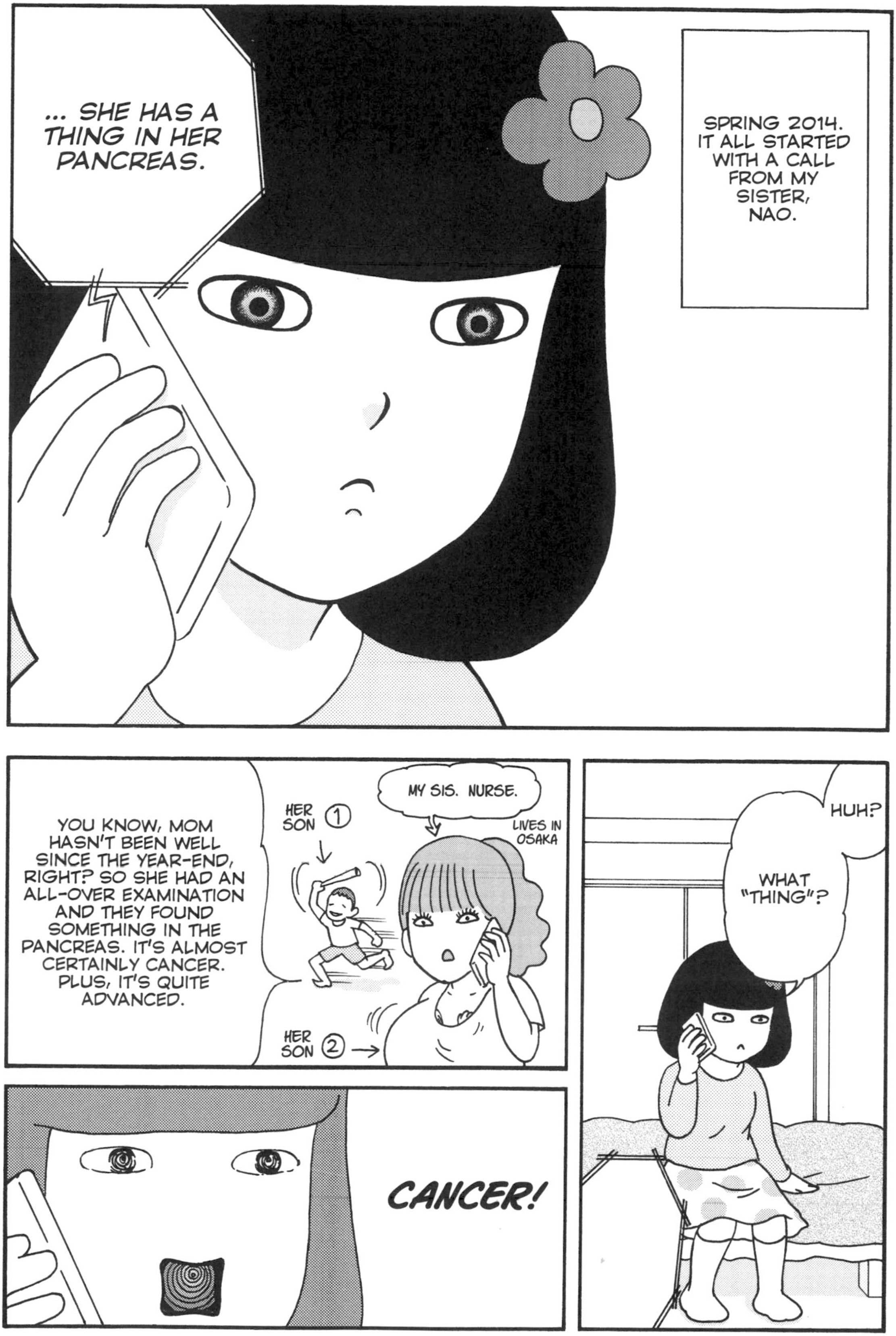
SPRING 2014. IT ALL STARTED WITH A CALL FROM MY SISTER, NAO.
... SHE HAS A THING IN HER PANCREAS.
HUH?
WHAT "THING"?
MY SIS. NURSE.
LIVES IN OSAKA
HER SON ①
YOU KNOW, MOM HASN'T BEEN WELL SINCE THE YEAR-END, RIGHT? SO SHE HAD AN ALL-OVER EXAMINATION AND THEY FOUND SOMETHING IN THE PANCREAS. IT'S ALMOST CERTAINLY CANCER. PLUS, IT'S QUITE ADVANCED.
HER SON ②
CANCER!

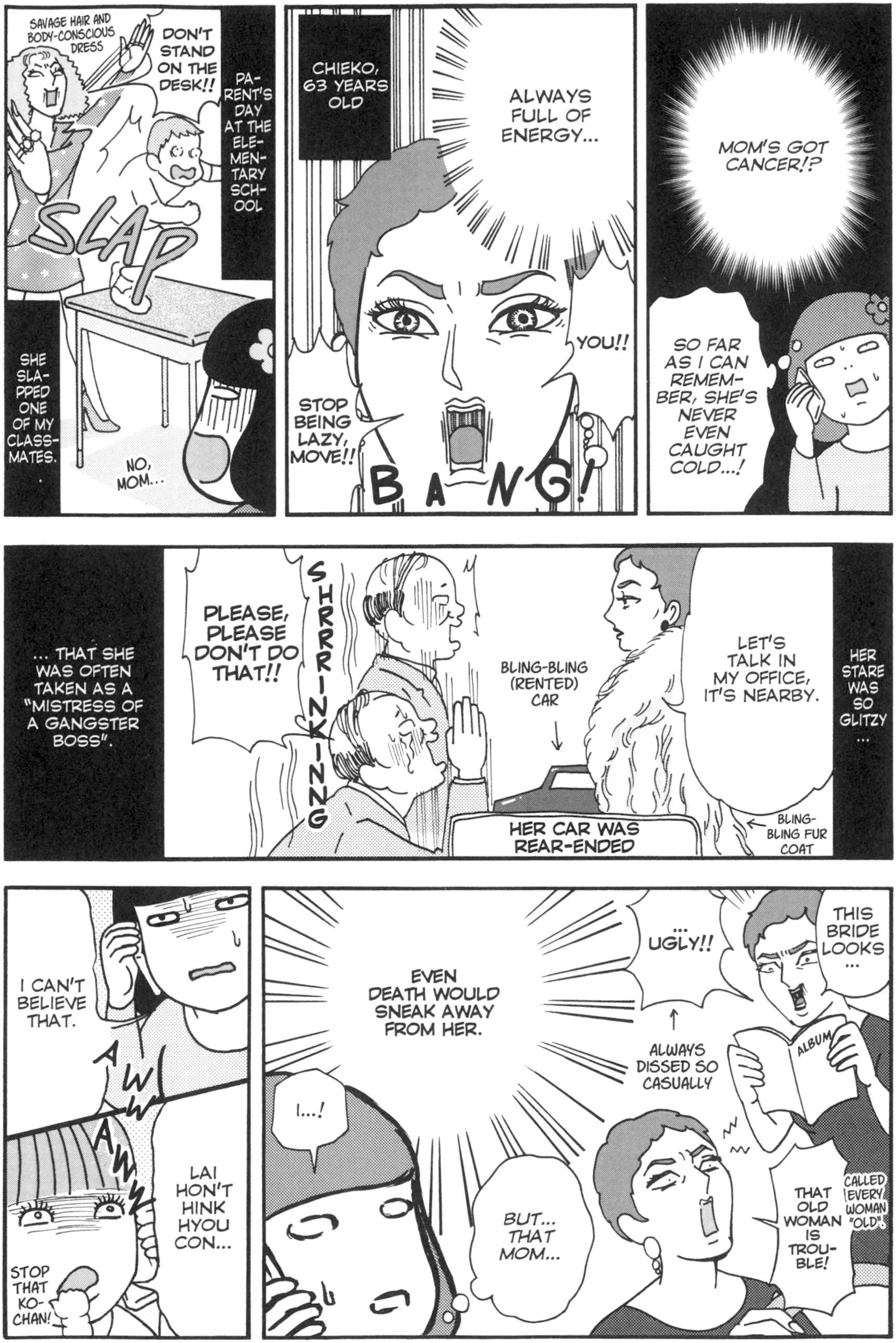
MOM'S GOT CANCER!?
SO FAR AS I CAN REMEMBER, SHE'S NEVER EVEN CAUGHT COLD...!
CHIEKO, 63 YEARS OLD
ALWAYS FULL OF ENERGY...
YOU!!
STOP BEING LAZY, MOVE!!
BANG!
PA-RENT'S DAY AT THE ELE-MEN-TARY SCH-OOL
DON'T STAND ON THE DESK!!
SAVAGE HAIR AND BODY-CONSCIOUS DRESS
SLAP
SHE SLA-PPED ONE OF MY CLASS-MATES.
NO, MOM...
HER STARE WAS SO GLITZY ...
LET'S TALK IN MY OFFICE, IT'S NEARBY.
BLING-BLING FUR COAT
HER CAR WAS REAR-ENDED
BLING-BLING (RENTED) CAR
PLEASE, PLEASE DON'T DO THAT!!
SHRRRINKINNG
... THAT SHE WAS OFTEN TAKEN AS A "MISTRESS OF A GANGSTER BOSS".
THIS BRIDE LOOKS ...
... UGLY!!
ALWAYS DISSED SO CASUALLY
EVEN DEATH WOULD SNEAK AWAY FROM HER.
CALLED EVERY WOMAN "OLD".
THAT OLD WOMAN IS TROU-BLE!
BUT... THAT MOM...
I...!
I CAN'T BELIEVE THAT.
AWWAWW
LAI HON'T HINK HYOU CON...
STOP THAT KO-CHAN!

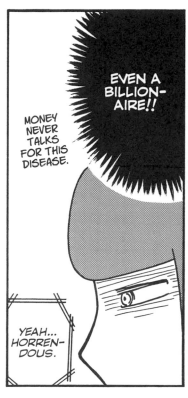

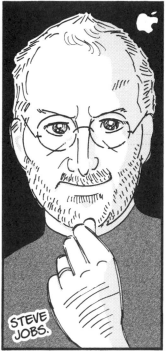

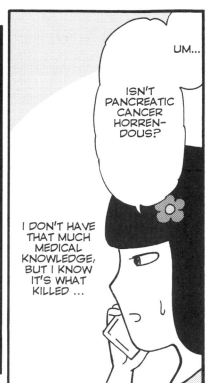

UM...
ISN'T PANCREATIC CANCER HORREN-DOUS?
I DON'T HAVE THAT MUCH MEDICAL KNOWLEDGE, BUT I KNOW IT'S WHAT KILLED ...
STEVE JOBS.
EVEN A BILLION-AIRE!!
MONEY NEVER TALKS FOR THIS DISEASE.
YEAH... HORREN-DOUS.
SHE STILL DOESN'T KNOW MUCH ABOUT IT, BUT ...
... WITHOUT PROPER, URGENT TREATMENT, SHE WON'T GET THROUGH ANOTHER 6 MONTHS.
IF THE CANCER DRUGS WORK, PERHAPS A FULL YEAR.

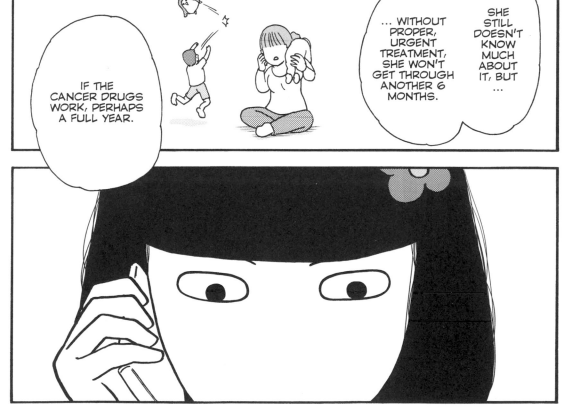

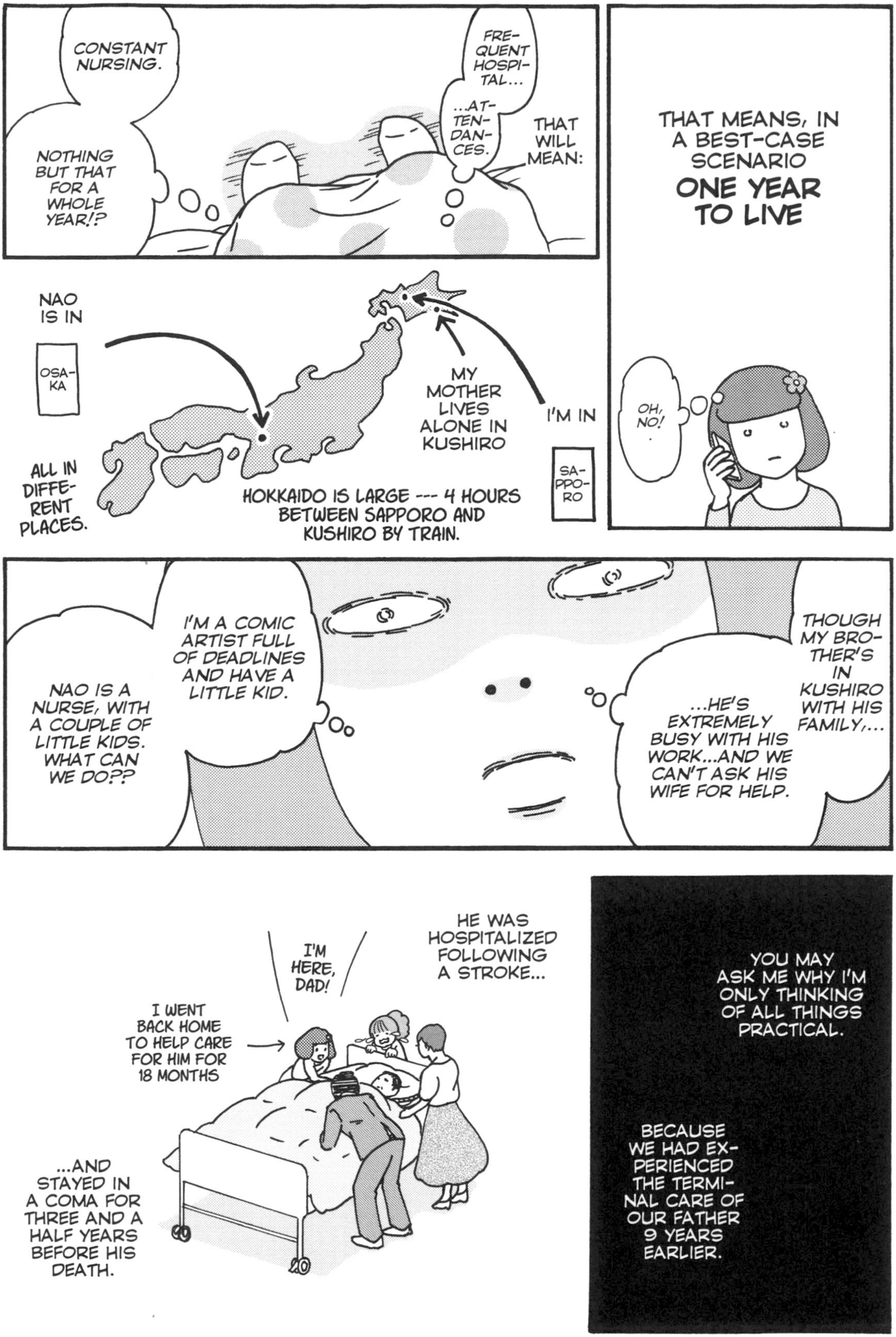
THAT MEANS, IN A BEST-CASE SCENARIO
ONE YEAR TO LIVE
OH, NO!
THAT WILL MEAN:
FREQUENT HOSPITAL...
...ATTENDANCES.
CONSTANT NURSING.
NOTHING BUT THAT FOR A WHOLE YEAR!?
I'M IN
SAPPORO
MY MOTHER LIVES ALONE IN KUSHIRO
NAO IS IN
OSAKA
HOKKAIDO IS LARGE --- 4 HOURS BETWEEN SAPPORO AND KUSHIRO BY TRAIN.
ALL IN DIFFERENT PLACES.
THOUGH MY BROTHER'S IN KUSHIRO WITH HIS FAMILY,...
...HE'S EXTREMELY BUSY WITH HIS WORK...AND WE CAN'T ASK HIS WIFE FOR HELP.
I'M A COMIC ARTIST FULL OF DEADLINES AND HAVE A LITTLE KID.
NAO IS A NURSE, WITH A COUPLE OF LITTLE KIDS. WHAT CAN WE DO??
YOU MAY ASK ME WHY I'M ONLY THINKING OF ALL THINGS PRACTICAL.
BECAUSE WE HAD EXPERIENCED THE TERMINAL CARE OF OUR FATHER 9 YEARS EARLIER.
HE WAS HOSPITALIZED FOLLOWING A STROKE...
I'M HERE, DAD!
I WENT BACK HOME TO HELP CARE FOR HIM FOR 18 MONTHS
...AND STAYED IN A COMA FOR THREE AND A HALF YEARS BEFORE HIS DEATH.

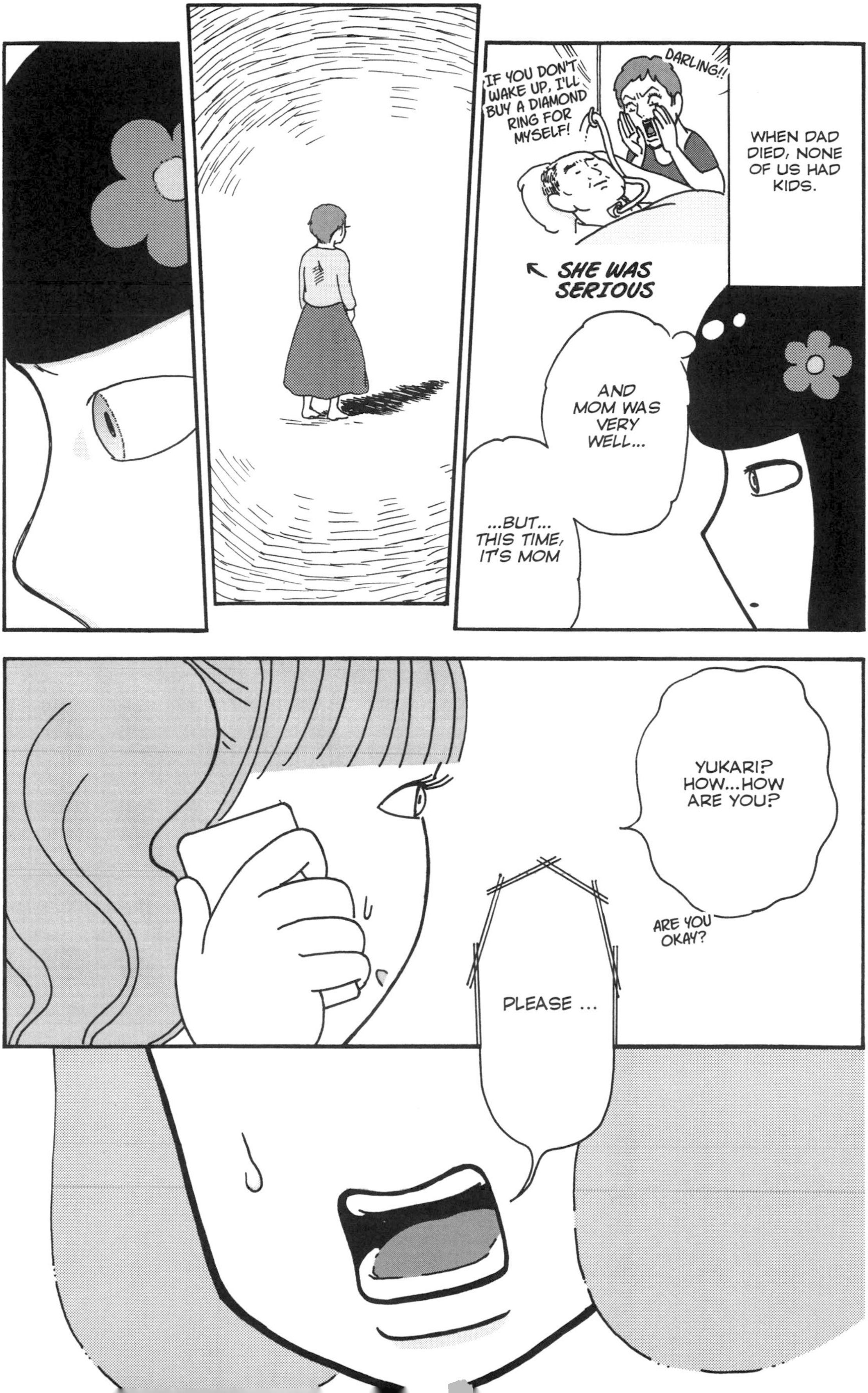
WHEN DAD DIED, NONE OF US HAD KIDS.
DARLING!!
IF YOU DON'T WAKE UP, I'LL BUY A DIAMOND RING FOR MYSELF!
SHE WAS SERIOUS
AND MOM WAS VERY WELL...
...BUT... THIS TIME, IT'S MOM
YUKARI? HOW...HOW ARE YOU?
ARE YOU OKAY?
PLEASE ...

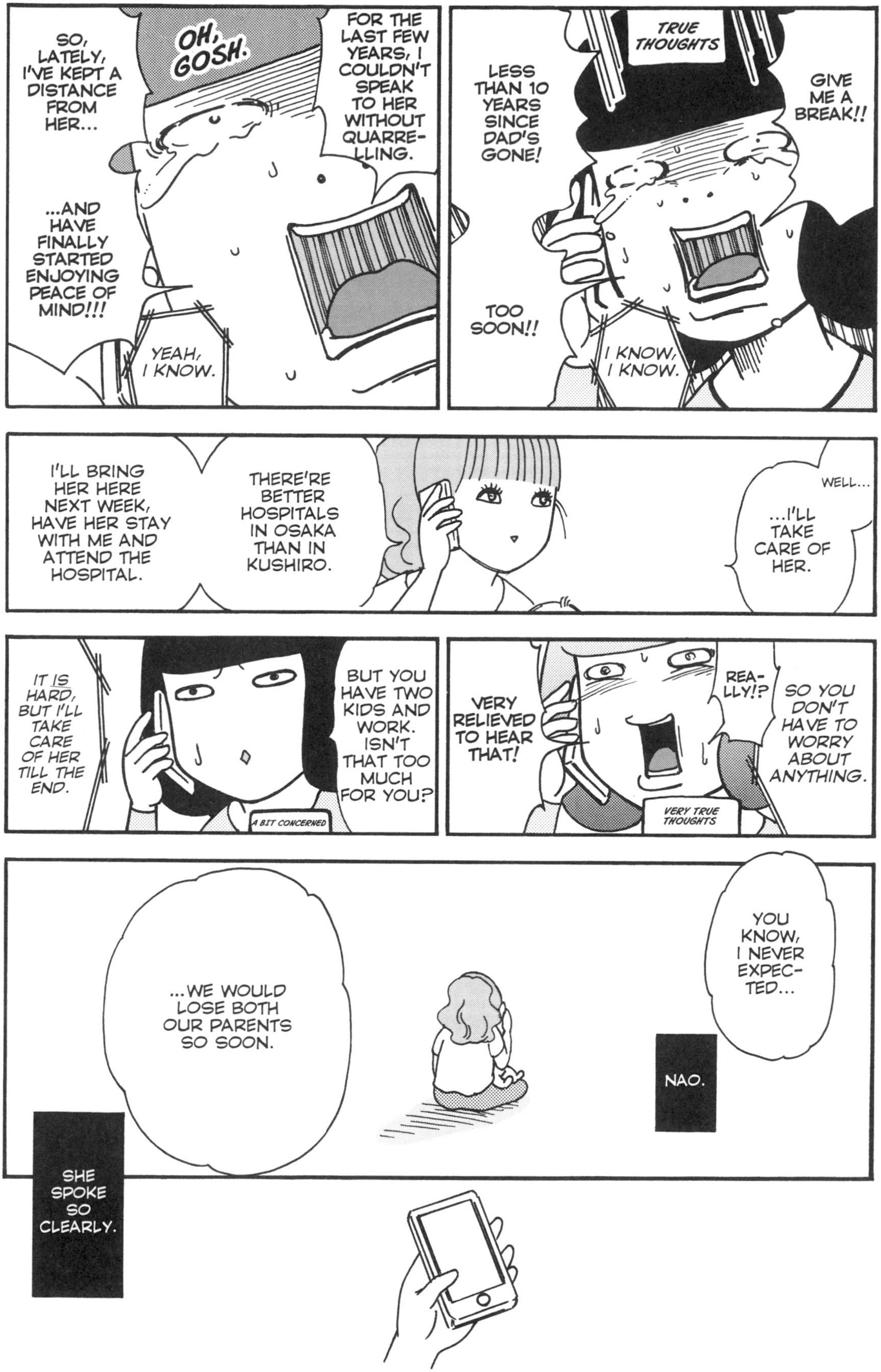
TRUE THOUGHTS
GIVE ME A BREAK!!
LESS THAN 10 YEARS SINCE DAD'S GONE!
I KNOW, I KNOW.
TOO SOON!!
FOR THE LAST FEW YEARS, I COULDN'T SPEAK TO HER WITHOUT QUARRELLING.
OH, GOSH.
SO, LATELY, I'VE KEPT A DISTANCE FROM HER...
...AND HAVE FINALLY STARTED ENJOYING PEACE OF MIND!!!
YEAH, I KNOW.
WELL...
...I'LL TAKE CARE OF HER.
THERE'RE BETTER HOSPITALS IN OSAKA THAN IN KUSHIRO.
I'LL BRING HER HERE NEXT WEEK, HAVE HER STAY WITH ME AND ATTEND THE HOSPITAL.
SO YOU DON'T HAVE TO WORRY ABOUT ANYTHING.
REALLY!?
VERY RELIEVED TO HEAR THAT!
VERY TRUE THOUGHTS
BUT YOU HAVE TWO KIDS AND WORK. ISN'T THAT TOO MUCH FOR YOU?
IT IS HARD, BUT I'LL TAKE CARE OF HER TILL THE END.
A BIT CONCERNED
YOU KNOW, I NEVER EXPECTED...
NAO.
...WE WOULD LOSE BOTH OUR PARENTS SO SOON.
SHE SPOKE SO CLEARLY.

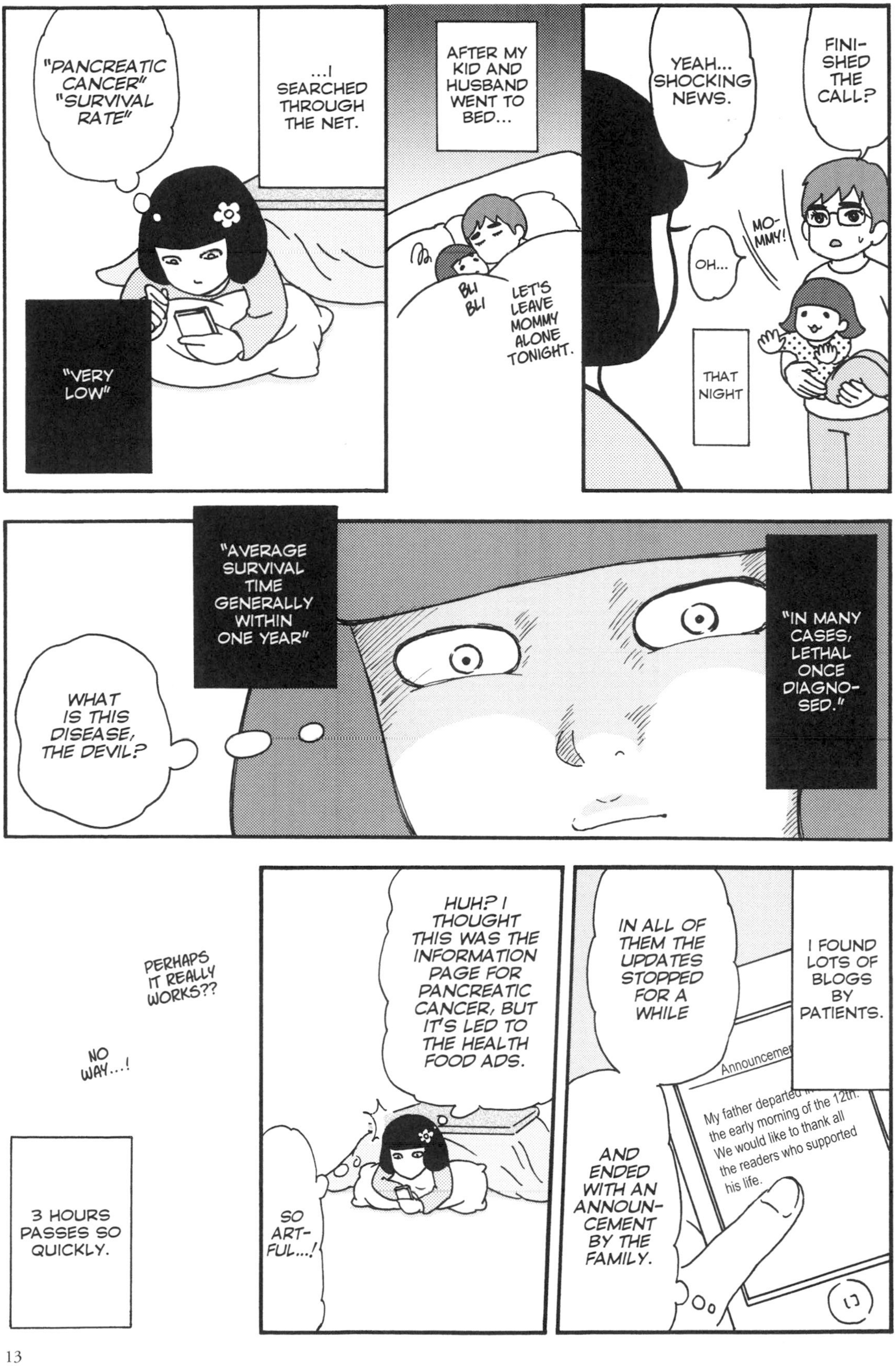
FINI-SHED THE CALL?
YEAH... SHOCKING NEWS.
MO-MMY!
OH...
THAT NIGHT
AFTER MY KID AND HUSBAND WENT TO BED...
LET'S LEAVE MOMMY ALONE TONIGHT.
BLI BLI
...I SEARCHED THROUGH THE NET.
"PANCREATIC CANCER" "SURVIVAL RATE"
"VERY LOW"
"IN MANY CASES, LETHAL ONCE DIAGNO-SED."
"AVERAGE SURVIVAL TIME GENERALLY WITHIN ONE YEAR"
WHAT IS THIS DISEASE, THE DEVIL?
I FOUND LOTS OF BLOGS BY PATIENTS.
IN ALL OF THEM THE UPDATES STOPPED FOR A WHILE
Announcem
My father departed
the early morning of the 12th.
We would like to thank all the readers who supported his life.
AND ENDED WITH AN ANNOUN-CEMENT BY THE FAMILY.
HUH? I THOUGHT THIS WAS THE INFORMATION PAGE FOR PANCREATIC CANCER, BUT IT'S LED TO THE HEALTH FOOD ADS.
SO ART-FUL...!
PERHAPS IT REALLY WORKS??
NO WAY...!
3 HOURS PASSES SO QUICKLY.

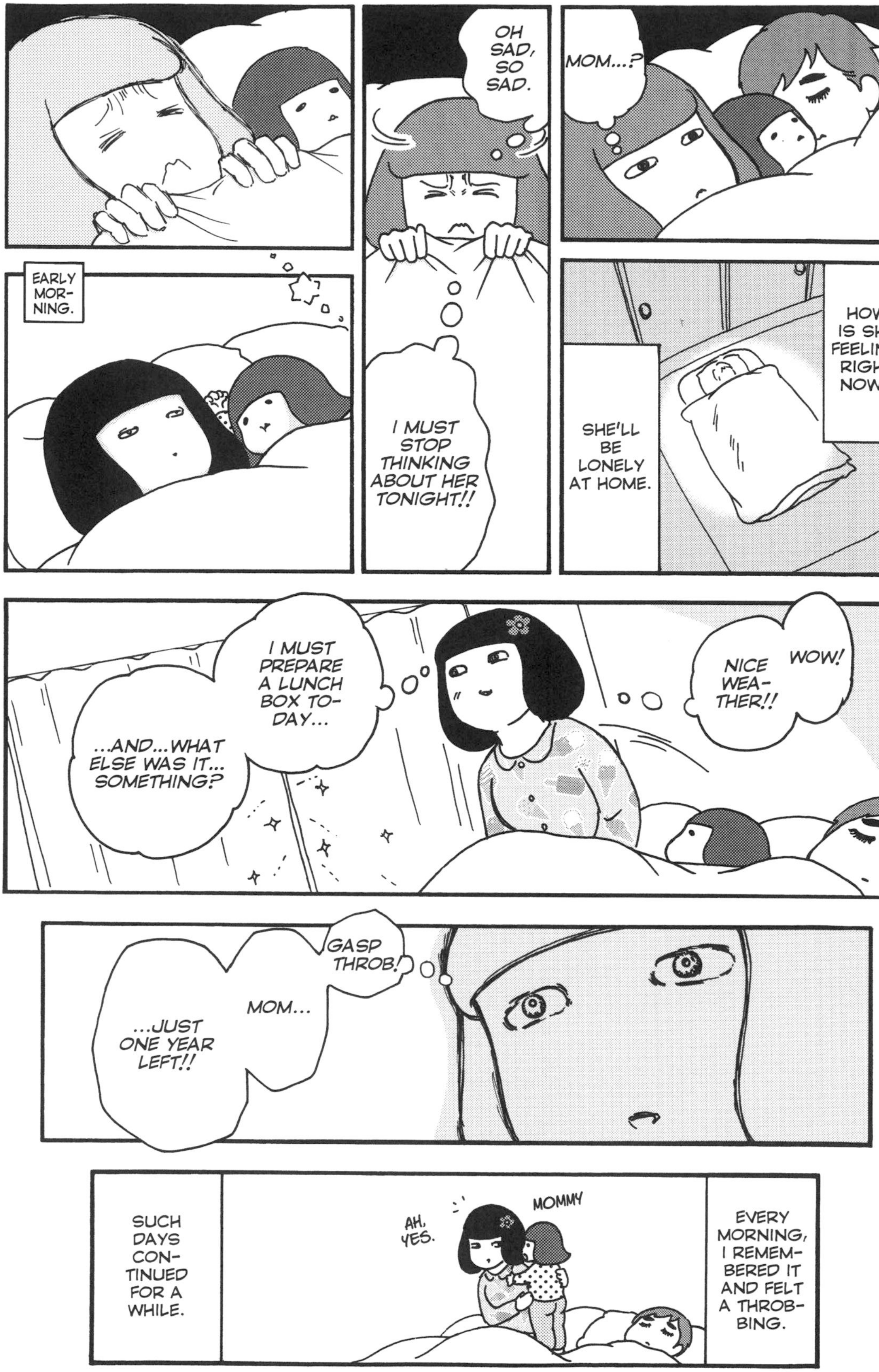
MOM...?
HOW IS SHE FEELING RIGHT NOW?
SHE'LL BE LONELY AT HOME.
OH SAD, SO SAD.
I MUST STOP THINKING ABOUT HER TONIGHT!!
EARLY MORNING.
WOW!
NICE WEATHER!!
I MUST PREPARE A LUNCH BOX TODAY...
...AND...WHAT ELSE WAS IT... SOMETHING?
GASP THROB!
MOM...
...JUST ONE YEAR LEFT!!
EVERY MORNING, I REMEMBERED IT AND FELT A THROBBING.
MOMMY
AH, YES.
SUCH DAYS CONTINUED FOR A WHILE.

CHAPTER 2

IT WAS
A VERY
GENTLE
VOICE

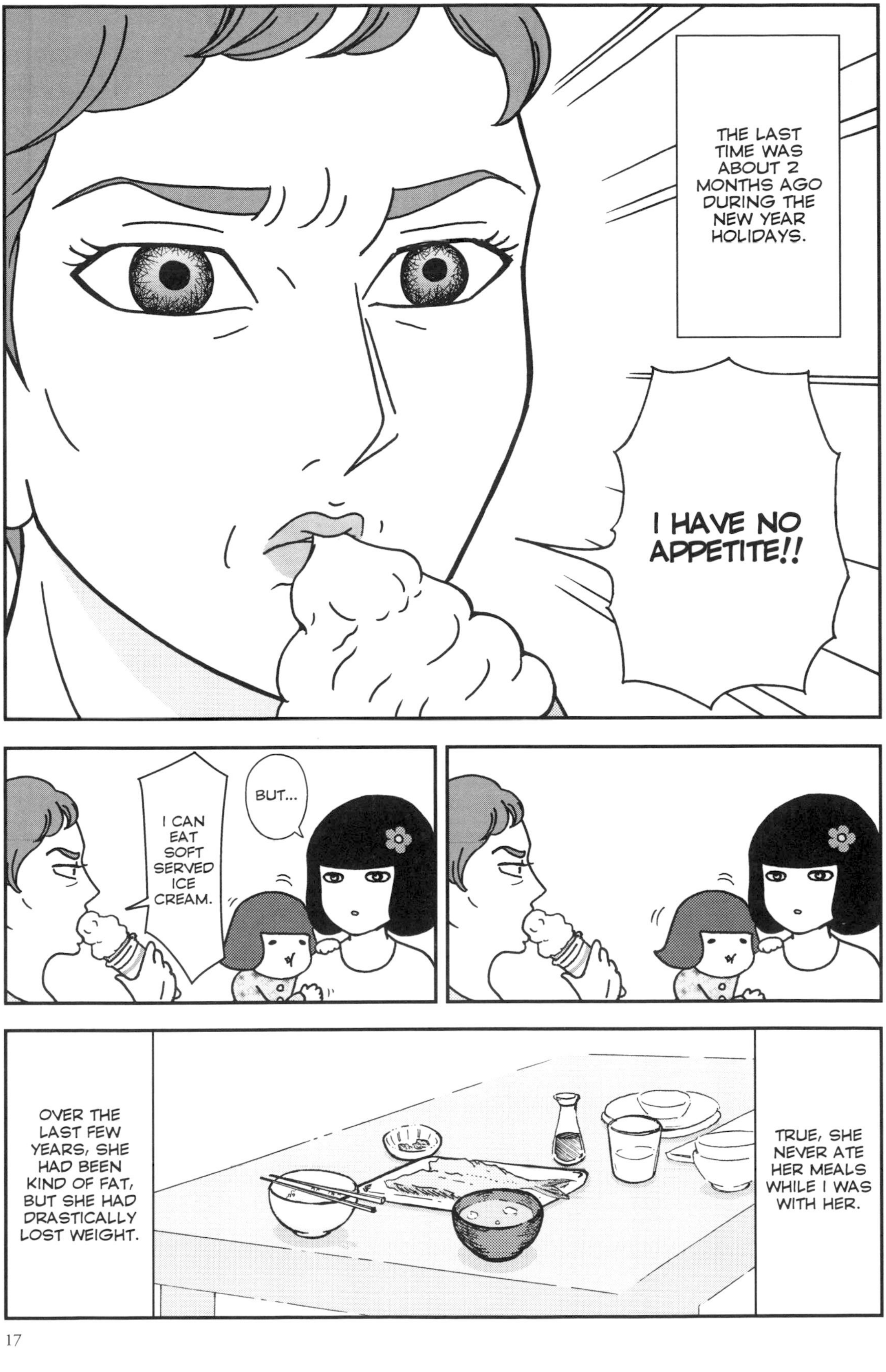
THE LAST TIME WAS ABOUT 2 MONTHS AGO DURING THE NEW YEAR HOLIDAYS.
I HAVE NO APPETITE!!
BUT...
I CAN EAT SOFT SERVED ICE CREAM.
TRUE, SHE NEVER ATE HER MEALS WHILE I WAS WITH HER.
OVER THE LAST FEW YEARS, SHE HAD BEEN KIND OF FAT, BUT SHE HAD DRASTICALLY LOST WEIGHT.

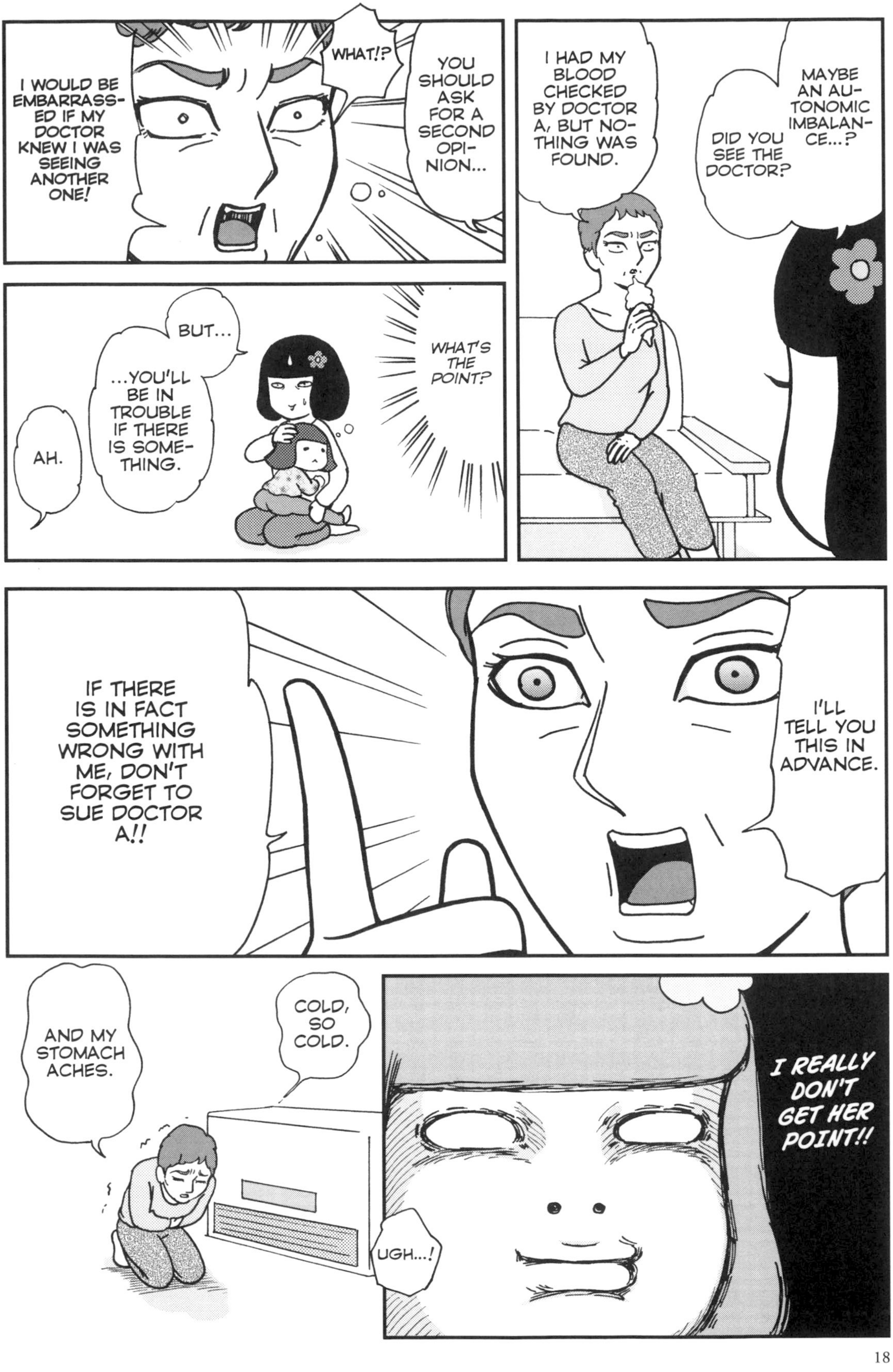
MAYBE AN AUTONOMIC IMBALANCE...?
DID YOU SEE THE DOCTOR?
I HAD MY BLOOD CHECKED BY DOCTOR A, BUT NOTHING WAS FOUND.
YOU SHOULD ASK FOR A SECOND OPINION...
WHAT!?
I WOULD BE EMBARRASSED IF MY DOCTOR KNEW I WAS SEEING ANOTHER ONE!
WHAT'S THE POINT?
BUT...
...YOU'LL BE IN TROUBLE IF THERE IS SOMETHING.
AH.
I'LL TELL YOU THIS IN ADVANCE.
IF THERE IS IN FACT SOMETHING WRONG WITH ME, DON'T FORGET TO SUE DOCTOR A!!
I REALLY DON'T GET HER POINT!!
UGH...!
COLD, SO COLD.
AND MY STOMACH ACHES.

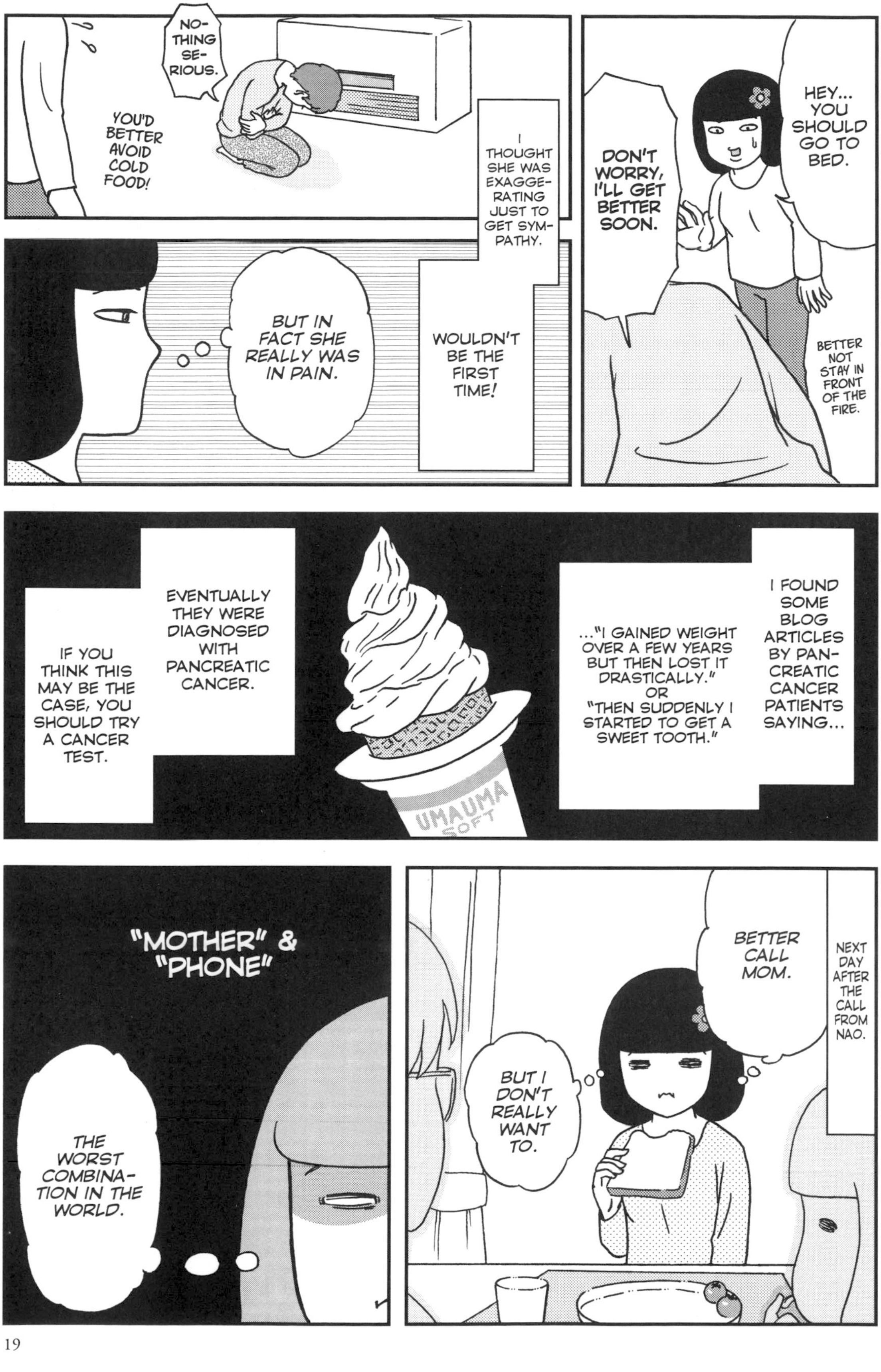
HEY... YOU SHOULD GO TO BED.
DON'T WORRY, I'LL GET BETTER SOON.
BETTER NOT STAY IN FRONT OF THE FIRE.
I THOUGHT SHE WAS EXAGGE-RATING JUST TO GET SYM-PATHY.
NO-THING SE-RIOUS.
YOU'D BETTER AVOID COLD FOOD!
WOULDN'T BE THE FIRST TIME!
BUT IN FACT SHE REALLY WAS IN PAIN.
I FOUND SOME BLOG ARTICLES BY PAN-CREATIC CANCER PATIENTS SAYING...
..."I GAINED WEIGHT OVER A FEW YEARS BUT THEN LOST IT DRASTICALLY." OR "THEN SUDDENLY I STARTED TO GET A SWEET TOOTH."
UMAUMA SOFT
EVENTUALLY THEY WERE DIAGNOSED WITH PANCREATIC CANCER.
IF YOU THINK THIS MAY BE THE CASE, YOU SHOULD TRY A CANCER TEST.
NEXT DAY AFTER THE CALL FROM NAO.
BETTER CALL MOM.
BUT I DON'T REALLY WANT TO.
"MOTHER" & "PHONE"
THE WORST COMBINA-TION IN THE WORLD.

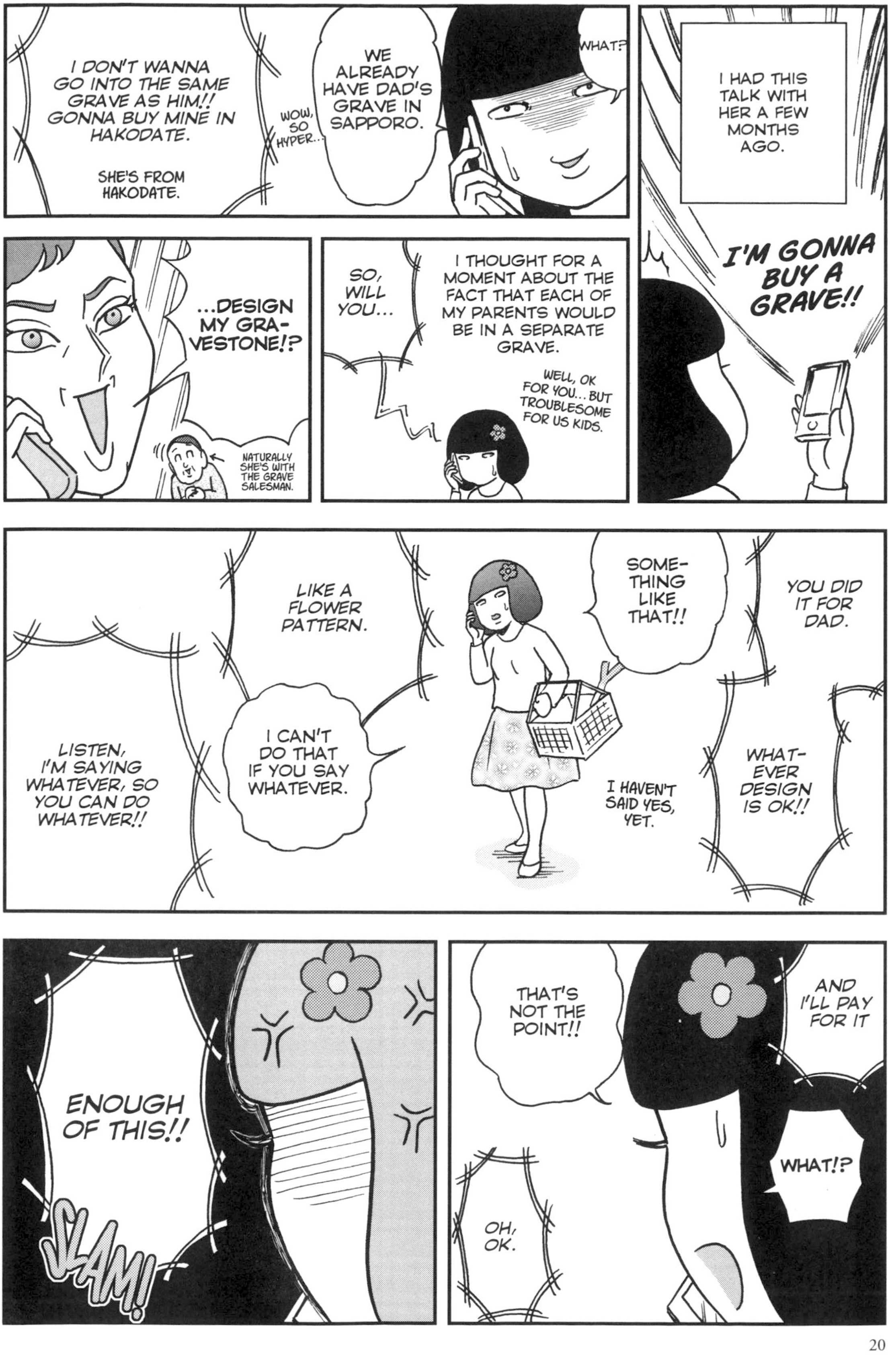
I HAD THIS TALK WITH HER A FEW MONTHS AGO.
I'M GONNA BUY A GRAVE!!
WHAT?
WE ALREADY HAVE DAD'S GRAVE IN SAPPORO.
WOW, SO HYPER...
I DON'T WANNA GO INTO THE SAME GRAVE AS HIM!! GONNA BUY MINE IN HAKODATE.
SHE'S FROM HAKODATE.
I THOUGHT FOR A MOMENT ABOUT THE FACT THAT EACH OF MY PARENTS WOULD BE IN A SEPARATE GRAVE.
SO, WILL YOU...
WELL, OK FOR YOU... BUT TROUBLESOME FOR US KIDS.
...DESIGN MY GRAVESTONE!?
NATURALLY SHE'S WITH THE GRAVE SALESMAN.
YOU DID IT FOR DAD.
WHAT-EVER DESIGN IS OK!!
SOME-THING LIKE THAT!!
I HAVEN'T SAID YES, YET.
LIKE A FLOWER PATTERN.
I CAN'T DO THAT IF YOU SAY WHATEVER.
LISTEN, I'M SAYING WHATEVER, SO YOU CAN DO WHATEVER!!
AND I'LL PAY FOR IT
THAT'S NOT THE POINT!!
WHAT!?
OH, OK.
ENOUGH OF THIS!!
SLAM!

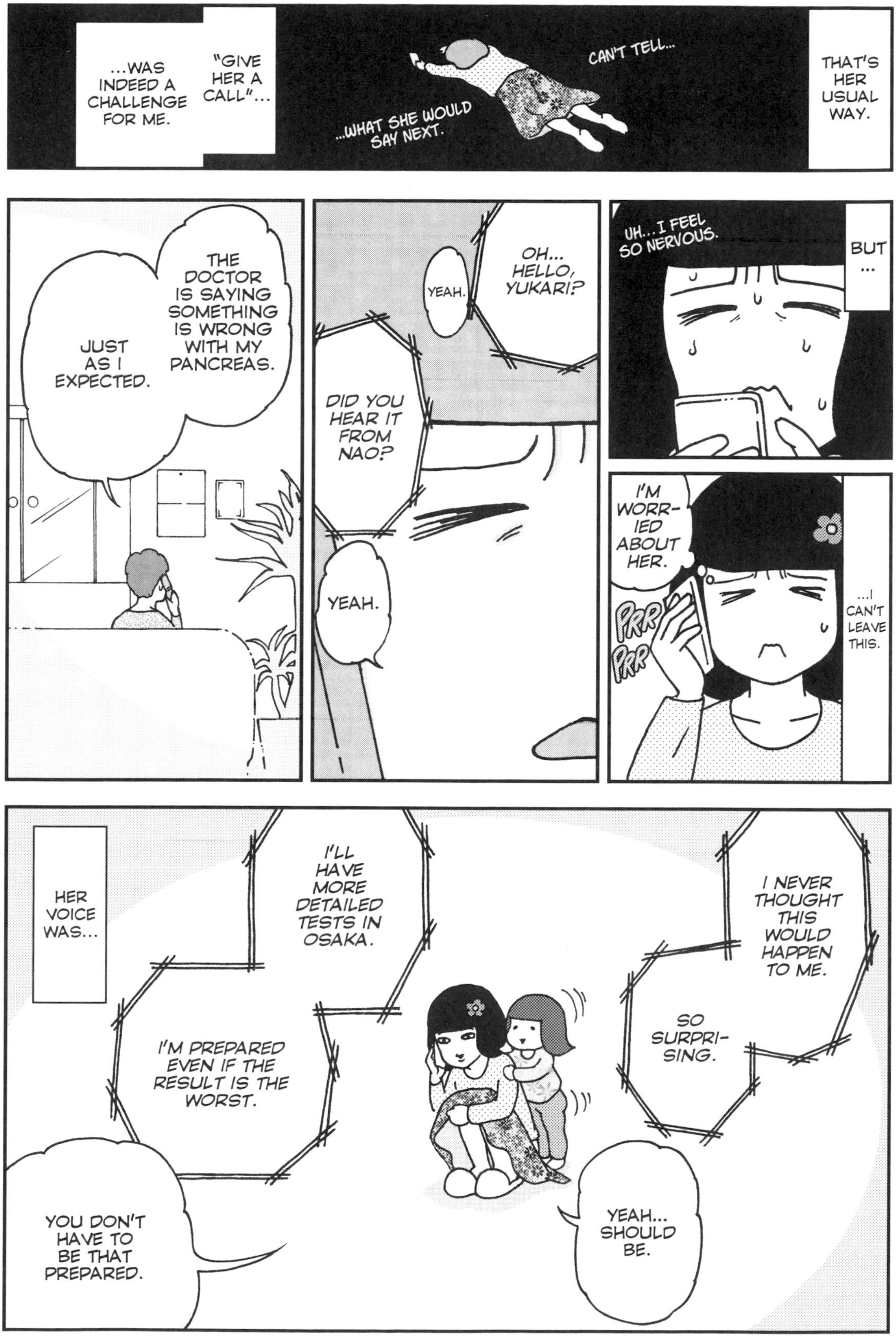
THAT'S HER USUAL WAY.
CAN'T TELL...
...WHAT SHE WOULD SAY NEXT.
"GIVE HER A CALL"...
...WAS INDEED A CHALLENGE FOR ME.
BUT...
UH... I FEEL SO NERVOUS.
...I CAN'T LEAVE THIS.
I'M WORR-IED ABOUT HER.
PRR PRR
OH... HELLO, YUKARI?
YEAH.
DID YOU HEAR IT FROM NAO?
YEAH.
THE DOCTOR IS SAYING SOMETHING IS WRONG WITH MY PANCREAS.
JUST AS I EXPECTED.
I NEVER THOUGHT THIS WOULD HAPPEN TO ME.
SO SURPRI-SING.
I'LL HAVE MORE DETAILED TESTS IN OSAKA.
HER VOICE WAS...
I'M PREPARED EVEN IF THE RESULT IS THE WORST.
YEAH... SHOULD BE.
YOU DON'T HAVE TO BE THAT PREPARED.

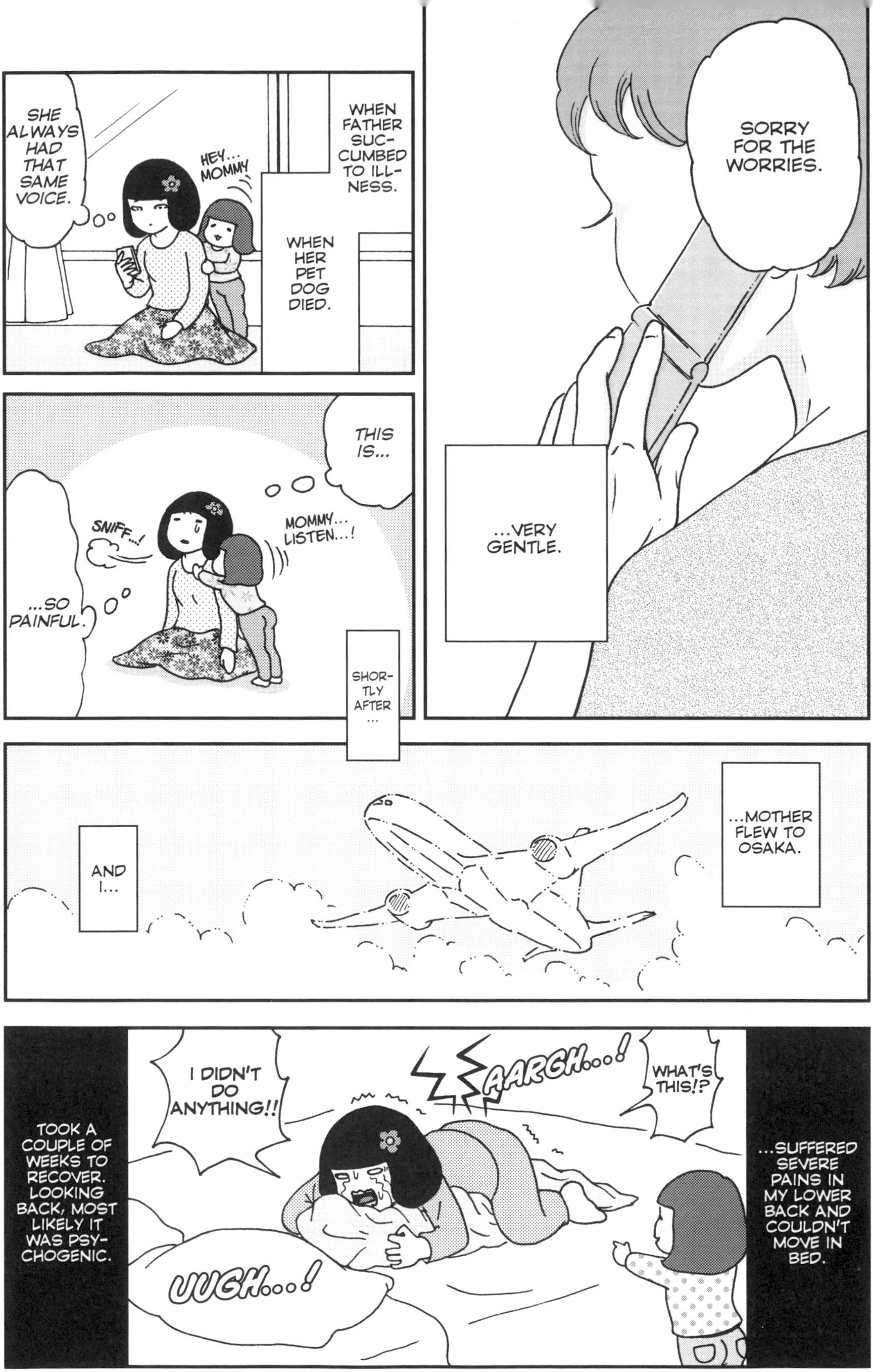
SORRY FOR THE WORRIES.
...VERY GENTLE.
WHEN FATHER SUC-CUMBED TO ILL-NESS.
WHEN HER PET DOG DIED.
HEY... MOMMY
SHE ALWAYS HAD THAT SAME VOICE.
THIS IS...
MOMMY... LISTEN...!
SNIFF...!
...SO PAINFUL.
SHOR-TLY AFTER ...
...MOTHER FLEW TO OSAKA.
AND I...
...SUFFERED SEVERE PAINS IN MY LOWER BACK AND COULDN'T MOVE IN BED.
WHAT'S THIS!?
AARGH...!
I DIDN'T DO ANYTHING!!
UUGH...!
TOOK A COUPLE OF WEEKS TO RECOVER. LOOKING BACK, MOST LIKELY IT WAS PSY-CHOGENIC.

CHAPTER 3

SHOULD WE TELL HER?

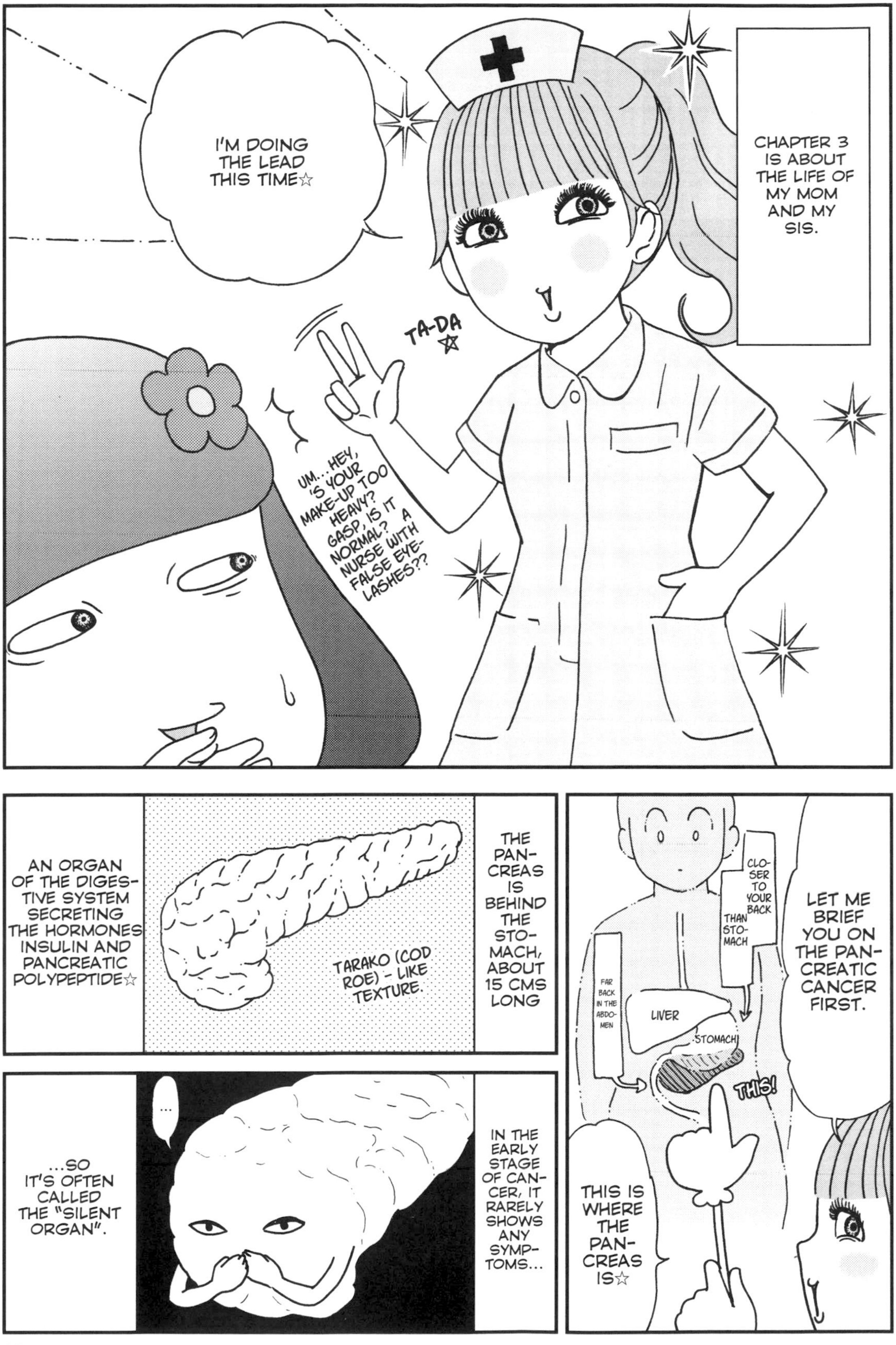

CHAPTER 3 IS ABOUT THE LIFE OF MY MOM AND MY SIS.
I'M DOING THE LEAD THIS TIME☆
TA-DA☆
UM... HEY, 'S YOUR MAKE-UP TOO HEAVY? GASP, IS IT NORMAL? A NURSE WITH FALSE EYE-LASHES??
LET ME BRIEF YOU ON THE PAN-CREATIC CANCER FIRST.
CLO-SER TO YOUR BACK THAN STO-MACH
FAR BACK IN THE ABDO-MEN
LIVER
STOMACH
THIS!
THIS IS WHERE THE PAN-CREAS IS☆
THE PAN-CREAS IS BEHIND THE STO-MACH, ABOUT 15 CMS LONG
TARAKO (COD ROE) - LIKE TEXTURE.
AN ORGAN OF THE DIGES-TIVE SYSTEM SECRETING THE HORMONES INSULIN AND PANCREATIC POLYPEPTIDE☆
IN THE EARLY STAGE OF CAN-CER, IT RARELY SHOWS ANY SYMP-TOMS...
...
...SO IT'S OFTEN CALLED THE "SILENT ORGAN".

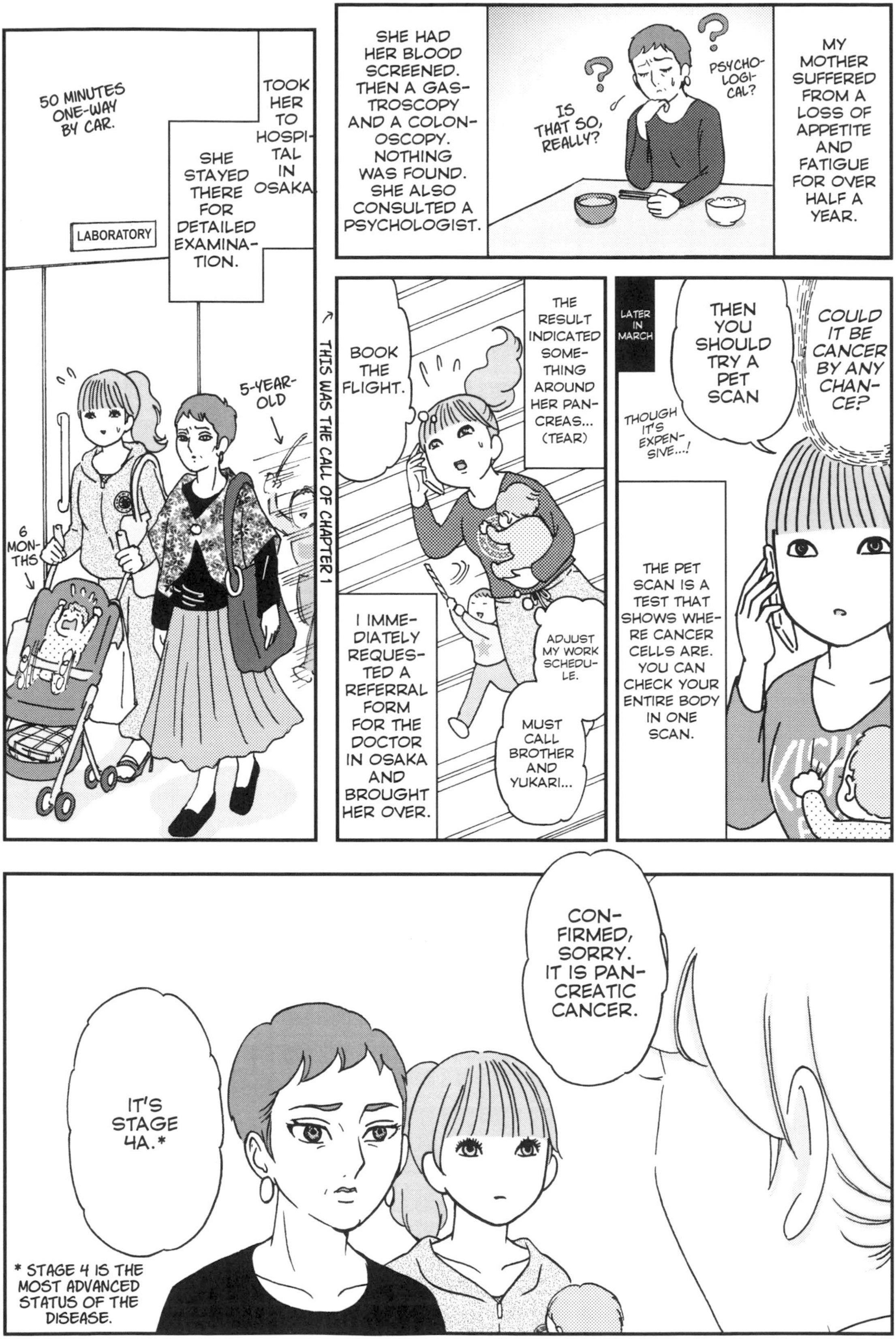

MY MOTHER SUFFERED FROM A LOSS OF APPETITE AND FATIGUE FOR OVER HALF A YEAR.
PSYCHO-LOGI-CAL?
IS THAT SO, REALLY?
SHE HAD HER BLOOD SCREENED. THEN A GAS-TROSCOPY AND A COLON-OSCOPY. NOTHING WAS FOUND. SHE ALSO CONSULTED A PSYCHOLOGIST.
LATER IN MARCH
COULD IT BE CANCER BY ANY CHAN-CE?
THEN YOU SHOULD TRY A PET SCAN
THOUGH IT'S EXPEN-SIVE...!
THE PET SCAN IS A TEST THAT SHOWS WHE-RE CANCER CELLS ARE. YOU CAN CHECK YOUR ENTIRE BODY IN ONE SCAN.
THE RESULT INDICATED SOME-THING AROUND HER PAN-CREAS... (TEAR)
BOOK THE FLIGHT.
ADJUST MY WORK SCHEDU-LE.
MUST CALL BROTHER AND YUKARI...
I IMME-DIATELY REQUES-TED A REFERRAL FORM FOR THE DOCTOR IN OSAKA AND BROUGHT HER OVER.
TOOK HER TO HOSPI-TAL IN OSAKA.
50 MINUTES ONE-WAY BY CAR.
SHE STAYED THERE FOR DETAILED EXAMINA-TION.
LABORATORY
5-YEAR-OLD
6 MON-THS
THIS WAS THE CALL OF CHAPTER 1
CON-FIRMED, SORRY. IT IS PAN-CREATIC CANCER.
IT'S STAGE 4A.*
* STAGE 4 IS THE MOST ADVANCED STATUS OF THE DISEASE.

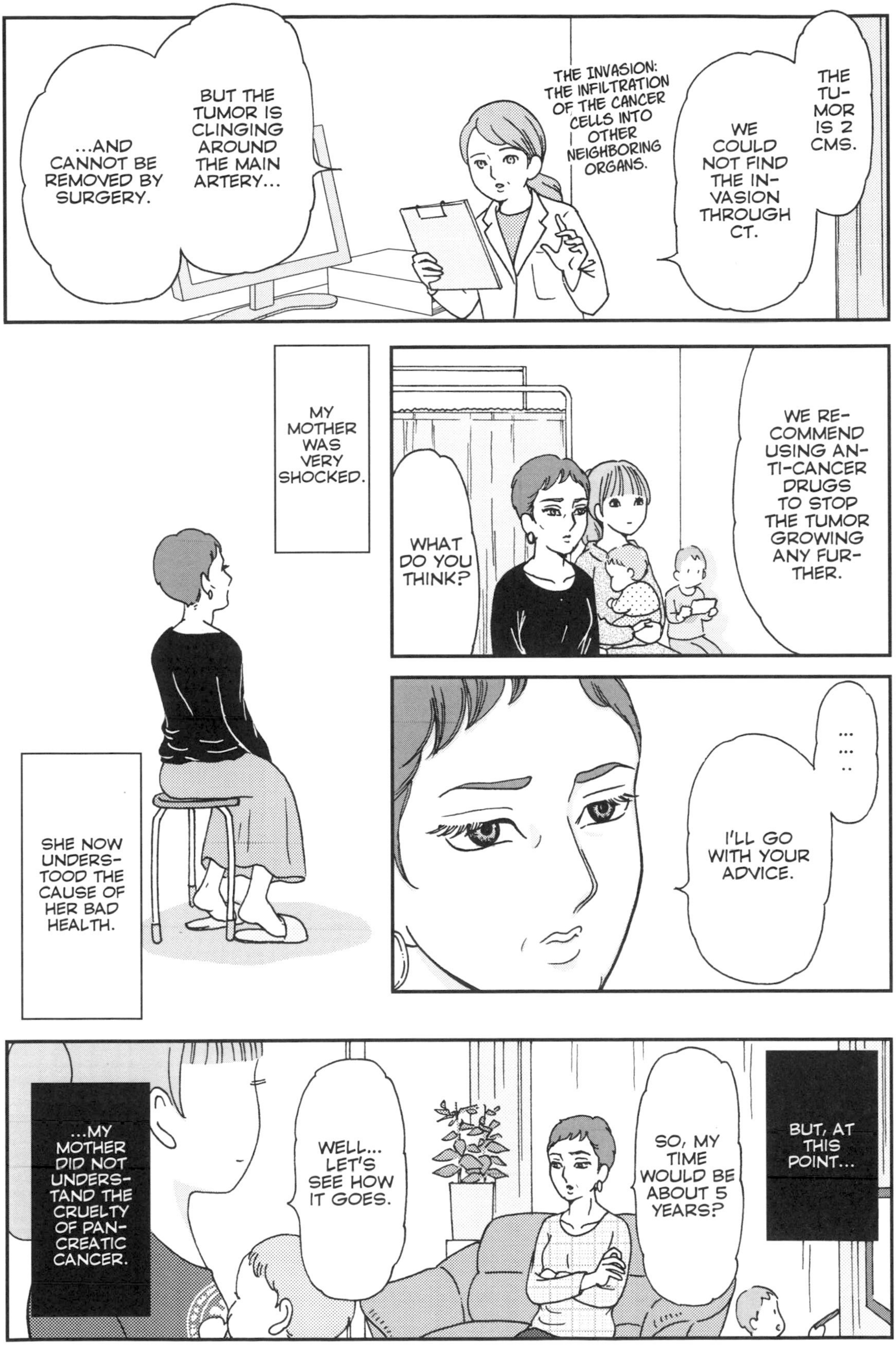
THE TUMOR IS 2 CMS.
WE COULD NOT FIND THE INVASION THROUGH CT.
THE INVASION: THE INFILTRATION OF THE CANCER CELLS INTO OTHER NEIGHBORING ORGANS.
BUT THE TUMOR IS CLINGING AROUND THE MAIN ARTERY...
...AND CANNOT BE REMOVED BY SURGERY.
WE RECOMMEND USING ANTI-CANCER DRUGS TO STOP THE TUMOR GROWING ANY FURTHER.
WHAT DO YOU THINK?
... .
I'LL GO WITH YOUR ADVICE.
MY MOTHER WAS VERY SHOCKED.
SHE NOW UNDERSTOOD THE CAUSE OF HER BAD HEALTH.
BUT, AT THIS POINT...
SO, MY TIME WOULD BE ABOUT 5 YEARS?
WELL... LET'S SEE HOW IT GOES.
...MY MOTHER DID NOT UNDERSTAND THE CRUELTY OF PANCREATIC CANCER.

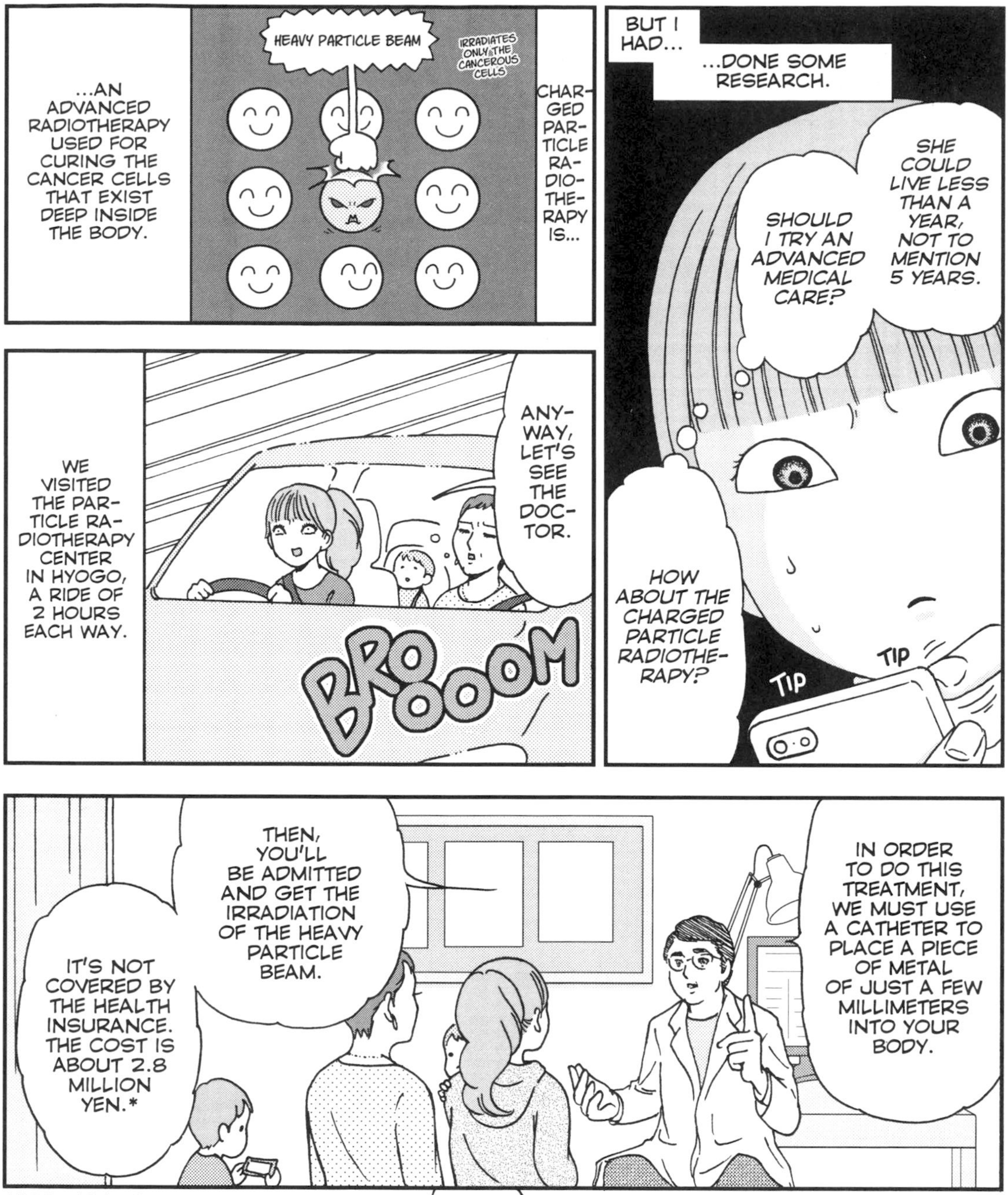
BUT I HAD...
...DONE SOME RESEARCH.
SHE COULD LIVE LESS THAN A YEAR, NOT TO MENTION 5 YEARS.
SHOULD I TRY AN ADVANCED MEDICAL CARE?
HOW ABOUT THE CHARGED PARTICLE RADIOTHERAPY?
TIP
TIP
CHARGED PARTICLE RADIOTHERAPY IS...
IRRADIATES ONLY THE CANCEROUS CELLS
HEAVY PARTICLE BEAM
...AN ADVANCED RADIOTHERAPY USED FOR CURING THE CANCER CELLS THAT EXIST DEEP INSIDE THE BODY.
ANYWAY, LET'S SEE THE DOCTOR.
BROOOOM
WE VISITED THE PARTICLE RADIOTHERAPY CENTER IN HYOGO, A RIDE OF 2 HOURS EACH WAY.
IN ORDER TO DO THIS TREATMENT, WE MUST USE A CATHETER TO PLACE A PIECE OF METAL OF JUST A FEW MILLIMETERS INTO YOUR BODY.
THEN, YOU'LL BE ADMITTED AND GET THE IRRADIATION OF THE HEAVY PARTICLE BEAM.
IT'S NOT COVERED BY THE HEALTH INSURANCE. THE COST IS ABOUT 2.8 MILLION YEN.*

*AROUND $25,000

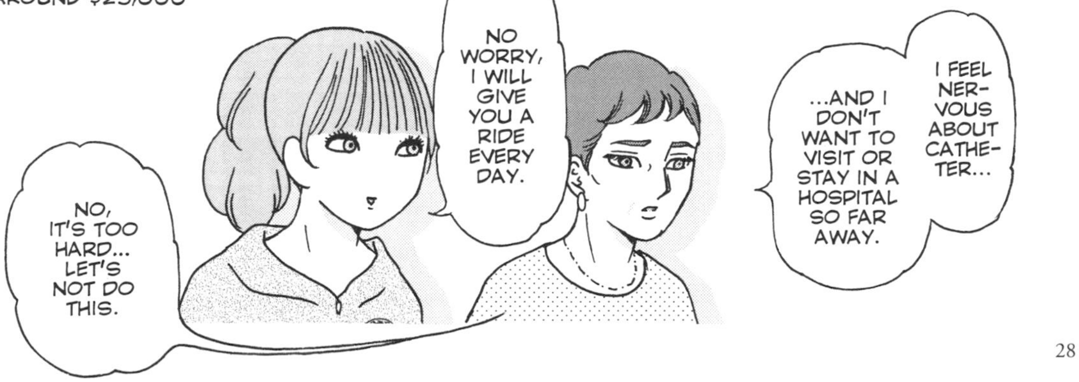
I FEEL NERVOUS ABOUT CATHETER...
...AND I DON'T WANT TO VISIT OR STAY IN A HOSPITAL SO FAR AWAY.
NO WORRY, I WILL GIVE YOU A RIDE EVERY DAY.
NO, IT'S TOO HARD... LET'S NOT DO THIS.

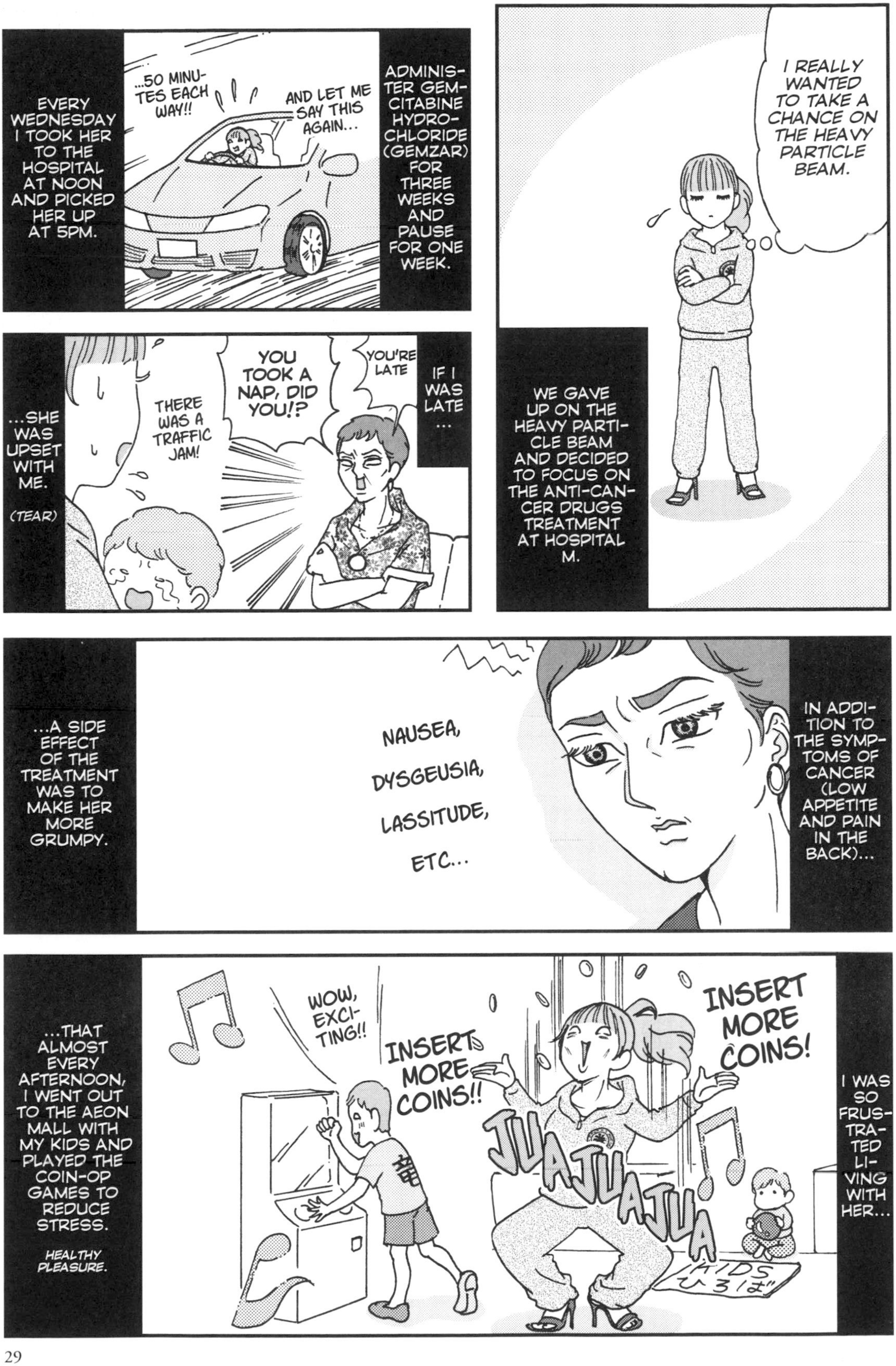
I REALLY WANTED TO TAKE A CHANCE ON THE HEAVY PARTICLE BEAM.
WE GAVE UP ON THE HEAVY PARTICLE BEAM AND DECIDED TO FOCUS ON THE ANTI-CANCER DRUGS TREATMENT AT HOSPITAL M.
ADMINISTER GEMCITABINE HYDROCHLORIDE (GEMZAR) FOR THREE WEEKS AND PAUSE FOR ONE WEEK.
AND LET ME SAY THIS AGAIN...
...50 MINUTES EACH WAY!!
EVERY WEDNESDAY I TOOK HER TO THE HOSPITAL AT NOON AND PICKED HER UP AT 5PM.
IF I WAS LATE ...
YOU'RE LATE
YOU TOOK A NAP, DID YOU!?
THERE WAS A TRAFFIC JAM!
...SHE WAS UPSET WITH ME.
(TEAR)
IN ADDITION TO THE SYMPTOMS OF CANCER (LOW APPETITE AND PAIN IN THE BACK)...
NAUSEA,
DYSGEUSIA,
LASSITUDE,
ETC...
...A SIDE EFFECT OF THE TREATMENT WAS TO MAKE HER MORE GRUMPY.
I WAS SO FRUSTRATED LIVING WITH HER...
INSERT MORE COINS!
JUAJUAJUA
KIDS ひろば
INSERT MORE COINS!!
WOW, EXCITING!!
...THAT ALMOST EVERY AFTERNOON, I WENT OUT TO THE AEON MALL WITH MY KIDS AND PLAYED THE COIN-OP GAMES TO REDUCE STRESS.
HEALTHY PLEASURE.

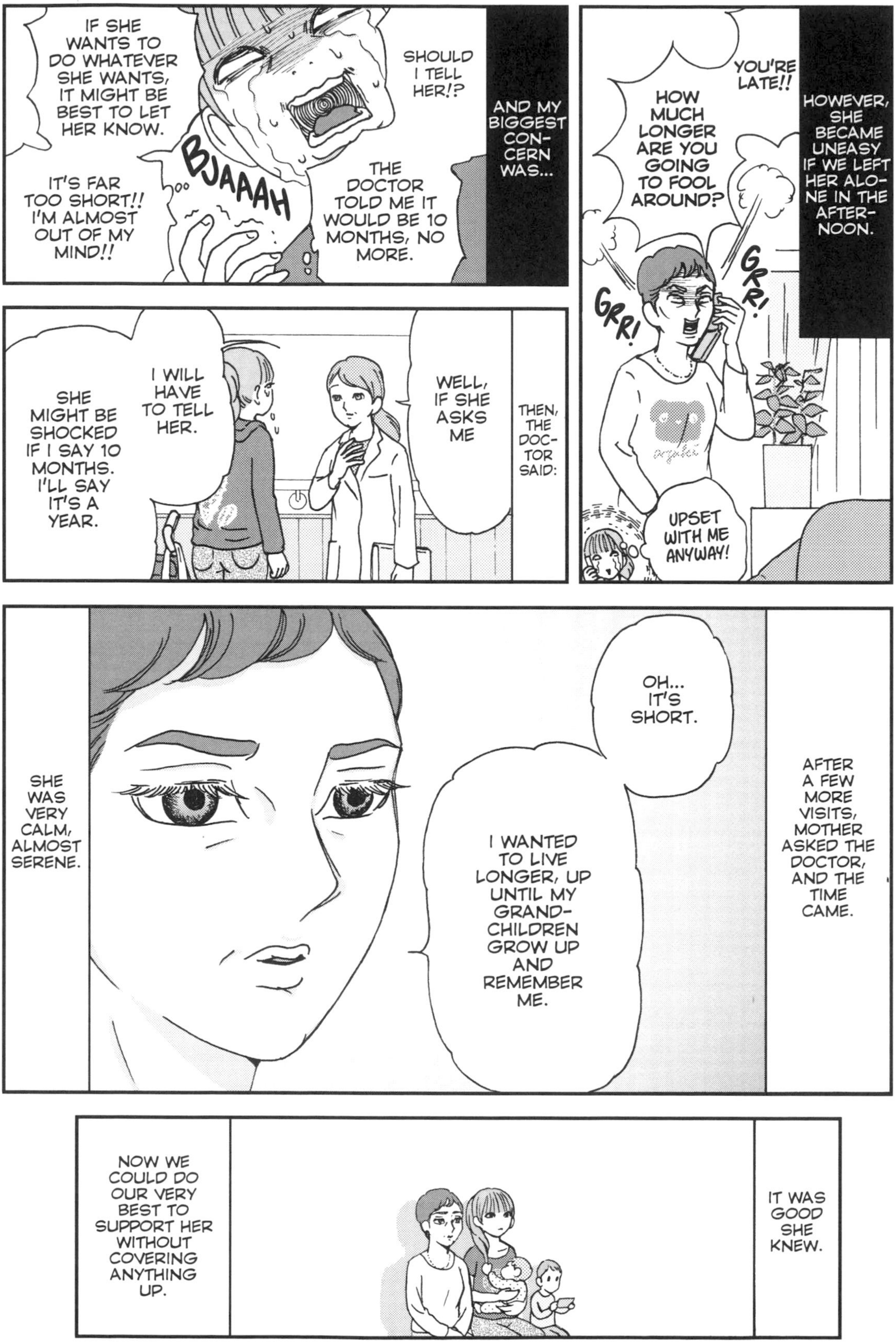
HOWEVER, SHE BECAME UNEASY IF WE LEFT HER ALONE IN THE AFTERNOON.
YOU'RE LATE!!
HOW MUCH LONGER ARE YOU GOING TO FOOL AROUND?
GRR!
GRR!
UPSET WITH ME ANYWAY!
AND MY BIGGEST CONCERN WAS...
SHOULD I TELL HER!?
THE DOCTOR TOLD ME IT WOULD BE 10 MONTHS, NO MORE.
IF SHE WANTS TO DO WHATEVER SHE WANTS, IT MIGHT BE BEST TO LET HER KNOW.
BJAAAH
IT'S FAR TOO SHORT!! I'M ALMOST OUT OF MY MIND!!
THEN, THE DOCTOR SAID:
WELL, IF SHE ASKS ME
I WILL HAVE TO TELL HER.
SHE MIGHT BE SHOCKED IF I SAY 10 MONTHS. I'LL SAY IT'S A YEAR.
AFTER A FEW MORE VISITS, MOTHER ASKED THE DOCTOR, AND THE TIME CAME.
OH... IT'S SHORT.
I WANTED TO LIVE LONGER, UP UNTIL MY GRAND-CHILDREN GROW UP AND REMEMBER ME.
SHE WAS VERY CALM, ALMOST SERENE.
IT WAS GOOD SHE KNEW.
NOW WE COULD DO OUR VERY BEST TO SUPPORT HER WITHOUT COVERING ANYTHING UP.

CHAPTER 4

MOM
SHUT HER
HEART

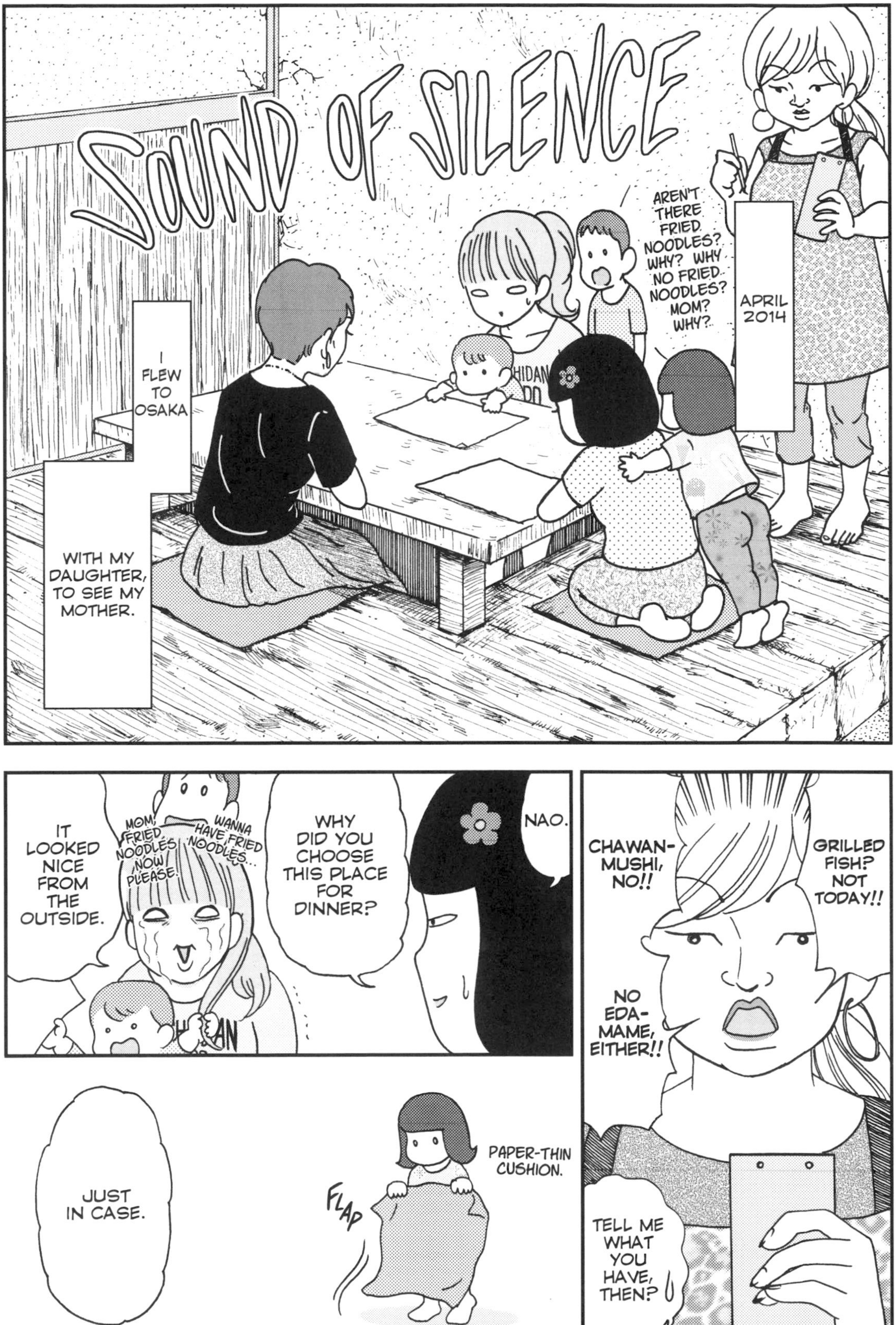
SOUND OF SILENCE
APRIL 2014
AREN'T THERE FRIED NOODLES? WHY? WHY NO FRIED NOODLES? MOM? WHY?
I FLEW TO OSAKA
WITH MY DAUGHTER, TO SEE MY MOTHER.
GRILLED FISH? NOT TODAY!!
CHAWAN-MUSHI, NO!!
NO EDA-MAME, EITHER!!
TELL ME WHAT YOU HAVE, THEN?
NAO.
WHY DID YOU CHOOSE THIS PLACE FOR DINNER?
WANNA HAVE FRIED NOODLES...
MOM, FRIED NOODLES NOW PLEASE.
IT LOOKED NICE FROM THE OUTSIDE.
PAPER-THIN CUSHION.
FLAP
JUST IN CASE.

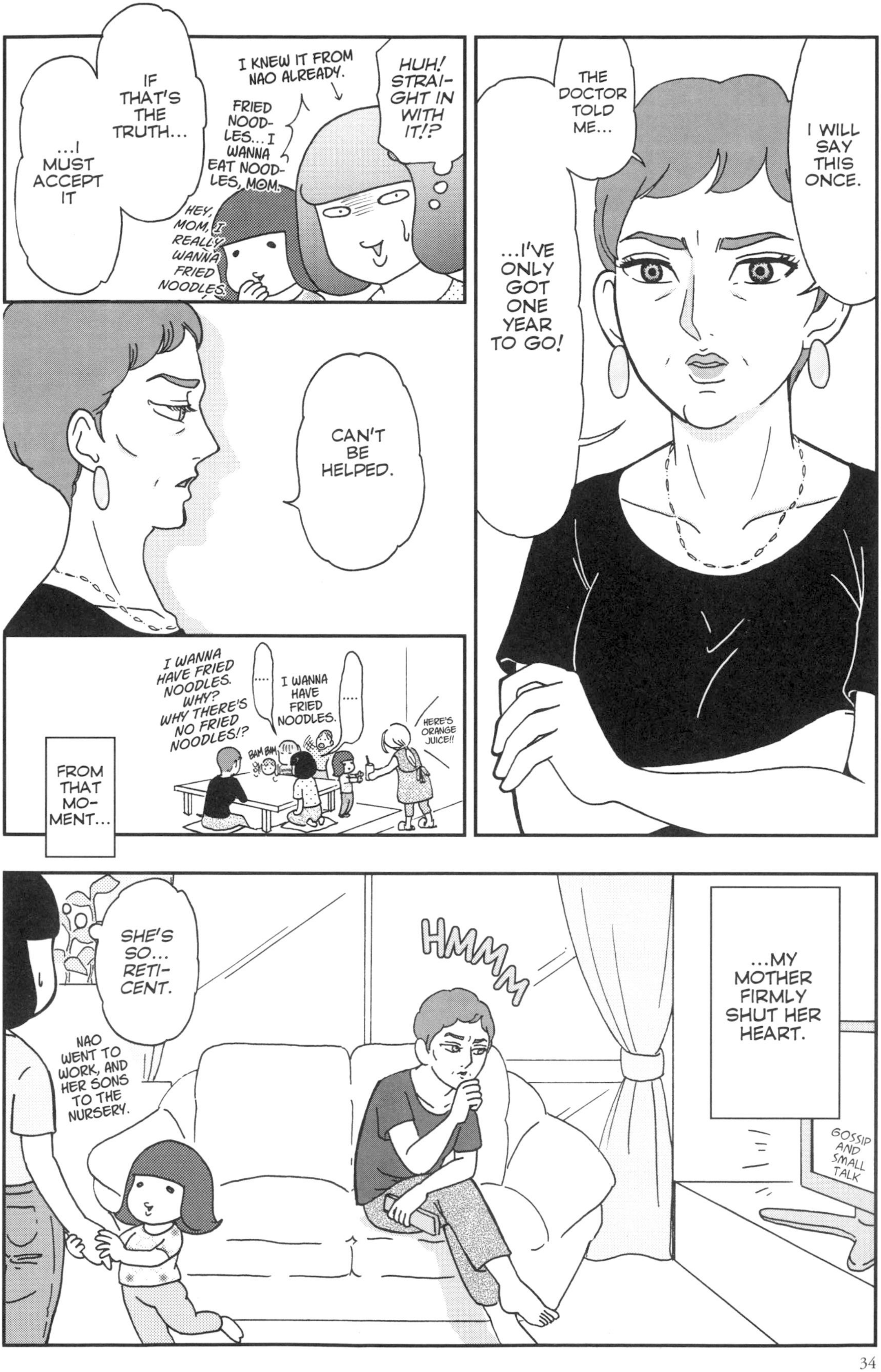
I WILL SAY THIS ONCE.
THE DOCTOR TOLD ME...
...I'VE ONLY GOT ONE YEAR TO GO!
HUH! STRAIGHT IN WITH IT!?
I KNEW IT FROM NAO ALREADY.
FRIED NOODLES... I WANNA EAT NOODLES, MOM.
IF THAT'S THE TRUTH...
...I MUST ACCEPT IT
HEY, MOM, I REALLY WANNA FRIED NOODLES.
CAN'T BE HELPED.
....
HERE'S ORANGE JUICE!!
I WANNA HAVE FRIED NOODLES.
....
BAM BAM
I WANNA HAVE FRIED NOODLES. WHY? WHY THERE'S NO FRIED NOODLES!?
FROM THAT MOMENT...
...MY MOTHER FIRMLY SHUT HER HEART.
GOSSIP AND SMALL TALK
HMMM
SHE'S SO... RETICENT.
NAO WENT TO WORK, AND HER SONS TO THE NURSERY.

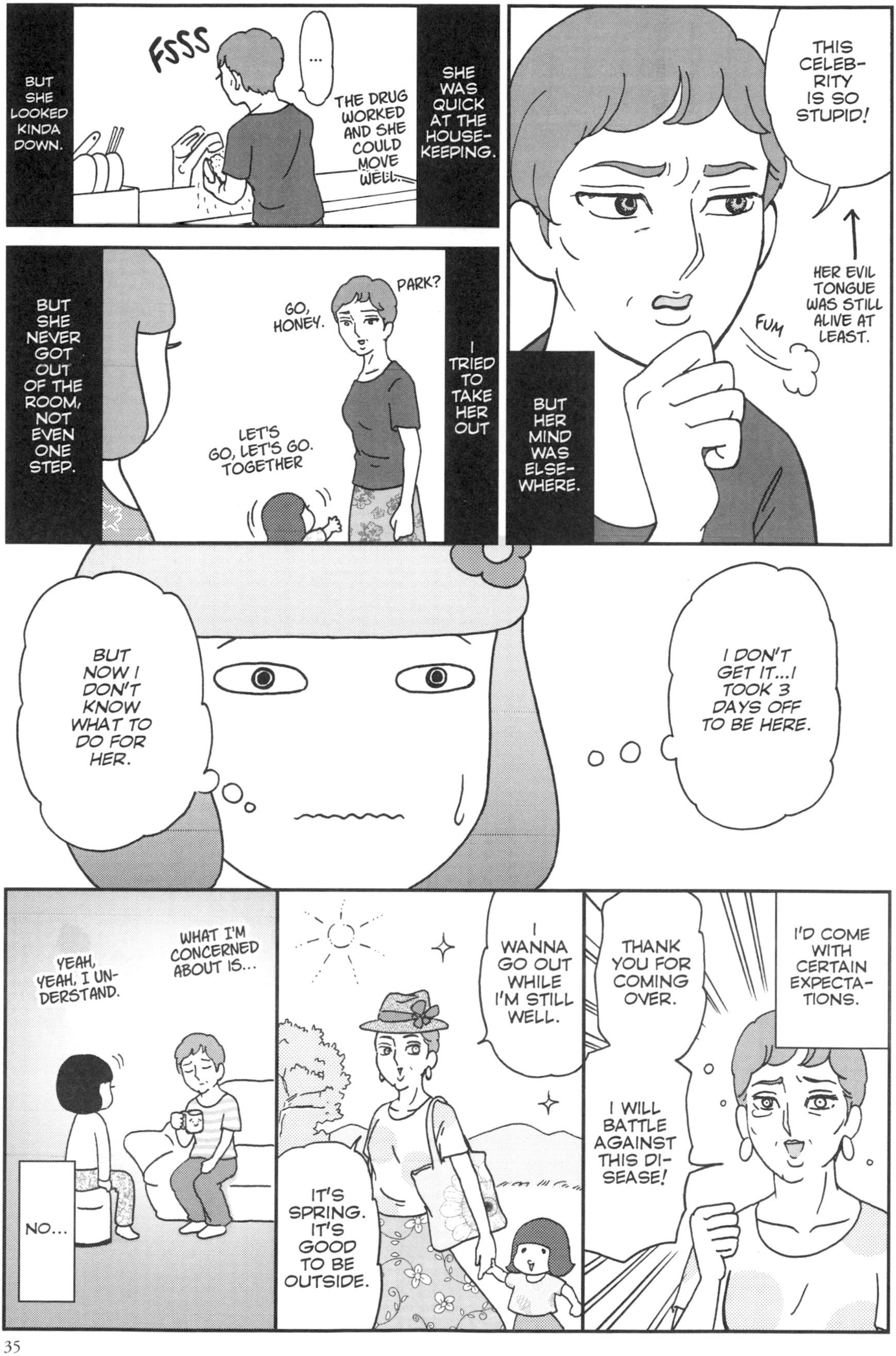
THIS CELEBRITY IS SO STUPID!
HER EVIL TONGUE WAS STILL ALIVE AT LEAST.
FUM
BUT HER MIND WAS ELSEWHERE.
SHE WAS QUICK AT THE HOUSEKEEPING.
...
THE DRUG WORKED AND SHE COULD MOVE WELL.
FSSS
BUT SHE LOOKED KINDA DOWN.
I TRIED TO TAKE HER OUT
PARK?
GO, HONEY.
LET'S GO, LET'S GO. TOGETHER
BUT SHE NEVER GOT OUT OF THE ROOM, NOT EVEN ONE STEP.
I DON'T GET IT...I TOOK 3 DAYS OFF TO BE HERE.
BUT NOW I DON'T KNOW WHAT TO DO FOR HER.
I'D COME WITH CERTAIN EXPECTATIONS.
THANK YOU FOR COMING OVER.
I WILL BATTLE AGAINST THIS DISEASE!
I WANNA GO OUT WHILE I'M STILL WELL.
IT'S SPRING. IT'S GOOD TO BE OUTSIDE.
WHAT I'M CONCERNED ABOUT IS...
YEAH, YEAH, I UNDERSTAND.
NO...

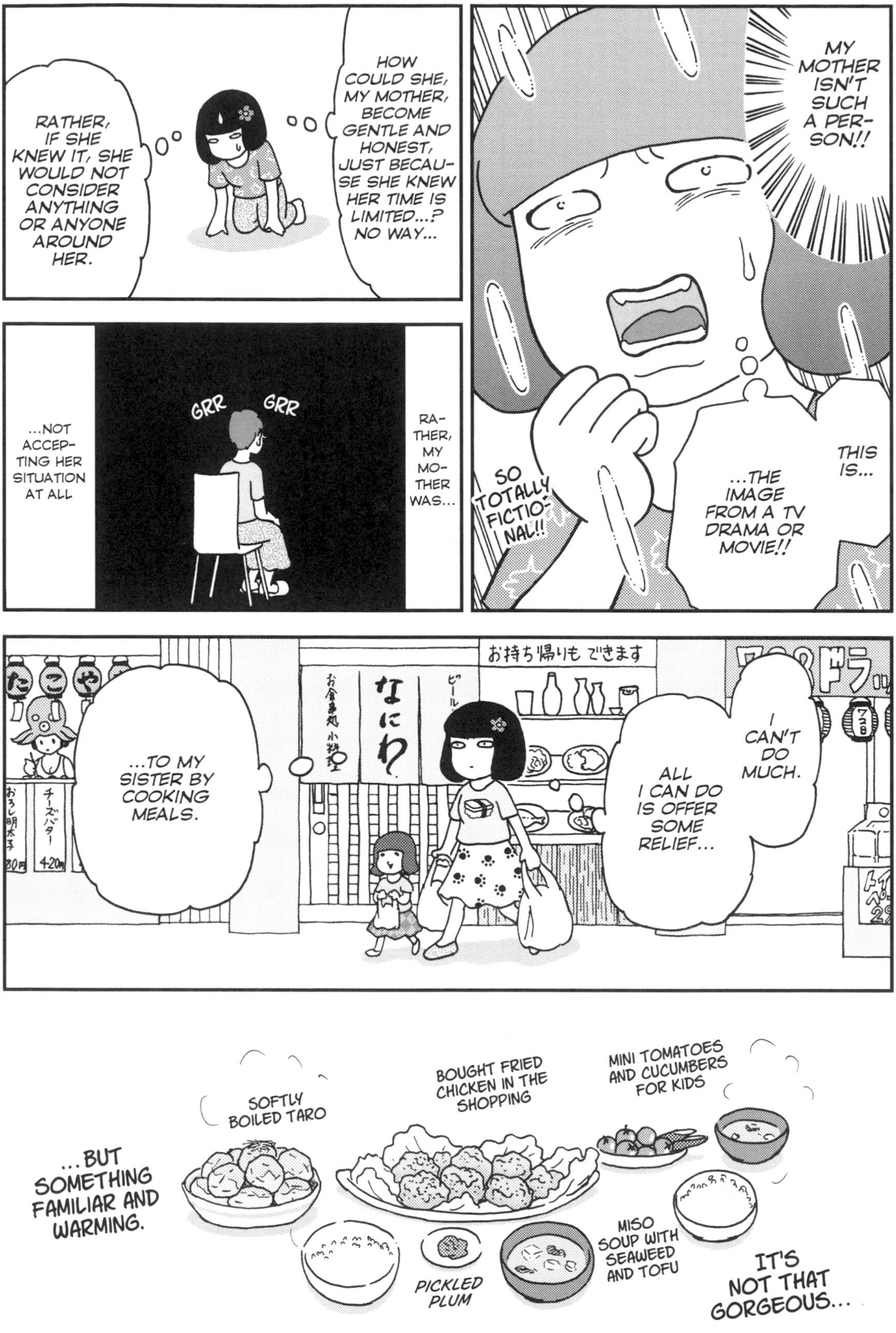

MY MOTHER ISN'T SUCH A PER-SON!!
THIS IS...
...THE IMAGE FROM A TV DRAMA OR MOVIE!!
SO TOTALLY FICTIO-NAL!!
HOW COULD SHE, MY MOTHER, BECOME GENTLE AND HONEST, JUST BECAU-SE SHE KNEW HER TIME IS LIMITED...? NO WAY...
RATHER, IF SHE KNEW IT, SHE WOULD NOT CONSIDER ANYTHING OR ANYONE AROUND HER.
RA-THER, MY MO-THER WAS...
GRR
GRR
...NOT ACCEP-TING HER SITUATION AT ALL
お持ち帰りも できます
ビール
なにわ
お食事処 小料理
おろし明太子
チーズバター
420円
I CAN'T DO MUCH.
ALL I CAN DO IS OFFER SOME RELIEF...
...TO MY SISTER BY COOKING MEALS.
MINI TOMATOES AND CUCUMBERS FOR KIDS
BOUGHT FRIED CHICKEN IN THE SHOPPING
SOFTLY BOILED TARO
MISO SOUP WITH SEAWEED AND TOFU
PICKLED PLUM
IT'S NOT THAT GORGEOUS...
...BUT SOMETHING FAMILIAR AND WARMING.

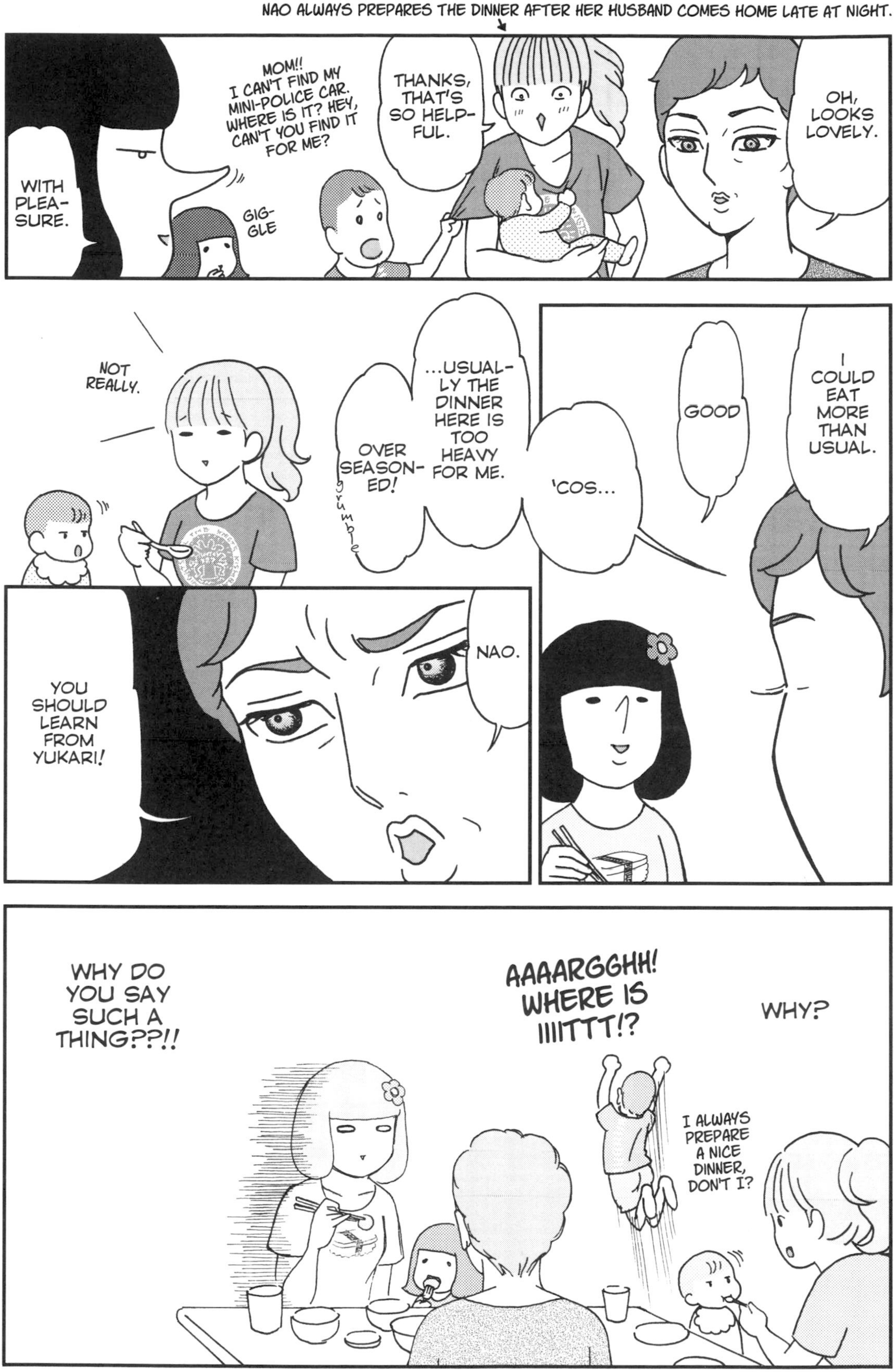
NAO ALWAYS PREPARES THE DINNER AFTER HER HUSBAND COMES HOME LATE AT NIGHT.
OH, LOOKS LOVELY.
THANKS, THAT'S SO HELPFUL.
MOM!! I CAN'T FIND MY MINI-POLICE CAR. WHERE IS IT? HEY, CAN'T YOU FIND IT FOR ME?
GIGGLE
WITH PLEASURE.
I COULD EAT MORE THAN USUAL.
GOOD
'COS...
...USUALLY THE DINNER HERE IS TOO HEAVY FOR ME.
OVER SEASONED!
grumble
NOT REALLY.
NAO.
YOU SHOULD LEARN FROM YUKARI!
WHY?
I ALWAYS PREPARE A NICE DINNER, DON'T I?
AAAARGGHH! WHERE IS IIIITTT!?
WHY DO YOU SAY SUCH A THING??!!

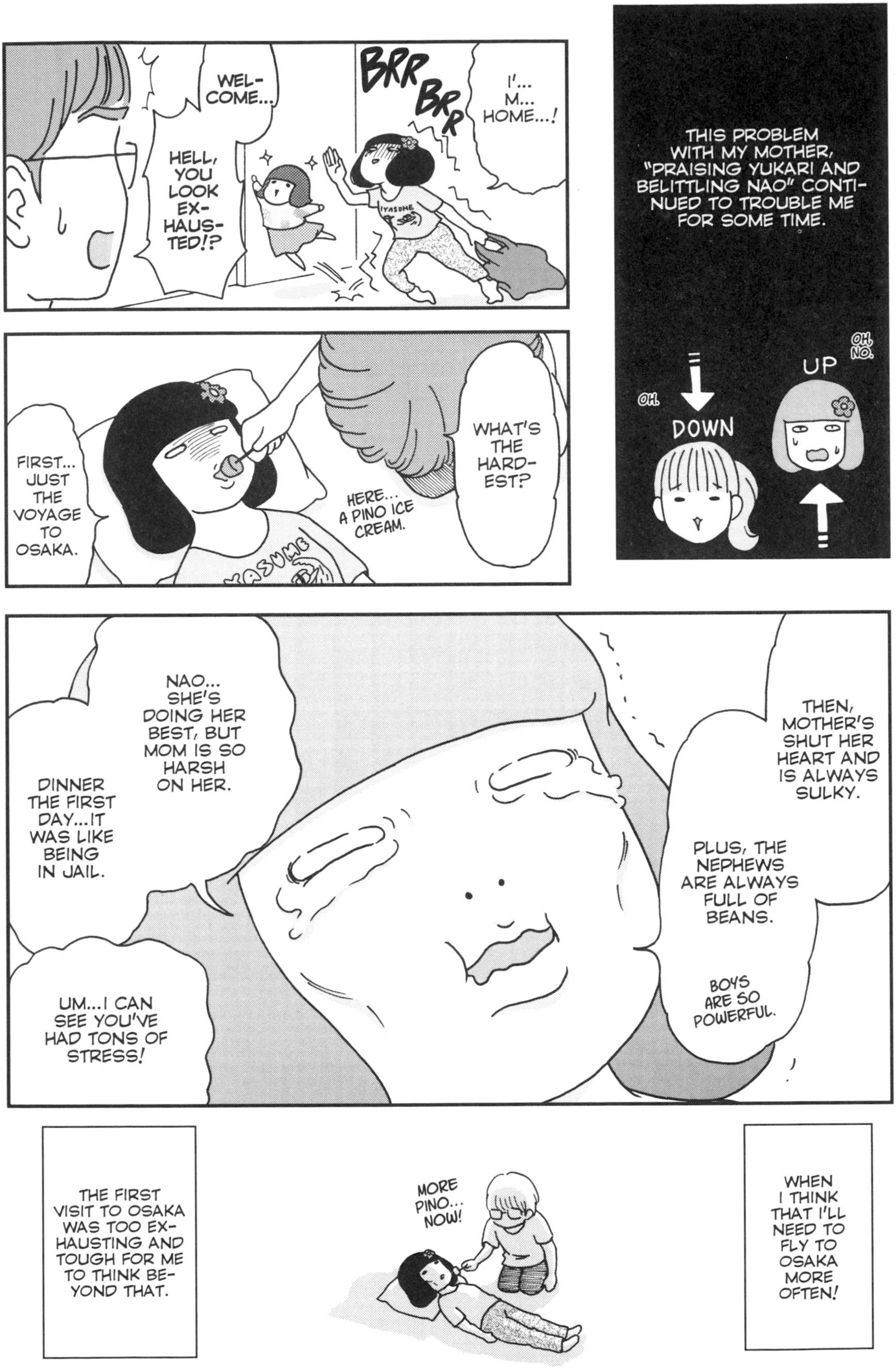
THIS PROBLEM WITH MY MOTHER, "PRAISING YUKARI AND BELITTLING NAO" CONTINUED TO TROUBLE ME FOR SOME TIME.
OH, NO.
UP
DOWN
OH.
I'... M... HOME...!
BRR BRR
WEL-COME...
HELL, YOU LOOK EX-HAUSTED!?
WHAT'S THE HARD-EST?
HERE... A PINO ICE CREAM.
FIRST... JUST THE VOYAGE TO OSAKA.
THEN, MOTHER'S SHUT HER HEART AND IS ALWAYS SULKY.
PLUS, THE NEPHEWS ARE ALWAYS FULL OF BEANS.
BOYS ARE SO POWERFUL.
NAO... SHE'S DOING HER BEST, BUT MOM IS SO HARSH ON HER.
DINNER THE FIRST DAY...IT WAS LIKE BEING IN JAIL.
UM...I CAN SEE YOU'VE HAD TONS OF STRESS!
WHEN I THINK THAT I'LL NEED TO FLY TO OSAKA MORE OFTEN!
MORE PINO... NOW!
THE FIRST VISIT TO OSAKA WAS TOO EX-HAUSTING AND TOUGH FOR ME TO THINK BE-YOND THAT.

CHAPTER 5

I DON'T WANT TO SAY THIS AGAIN

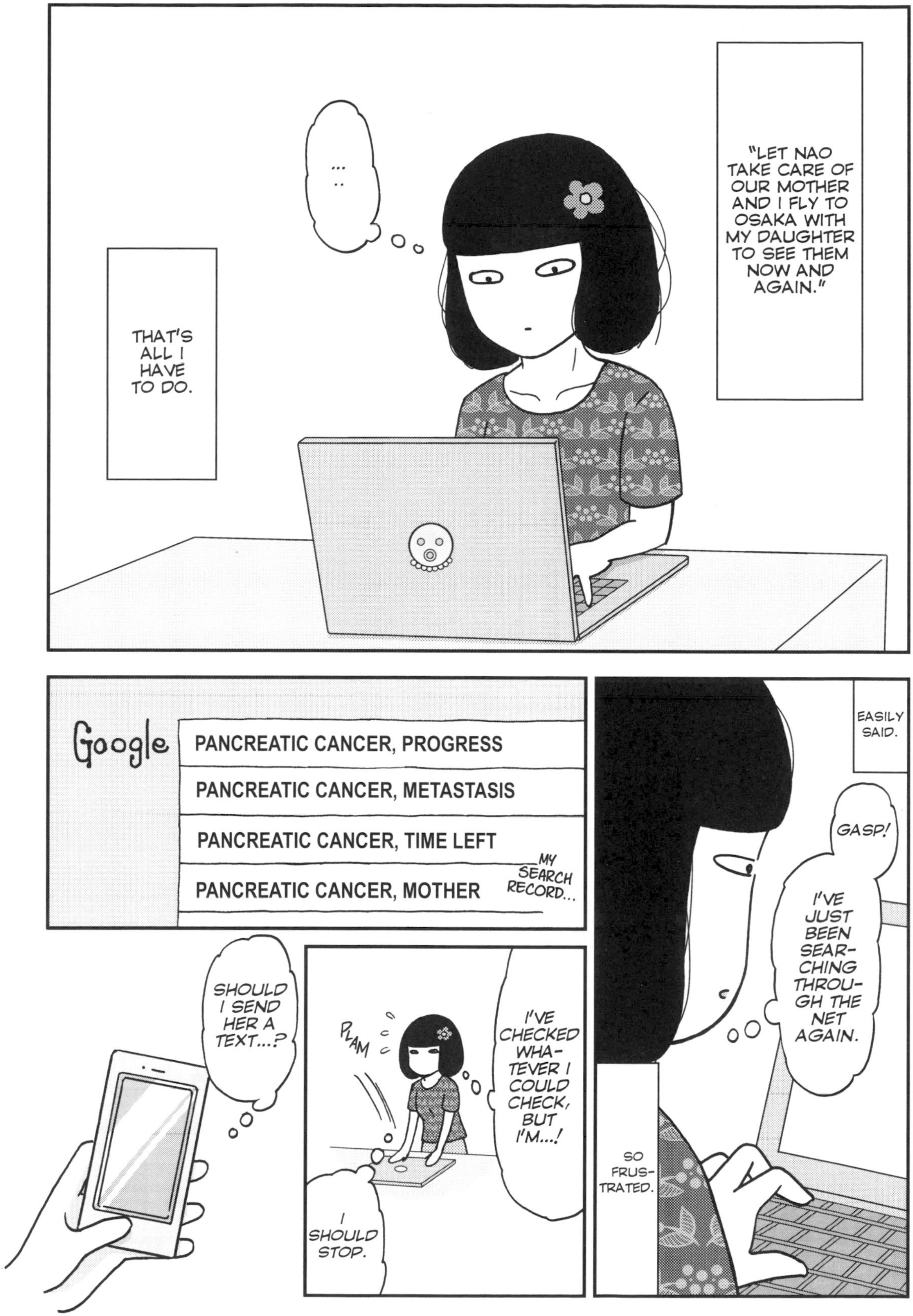
"LET NAO TAKE CARE OF OUR MOTHER AND I FLY TO OSAKA WITH MY DAUGHTER TO SEE THEM NOW AND AGAIN."
.....
THAT'S ALL I HAVE TO DO.
EASILY SAID.
GASP!
I'VE JUST BEEN SEARCHING THROUGH THE NET AGAIN.
SO FRUSTRATED.
Google
PANCREATIC CANCER, PROGRESS
PANCREATIC CANCER, METASTASIS
PANCREATIC CANCER, TIME LEFT
PANCREATIC CANCER, MOTHER
MY SEARCH RECORD...
I'VE CHECKED WHATEVER I COULD CHECK, BUT I'M...!
PLAM
I SHOULD STOP.
SHOULD I SEND HER A TEXT...?

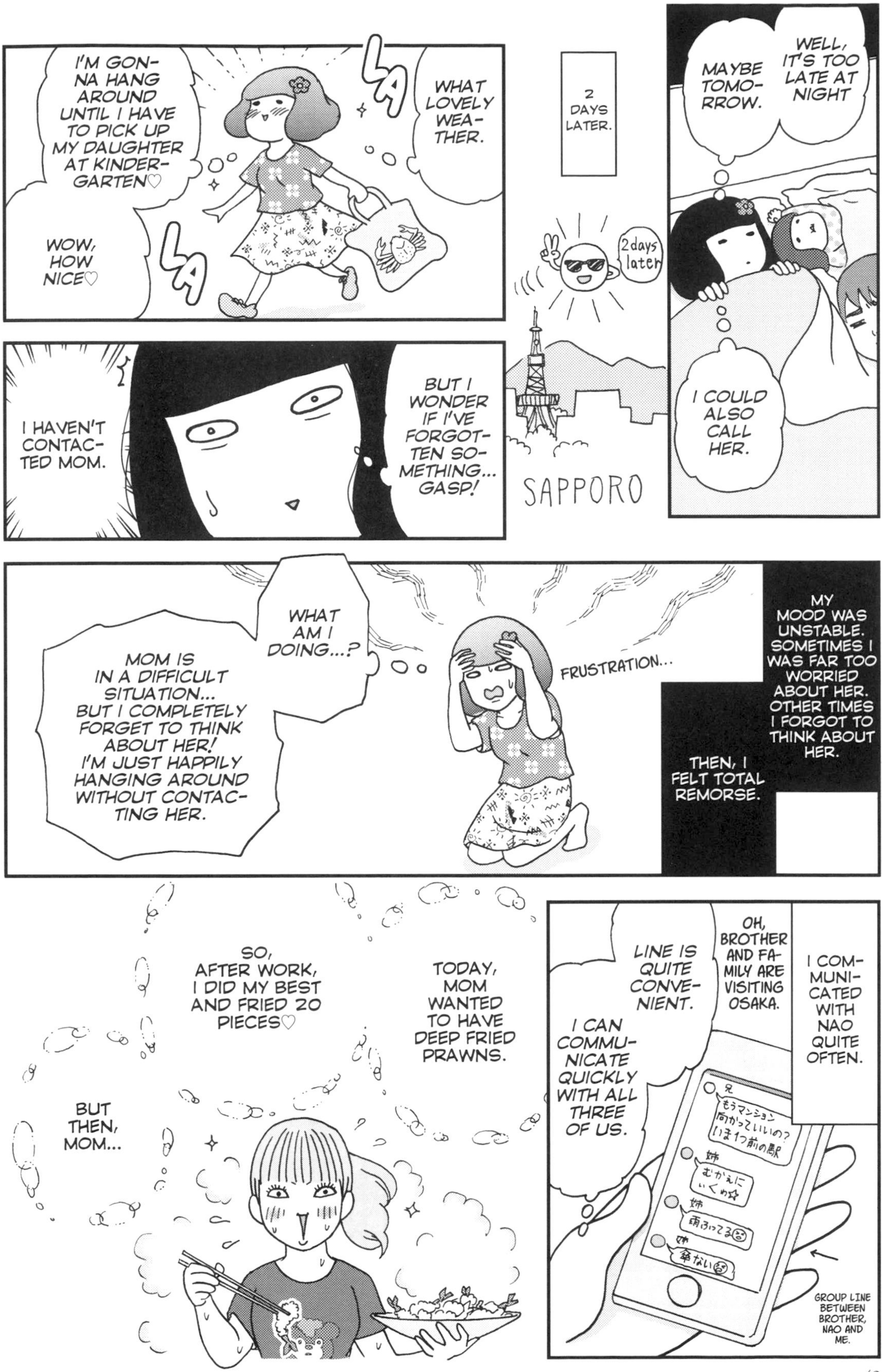
WELL, IT'S TOO LATE AT NIGHT
MAYBE TOMORROW.
I COULD ALSO CALL HER.
2 DAYS LATER.
2days later
SAPPORO
WHAT LOVELY WEATHER.
LA
I'M GONNA HANG AROUND UNTIL I HAVE TO PICK UP MY DAUGHTER AT KINDERGARTEN♡
LA
WOW, HOW NICE♡
BUT I WONDER IF I'VE FORGOTTEN SOMETHING... GASP!
I HAVEN'T CONTACTED MOM.
MY MOOD WAS UNSTABLE. SOMETIMES I WAS FAR TOO WORRIED ABOUT HER. OTHER TIMES I FORGOT TO THINK ABOUT HER.
THEN, I FELT TOTAL REMORSE.
FRUSTRATION...
WHAT AM I DOING...?
MOM IS IN A DIFFICULT SITUATION... BUT I COMPLETELY FORGET TO THINK ABOUT HER! I'M JUST HAPPILY HANGING AROUND WITHOUT CONTACTING HER.
I COMMUNICATED WITH NAO QUITE OFTEN.
OH, BROTHER AND FAMILY ARE VISITING OSAKA.
LINE IS QUITE CONVENIENT.
I CAN COMMUNICATE QUICKLY WITH ALL THREE OF US.
兄
もうマンション向かっていいの?いま1つ前の駅
姉
むかえにいくね☆
姉
雨ふってる
姉
傘ない
GROUP LINE BETWEEN BROTHER, NAO AND ME.
TODAY, MOM WANTED TO HAVE DEEP FRIED PRAWNS.
SO, AFTER WORK, I DID MY BEST AND FRIED 20 PIECES♡
BUT THEN, MOM...

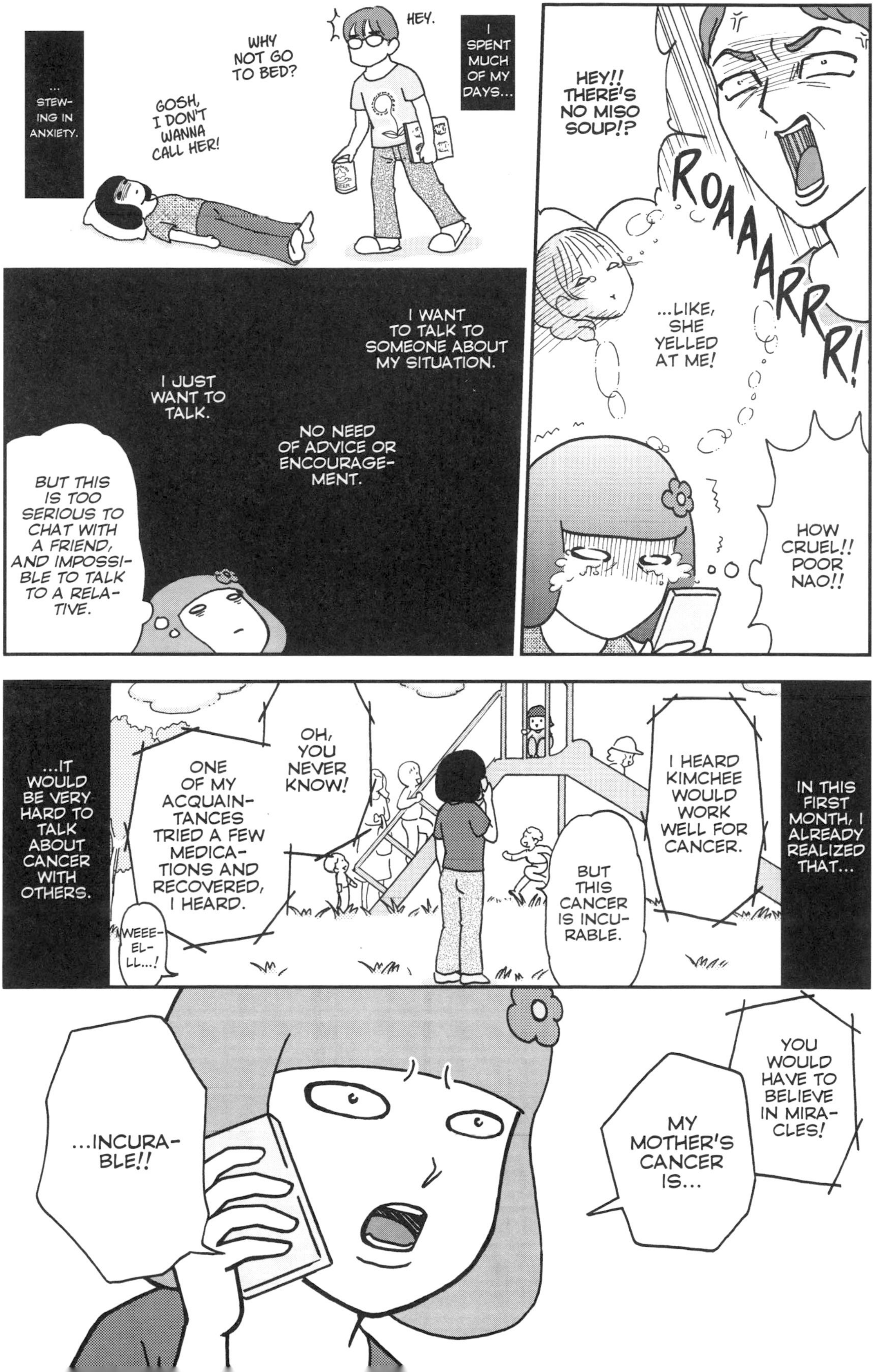
ROAAAARRRR!
HEY!! THERE'S NO MISO SOUP!?
...LIKE, SHE YELLED AT ME!
HOW CRUEL!! POOR NAO!!
I SPENT MUCH OF MY DAYS...
HEY.
WHY NOT GO TO BED?
GOSH, I DON'T WANNA CALL HER!
...STEWING IN ANXIETY.
I WANT TO TALK TO SOMEONE ABOUT MY SITUATION.
I JUST WANT TO TALK.
NO NEED OF ADVICE OR ENCOURAGEMENT.
BUT THIS IS TOO SERIOUS TO CHAT WITH A FRIEND, AND IMPOSSIBLE TO TALK TO A RELATIVE.
IN THIS FIRST MONTH, I ALREADY REALIZED THAT...
I HEARD KIMCHEE WOULD WORK WELL FOR CANCER.
BUT THIS CANCER IS INCURABLE.
OH, YOU NEVER KNOW!
ONE OF MY ACQUAINTANCES TRIED A FEW MEDICATIONS AND RECOVERED, I HEARD.
WEEE-EL-LL...!
...IT WOULD BE VERY HARD TO TALK ABOUT CANCER WITH OTHERS.
YOU WOULD HAVE TO BELIEVE IN MIRACLES!
MY MOTHER'S CANCER IS...
...INCURABLE!!

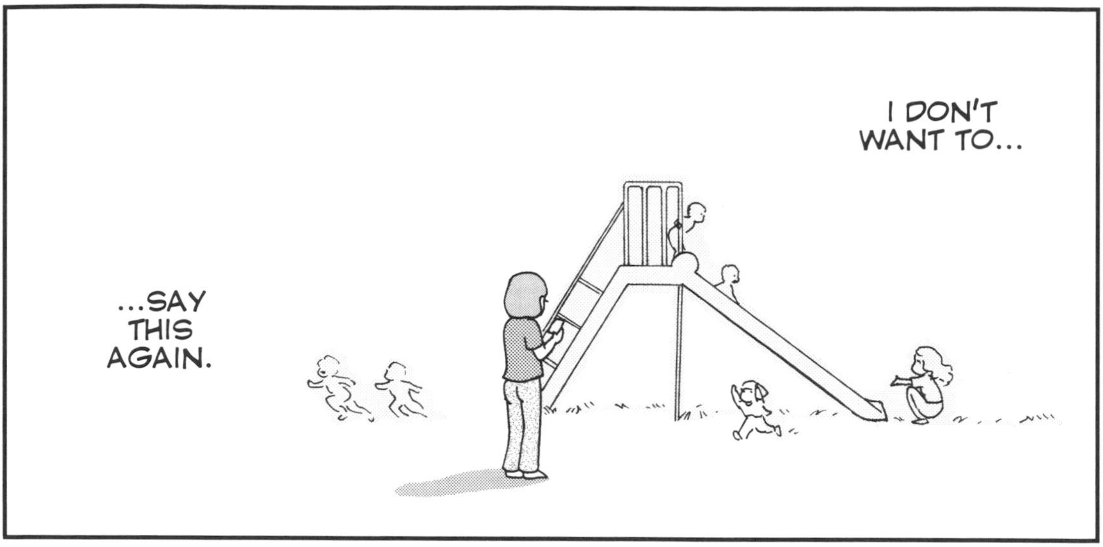
I DON'T WANT TO...
...SAY THIS AGAIN.

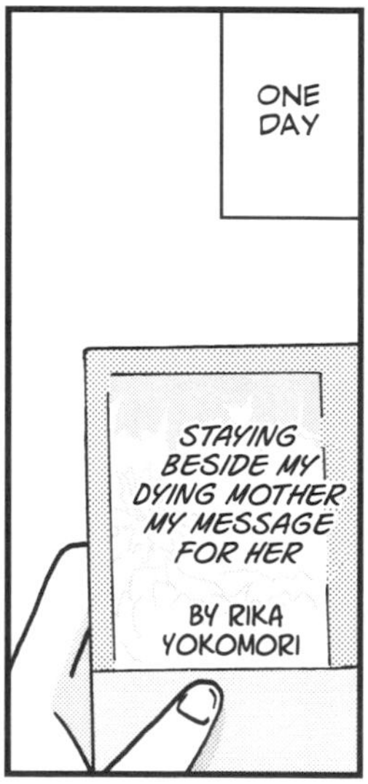
ONE DAY
STAYING BESIDE MY DYING MOTHER MY MESSAGE FOR HER
BY RIKA YOKOMORI

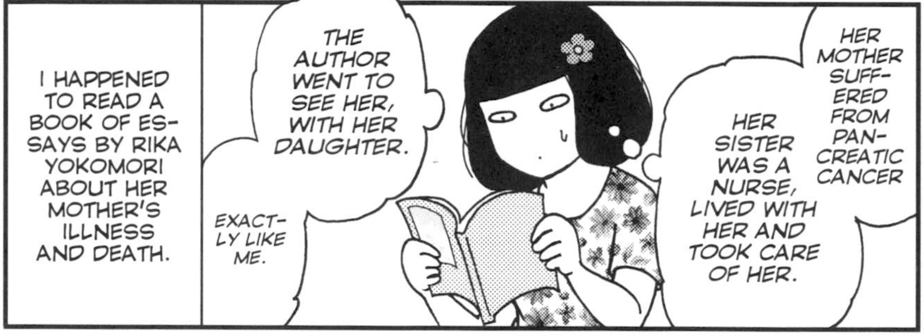
HER MOTHER SUFFERED FROM PANCREATIC CANCER
HER SISTER WAS A NURSE, LIVED WITH HER AND TOOK CARE OF HER.
THE AUTHOR WENT TO SEE HER, WITH HER DAUGHTER.
EXACTLY LIKE ME.
I HAPPENED TO READ A BOOK OF ESSAYS BY RIKA YOKOMORI ABOUT HER MOTHER'S ILLNESS AND DEATH.

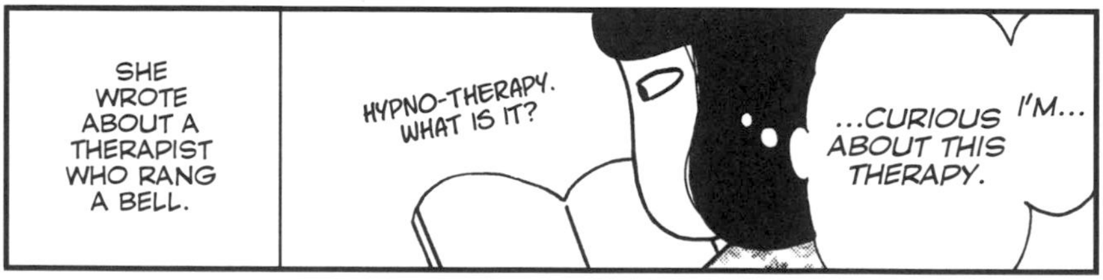
I'M...
...CURIOUS ABOUT THIS THERAPY.
HYPNO-THERAPY. WHAT IS IT?
SHE WROTE ABOUT A THERAPIST WHO RANG A BELL.

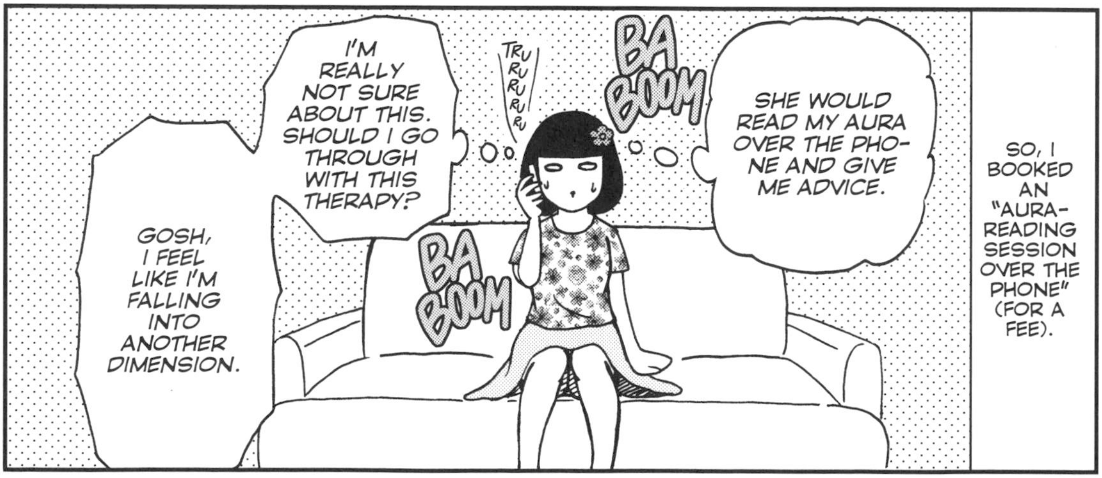
SO, I BOOKED AN "AURA-READING SESSION OVER THE PHONE" (FOR A FEE).
SHE WOULD READ MY AURA OVER THE PHONE AND GIVE ME ADVICE.
BA BOOM
TRU RU RU RU RU
I'M REALLY NOT SURE ABOUT THIS. SHOULD I GO THROUGH WITH THIS THERAPY?
BA BOOM
GOSH, I FEEL LIKE I'M FALLING INTO ANOTHER DIMENSION.

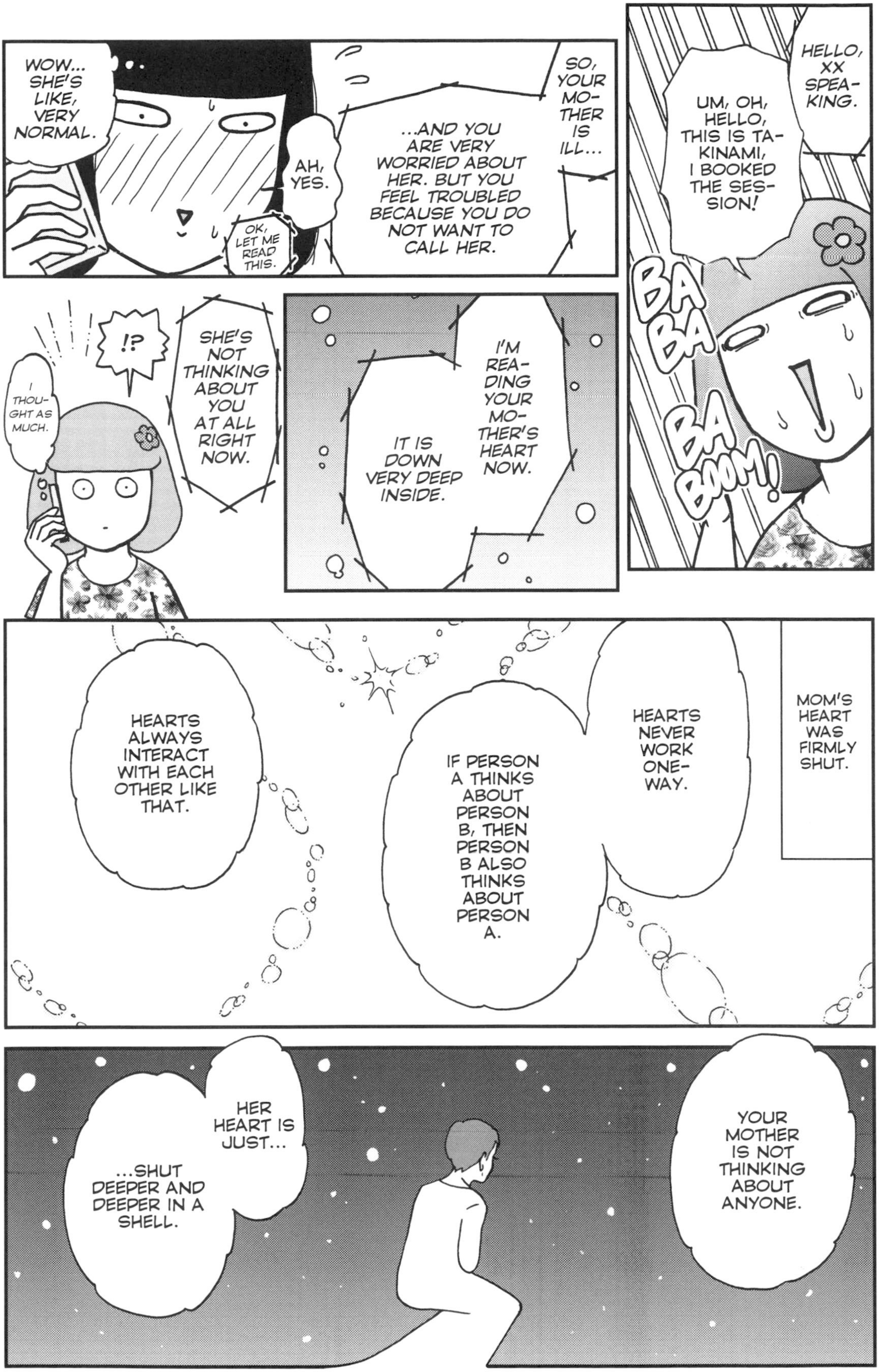
HELLO, XX SPEAKING.
UM, OH, HELLO, THIS IS TAKINAMI, I BOOKED THE SESSION!
BA BA BA BOOM!
SO, YOUR MOTHER IS ILL...
...AND YOU ARE VERY WORRIED ABOUT HER. BUT YOU FEEL TROUBLED BECAUSE YOU DO NOT WANT TO CALL HER.
AH, YES.
OK, LET ME READ THIS.
WOW... SHE'S LIKE, VERY NORMAL.
I'M READING YOUR MOTHER'S HEART NOW.
IT IS DOWN VERY DEEP INSIDE.
SHE'S NOT THINKING ABOUT YOU AT ALL RIGHT NOW.
!?
I THOUGHT AS MUCH.
MOM'S HEART WAS FIRMLY SHUT.
HEARTS NEVER WORK ONE-WAY.
IF PERSON A THINKS ABOUT PERSON B, THEN PERSON B ALSO THINKS ABOUT PERSON A.
HEARTS ALWAYS INTERACT WITH EACH OTHER LIKE THAT.
YOUR MOTHER IS NOT THINKING ABOUT ANYONE.
HER HEART IS JUST...
...SHUT DEEPER AND DEEPER IN A SHELL.

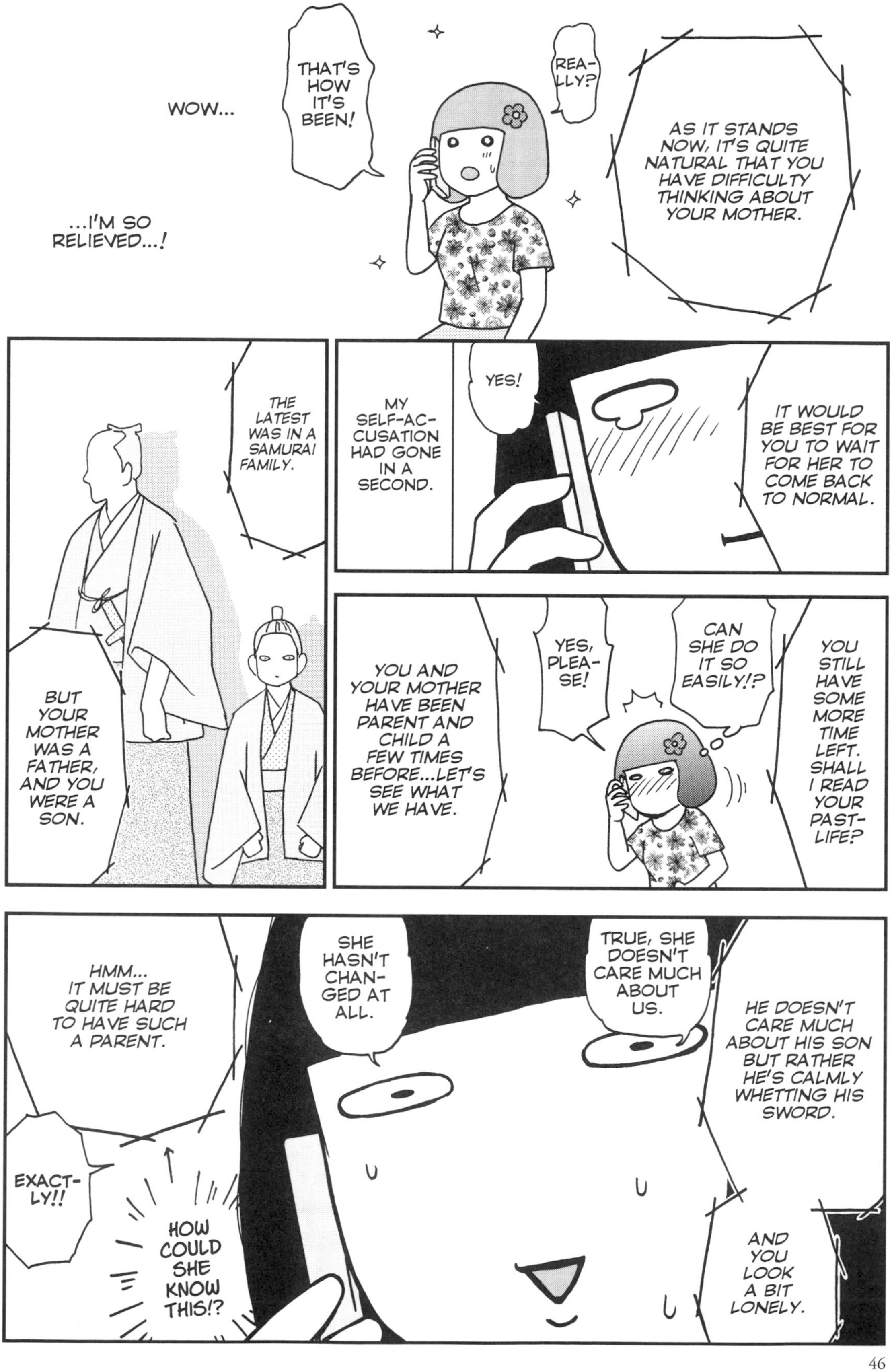
AS IT STANDS NOW, IT'S QUITE NATURAL THAT YOU HAVE DIFFICULTY THINKING ABOUT YOUR MOTHER.
REALLY?
THAT'S HOW IT'S BEEN!
WOW...
...I'M SO RELIEVED...!
IT WOULD BE BEST FOR YOU TO WAIT FOR HER TO COME BACK TO NORMAL.
YES!
MY SELF-ACCUSATION HAD GONE IN A SECOND.
YOU STILL HAVE SOME MORE TIME LEFT. SHALL I READ YOUR PAST-LIFE?
CAN SHE DO IT SO EASILY!?
YES, PLEASE!
YOU AND YOUR MOTHER HAVE BEEN PARENT AND CHILD A FEW TIMES BEFORE...LET'S SEE WHAT WE HAVE.
THE LATEST WAS IN A SAMURAI FAMILY.
BUT YOUR MOTHER WAS A FATHER, AND YOU WERE A SON.
HE DOESN'T CARE MUCH ABOUT HIS SON BUT RATHER HE'S CALMLY WHETTING HIS SWORD.
AND YOU LOOK A BIT LONELY.
TRUE, SHE DOESN'T CARE MUCH ABOUT US.
SHE HASN'T CHANGED AT ALL.
HMM... IT MUST BE QUITE HARD TO HAVE SUCH A PARENT.
HOW COULD SHE KNOW THIS!?
EXACTLY!!

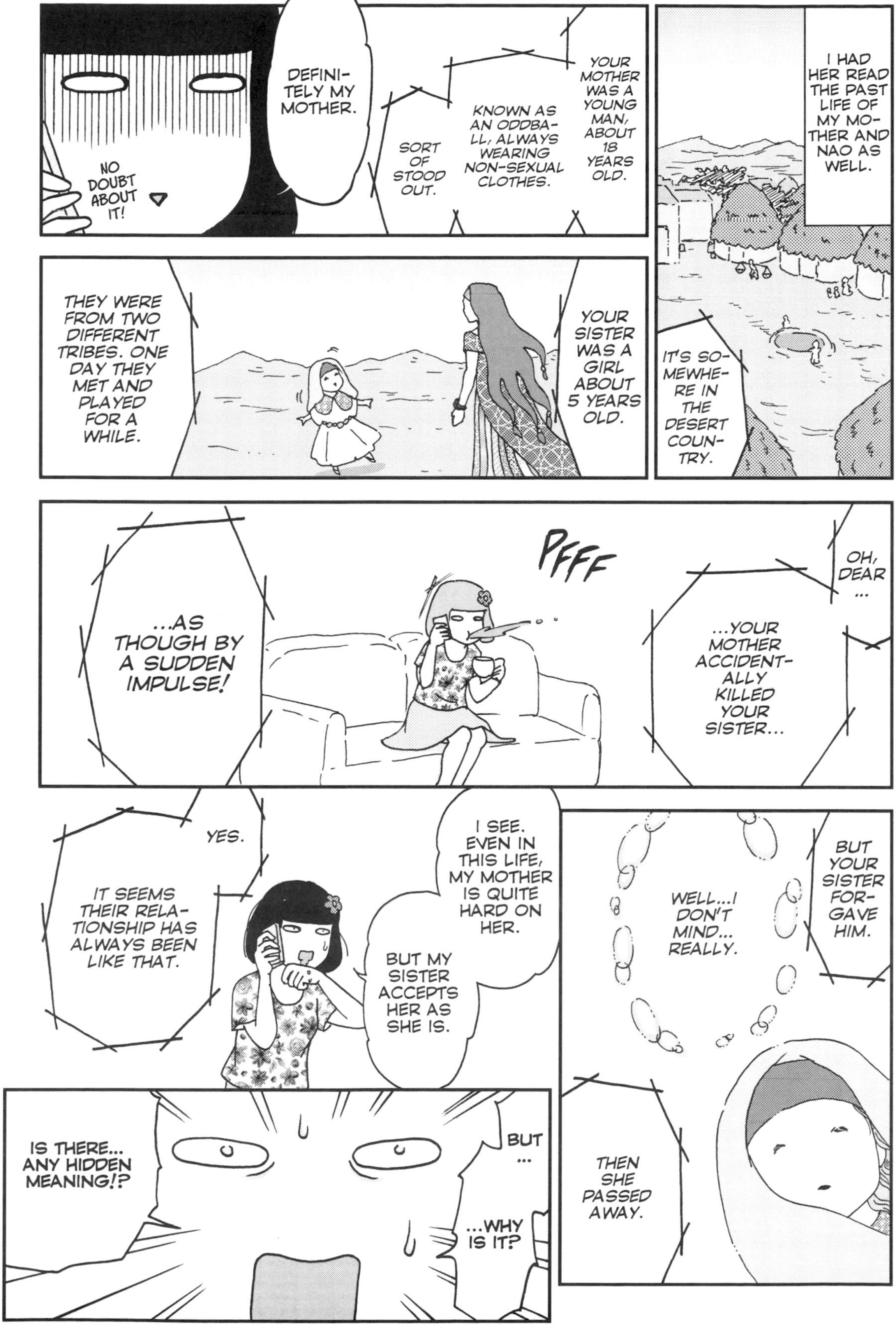
I HAD HER READ THE PAST LIFE OF MY MOTHER AND NAO AS WELL.
IT'S SOMEWHERE IN THE DESERT COUNTRY.
YOUR MOTHER WAS A YOUNG MAN, ABOUT 18 YEARS OLD.
KNOWN AS AN ODDBALL, ALWAYS WEARING NON-SEXUAL CLOTHES.
SORT OF STOOD OUT.
DEFINITELY MY MOTHER.
NO DOUBT ABOUT IT!
YOUR SISTER WAS A GIRL ABOUT 5 YEARS OLD.
THEY WERE FROM TWO DIFFERENT TRIBES. ONE DAY THEY MET AND PLAYED FOR A WHILE.
OH, DEAR ...
...YOUR MOTHER ACCIDENTALLY KILLED YOUR SISTER...
PFFF
...AS THOUGH BY A SUDDEN IMPULSE!
BUT YOUR SISTER FORGAVE HIM.
WELL...I DON'T MIND... REALLY.
THEN SHE PASSED AWAY.
I SEE. EVEN IN THIS LIFE, MY MOTHER IS QUITE HARD ON HER.
BUT MY SISTER ACCEPTS HER AS SHE IS.
YES.
IT SEEMS THEIR RELATIONSHIP HAS ALWAYS BEEN LIKE THAT.
BUT ...
...WHY IS IT?
IS THERE... ANY HIDDEN MEANING!?

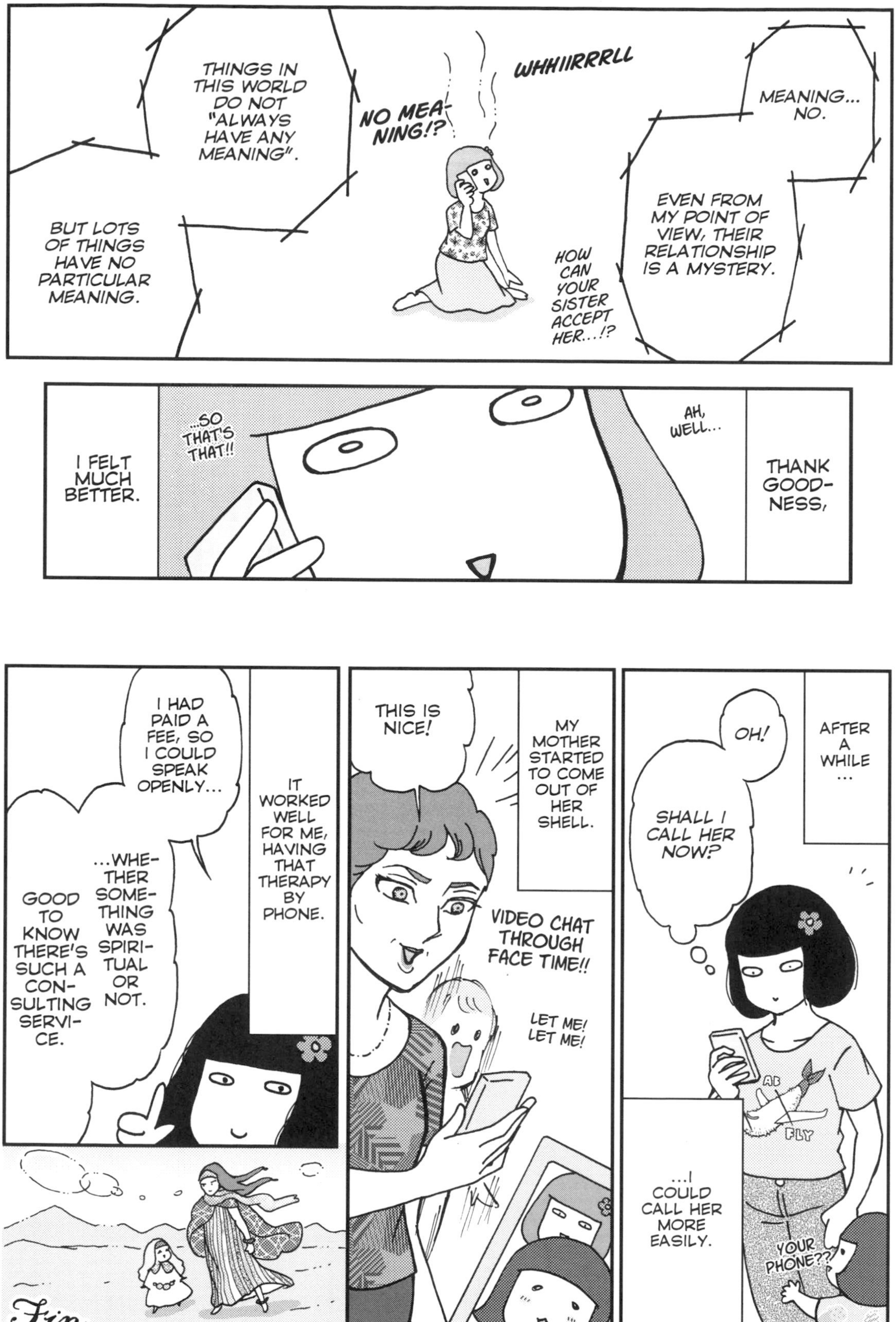
MEANING... NO.
EVEN FROM MY POINT OF VIEW, THEIR RELATIONSHIP IS A MYSTERY.
HOW CAN YOUR SISTER ACCEPT HER...!?
WHHIIRRRLL
NO MEA-NING!?
THINGS IN THIS WORLD DO NOT "ALWAYS HAVE ANY MEANING".
BUT LOTS OF THINGS HAVE NO PARTICULAR MEANING.
THANK GOOD-NESS,
AH, WELL...
...SO THAT'S THAT!!
I FELT MUCH BETTER.
AFTER A WHILE...
OH!
SHALL I CALL HER NOW?
...I COULD CALL HER MORE EASILY.
YOUR PHONE??
MY MOTHER STARTED TO COME OUT OF HER SHELL.
THIS IS NICE!
VIDEO CHAT THROUGH FACE TIME!!
LET ME! LET ME!
IT WORKED WELL FOR ME, HAVING THAT THERAPY BY PHONE.
I HAD PAID A FEE, SO I COULD SPEAK OPENLY...
...WHE-THER SOME-THING WAS SPIRI-TUAL OR NOT.
GOOD TO KNOW THERE'S SUCH A CON-SULTING SERVI-CE.
Fin.

CHAPTER 6

SELLING
OUR HOME

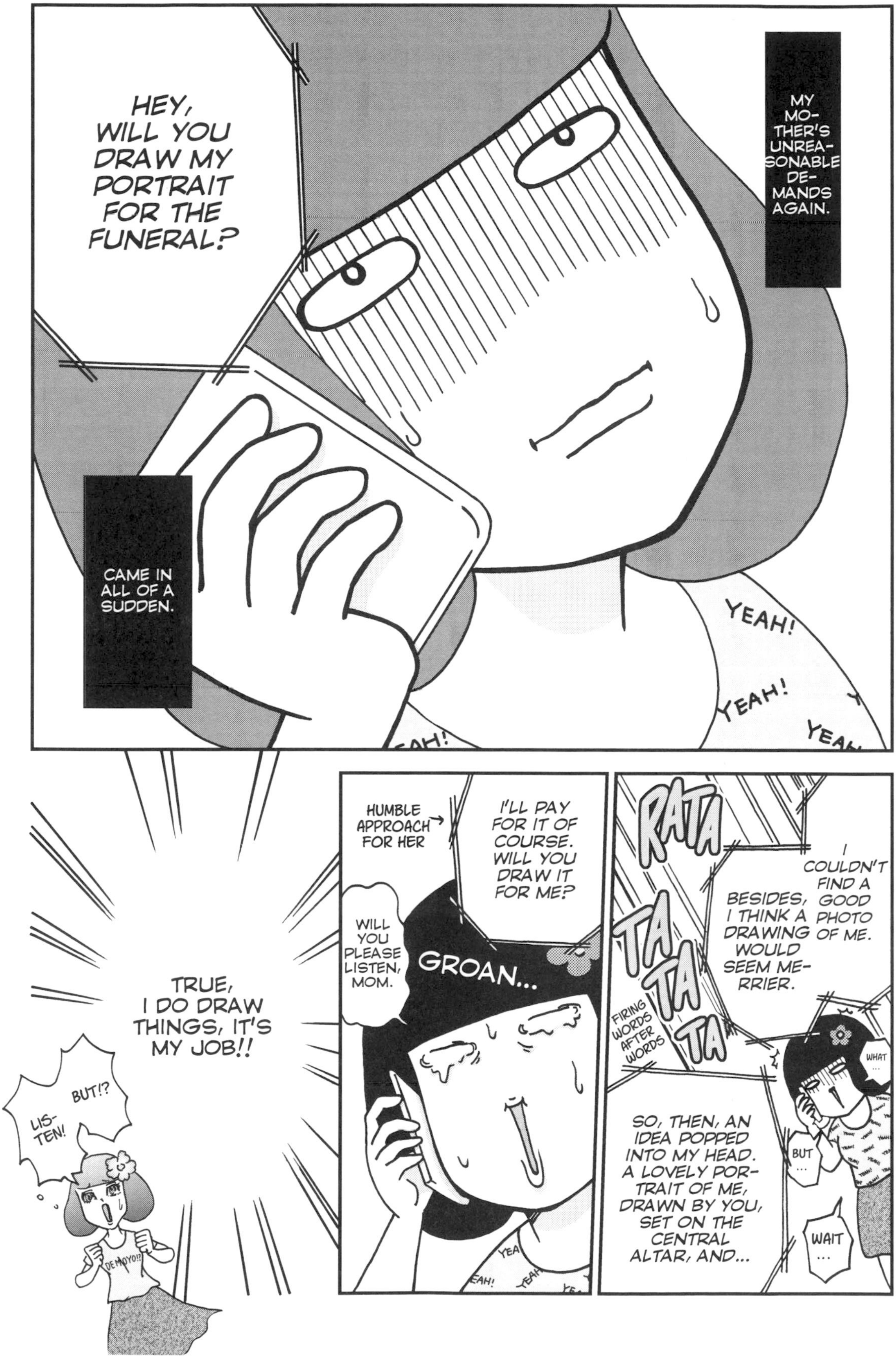
MY MOTHER'S UNREASONABLE DEMANDS AGAIN.
HEY, WILL YOU DRAW MY PORTRAIT FOR THE FUNERAL?
CAME IN ALL OF A SUDDEN.
YEAH! YEAH! YEAH!
RATA TA TA TA
I COULDN'T FIND A GOOD PHOTO OF ME.
BESIDES, I THINK A DRAWING WOULD SEEM MERRIER.
FIRING WORDS AFTER WORDS
WHAT ...
SO, THEN, AN IDEA POPPED INTO MY HEAD. A LOVELY PORTRAIT OF ME, DRAWN BY YOU, SET ON THE CENTRAL ALTAR, AND...
BUT ...
WAIT ...
I'LL PAY FOR IT OF COURSE. WILL YOU DRAW IT FOR ME?
HUMBLE APPROACH FOR HER
WILL YOU PLEASE LISTEN, MOM.
GROAN...
TRUE, I DO DRAW THINGS, IT'S MY JOB!!
BUT!?
LISTEN!
DEMOYO!!

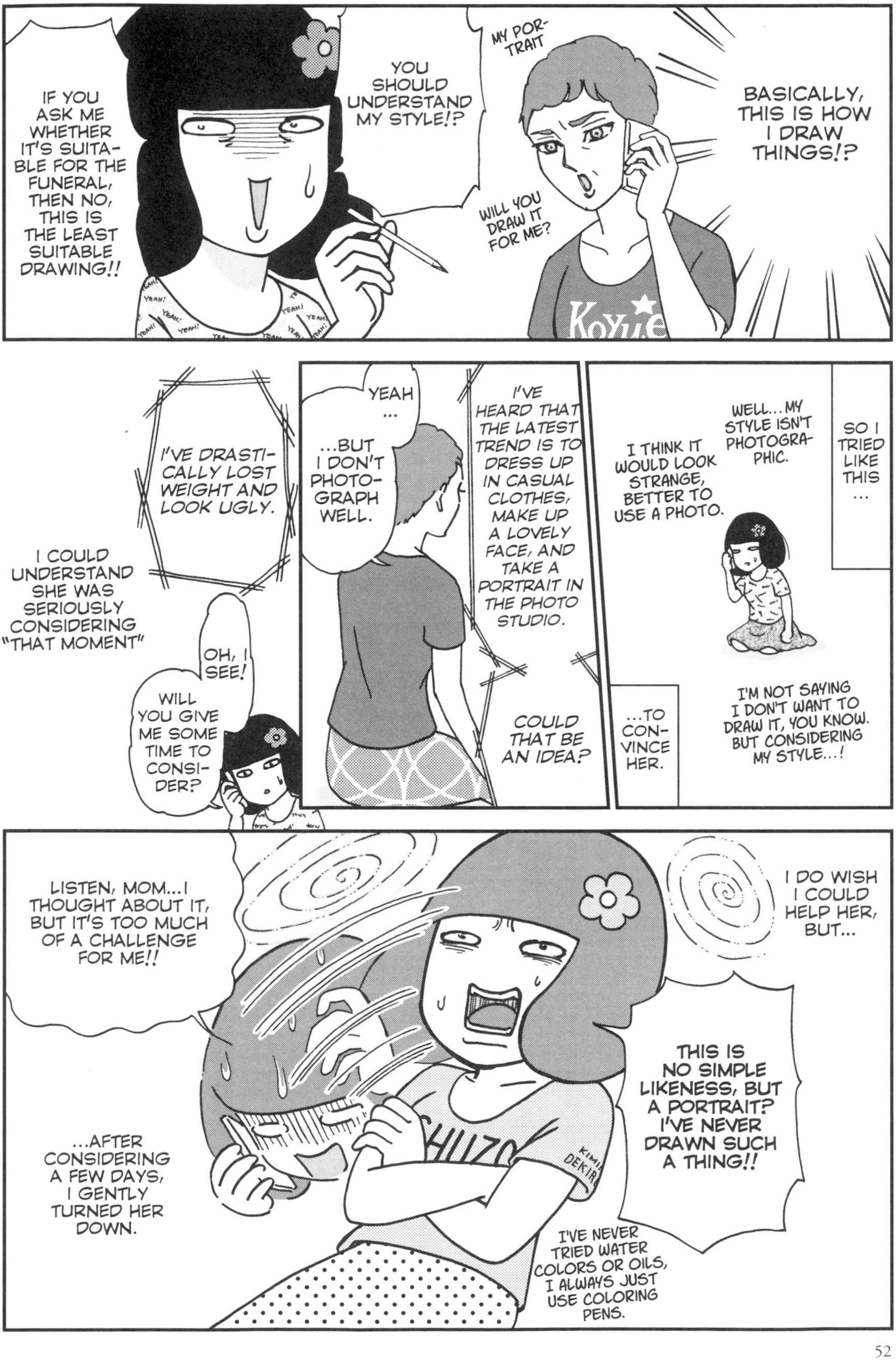
BASICALLY, THIS IS HOW I DRAW THINGS!?
MY PORTRAIT
WILL YOU DRAW IT FOR ME?
YOU SHOULD UNDERSTAND MY STYLE!?
IF YOU ASK ME WHETHER IT'S SUITABLE FOR THE FUNERAL, THEN NO, THIS IS THE LEAST SUITABLE DRAWING!!
SO I TRIED LIKE THIS ...
WELL... MY STYLE ISN'T PHOTOGRAPHIC.
I THINK IT WOULD LOOK STRANGE, BETTER TO USE A PHOTO.
I'M NOT SAYING I DON'T WANT TO DRAW IT, YOU KNOW. BUT CONSIDERING MY STYLE...!
...TO CONVINCE HER.
I'VE HEARD THAT THE LATEST TREND IS TO DRESS UP IN CASUAL CLOTHES, MAKE UP A LOVELY FACE, AND TAKE A PORTRAIT IN THE PHOTO STUDIO.
YEAH ...
...BUT I DON'T PHOTOGRAPH WELL.
COULD THAT BE AN IDEA?
I'VE DRASTICALLY LOST WEIGHT AND LOOK UGLY.
I COULD UNDERSTAND SHE WAS SERIOUSLY CONSIDERING "THAT MOMENT"
OH, I SEE!
WILL YOU GIVE ME SOME TIME TO CONSIDER?
I DO WISH I COULD HELP HER, BUT...
LISTEN, MOM...I THOUGHT ABOUT IT, BUT IT'S TOO MUCH OF A CHALLENGE FOR ME!!
THIS IS NO SIMPLE LIKENESS, BUT A PORTRAIT? I'VE NEVER DRAWN SUCH A THING!!
I'VE NEVER TRIED WATER COLORS OR OILS, I ALWAYS JUST USE COLORING PENS.
...AFTER CONSIDERING A FEW DAYS, I GENTLY TURNED HER DOWN.

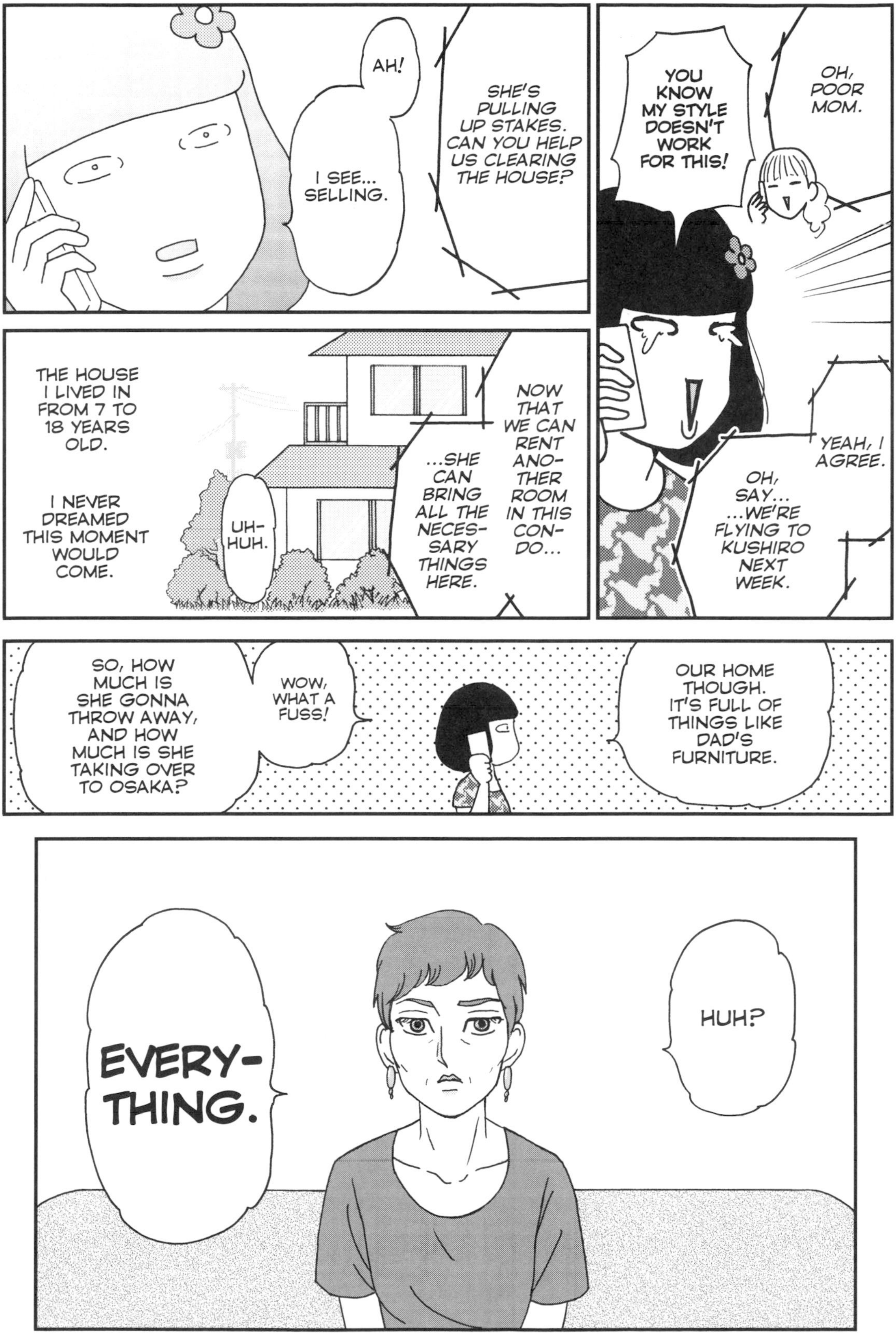
OH, POOR MOM.
YOU KNOW MY STYLE DOESN'T WORK FOR THIS!
YEAH, I AGREE.
OH, SAY... ...WE'RE FLYING TO KUSHIRO NEXT WEEK.
SHE'S PULLING UP STAKES. CAN YOU HELP US CLEARING THE HOUSE?
AH!
I SEE... SELLING.
NOW THAT WE CAN RENT ANOTHER ROOM IN THIS CONDO...
...SHE CAN BRING ALL THE NECESSARY THINGS HERE.
UH-HUH.
THE HOUSE I LIVED IN FROM 7 TO 18 YEARS OLD.
I NEVER DREAMED THIS MOMENT WOULD COME.
OUR HOME THOUGH. IT'S FULL OF THINGS LIKE DAD'S FURNITURE.
WOW, WHAT A FUSS!
SO, HOW MUCH IS SHE GONNA THROW AWAY, AND HOW MUCH IS SHE TAKING OVER TO OSAKA?
HUH?
EVERYTHING.

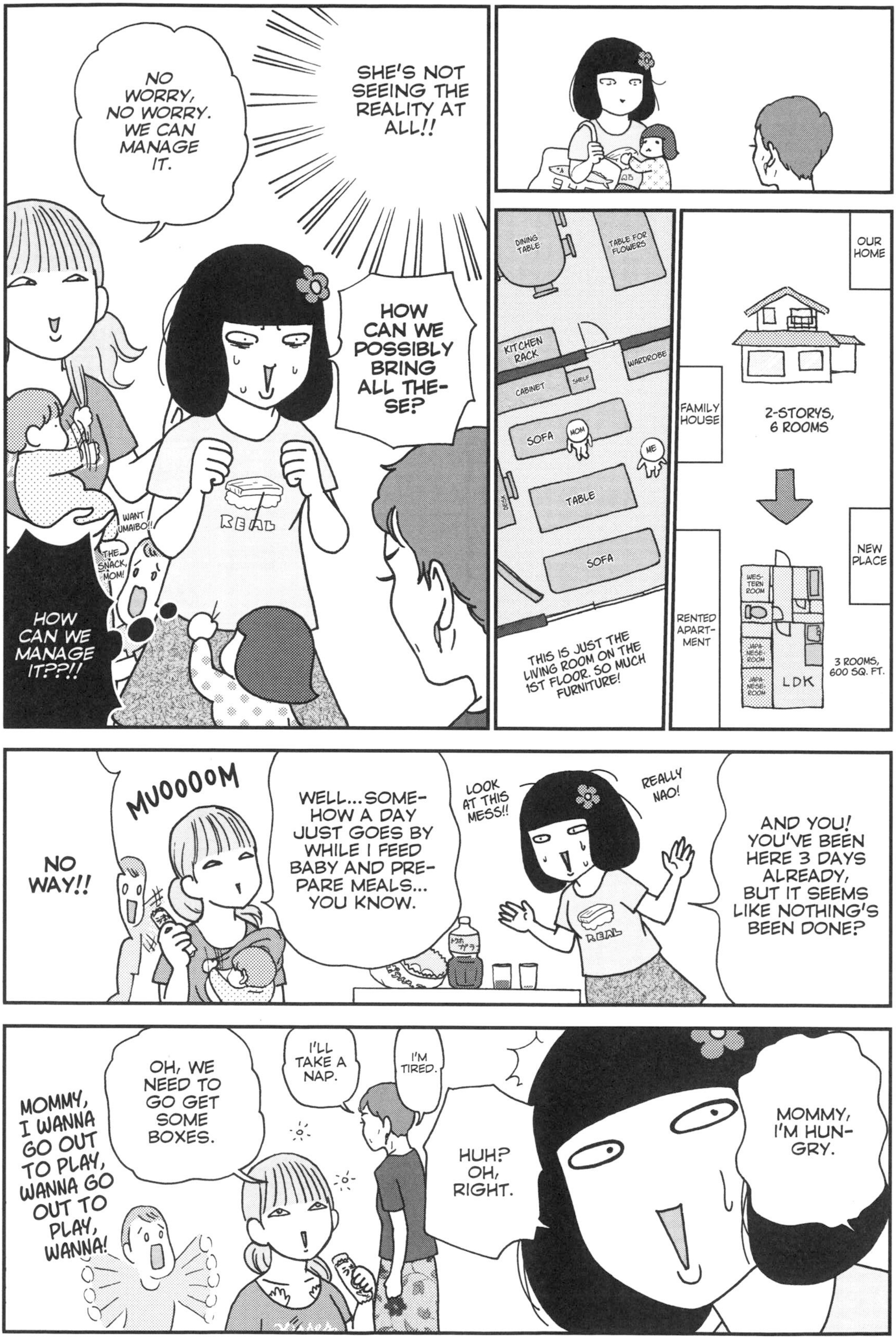
OUR HOME
2-STORYS, 6 ROOMS
FAMILY HOUSE
NEW PLACE
WESTERN ROOM
JAPANESE ROOM
JAPANESE ROOM
LDK
3 ROOMS, 600 SQ. FT.
RENTED APARTMENT
TABLE FOR FLOWERS
DINING TABLE
WARDROBE
KITCHEN RACK
SHELF
CABINET
ME
MOM
SOFA
TABLE
SOFA
DESK
THIS IS JUST THE LIVING ROOM ON THE 1ST FLOOR. SO MUCH FURNITURE!
SHE'S NOT SEEING THE REALITY AT ALL!!
NO WORRY, NO WORRY. WE CAN MANAGE IT.
HOW CAN WE POSSIBLY BRING ALL THESE?
WANT UMAIBO!!
THE SNACK, MOM!
HOW CAN WE MANAGE IT??!!
AND YOU! YOU'VE BEEN HERE 3 DAYS ALREADY, BUT IT SEEMS LIKE NOTHING'S BEEN DONE?
REALLY NAO!
LOOK AT THIS MESS!!
WELL...SOMEHOW A DAY JUST GOES BY WHILE I FEED BABY AND PREPARE MEALS... YOU KNOW.
MUOOOOM
NO WAY!!
MOMMY, I'M HUNGRY.
HUH? OH, RIGHT.
I'M TIRED.
I'LL TAKE A NAP.
OH, WE NEED TO GO GET SOME BOXES.
MOMMY, I WANNA GO OUT TO PLAY, WANNA GO OUT TO PLAY, WANNA!

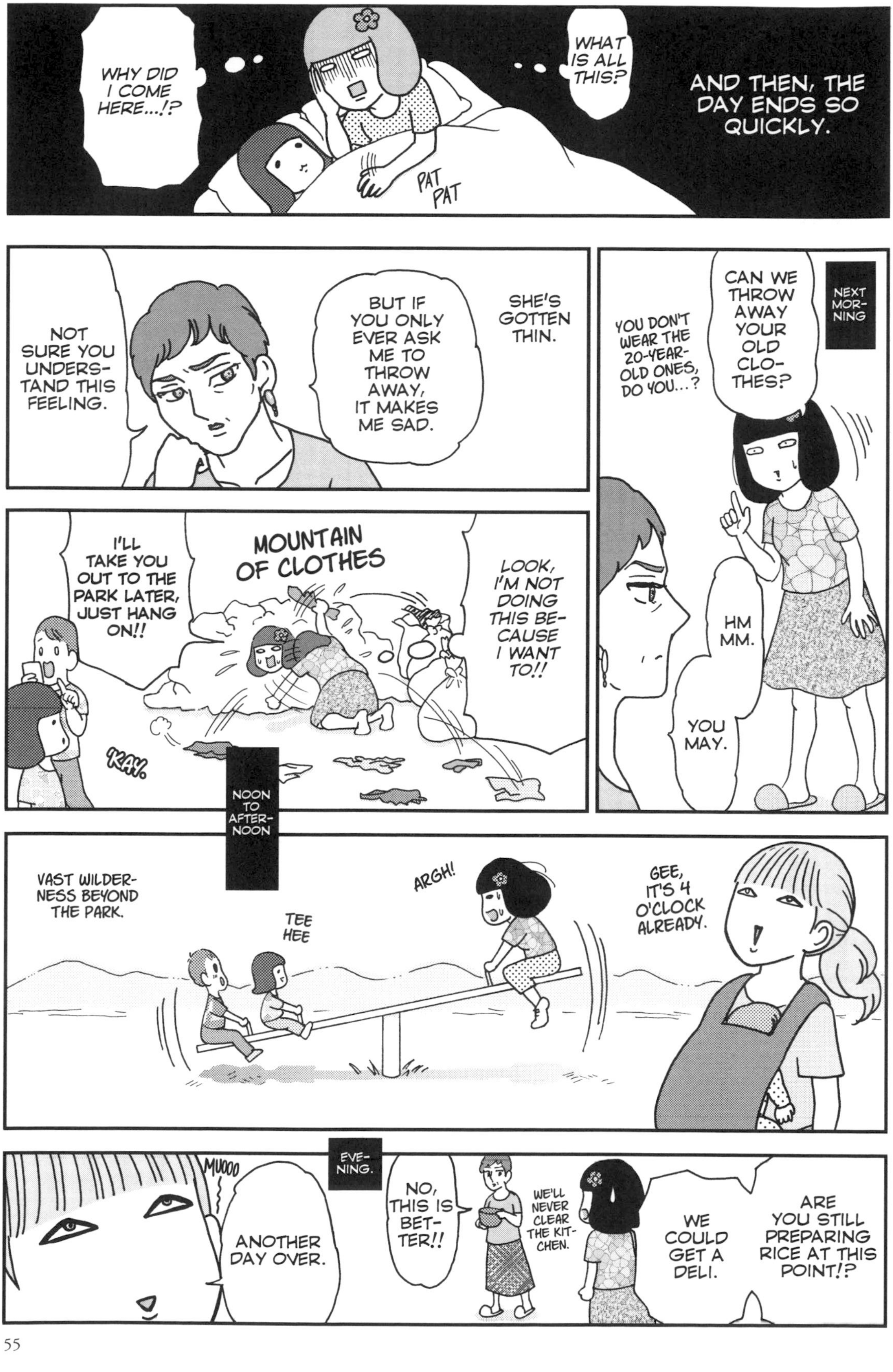
AND THEN, THE DAY ENDS SO QUICKLY.
WHAT IS ALL THIS?
WHY DID I COME HERE...!?
PAT PAT
NEXT MORNING
CAN WE THROW AWAY YOUR OLD CLOTHES?
YOU DON'T WEAR THE 20-YEAR-OLD ONES, DO YOU...?
HM MM.
YOU MAY.
SHE'S GOTTEN THIN.
BUT IF YOU ONLY EVER ASK ME TO THROW AWAY, IT MAKES ME SAD.
NOT SURE YOU UNDERSTAND THIS FEELING.
LOOK, I'M NOT DOING THIS BECAUSE I WANT TO!!
MOUNTAIN OF CLOTHES
I'LL TAKE YOU OUT TO THE PARK LATER, JUST HANG ON!!
'KAY.
NOON TO AFTERNOON
GEE, IT'S 4 O'CLOCK ALREADY.
ARGH!
TEE HEE
VAST WILDERNESS BEYOND THE PARK.
ARE YOU STILL PREPARING RICE AT THIS POINT!?
WE COULD GET A DELI.
WE'LL NEVER CLEAR THE KITCHEN.
NO, THIS IS BETTER!!
EVENING.
ANOTHER DAY OVER.
MUOOO

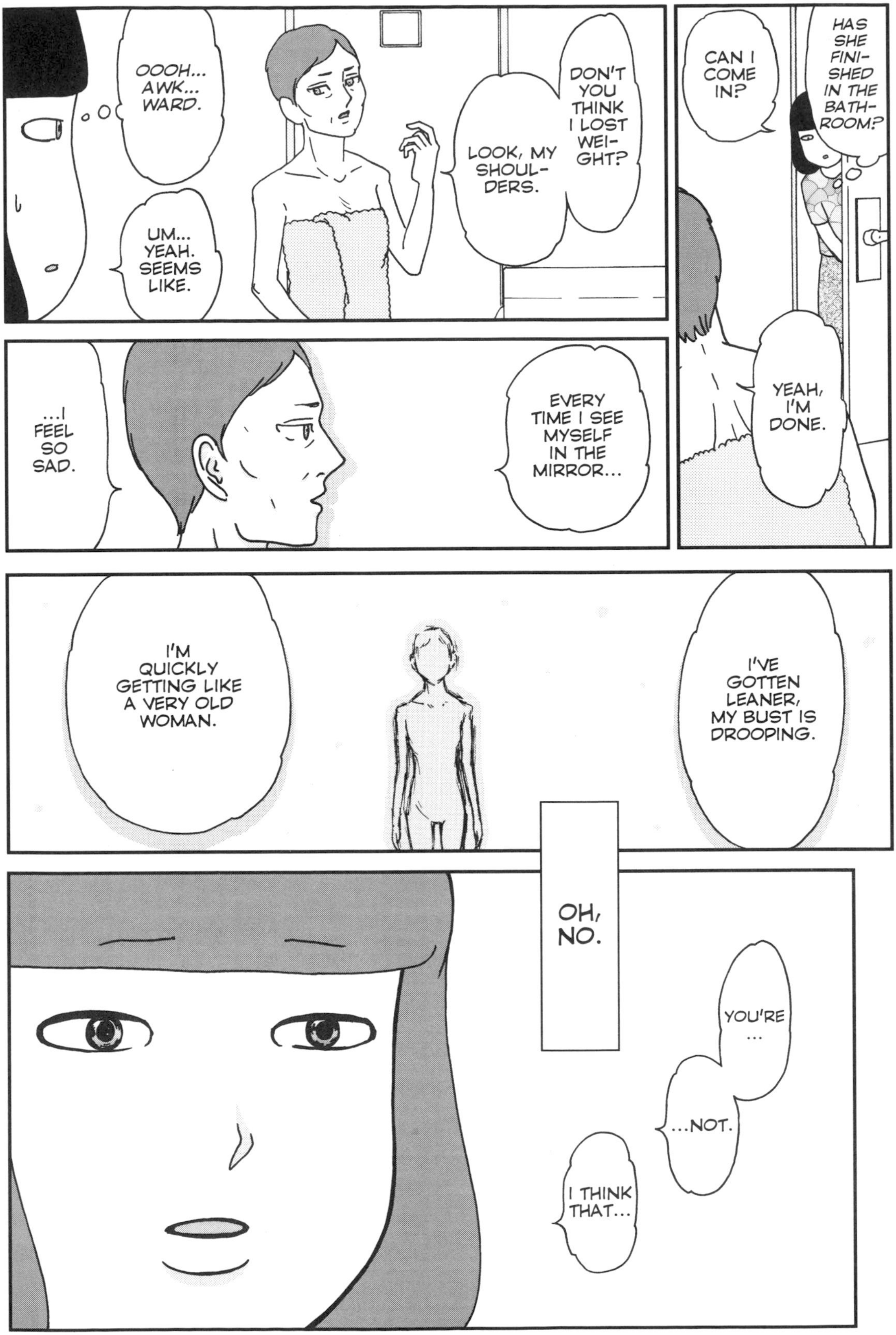
HAS SHE FINISHED IN THE BATHROOM?
CAN I COME IN?
YEAH, I'M DONE.
DON'T YOU THINK I LOST WEIGHT?
LOOK, MY SHOULDERS.
OOOH... AWK... WARD.
UM... YEAH. SEEMS LIKE.
EVERY TIME I SEE MYSELF IN THE MIRROR...
...I FEEL SO SAD.
I'VE GOTTEN LEANER, MY BUST IS DROOPING.
I'M QUICKLY GETTING LIKE A VERY OLD WOMAN.
OH, NO.
YOU'RE ...
...NOT.
I THINK THAT...

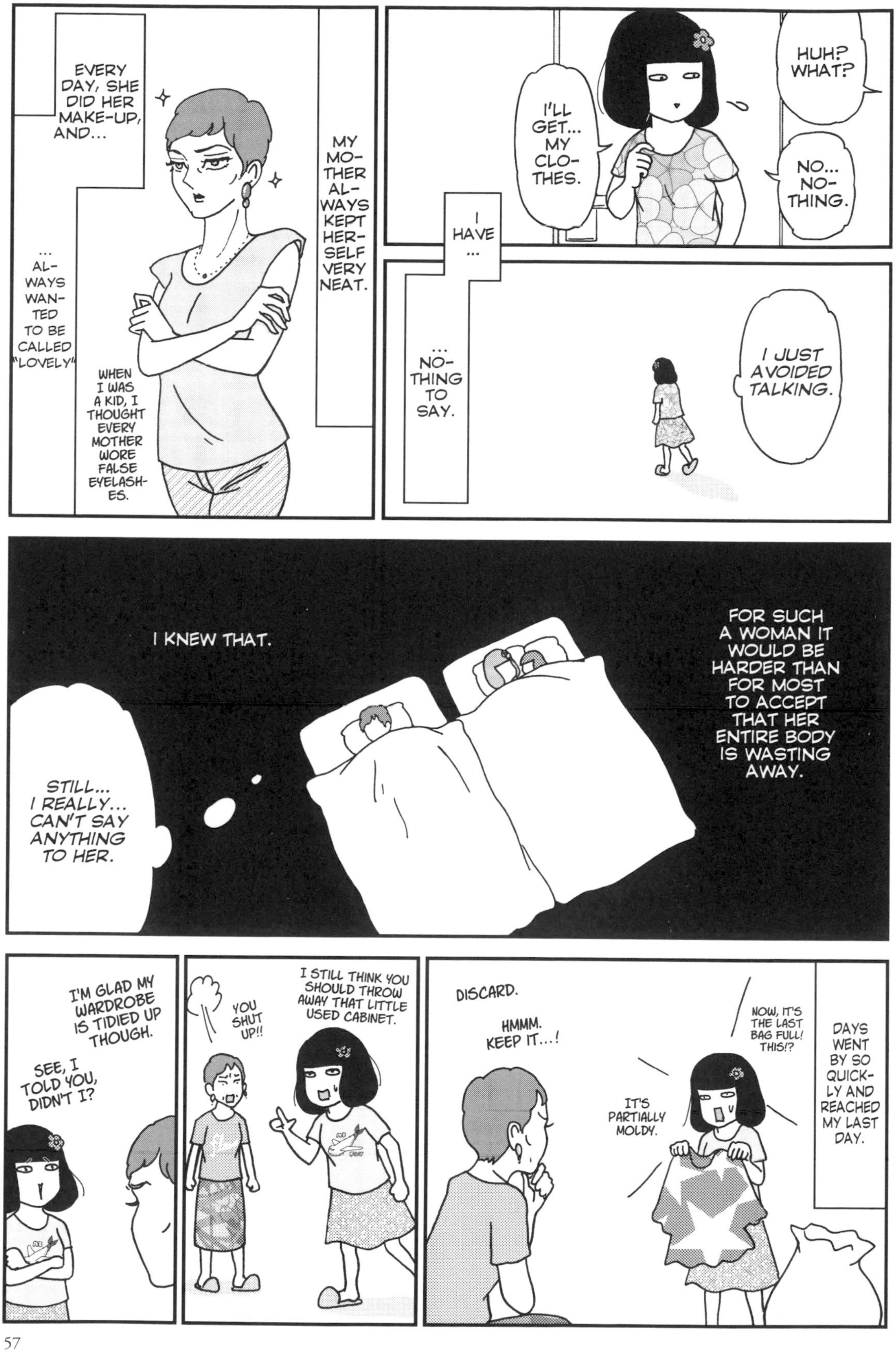
HUH? WHAT?
NO... NOTHING.
I'LL GET... MY CLOTHES.
I HAVE...
...NOTHING TO SAY.
I JUST AVOIDED TALKING.
MY MOTHER ALWAYS KEPT HERSELF VERY NEAT.
EVERY DAY, SHE DID HER MAKE-UP, AND...
...ALWAYS WANTED TO BE CALLED "LOVELY"
WHEN I WAS A KID, I THOUGHT EVERY MOTHER WORE FALSE EYELASHES.
FOR SUCH A WOMAN IT WOULD BE HARDER THAN FOR MOST TO ACCEPT THAT HER ENTIRE BODY IS WASTING AWAY.
I KNEW THAT.
STILL... I REALLY... CAN'T SAY ANYTHING TO HER.
DAYS WENT BY SO QUICKLY AND REACHED MY LAST DAY.
NOW, IT'S THE LAST BAG FULL! THIS!?
IT'S PARTIALLY MOLDY.
DISCARD.
HMMM. KEEP IT...!
I STILL THINK YOU SHOULD THROW AWAY THAT LITTLE USED CABINET.
YOU SHUT UP!!
I'M GLAD MY WARDROBE IS TIDIED UP THOUGH.
SEE, I TOLD YOU, DIDN'T I?

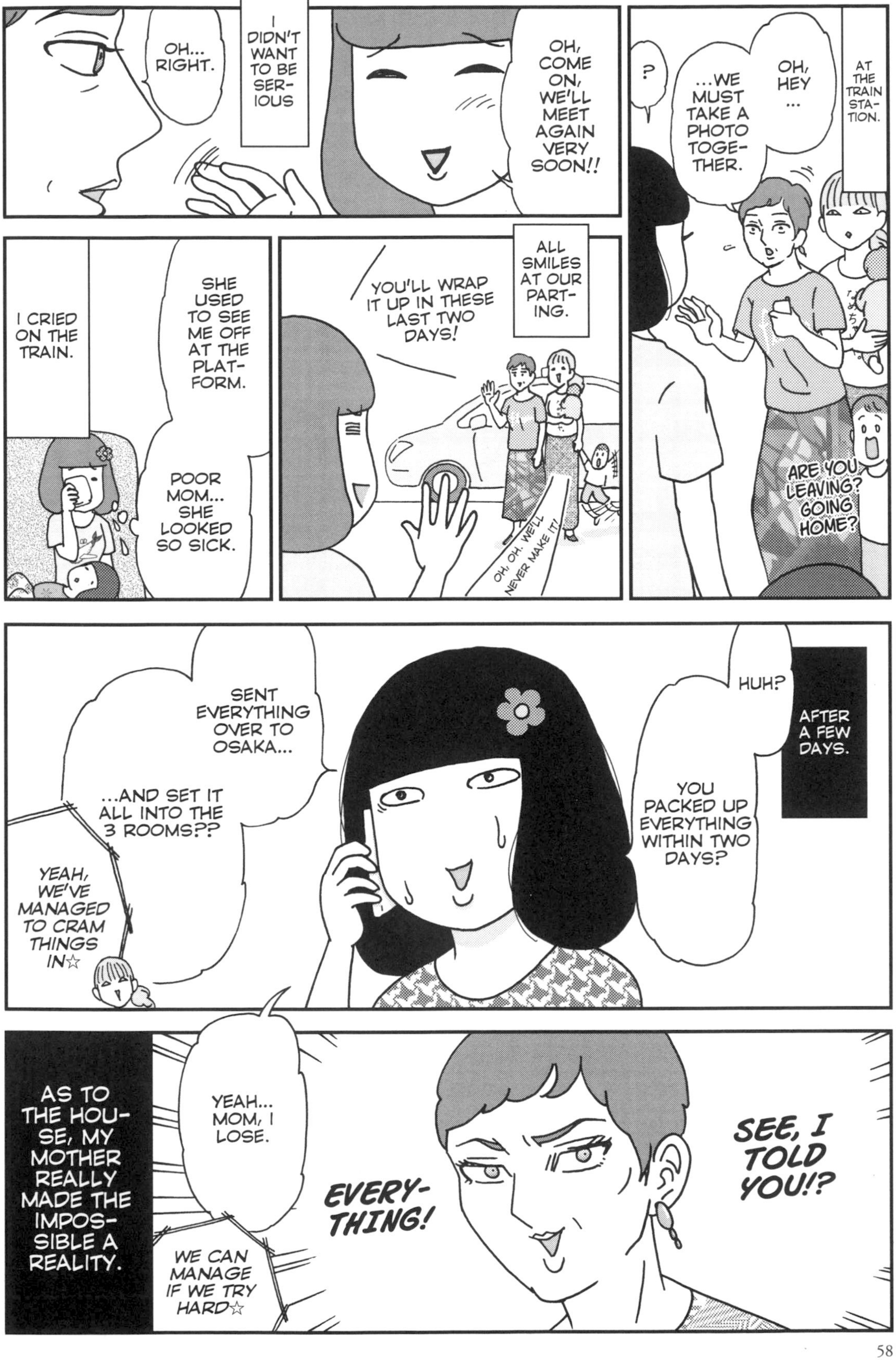

AT THE TRAIN STATION.
OH, HEY ...
...WE MUST TAKE A PHOTO TOGE-THER.
?
ARE YOU LEAVING? GOING HOME?
OH, COME ON, WE'LL MEET AGAIN VERY SOON!!
I DIDN'T WANT TO BE SER-IOUS
OH... RIGHT.
ALL SMILES AT OUR PART-ING.
YOU'LL WRAP IT UP IN THESE LAST TWO DAYS!
OH, OH. WE'LL NEVER MAKE IT!
SHE USED TO SEE ME OFF AT THE PLAT-FORM.
POOR MOM... SHE LOOKED SO SICK.
I CRIED ON THE TRAIN.
AFTER A FEW DAYS.
HUH?
YOU PACKED UP EVERYTHING WITHIN TWO DAYS?
SENT EVERYTHING OVER TO OSAKA...
...AND SET IT ALL INTO THE 3 ROOMS??
YEAH, WE'VE MANAGED TO CRAM THINGS IN☆
SEE, I TOLD YOU!?
EVERY-THING!
YEAH... MOM, I LOSE.
WE CAN MANAGE IF WE TRY HARD☆
AS TO THE HOU-SE, MY MOTHER REALLY MADE THE IMPOS-SIBLE A REALITY.

CHAPTER 7.

HOW LONG CAN WE GO OUT TOGETHER?

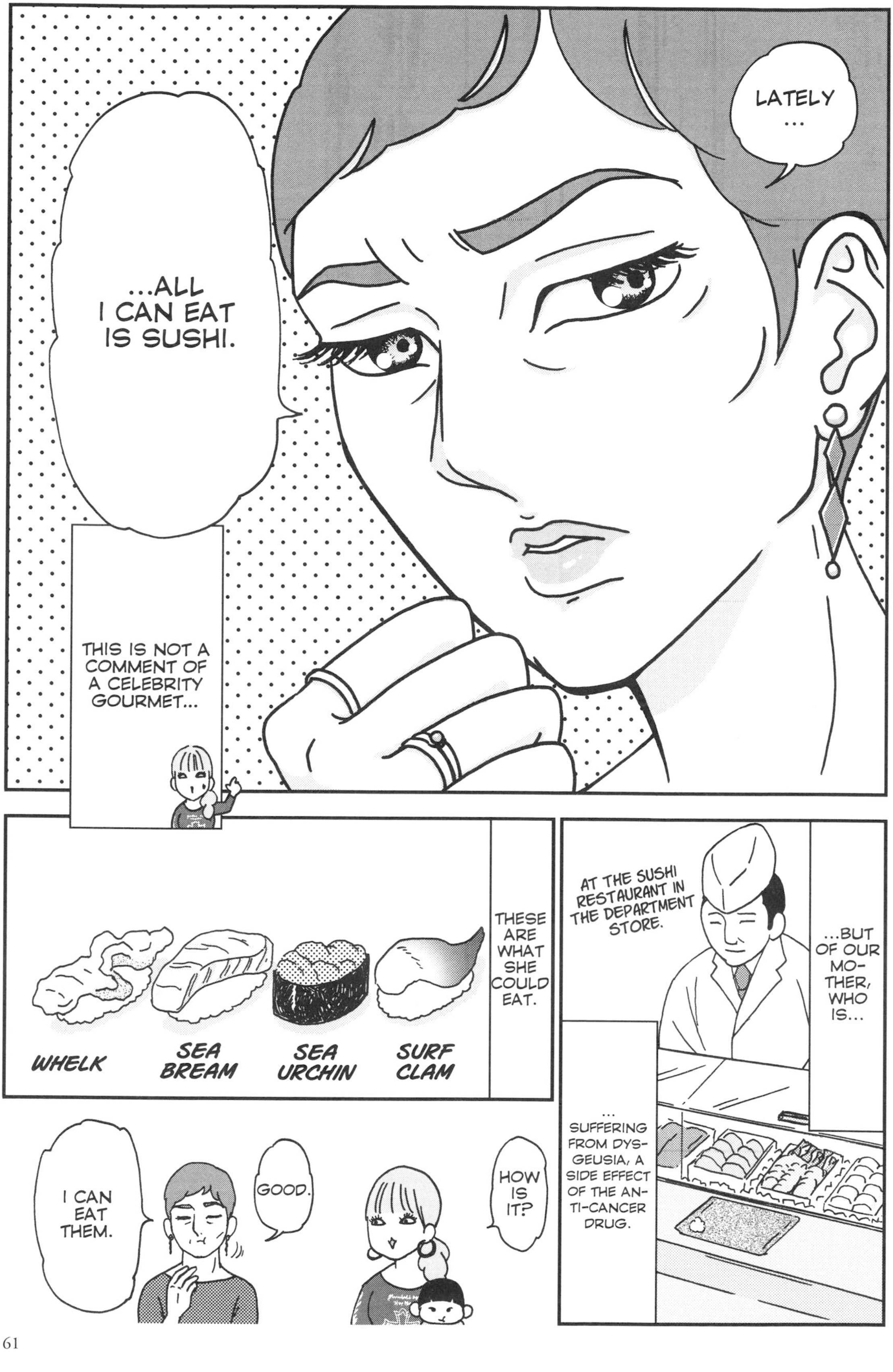

LATELY ...
...ALL I CAN EAT IS SUSHI.
THIS IS NOT A COMMENT OF A CELEBRITY GOURMET...
...BUT OF OUR MOTHER, WHO IS...
AT THE SUSHI RESTAURANT IN THE DEPARTMENT STORE.
... SUFFERING FROM DYSGEUSIA, A SIDE EFFECT OF THE ANTI-CANCER DRUG.
THESE ARE WHAT SHE COULD EAT.
SURF CLAM
SEA URCHIN
SEA BREAM
WHELK
HOW IS IT?
GOOD.
I CAN EAT THEM.

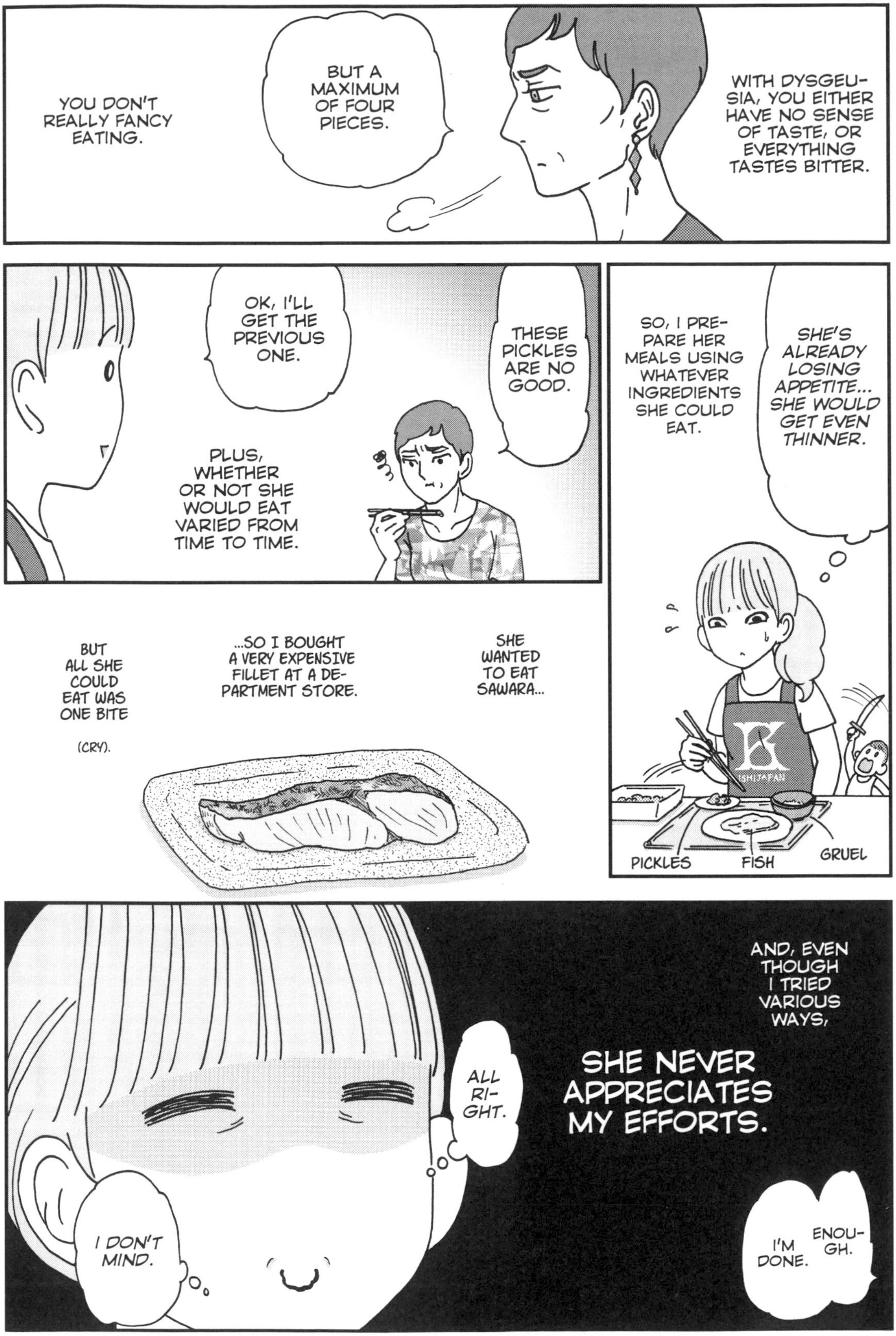
WITH DYSGEUSIA, YOU EITHER HAVE NO SENSE OF TASTE, OR EVERYTHING TASTES BITTER.
BUT A MAXIMUM OF FOUR PIECES.
YOU DON'T REALLY FANCY EATING.
SHE'S ALREADY LOSING APPETITE... SHE WOULD GET EVEN THINNER.
SO, I PREPARE HER MEALS USING WHATEVER INGREDIENTS SHE COULD EAT.
GRUEL
FISH
PICKLES
THESE PICKLES ARE NO GOOD.
OK, I'LL GET THE PREVIOUS ONE.
PLUS, WHETHER OR NOT SHE WOULD EAT VARIED FROM TIME TO TIME.
SHE WANTED TO EAT SAWARA...
...SO I BOUGHT A VERY EXPENSIVE FILLET AT A DEPARTMENT STORE.
BUT ALL SHE COULD EAT WAS ONE BITE
(CRY).
AND, EVEN THOUGH I TRIED VARIOUS WAYS,
SHE NEVER APPRECIATES MY EFFORTS.
ENOUGH.
I'M DONE.
ALL RIGHT.
I DON'T MIND.

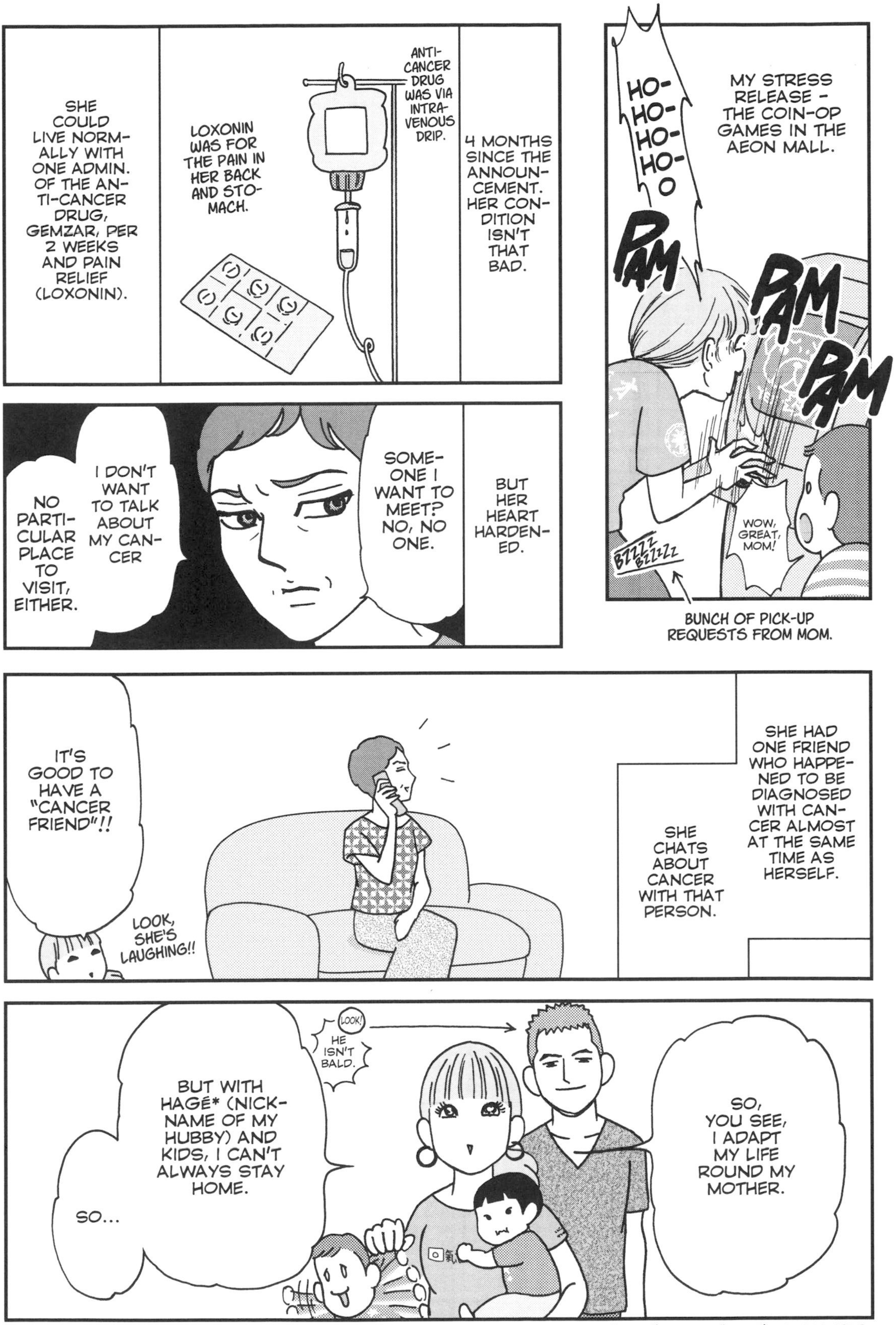
MY STRESS RELEASE – THE COIN-OP GAMES IN THE AEON MALL.
HO-HO-HO-HO-O
PAM
PAM PAM PAM
WOW, GREAT, MOM!
BZZZZZ BZZZZZ
BUNCH OF PICK-UP REQUESTS FROM MOM.
4 MONTHS SINCE THE ANNOUNCEMENT. HER CONDITION ISN'T THAT BAD.
ANTI-CANCER DRUG WAS VIA INTRAVENOUS DRIP.
LOXONIN WAS FOR THE PAIN IN HER BACK AND STOMACH.
SHE COULD LIVE NORMALLY WITH ONE ADMIN. OF THE ANTI-CANCER DRUG, GEMZAR, PER 2 WEEKS AND PAIN RELIEF (LOXONIN).
BUT HER HEART HARDENED.
SOMEONE I WANT TO MEET? NO, NO ONE.
I DON'T WANT TO TALK ABOUT MY CANCER
NO PARTICULAR PLACE TO VISIT, EITHER.
SHE HAD ONE FRIEND WHO HAPPENED TO BE DIAGNOSED WITH CANCER ALMOST AT THE SAME TIME AS HERSELF.
SHE CHATS ABOUT CANCER WITH THAT PERSON.
IT'S GOOD TO HAVE A "CANCER FRIEND"!!
LOOK, SHE'S LAUGHING!!
SO, YOU SEE, I ADAPT MY LIFE ROUND MY MOTHER.
LOOK! HE ISN'T BALD.
BUT WITH HAGÉ* (NICKNAME OF MY HUBBY) AND KIDS, I CAN'T ALWAYS STAY HOME.
SO...

* "HAGÉ" MEANS "BALD" IN JAPANESE.

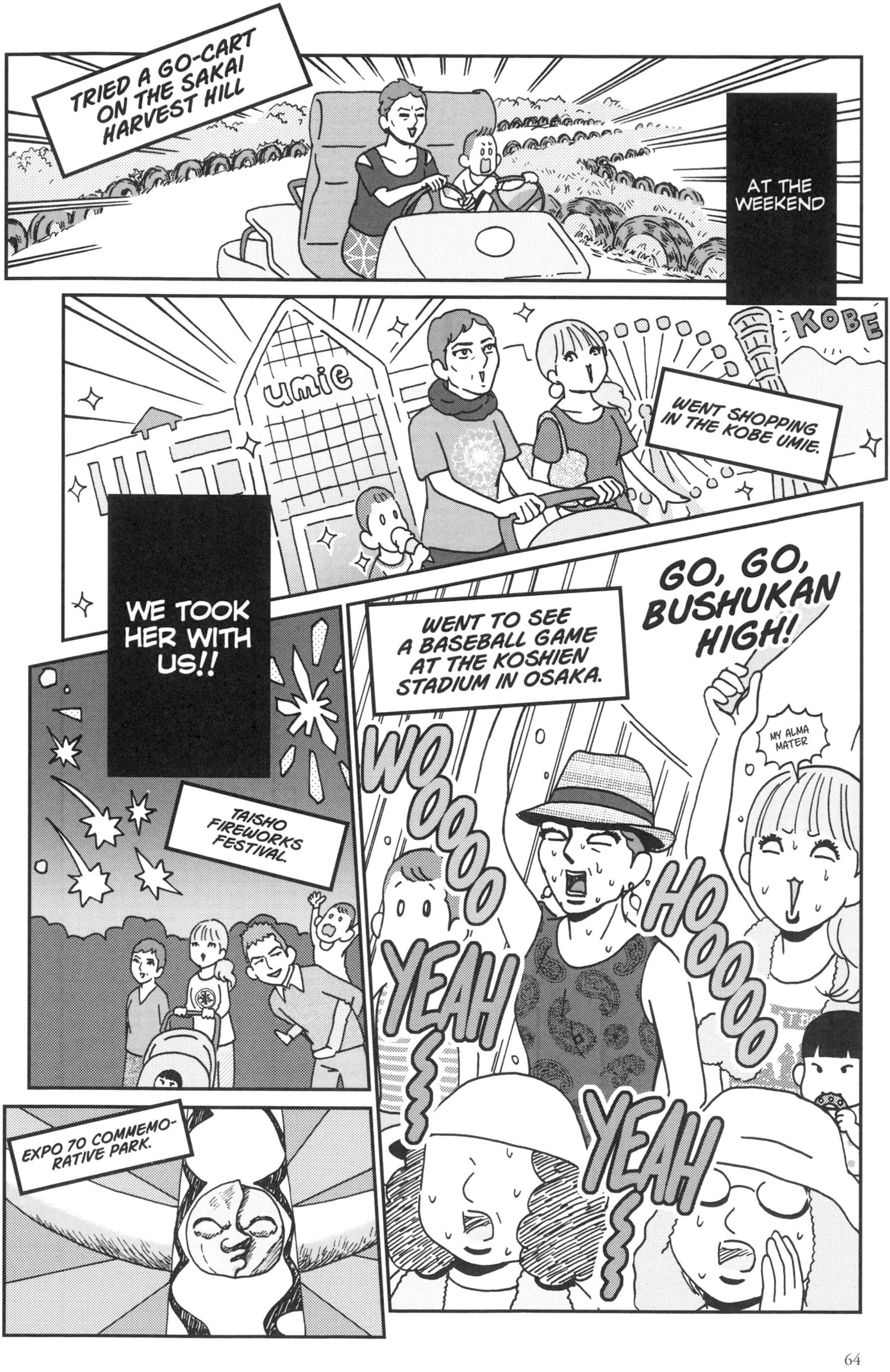

AT THE WEEKEND
TRIED A GO-CART ON THE SAKAI HARVEST HILL
KOBE
WENT SHOPPING IN THE KOBE UMIE.
umie
WE TOOK HER WITH US!!
GO, GO, BUSHUKAN HIGH!
WENT TO SEE A BASEBALL GAME AT THE KOSHIEN STADIUM IN OSAKA.
MY ALMA MATER
HOOOOOO
YEAH
WOOOOOO
YEAH
TAISHO FIREWORKS FESTIVAL.
EXPO 70 COMMEMO-RATIVE PARK.

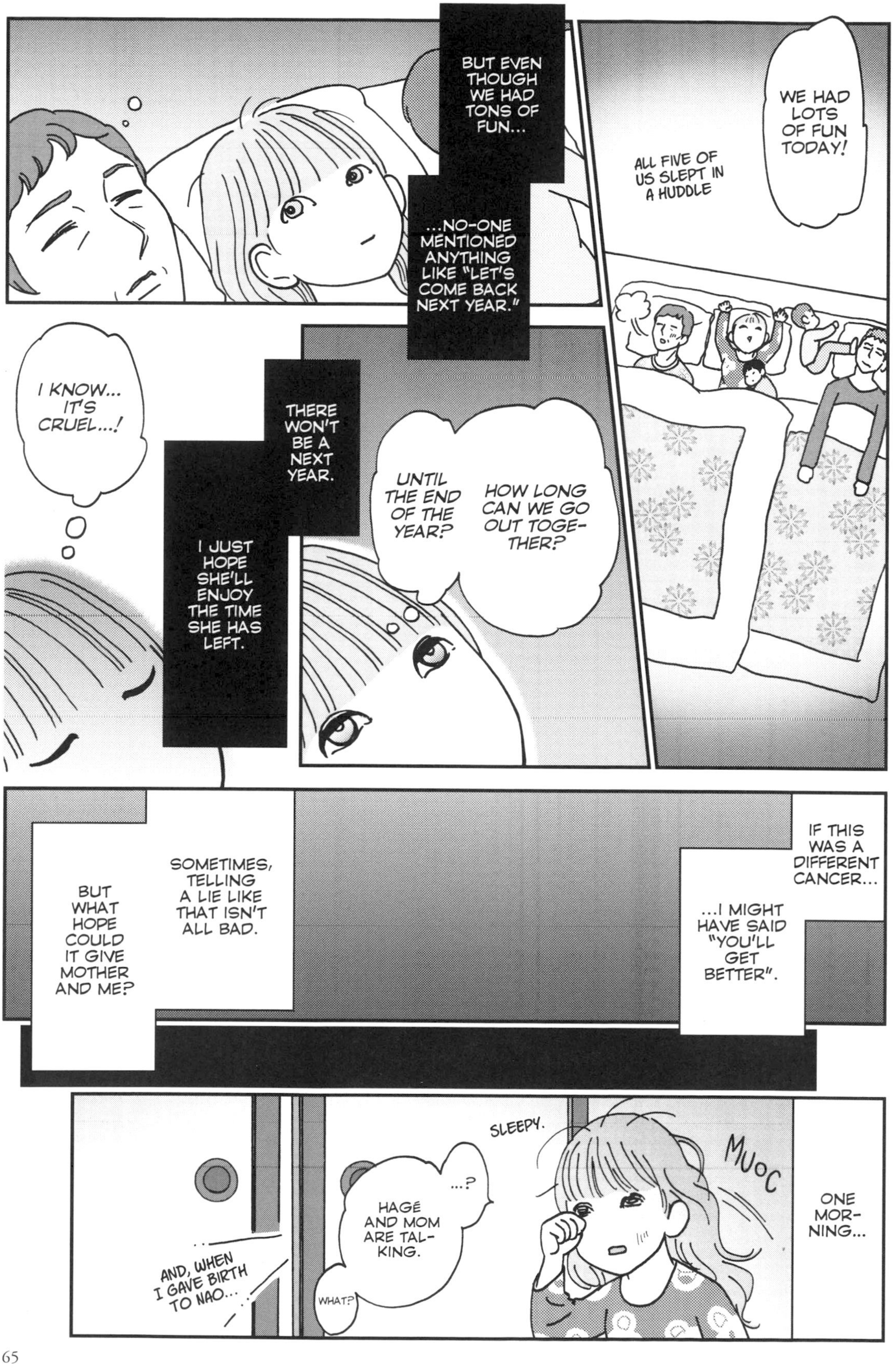
WE HAD LOTS OF FUN TODAY!
ALL FIVE OF US SLEPT IN A HUDDLE
BUT EVEN THOUGH WE HAD TONS OF FUN...
...NO-ONE MENTIONED ANYTHING LIKE "LET'S COME BACK NEXT YEAR."
THERE WON'T BE A NEXT YEAR.
HOW LONG CAN WE GO OUT TOGE-THER?
UNTIL THE END OF THE YEAR?
I JUST HOPE SHE'LL ENJOY THE TIME SHE HAS LEFT.
I KNOW... IT'S CRUEL...!
IF THIS WAS A DIFFERENT CANCER...
...I MIGHT HAVE SAID "YOU'LL GET BETTER".
SOMETIMES, TELLING A LIE LIKE THAT ISN'T ALL BAD.
BUT WHAT HOPE COULD IT GIVE MOTHER AND ME?
ONE MORN-NING...
MUOC
SLEEPY.
...?
HAGE AND MOM ARE TAL-KING.
WHAT?
AND, WHEN I GAVE BIRTH TO NAO...

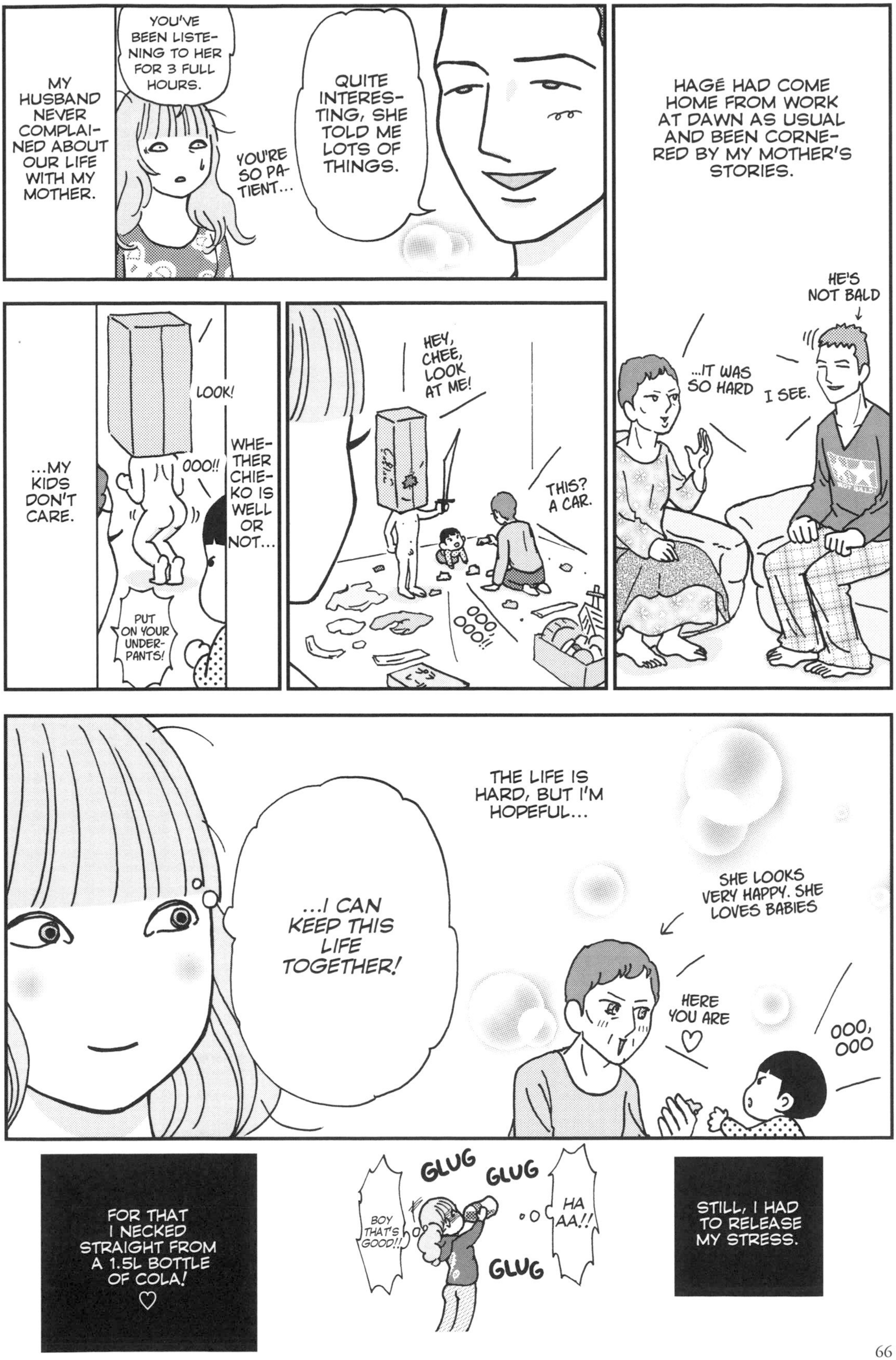
HAGE HAD COME HOME FROM WORK AT DAWN AS USUAL AND BEEN CORNERED BY MY MOTHER'S STORIES.
HE'S NOT BALD
...IT WAS SO HARD
I SEE.
QUITE INTERESTING, SHE TOLD ME LOTS OF THINGS.
YOU'RE SO PATIENT...
YOU'VE BEEN LISTENING TO HER FOR 3 FULL HOURS.
MY HUSBAND NEVER COMPLAINED ABOUT OUR LIFE WITH MY MOTHER.
HEY, CHEE, LOOK AT ME!
THIS? A CAR.
OOO, OOO!!
LOOK!
OOO!!
WHETHER CHIEKO IS WELL OR NOT...
PUT ON YOUR UNDERPANTS!
...MY KIDS DON'T CARE.
THE LIFE IS HARD, BUT I'M HOPEFUL...
SHE LOOKS VERY HAPPY. SHE LOVES BABIES
OOO, OOO
HERE YOU ARE ♡
...I CAN KEEP THIS LIFE TOGETHER!
STILL, I HAD TO RELEASE MY STRESS.
GLUG
GLUG
HA AA!!
GLUG
BOY THAT'S GOOD!!
FOR THAT I NECKED STRAIGHT FROM A 1.5L BOTTLE OF COLA! ♡

CHAPTER 8

WE WERE
IN THE
"PERFECT
HAPPINESS"

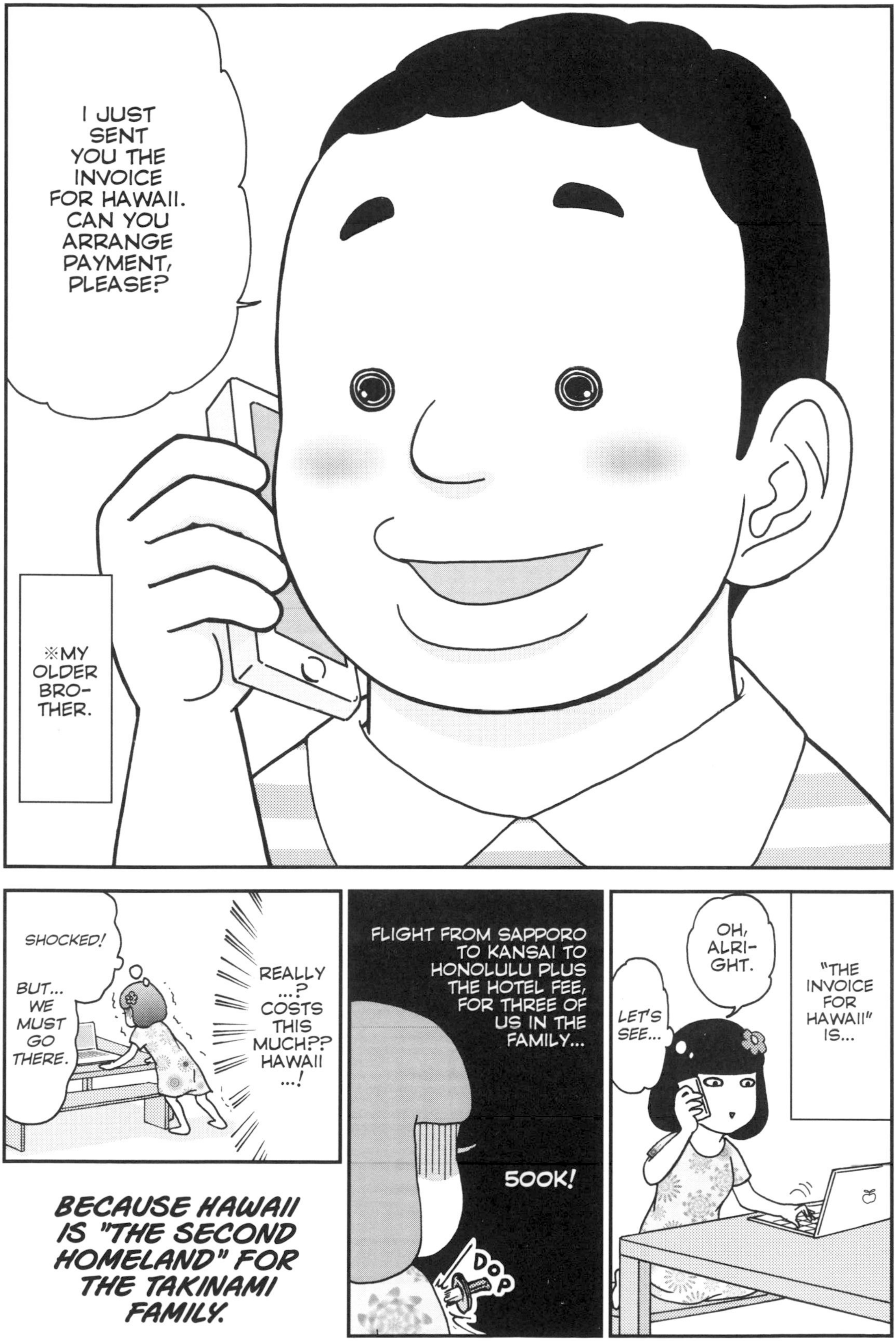
I JUST SENT YOU THE INVOICE FOR HAWAII. CAN YOU ARRANGE PAYMENT, PLEASE?
※MY OLDER BRO-THER.
"THE INVOICE FOR HAWAII" IS...
OH, ALRI-GHT.
LET'S SEE...
FLIGHT FROM SAPPORO TO KANSAI TO HONOLULU PLUS THE HOTEL FEE, FOR THREE OF US IN THE FAMILY...
500K!
DOP
REALLY ...? COSTS THIS MUCH?? HAWAII ...!
SHOCKED!
BUT... WE MUST GO THERE.
BECAUSE HAWAII IS "THE SECOND HOMELAND" FOR THE TAKINAMI FAMILY.

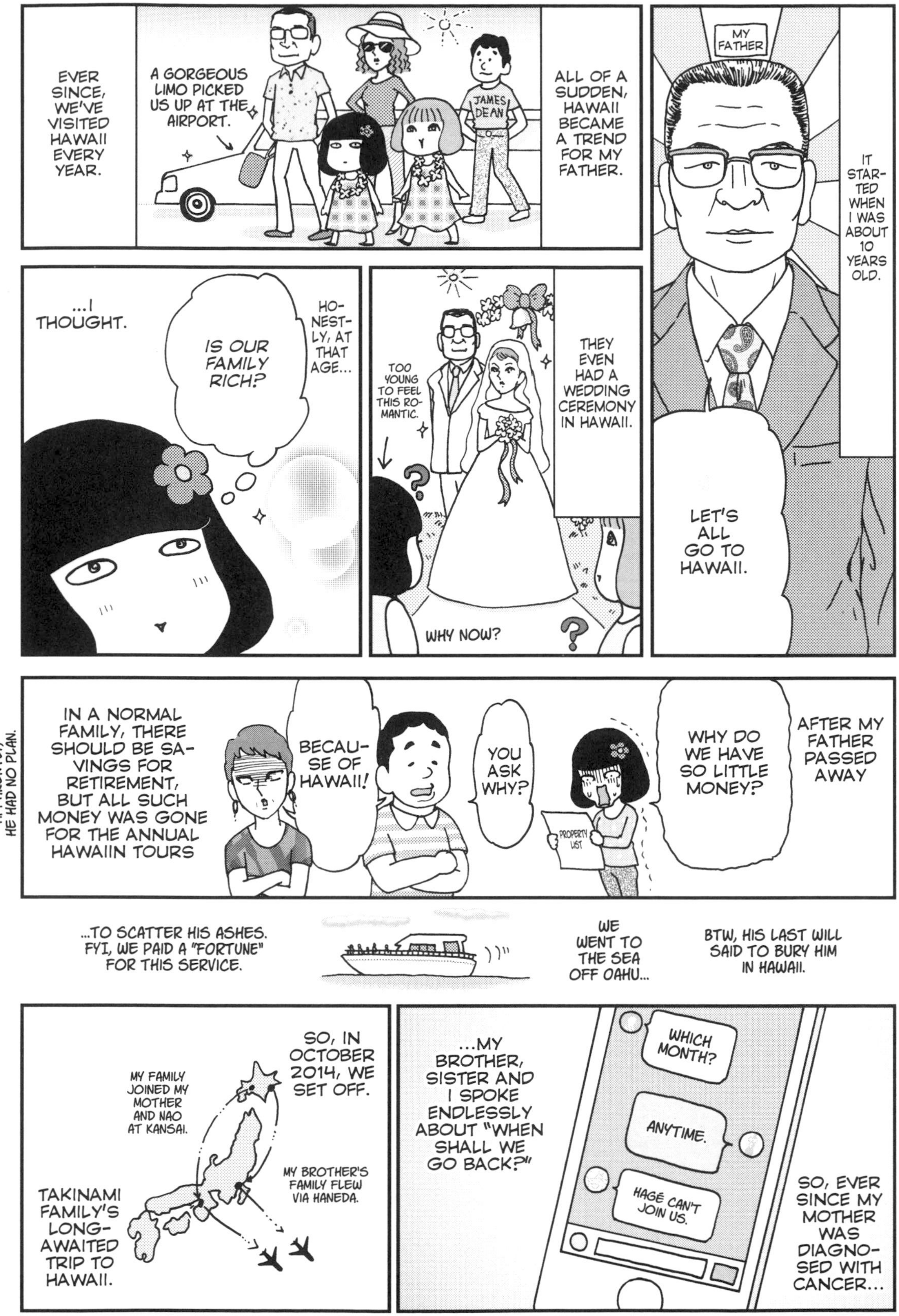

MY FATHER
IT STARTED WHEN I WAS ABOUT 10 YEARS OLD.
LET'S ALL GO TO HAWAII.
ALL OF A SUDDEN, HAWAII BECAME A TREND FOR MY FATHER.
JAMES DEAN
A GORGEOUS LIMO PICKED US UP AT THE AIRPORT.
EVER SINCE, WE'VE VISITED HAWAII EVERY YEAR.
THEY EVEN HAD A WEDDING CEREMONY IN HAWAII.
TOO YOUNG TO FEEL THIS ROMANTIC.
WHY NOW?
HONESTLY, AT THAT AGE...
IS OUR FAMILY RICH?
...I THOUGHT.
AFTER MY FATHER PASSED AWAY
WHY DO WE HAVE SO LITTLE MONEY?
PROPERTY LIST
YOU ASK WHY?
BECAUSE OF HAWAII!
IN A NORMAL FAMILY, THERE SHOULD BE SAVINGS FOR RETIREMENT, BUT ALL SUCH MONEY WAS GONE FOR THE ANNUAL HAWAIIN TOURS
APPARENTLY, HE HAD NO PLAN.
BTW, HIS LAST WILL SAID TO BURY HIM IN HAWAII.
WE WENT TO THE SEA OFF OAHU...
...TO SCATTER HIS ASHES. FYI, WE PAID A "FORTUNE" FOR THIS SERVICE.
SO, EVER SINCE MY MOTHER WAS DIAGNOSED WITH CANCER...
WHICH MONTH?
ANYTIME.
HAGÉ CAN'T JOIN US.
...MY BROTHER, SISTER AND I SPOKE ENDLESSLY ABOUT "WHEN SHALL WE GO BACK?"
SO, IN OCTOBER 2014, WE SET OFF.
MY FAMILY JOINED MY MOTHER AND NAO AT KANSAI.
MY BROTHER'S FAMILY FLEW VIA HANEDA.
TAKINAMI FAMILY'S LONG-AWAITED TRIP TO HAWAII.

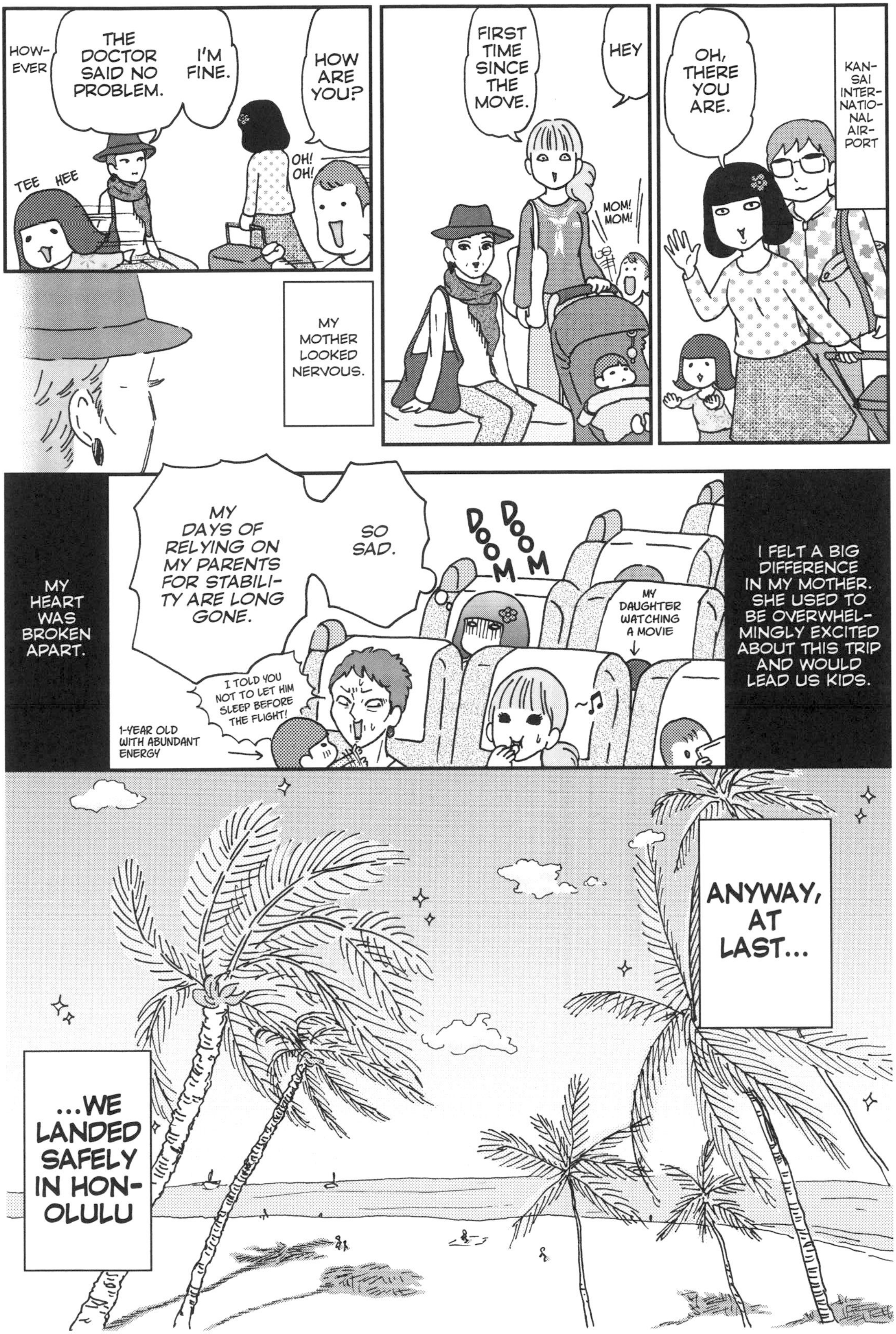
KANSAI INTERNATIONAL AIRPORT
OH, THERE YOU ARE.
HEY
FIRST TIME SINCE THE MOVE.
MOM! MOM!
HOW ARE YOU?
OH! OH!
I'M FINE.
THE DOCTOR SAID NO PROBLEM.
HOWEVER
TEE HEE
MY MOTHER LOOKED NERVOUS.
I FELT A BIG DIFFERENCE IN MY MOTHER. SHE USED TO BE OVERWHELMINGLY EXCITED ABOUT THIS TRIP AND WOULD LEAD US KIDS.
DOOM DOOM
SO SAD.
MY DAYS OF RELYING ON MY PARENTS FOR STABILITY ARE LONG GONE.
MY DAUGHTER WATCHING A MOVIE
~♪
I TOLD YOU NOT TO LET HIM SLEEP BEFORE THE FLIGHT!
1-YEAR OLD WITH ABUNDANT ENERGY
MY HEART WAS BROKEN APART.
ANYWAY, AT LAST...
...WE LANDED SAFELY IN HONOLULU

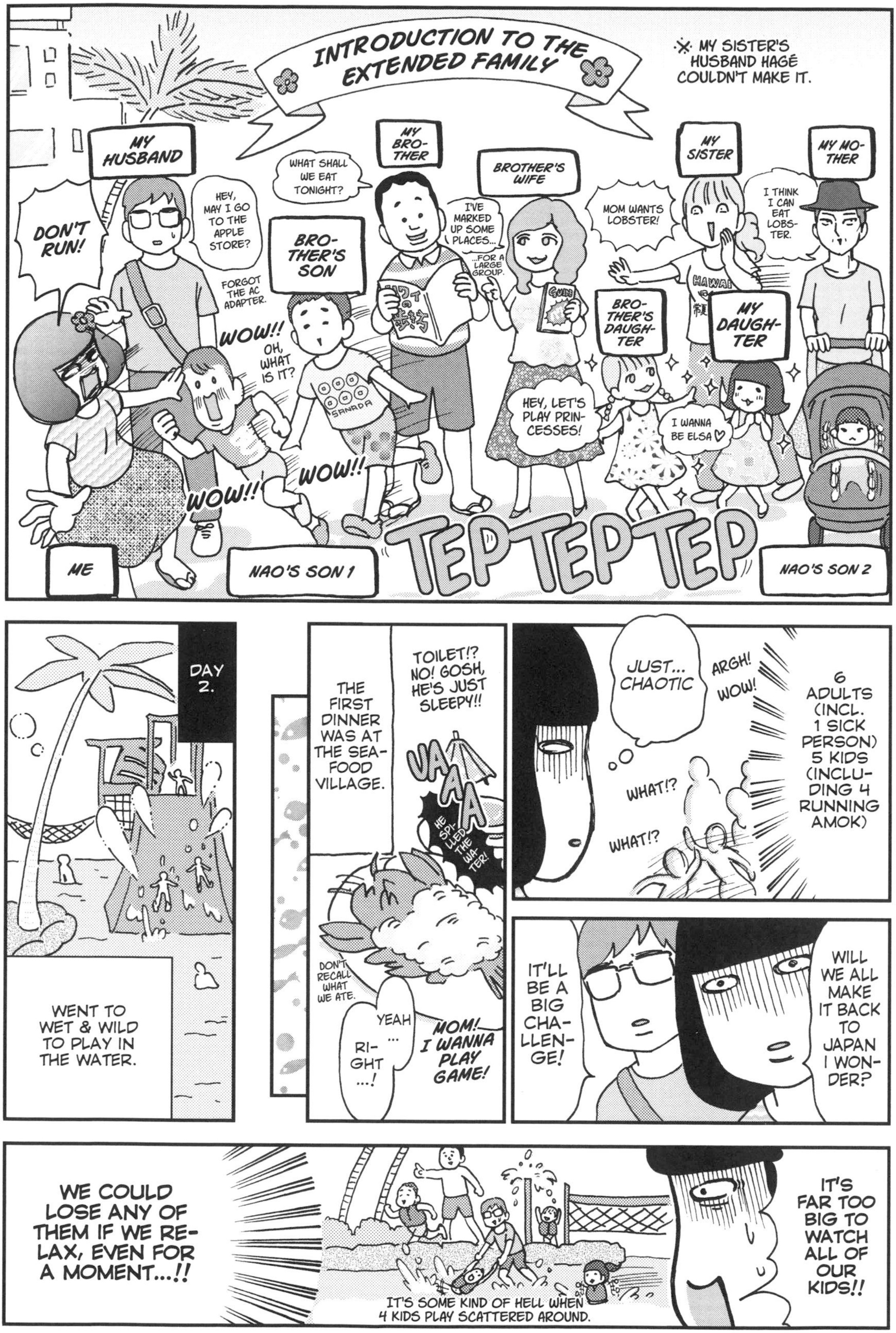
INTRODUCTION TO THE EXTENDED FAMILY
※ MY SISTER'S HUSBAND HAGÉ COULDN'T MAKE IT.
MY MOTHER
I THINK I CAN EAT LOBSTER.
MY SISTER
MOM WANTS LOBSTER!
BROTHER'S WIFE
I'VE MARKED UP SOME PLACES...
...FOR A LARGE GROUP.
MY BROTHER
WHAT SHALL WE EAT TONIGHT?
MY HUSBAND
HEY, MAY I GO TO THE APPLE STORE?
DON'T RUN!
BROTHER'S SON
FORGOT THE AC ADAPTER.
MY DAUGHTER
BROTHER'S DAUGHTER
I WANNA BE ELSA ♡
HEY, LET'S PLAY PRINCESSES!
WOW!!
OH, WHAT IS IT?
WOW!!
WOW!!
TEP TEP TEP
NAO'S SON 2
NAO'S SON 1
ME
6 ADULTS (INCL. 1 SICK PERSON) 5 KIDS (INCLUDING 4 RUNNING AMOK)
ARGH!
WOW!
JUST... CHAOTIC
WHAT!?
WHAT!?
WILL WE ALL MAKE IT BACK TO JAPAN I WONDER?
IT'LL BE A BIG CHALLENGE!
TOILET!? NO! GOSH, HE'S JUST SLEEPY!!
THE FIRST DINNER WAS AT THE SEAFOOD VILLAGE.
VAAAA
HE SPILLED THE WATER!
DON'T RECALL WHAT WE ATE.
MOM! I WANNA PLAY GAME!
YEAH...
RIGHT...!
DAY 2.
WENT TO WET & WILD TO PLAY IN THE WATER.
IT'S FAR TOO BIG TO WATCH ALL OF OUR KIDS!!
IT'S SOME KIND OF HELL WHEN 4 KIDS PLAY SCATTERED AROUND.
WE COULD LOSE ANY OF THEM IF WE RELAX, EVEN FOR A MOMENT...!!

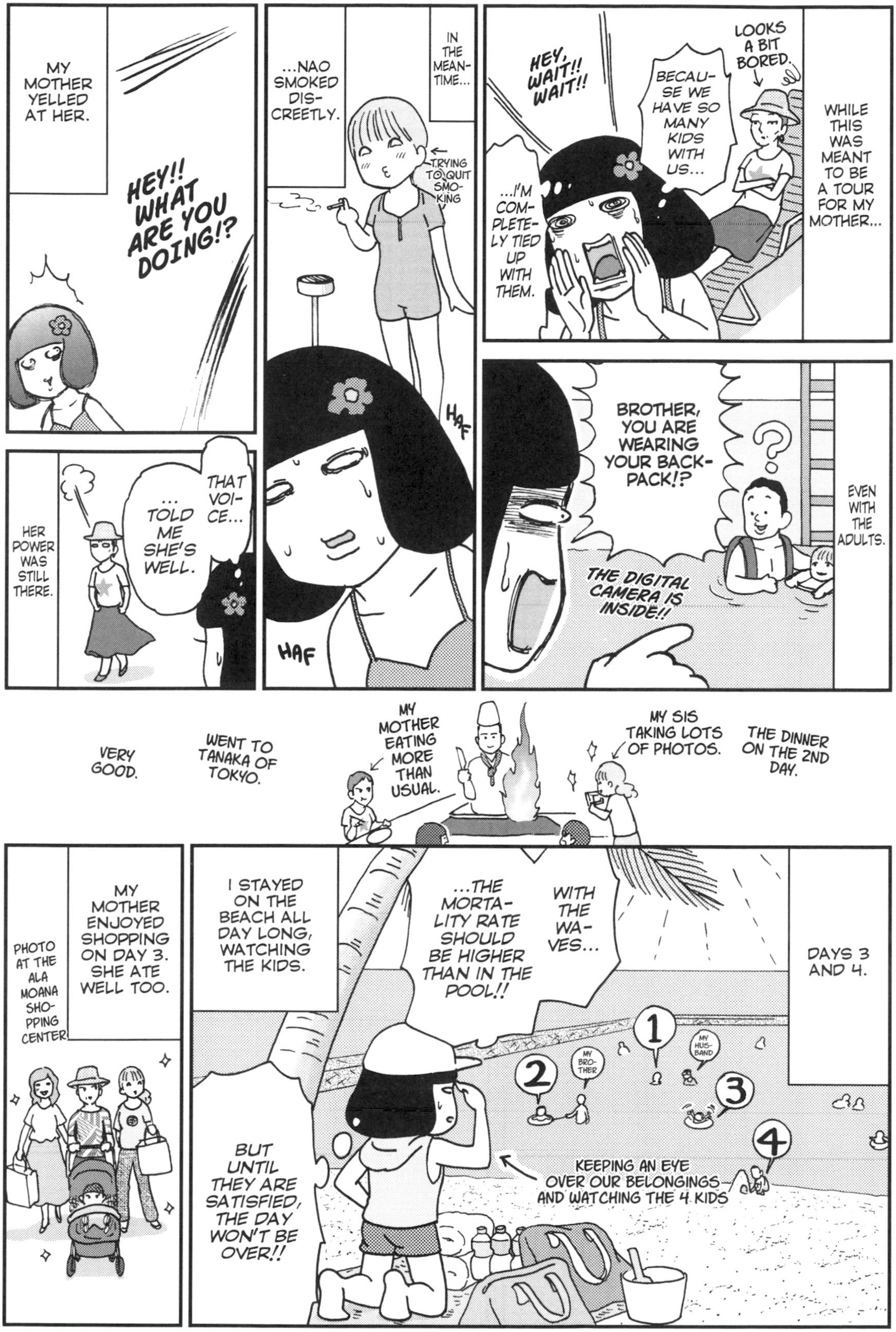
WHILE THIS WAS MEANT TO BE A TOUR FOR MY MOTHER...
LOOKS A BIT BORED.
BECAUSE WE HAVE SO MANY KIDS WITH US...
HEY, WAIT!! WAIT!!
...I'M COMPLETELY TIED UP WITH THEM.
EVEN WITH THE ADULTS.
BROTHER, YOU ARE WEARING YOUR BACKPACK!?
THE DIGITAL CAMERA IS INSIDE!!
IN THE MEANTIME...
...NAO SMOKED DISCREETLY.
TRYING TO QUIT SMOKING
HAF
HAF
HEY!! WHAT ARE YOU DOING!?
MY MOTHER YELLED AT HER.
THAT VOICE...
...TOLD ME SHE'S WELL.
HER POWER WAS STILL THERE.
THE DINNER ON THE 2ND DAY.
MY SIS TAKING LOTS OF PHOTOS.
MY MOTHER EATING MORE THAN USUAL.
WENT TO TANAKA OF TOKYO.
VERY GOOD.
DAYS 3 AND 4.
WITH THE WAVES...
...THE MORTALITY RATE SHOULD BE HIGHER THAN IN THE POOL!!
I STAYED ON THE BEACH ALL DAY LONG, WATCHING THE KIDS.
1
MY HUSBAND
MY BROTHER
2
3
4
KEEPING AN EYE OVER OUR BELONGINGS AND WATCHING THE 4 KIDS
BUT UNTIL THEY ARE SATISFIED, THE DAY WON'T BE OVER!!
MY MOTHER ENJOYED SHOPPING ON DAY 3. SHE ATE WELL TOO.
PHOTO AT THE ALA MOANA SHOPPING CENTER

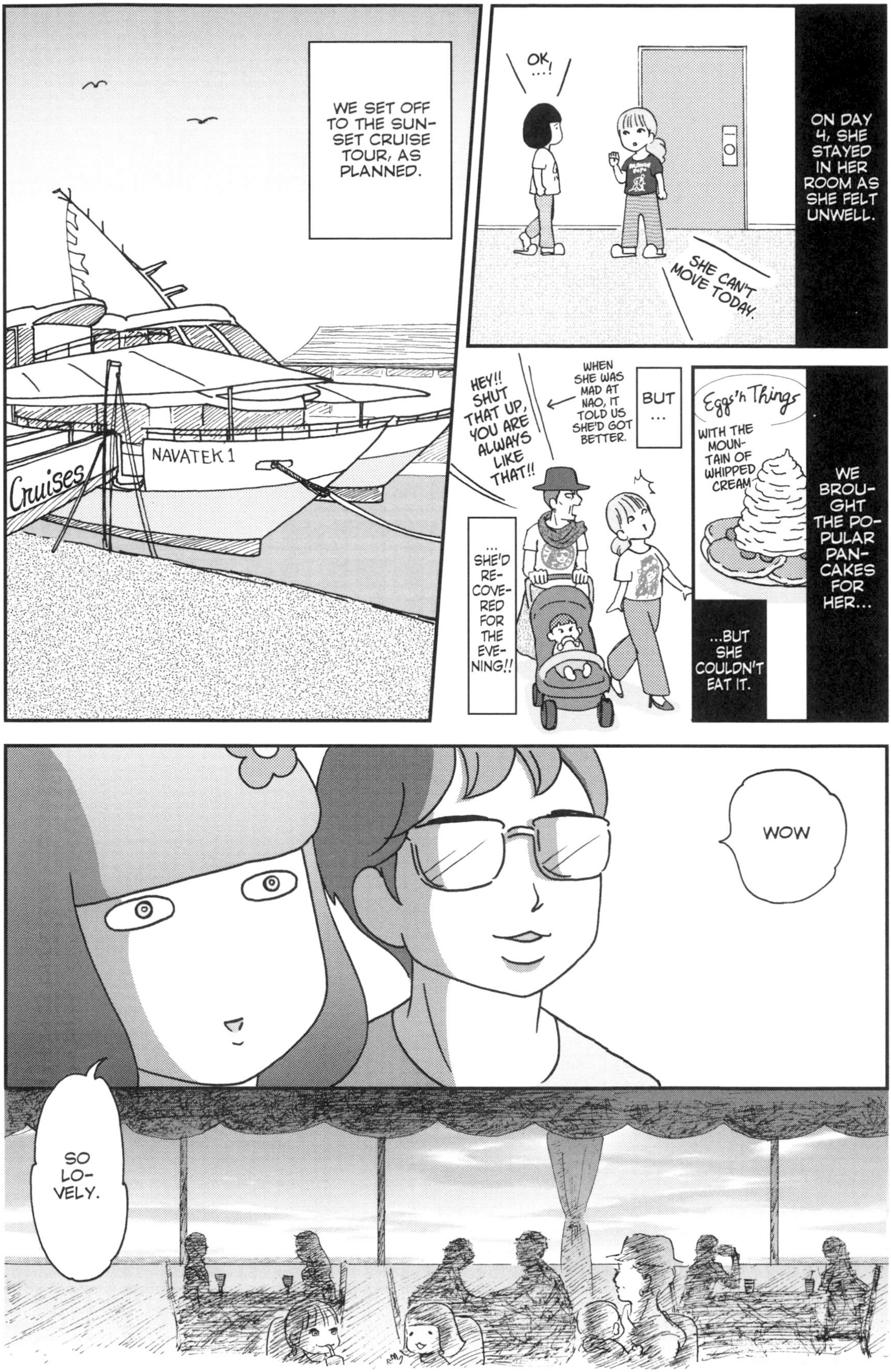
ON DAY 4, SHE STAYED IN HER ROOM AS SHE FELT UNWELL.
OK ...!
SHE CAN'T MOVE TODAY.
WE BROUGHT THE POPULAR PAN-CAKES FOR HER...
Eggs'n Things
WITH THE MOUN-TAIN OF WHIPPED CREAM
...BUT SHE COULDN'T EAT IT.
BUT ...
WHEN SHE WAS MAD AT NAO, IT TOLD US SHE'D GOT BETTER.
HEY!! SHUT THAT UP, YOU ARE ALWAYS LIKE THAT!!
... SHE'D RE-COVE-RED FOR THE EVE-NING!!
WE SET OFF TO THE SUN-SET CRUISE TOUR, AS PLANNED.
NAVATEK 1
Cruises
WOW
SO LO-VELY.

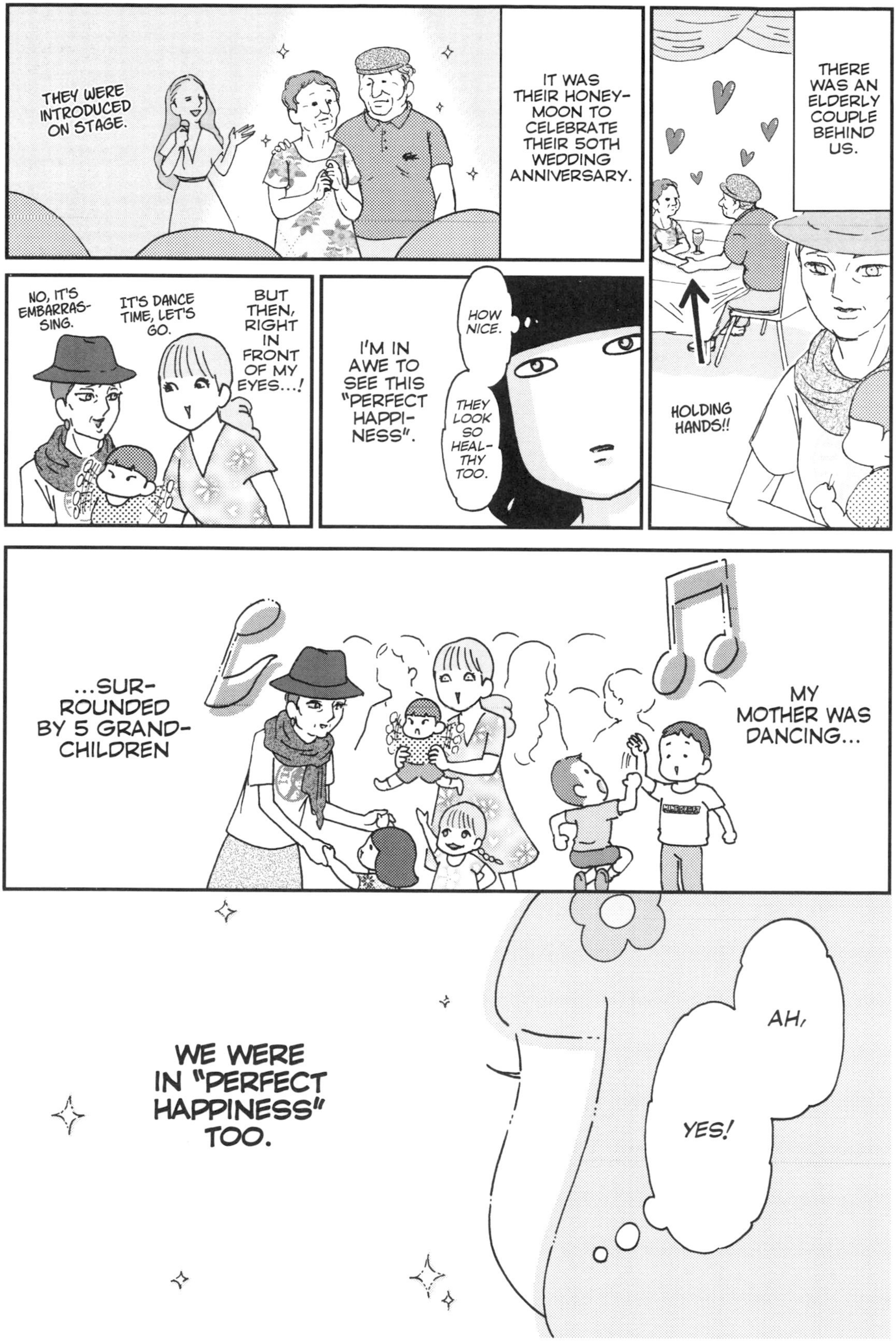

THERE WAS AN ELDERLY COUPLE BEHIND US.
HOLDING HANDS!!
IT WAS THEIR HONEY-MOON TO CELEBRATE THEIR 50TH WEDDING ANNIVERSARY.
THEY WERE INTRODUCED ON STAGE.
HOW NICE.
THEY LOOK SO HEAL-THY TOO.
I'M IN AWE TO SEE THIS "PERFECT HAPPI-NESS".
BUT THEN, RIGHT IN FRONT OF MY EYES...!
IT'S DANCE TIME, LET'S GO.
NO, IT'S EMBARRAS-SING.
MY MOTHER WAS DANCING...
...SUR-ROUNDED BY 5 GRAND-CHILDREN
AH,
YES!
WE WERE IN "PERFECT HAPPINESS" TOO.

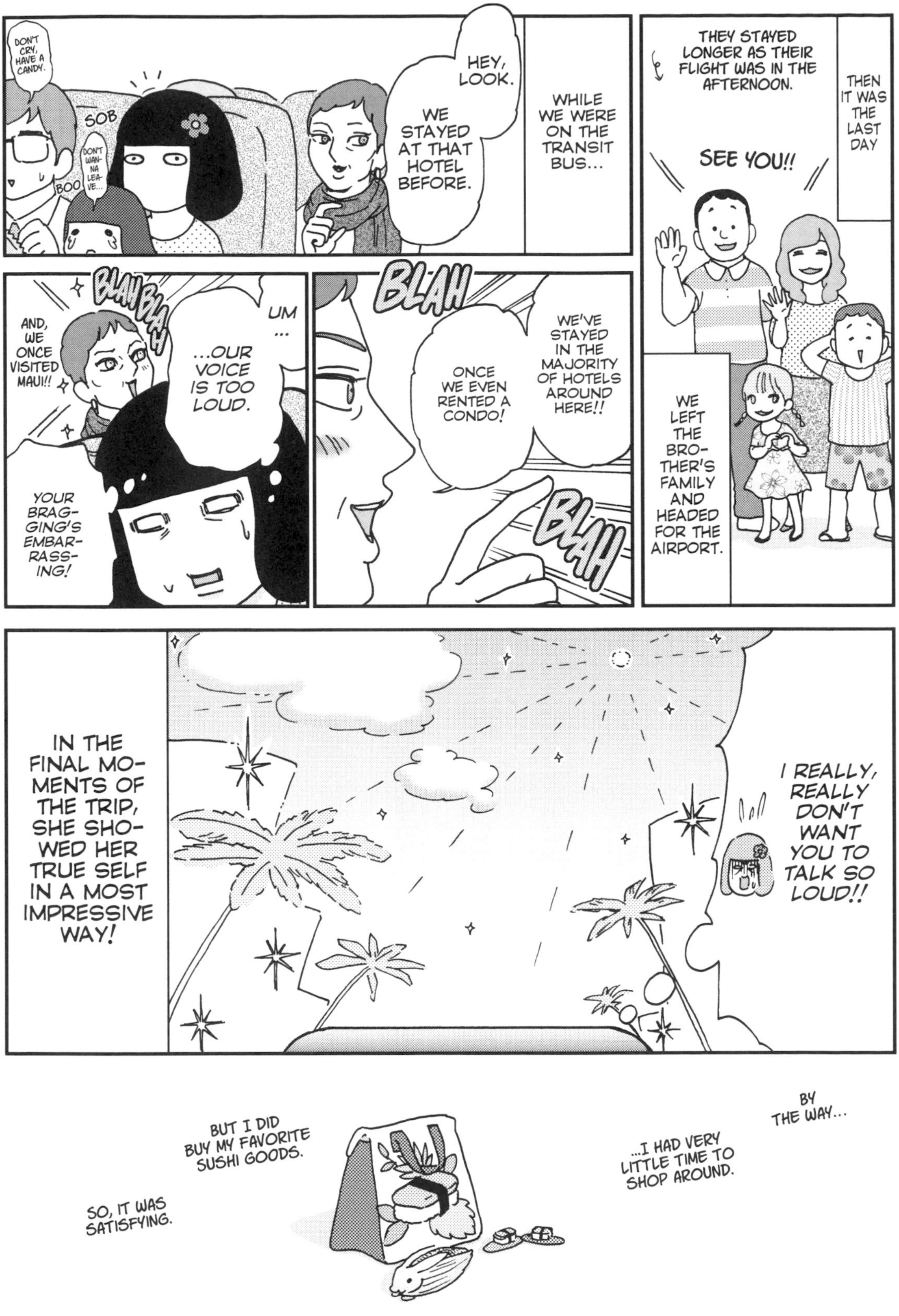
THEN IT WAS THE LAST DAY
THEY STAYED LONGER AS THEIR FLIGHT WAS IN THE AFTERNOON.
SEE YOU!!
WE LEFT THE BROTHER'S FAMILY AND HEADED FOR THE AIRPORT.
WHILE WE WERE ON THE TRANSIT BUS...
HEY, LOOK.
WE STAYED AT THAT HOTEL BEFORE.
DON'T CRY, HAVE A CANDY.
SOB
DON'T WANNA LEAVE...
BOO
BLAH
WE'VE STAYED IN THE MAJORITY OF HOTELS AROUND HERE!!
ONCE WE EVEN RENTED A CONDO!
BLAH
UM ...
BLAH BLAH
...OUR VOICE IS TOO LOUD.
AND, WE ONCE VISITED MAUI!!
YOUR BRAGGING'S EMBARRASSING!
I REALLY, REALLY DON'T WANT YOU TO TALK SO LOUD!!
IN THE FINAL MOMENTS OF THE TRIP, SHE SHOWED HER TRUE SELF IN A MOST IMPRESSIVE WAY!
BY THE WAY...
...I HAD VERY LITTLE TIME TO SHOP AROUND.
BUT I DID BUY MY FAVORITE SUSHI GOODS.
SO, IT WAS SATISFYING.

CHAPTER 9

I DON'T
WANT TO
DISLIKE YOU
ANYMORE

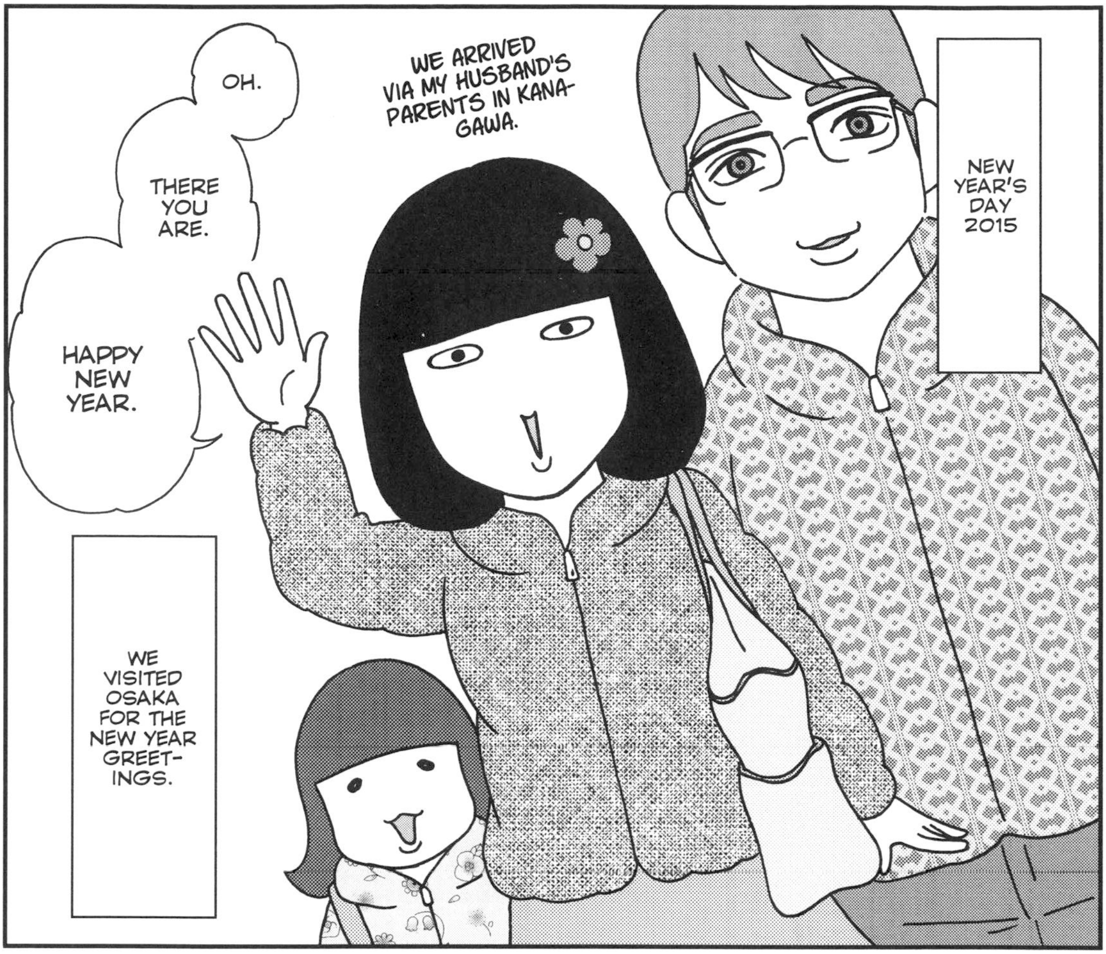
NEW YEAR'S DAY 2015
WE ARRIVED VIA MY HUSBAND'S PARENTS IN KANA-GAWA.
OH.
THERE YOU ARE.
HAPPY NEW YEAR.
WE VISITED OSAKA FOR THE NEW YEAR GREET-INGS.

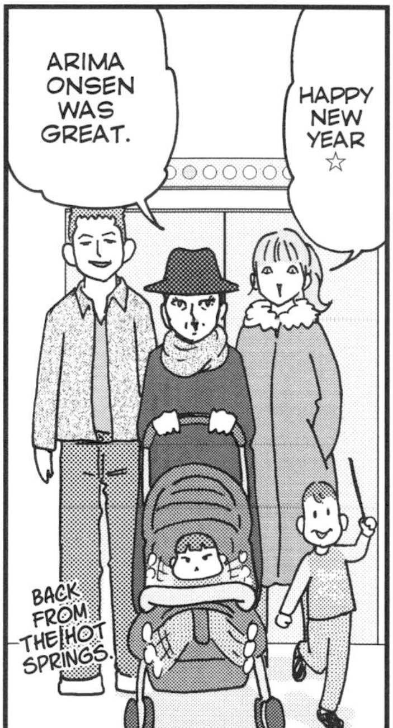
HAPPY NEW YEAR ☆
ARIMA ONSEN WAS GREAT.
BACK FROM THE HOT SPRINGS.

IN THE RESTAURANT FLOOR OF THE STATION BUILDING.

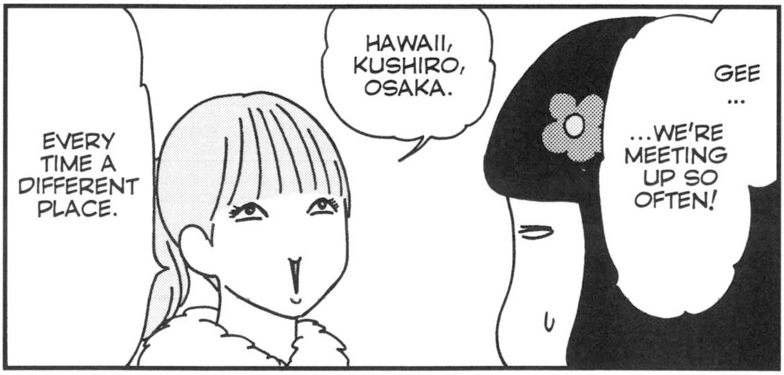
GEE ...
...WE'RE MEETING UP SO OFTEN!
HAWAII, KUSHIRO, OSAKA.
EVERY TIME A DIFFERENT PLACE.

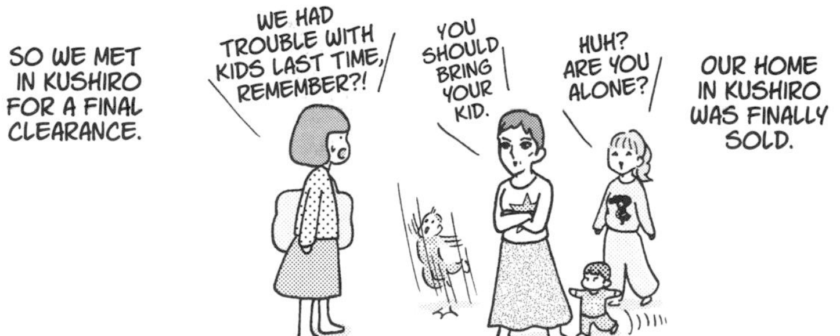
OUR HOME IN KUSHIRO WAS FINALLY SOLD.
HUH? ARE YOU ALONE?
YOU SHOULD BRING YOUR KID.
WE HAD TROUBLE WITH KIDS LAST TIME, REMEMBER?!
SO WE MET IN KUSHIRO FOR A FINAL CLEARANCE.

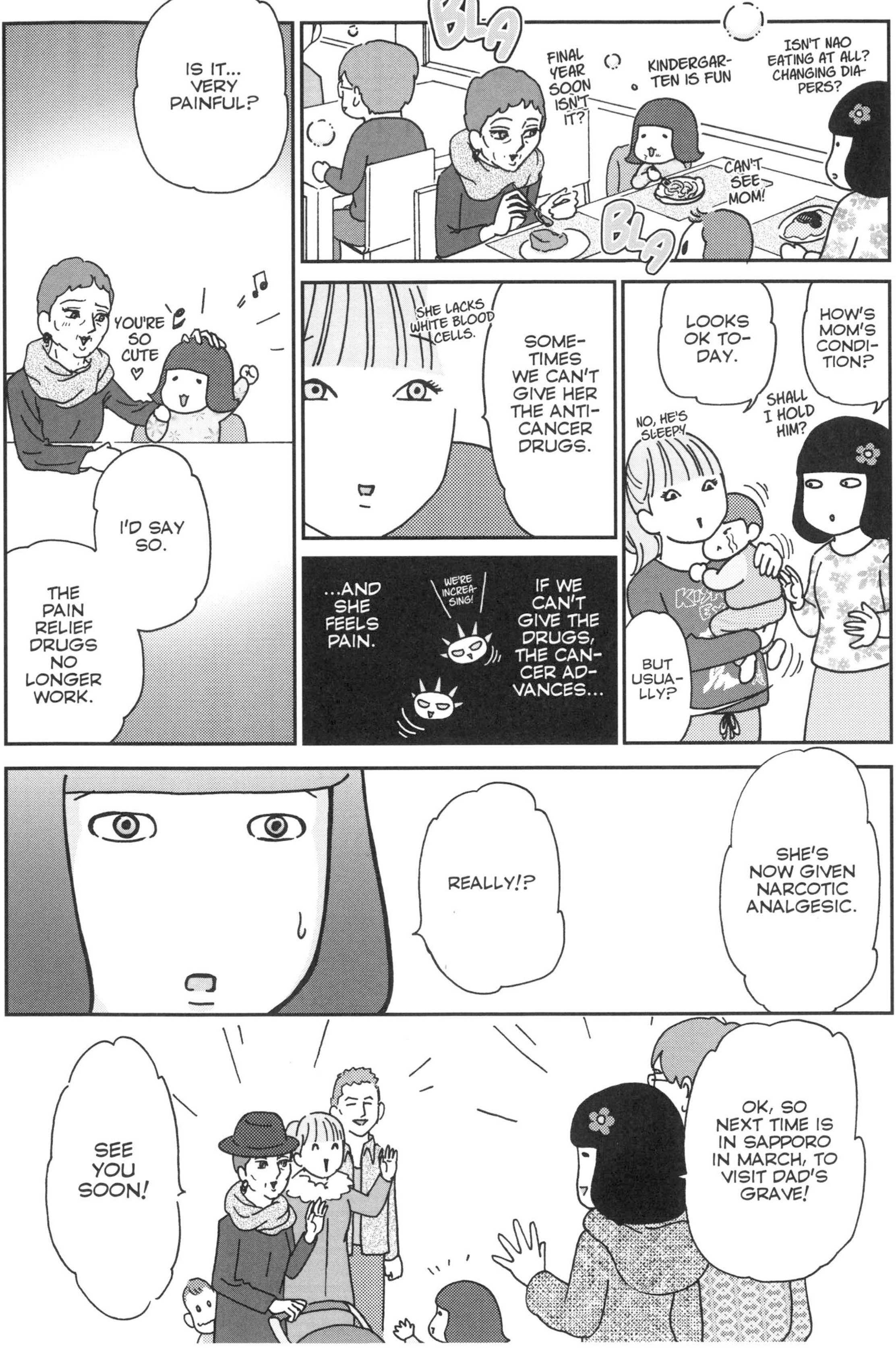
BLA
ISN'T NAO EATING AT ALL? CHANGING DIAPERS?
KINDERGARTEN IS FUN
FINAL YEAR SOON ISN'T IT?
CAN'T SEE MOM!
BLA
HOW'S MOM'S CONDITION?
LOOKS OK TODAY.
BUT USUALLY?
SHALL I HOLD HIM?
NO, HE'S SLEEPY
SOMETIMES WE CAN'T GIVE HER THE ANTI-CANCER DRUGS.
SHE LACKS WHITE BLOOD CELLS.
IF WE CAN'T GIVE THE DRUGS, THE CANCER ADVANCES...
WE'RE INCREASING!
...AND SHE FEELS PAIN.
IS IT... VERY PAINFUL?
YOU'RE SO CUTE ♡
I'D SAY SO.
THE PAIN RELIEF DRUGS NO LONGER WORK.
SHE'S NOW GIVEN NARCOTIC ANALGESIC.
REALLY!?
OK, SO NEXT TIME IS IN SAPPORO IN MARCH, TO VISIT DAD'S GRAVE!
SEE YOU SOON!

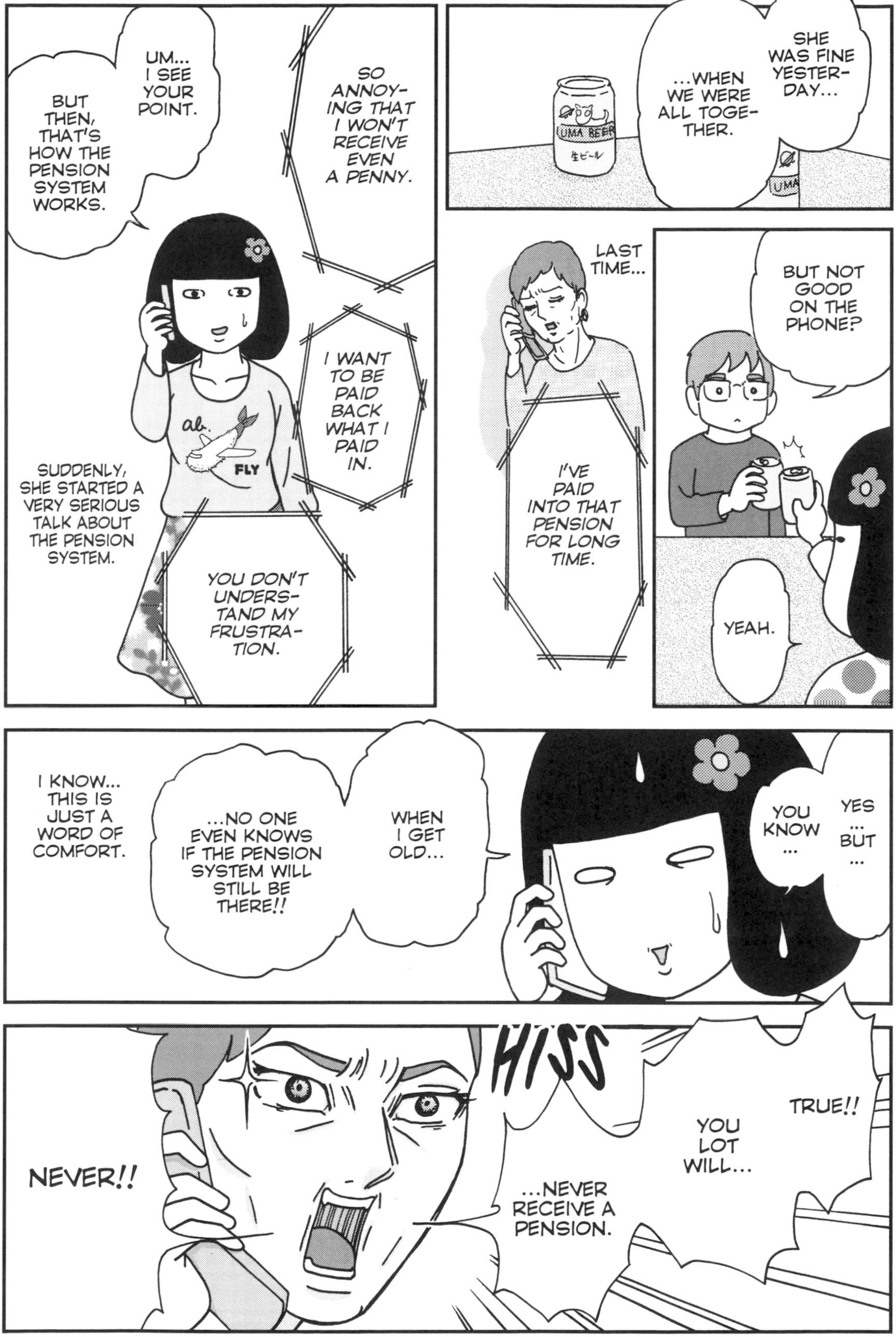

SHE WAS FINE YESTER-DAY...
...WHEN WE WERE ALL TOGE-THER.
UMA BEER
生ビール
UMA
BUT NOT GOOD ON THE PHONE?
YEAH.
LAST TIME...
I'VE PAID INTO THAT PENSION FOR LONG TIME.
SO ANNOY-ING THAT I WON'T RECEIVE EVEN A PENNY.
UM... I SEE YOUR POINT.
BUT THEN, THAT'S HOW THE PENSION SYSTEM WORKS.
I WANT TO BE PAID BACK WHAT I PAID IN.
ab.
FLY
SUDDENLY, SHE STARTED A VERY SERIOUS TALK ABOUT THE PENSION SYSTEM.
YOU DON'T UNDERS-TAND MY FRUSTRA-TION.
YES ... BUT ...
YOU KNOW ...
WHEN I GET OLD...
...NO ONE EVEN KNOWS IF THE PENSION SYSTEM WILL STILL BE THERE!!
I KNOW... THIS IS JUST A WORD OF COMFORT.
HISS
TRUE!!
YOU LOT WILL...
...NEVER RECEIVE A PENSION.
NEVER!!

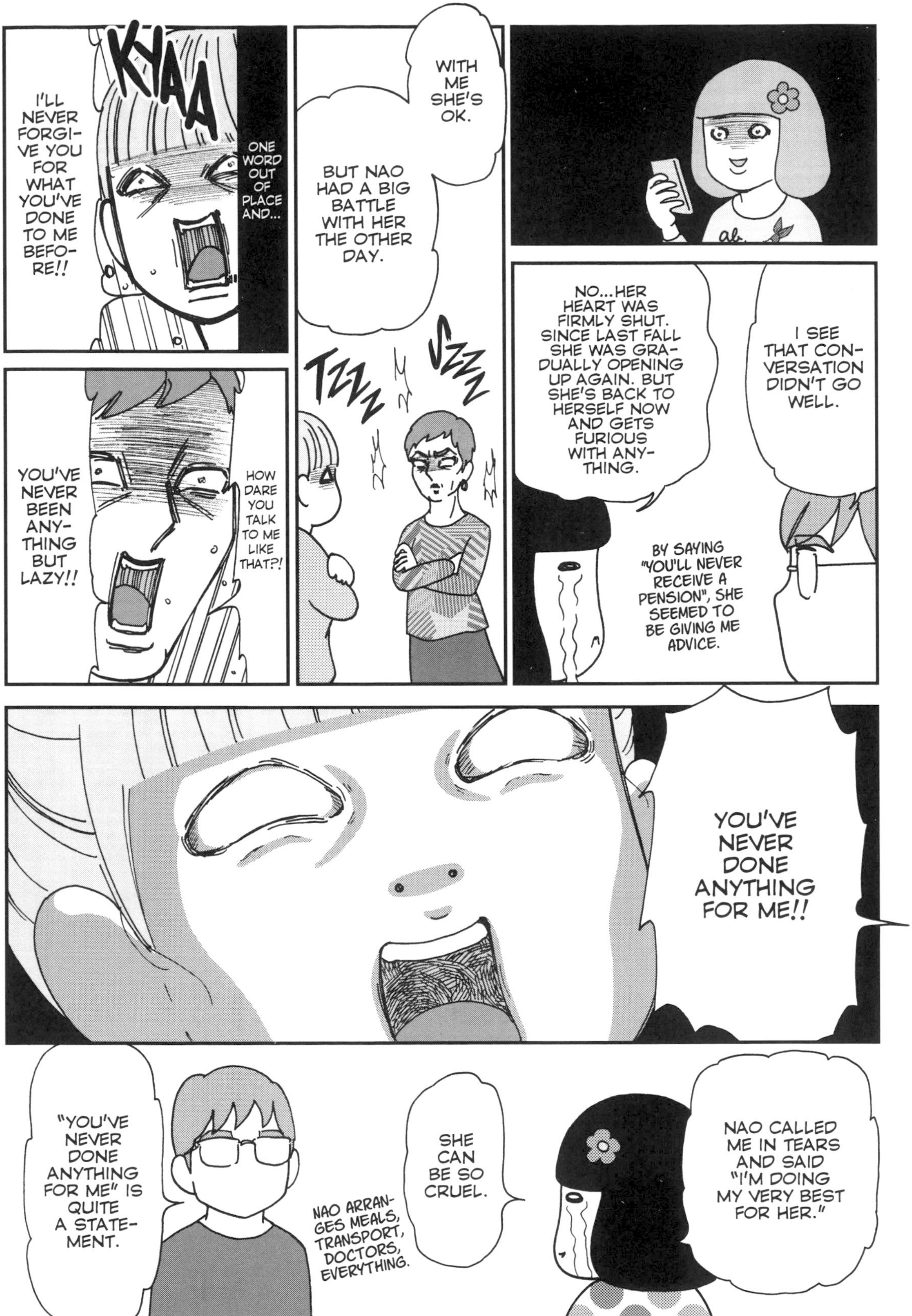
I SEE THAT CONVERSATION DIDN'T GO WELL.
NO...HER HEART WAS FIRMLY SHUT. SINCE LAST FALL SHE WAS GRADUALLY OPENING UP AGAIN. BUT SHE'S BACK TO HERSELF NOW AND GETS FURIOUS WITH ANYTHING.
BY SAYING "YOU'LL NEVER RECEIVE A PENSION", SHE SEEMED TO BE GIVING ME ADVICE.
WITH ME SHE'S OK.
BUT NAO HAD A BIG BATTLE WITH HER THE OTHER DAY.
SZZZ
TZZZ
KYAA
ONE WORD OUT OF PLACE AND...
I'LL NEVER FORGIVE YOU FOR WHAT YOU'VE DONE TO ME BEFORE!!
HOW DARE YOU TALK TO ME LIKE THAT?!
YOU'VE NEVER BEEN ANYTHING BUT LAZY!!
YOU'VE NEVER DONE ANYTHING FOR ME!!
NAO CALLED ME IN TEARS AND SAID "I'M DOING MY VERY BEST FOR HER."
SHE CAN BE SO CRUEL.
NAO ARRANGES MEALS, TRANSPORT, DOCTORS, EVERYTHING.
"YOU'VE NEVER DONE ANYTHING FOR ME" IS QUITE A STATEMENT.

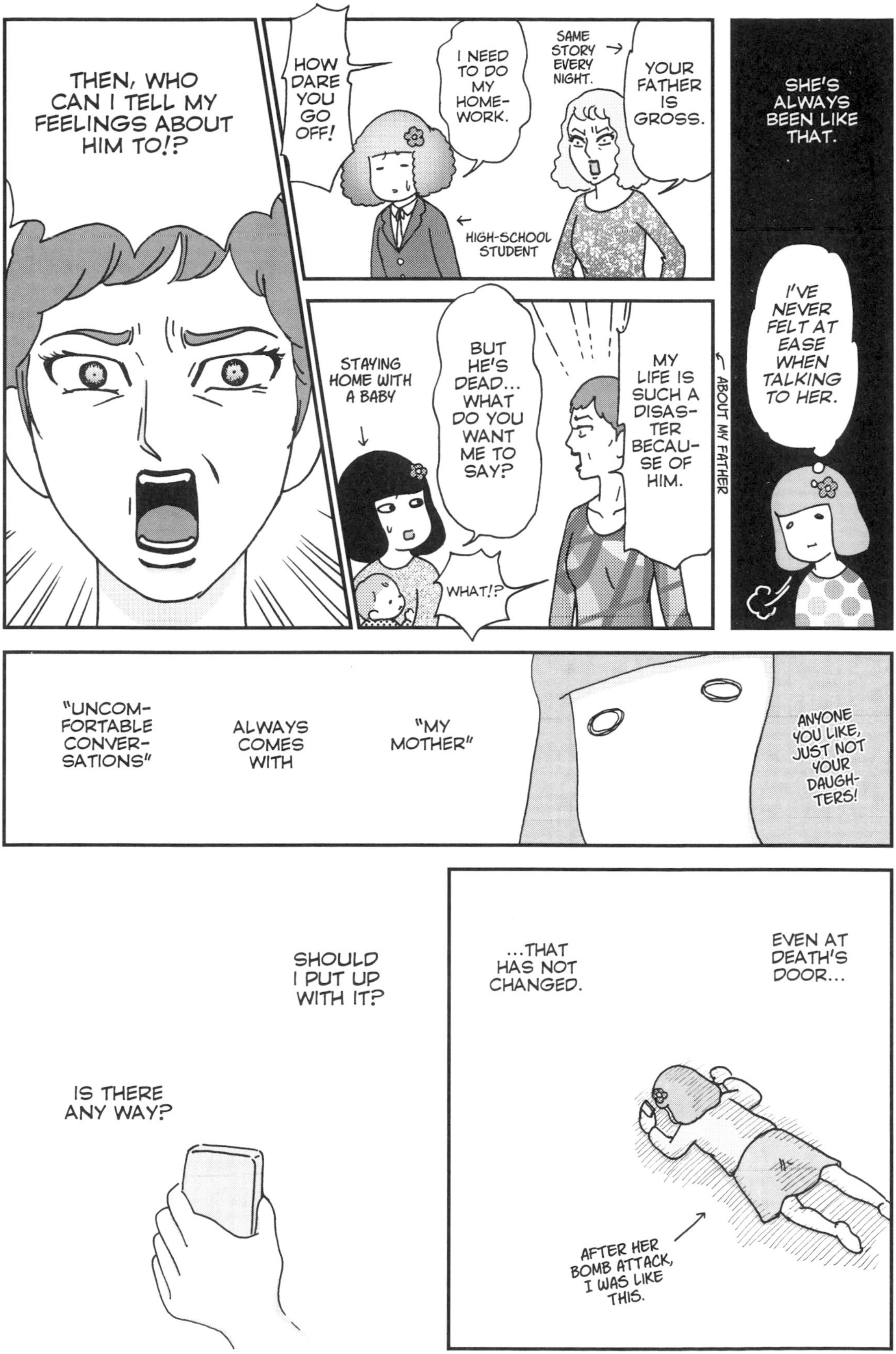
SHE'S ALWAYS BEEN LIKE THAT.
I'VE NEVER FELT AT EASE WHEN TALKING TO HER.
SAME STORY EVERY NIGHT.
YOUR FATHER IS GROSS.
I NEED TO DO MY HOMEWORK.
HOW DARE YOU GO OFF!
HIGH-SCHOOL STUDENT
ABOUT MY FATHER
MY LIFE IS SUCH A DISASTER BECAUSE OF HIM.
BUT HE'S DEAD... WHAT DO YOU WANT ME TO SAY?
STAYING HOME WITH A BABY
WHAT!?
THEN, WHO CAN I TELL MY FEELINGS ABOUT HIM TO!?
ANYONE YOU LIKE, JUST NOT YOUR DAUGHTERS!
"MY MOTHER"
ALWAYS COMES WITH
"UNCOMFORTABLE CONVERSATIONS"
EVEN AT DEATH'S DOOR...
...THAT HAS NOT CHANGED.
AFTER HER BOMB ATTACK, I WAS LIKE THIS.
SHOULD I PUT UP WITH IT?
IS THERE ANY WAY?

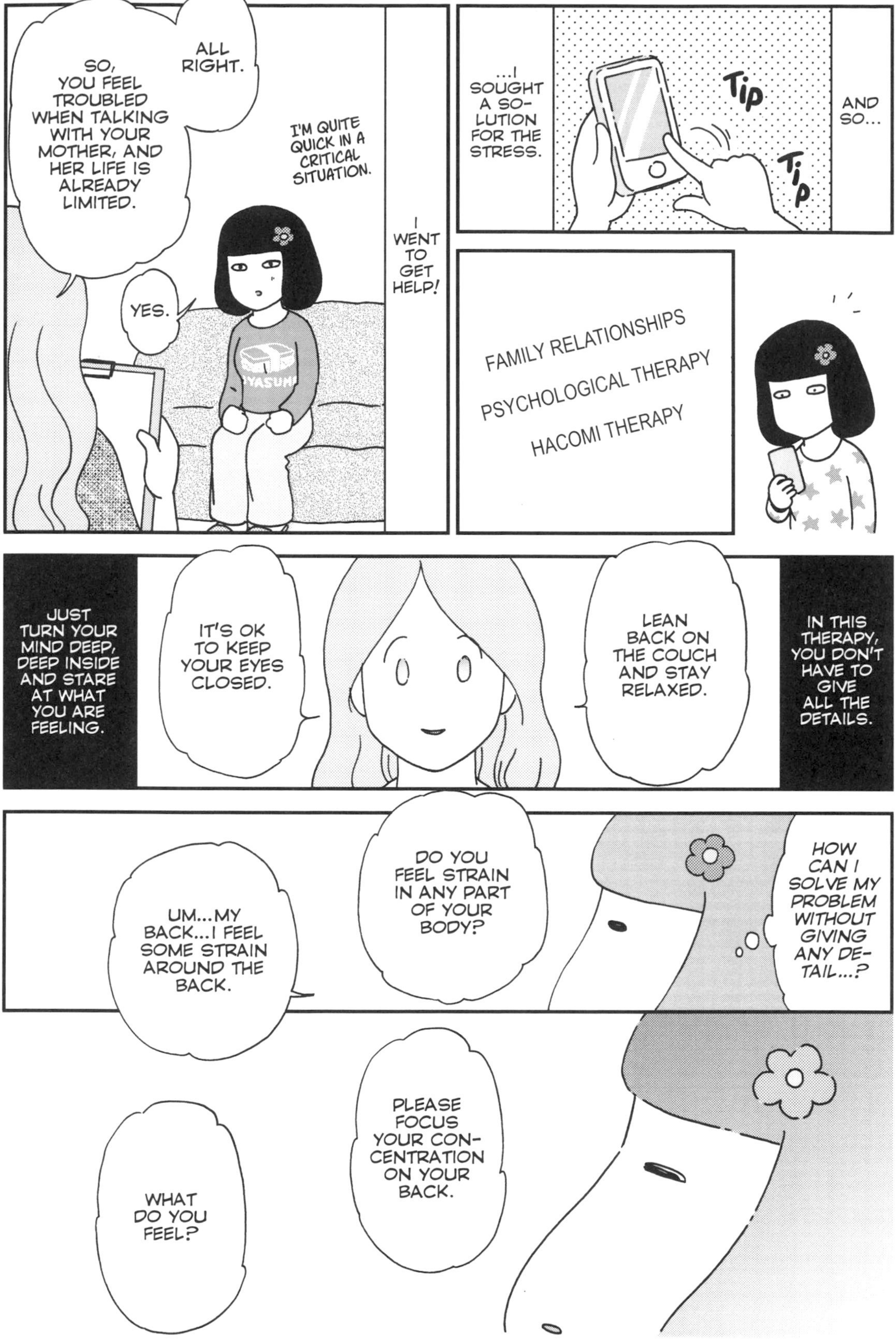
AND SO…
Tip
Tip
…I SOUGHT A SOLUTION FOR THE STRESS.
FAMILY RELATIONSHIPS
PSYCHOLOGICAL THERAPY
HACOMI THERAPY
I WENT TO GET HELP!
ALL RIGHT.
I'M QUITE QUICK IN A CRITICAL SITUATION.
SO, YOU FEEL TROUBLED WHEN TALKING WITH YOUR MOTHER, AND HER LIFE IS ALREADY LIMITED.
YES.
IN THIS THERAPY, YOU DON'T HAVE TO GIVE ALL THE DETAILS.
LEAN BACK ON THE COUCH AND STAY RELAXED.
IT'S OK TO KEEP YOUR EYES CLOSED.
JUST TURN YOUR MIND DEEP, DEEP INSIDE AND STARE AT WHAT YOU ARE FEELING.
HOW CAN I SOLVE MY PROBLEM WITHOUT GIVING ANY DETAIL…?
DO YOU FEEL STRAIN IN ANY PART OF YOUR BODY?
UM…MY BACK…I FEEL SOME STRAIN AROUND THE BACK.
PLEASE FOCUS YOUR CONCENTRATION ON YOUR BACK.
WHAT DO YOU FEEL?

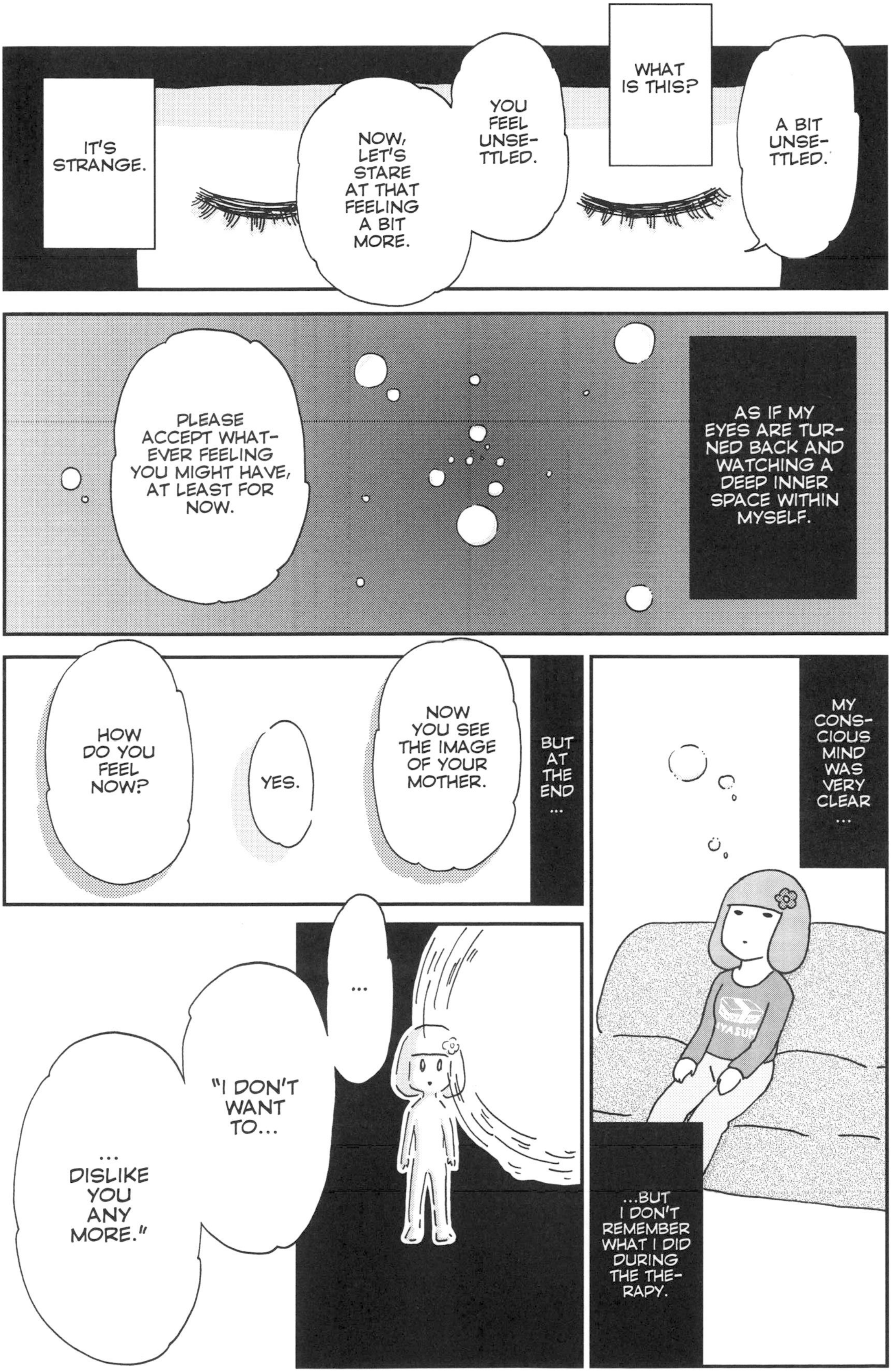
A BIT UNSE-TTLED.
WHAT IS THIS?
YOU FEEL UNSE-TTLED.
NOW, LET'S STARE AT THAT FEELING A BIT MORE.
IT'S STRANGE.
AS IF MY EYES ARE TUR-NED BACK AND WATCHING A DEEP INNER SPACE WITHIN MYSELF.
PLEASE ACCEPT WHAT-EVER FEELING YOU MIGHT HAVE, AT LEAST FOR NOW.
MY CONS-CIOUS MIND WAS VERY CLEAR ...
...BUT I DON'T REMEMBER WHAT I DID DURING THE THE-RAPY.
BUT AT THE END ...
NOW YOU SEE THE IMAGE OF YOUR MOTHER.
YES.
HOW DO YOU FEEL NOW?
...
"I DON'T WANT TO...
... DISLIKE YOU ANY MORE."

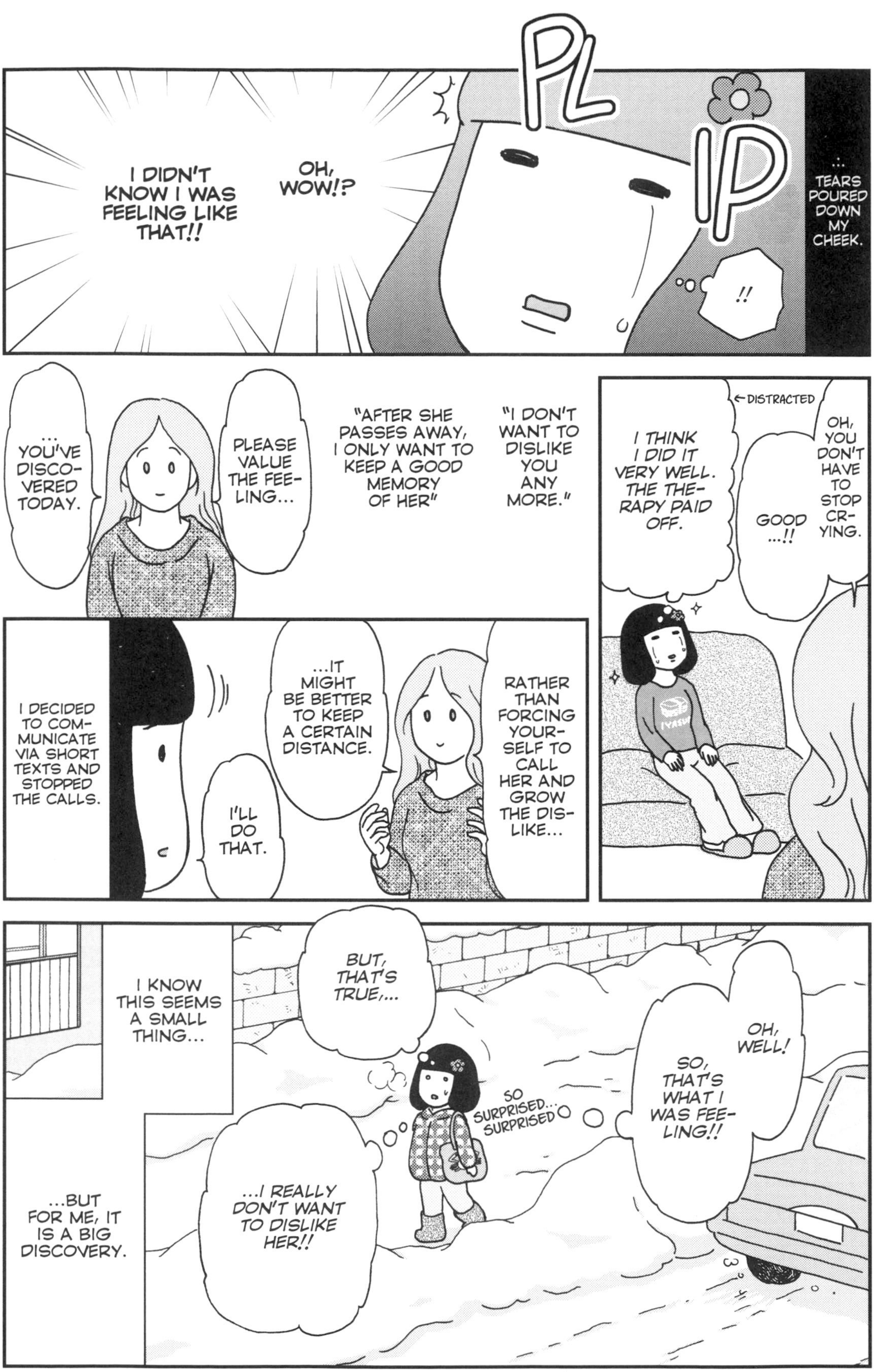

...TEARS POURED DOWN MY CHEEK.
PLIP
!!
OH, WOW!?
I DIDN'T KNOW I WAS FEELING LIKE THAT!!
OH, YOU DON'T HAVE TO STOP CRYING.
← DISTRACTED
GOOD ...!!
I THINK I DID IT VERY WELL. THE THERAPY PAID OFF.
"I DON'T WANT TO DISLIKE YOU ANY MORE."
"AFTER SHE PASSES AWAY, I ONLY WANT TO KEEP A GOOD MEMORY OF HER"
PLEASE VALUE THE FEELING...
...YOU'VE DISCOVERED TODAY.
RATHER THAN FORCING YOURSELF TO CALL HER AND GROW THE DISLIKE...
...IT MIGHT BE BETTER TO KEEP A CERTAIN DISTANCE.
I'LL DO THAT.
I DECIDED TO COMMUNICATE VIA SHORT TEXTS AND STOPPED THE CALLS.
OH, WELL!
SO, THAT'S WHAT I WAS FEELING!!
SO SURPRISED... SURPRISED
BUT, THAT'S TRUE,...
I KNOW THIS SEEMS A SMALL THING...
...I REALLY DON'T WANT TO DISLIKE HER!!
...BUT FOR ME, IT IS A BIG DISCOVERY.

CHAPTER10

IS SHE DYING?

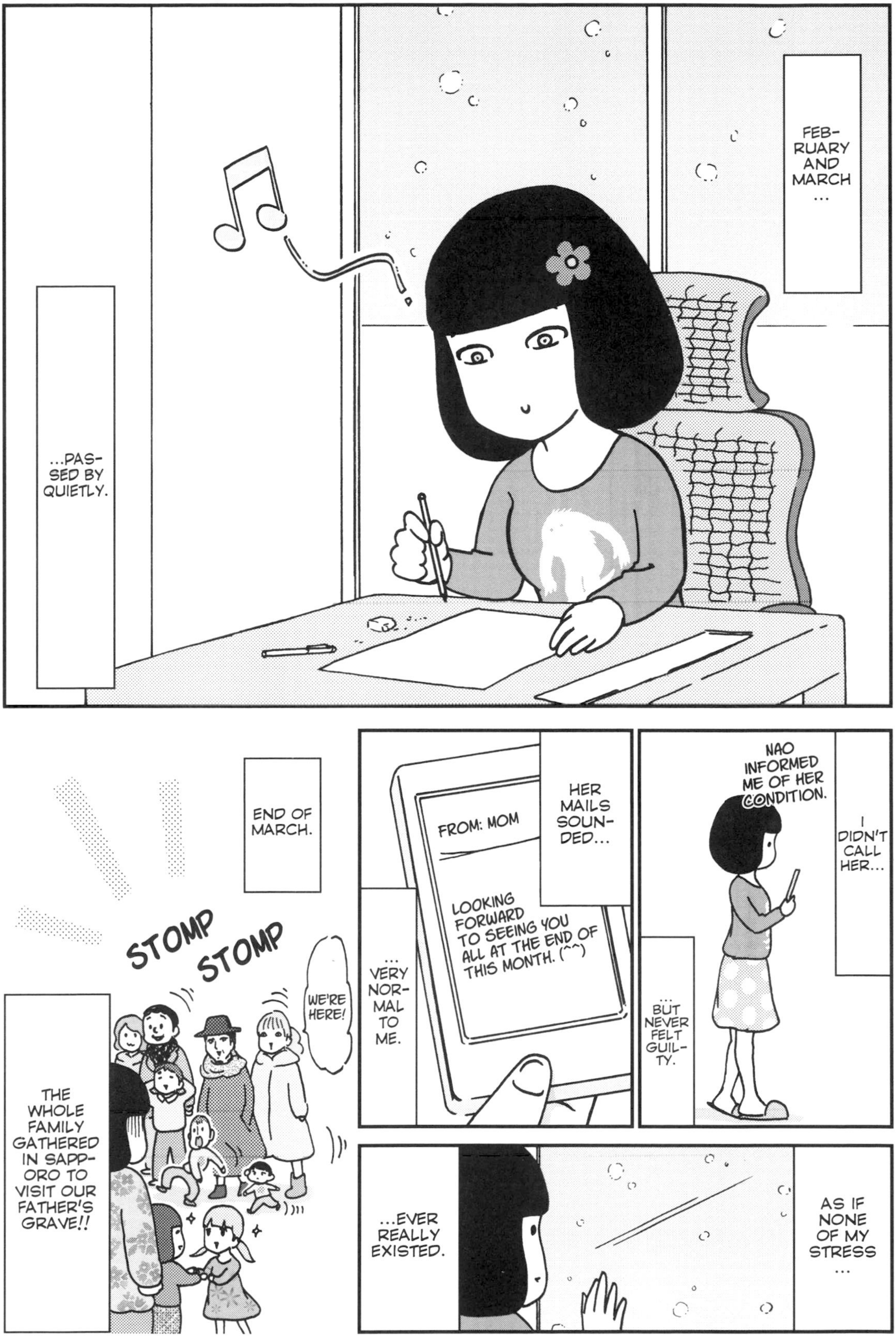

FEB-RUARY AND MARCH ...
...PAS-SED BY QUIETLY.
NAO INFORMED ME OF HER CONDITION.
I DIDN'T CALL HER...
...BUT NEVER FELT GUIL-TY.
HER MAILS SOUN-DED...
FROM: MOM
LOOKING FORWARD TO SEEING YOU ALL AT THE END OF THIS MONTH. (^^)
...VERY NOR-MAL TO ME.
AS IF NONE OF MY STRESS ...
...EVER REALLY EXISTED.
END OF MARCH.
STOMP STOMP
... WE'RE HERE!
THE WHOLE FAMILY GATHERED IN SAPP-ORO TO VISIT OUR FATHER'S GRAVE!!

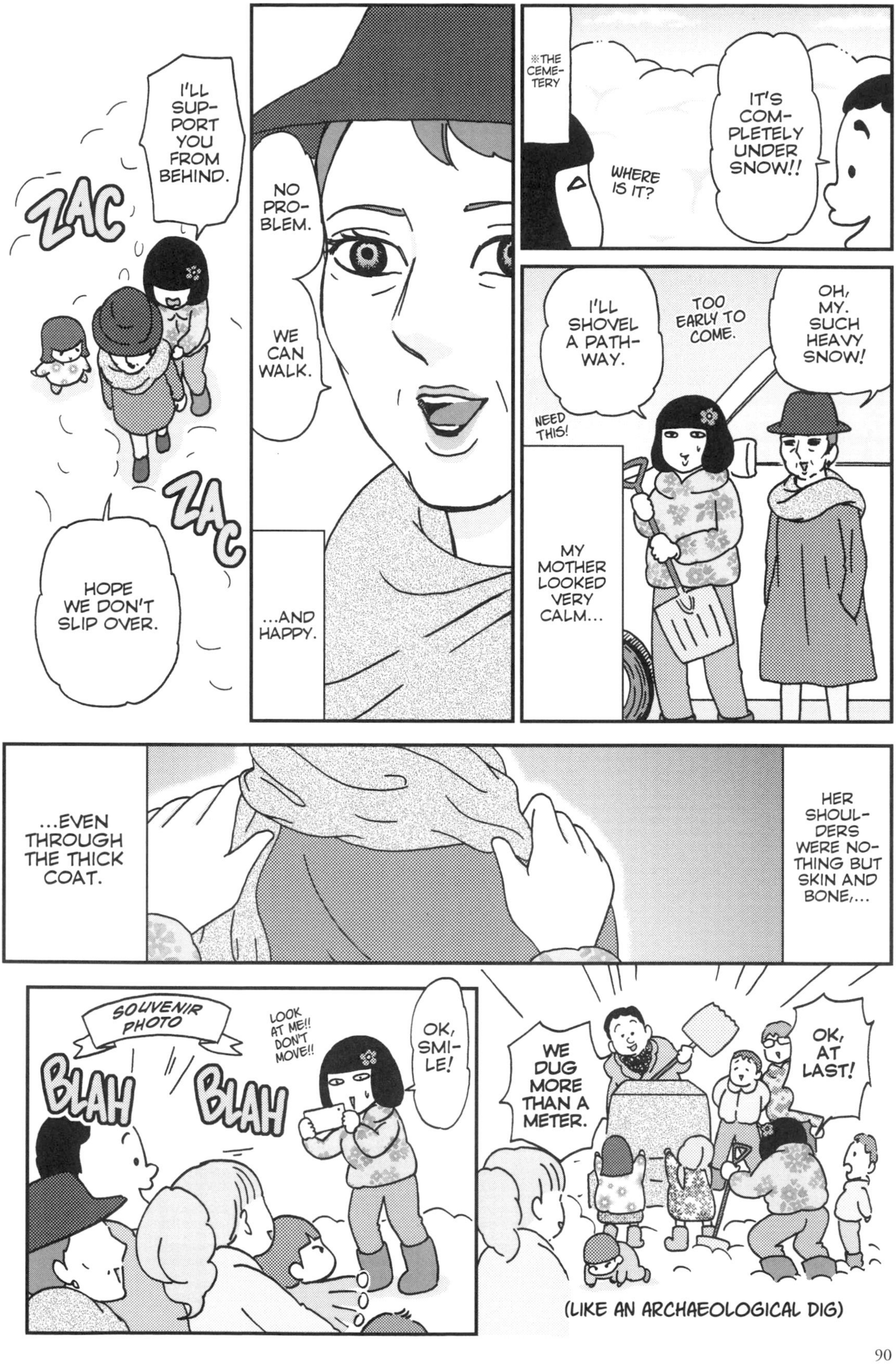
※THE CEMETERY
IT'S COMPLETELY UNDER SNOW!!
WHERE IS IT?
OH, MY. SUCH HEAVY SNOW!
TOO EARLY TO COME.
I'LL SHOVEL A PATHWAY.
NEED THIS!
MY MOTHER LOOKED VERY CALM...
NO PROBLEM.
WE CAN WALK.
...AND HAPPY.
I'LL SUPPORT YOU FROM BEHIND.
ZAC
ZAC
HOPE WE DON'T SLIP OVER.
HER SHOULDERS WERE NOTHING BUT SKIN AND BONE,...
...EVEN THROUGH THE THICK COAT.
OK, AT LAST!
WE DUG MORE THAN A METER.
(LIKE AN ARCHAEOLOGICAL DIG)
OK, SMILE!
LOOK AT ME!! DON'T MOVE!!
SOUVENIR PHOTO
BLAH
BLAH

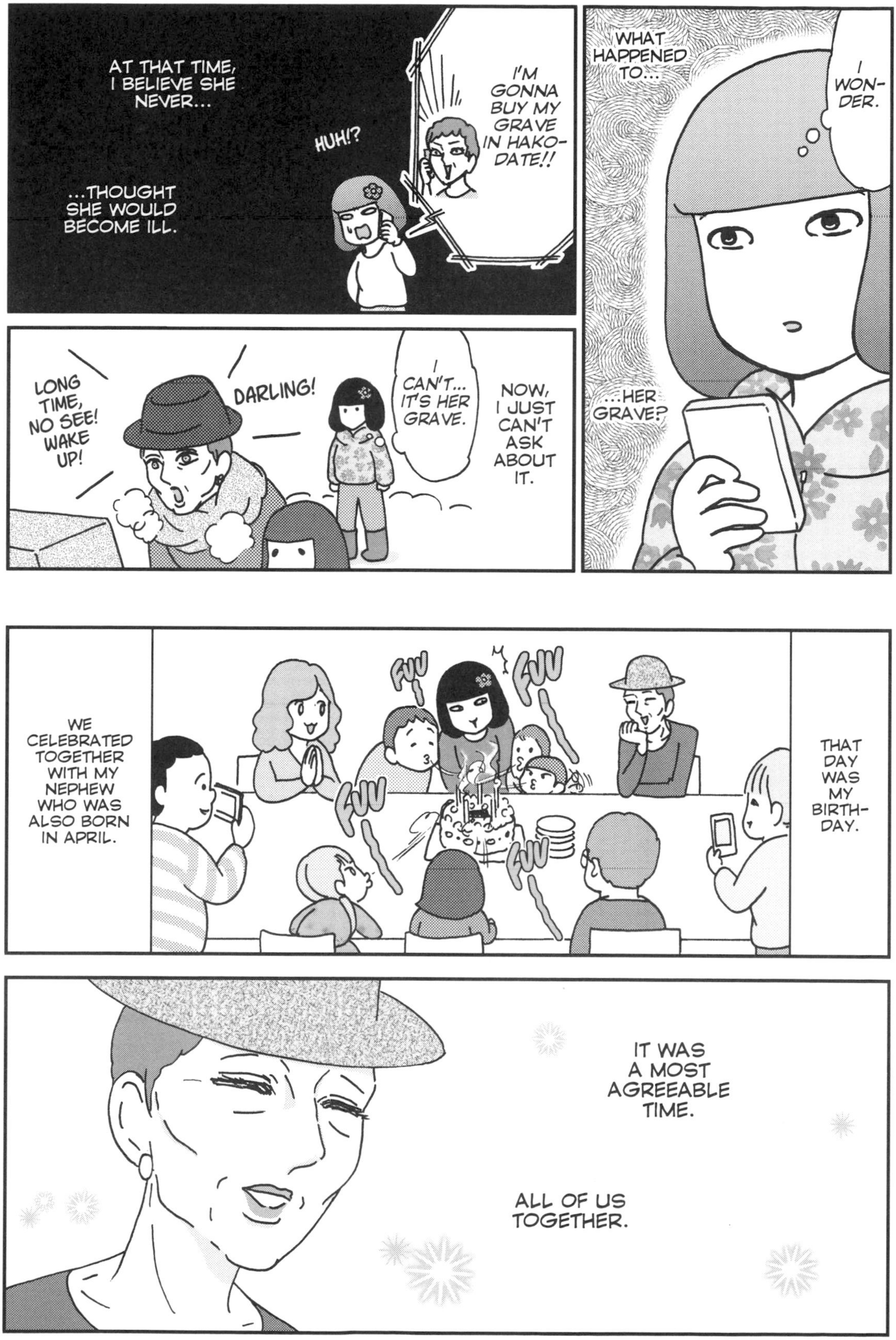
I WON-DER.
WHAT HAPPENED TO...
...HER GRAVE?
I'M GONNA BUY MY GRAVE IN HAKO-DATE!!
HUH!?
AT THAT TIME, I BELIEVE SHE NEVER...
...THOUGHT SHE WOULD BECOME ILL.
NOW, I JUST CAN'T ASK ABOUT IT.
I CAN'T... IT'S HER GRAVE.
DARLING!
LONG TIME, NO SEE! WAKE UP!
THAT DAY WAS MY BIRTH-DAY.
FUU
FUU
FUU
FUU
WE CELEBRATED TOGETHER WITH MY NEPHEW WHO WAS ALSO BORN IN APRIL.
IT WAS A MOST AGREEABLE TIME.
ALL OF US TOGETHER.

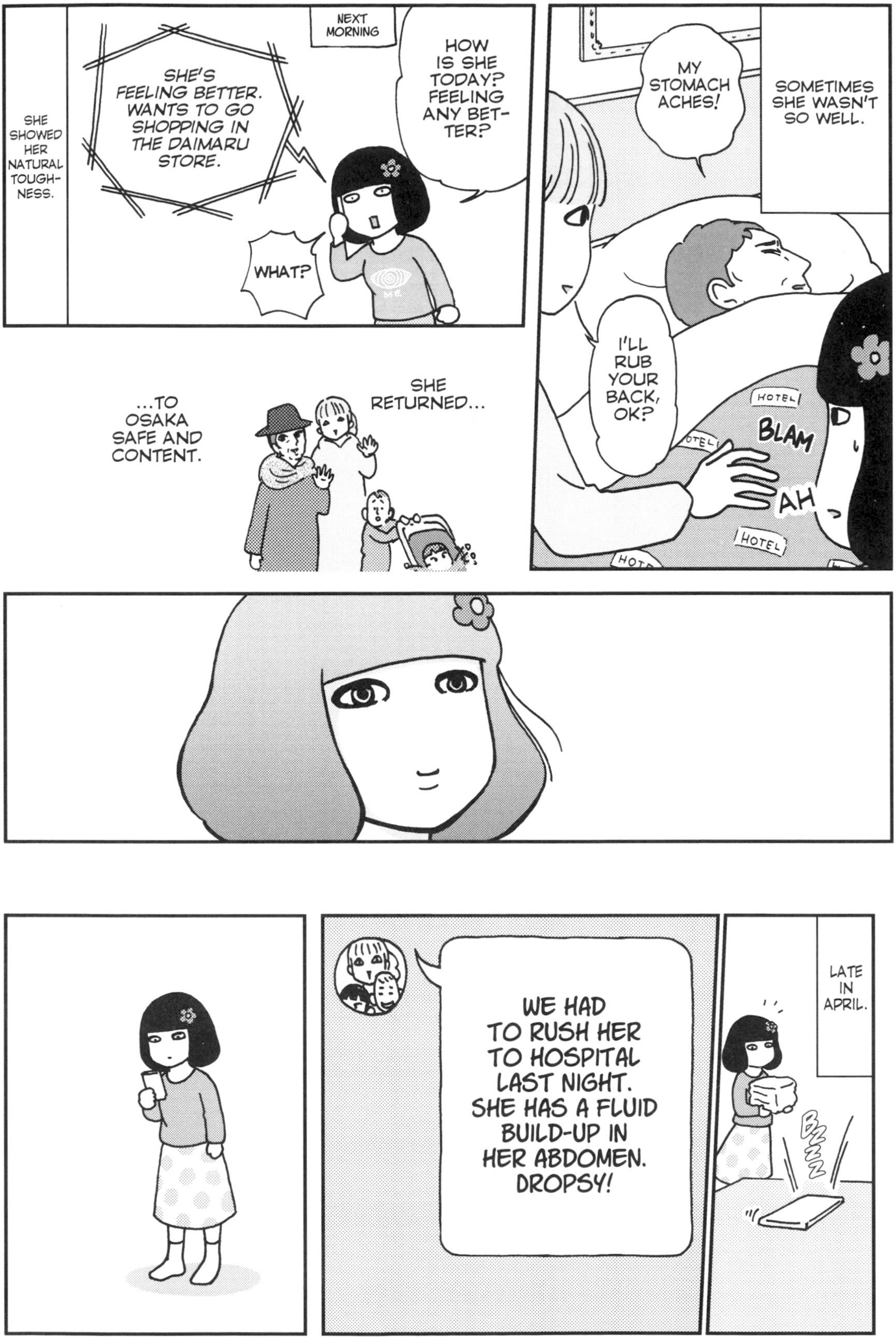
SOMETIMES SHE WASN'T SO WELL.
MY STOMACH ACHES!
I'LL RUB YOUR BACK, OK?
HOTEL
BLAM
AH
HOTEL
NEXT MORNING
HOW IS SHE TODAY? FEELING ANY BET-TER?
SHE'S FEELING BETTER. WANTS TO GO SHOPPING IN THE DAIMARU STORE.
WHAT?
SHE SHOWED HER NATURAL TOUGH-NESS.
SHE RETURNED...
...TO OSAKA SAFE AND CONTENT.
LATE IN APRIL.
BZZZ
WE HAD TO RUSH HER TO HOSPITAL LAST NIGHT. SHE HAS A FLUID BUILD-UP IN HER ABDOMEN. DROPSY!

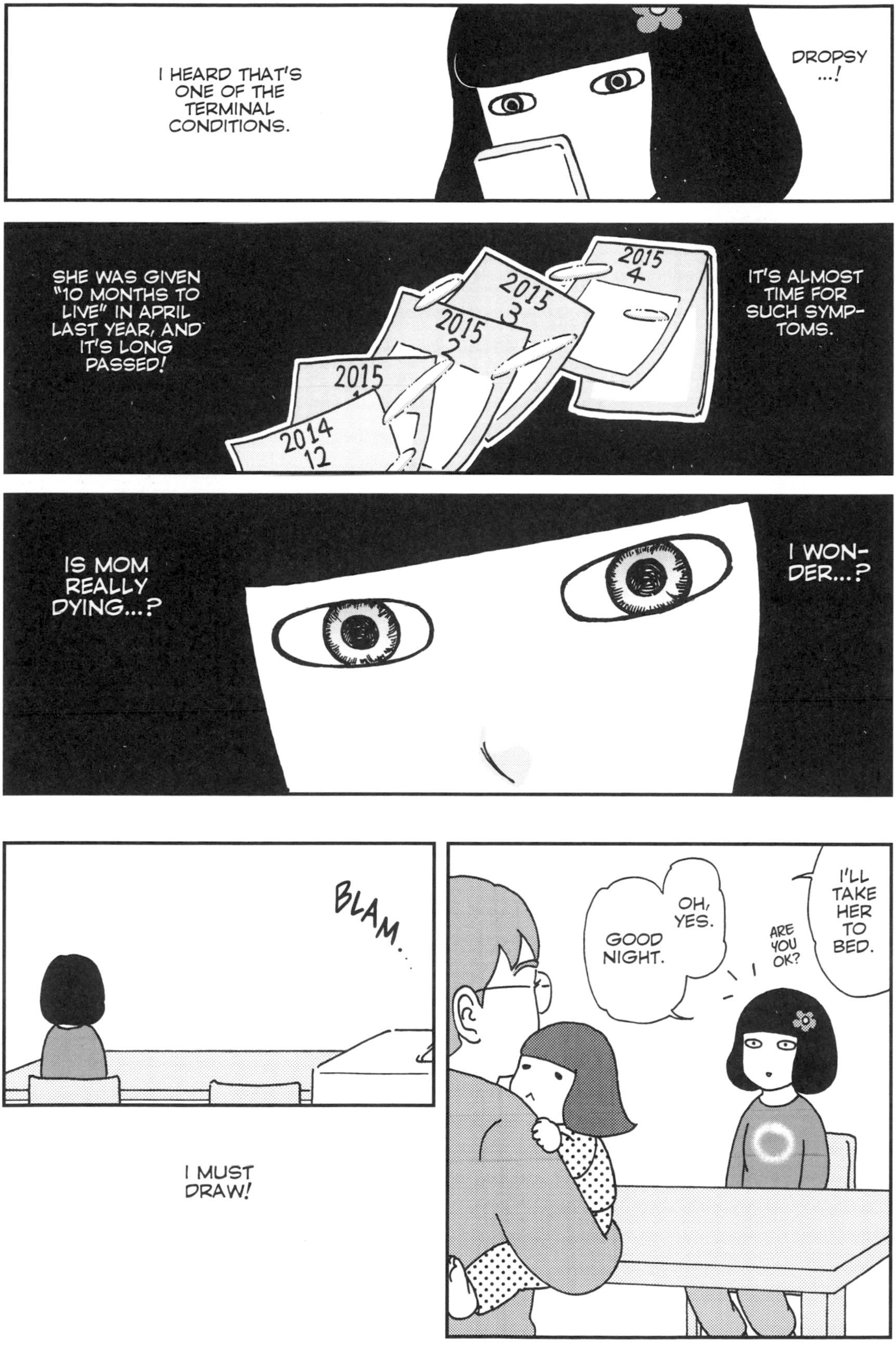
DROPSY ...!
I HEARD THAT'S ONE OF THE TERMINAL CONDITIONS.
IT'S ALMOST TIME FOR SUCH SYMP-TOMS.
SHE WAS GIVEN "10 MONTHS TO LIVE" IN APRIL LAST YEAR, AND IT'S LONG PASSED!
2015 4
2015 3
2015 2
2015 1
2014 12
I WON-DER...?
IS MOM REALLY DYING...?
I'LL TAKE HER TO BED.
ARE YOU OK?
OH, YES.
GOOD NIGHT.
BLAM...
I MUST DRAW!

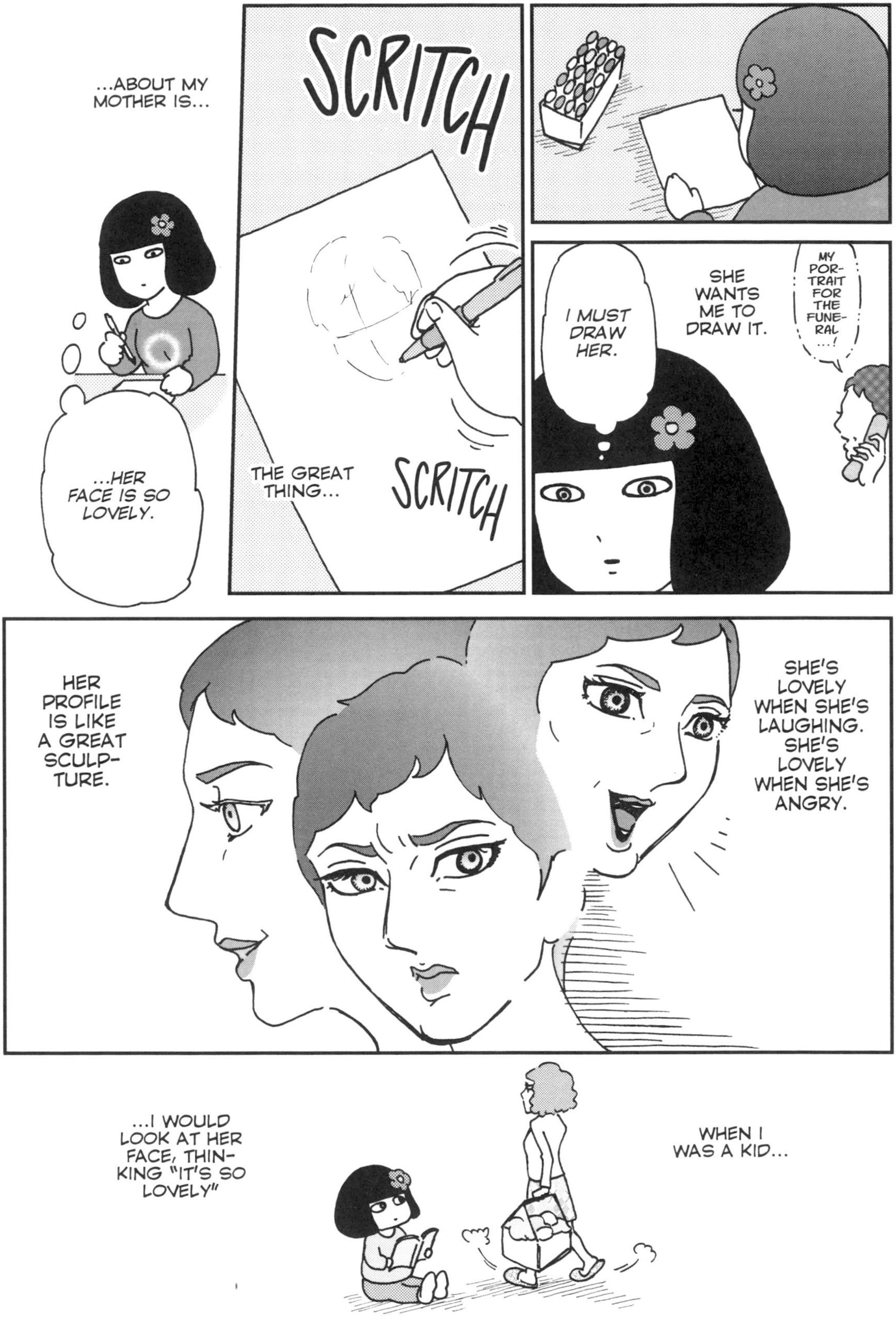
MY POR-TRAIT FOR THE FUNE-RAL ...!
SHE WANTS ME TO DRAW IT.
I MUST DRAW HER.
SCRITCH
THE GREAT THING...
SCRITCH
...ABOUT MY MOTHER IS...
...HER FACE IS SO LOVELY.
SHE'S LOVELY WHEN SHE'S LAUGHING. SHE'S LOVELY WHEN SHE'S ANGRY.
HER PROFILE IS LIKE A GREAT SCULP-TURE.
WHEN I WAS A KID...
...I WOULD LOOK AT HER FACE, THIN-KING "IT'S SO LOVELY"

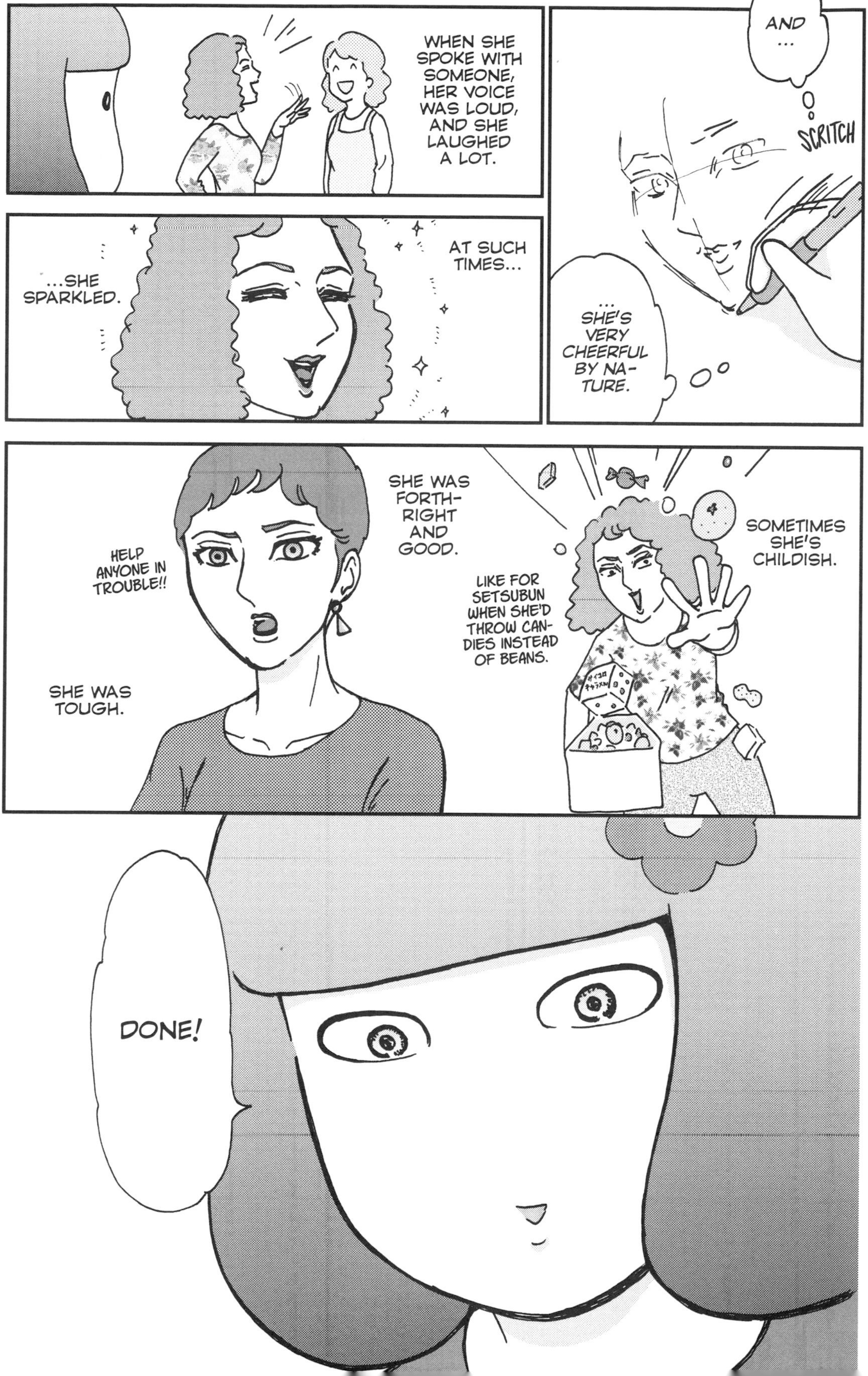
AND ...
SCRITCH
... SHE'S VERY CHEERFUL BY NA-TURE.
WHEN SHE SPOKE WITH SOMEONE, HER VOICE WAS LOUD, AND SHE LAUGHED A LOT.
AT SUCH TIMES...
...SHE SPARKLED.
SOMETIMES SHE'S CHILDISH.
LIKE FOR SETSUBUN WHEN SHE'D THROW CAN-DIES INSTEAD OF BEANS.
SHE WAS FORTH-RIGHT AND GOOD.
HELP ANYONE IN TROUBLE!!
SHE WAS TOUGH.
DONE!

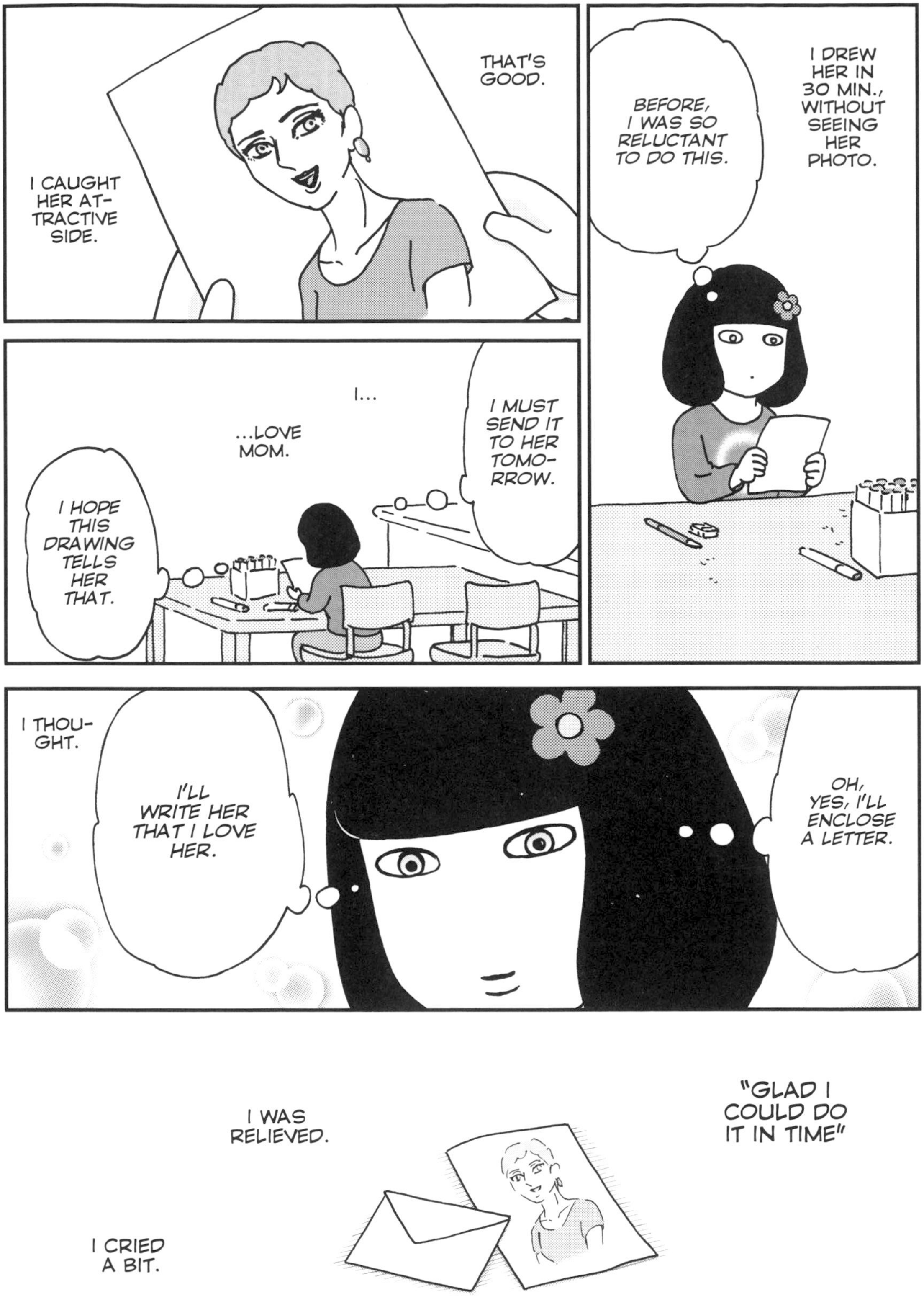
I DREW HER IN 30 MIN., WITHOUT SEEING HER PHOTO.
BEFORE, I WAS SO RELUCTANT TO DO THIS.
THAT'S GOOD.
I CAUGHT HER ATTRACTIVE SIDE.
I MUST SEND IT TO HER TOMORROW.
I...
...LOVE MOM.
I HOPE THIS DRAWING TELLS HER THAT.
OH, YES, I'LL ENCLOSE A LETTER.
I'LL WRITE HER THAT I LOVE HER.
I THOUGHT.
"GLAD I COULD DO IT IN TIME"
I WAS RELIEVED.
I CRIED A BIT.

CHAPTER 11

WE MAY
NOT MEET
AGAIN

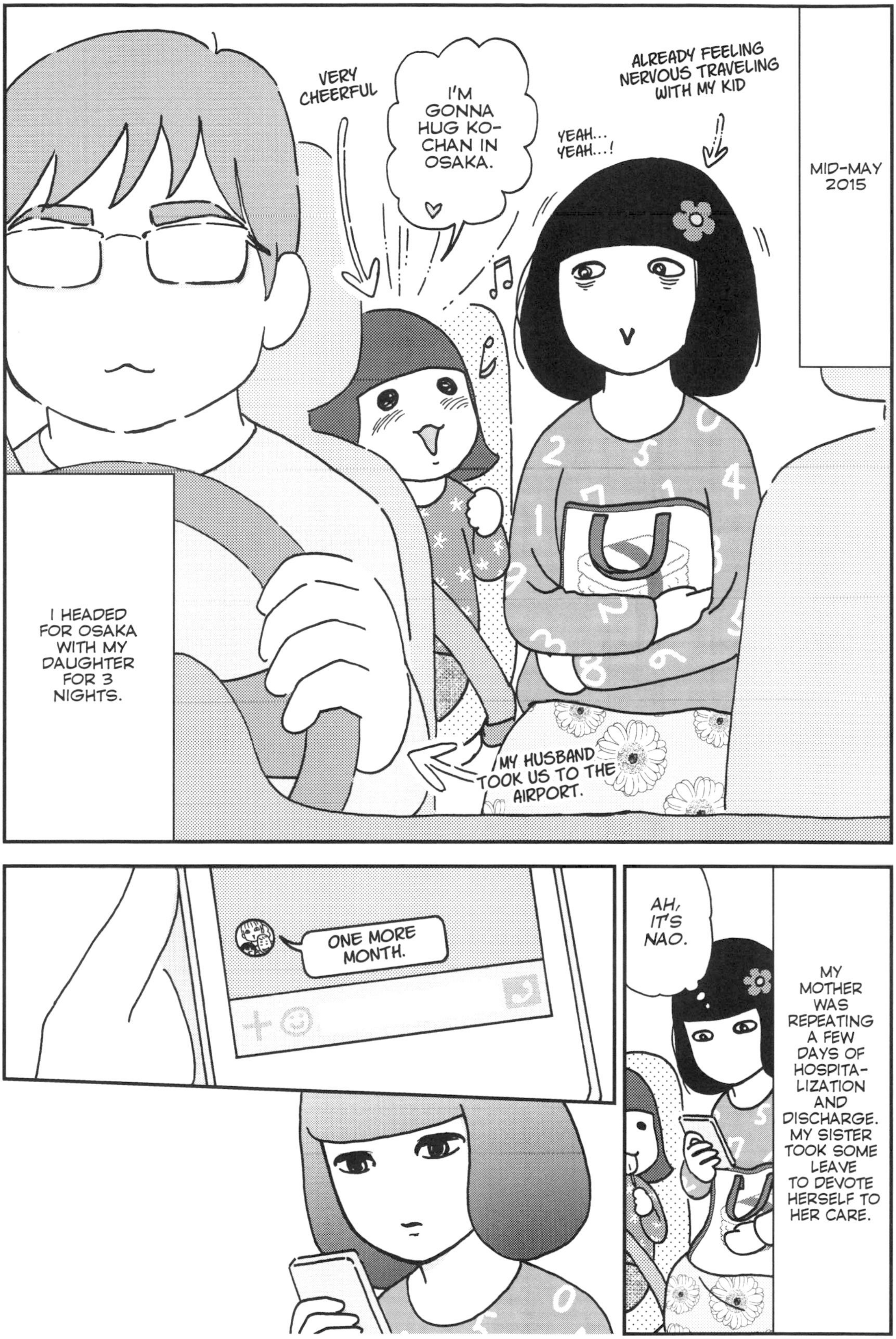
MID-MAY 2015
ALREADY FEELING NERVOUS TRAVELING WITH MY KID
YEAH... YEAH...!
I'M GONNA HUG KO-CHAN IN OSAKA.
VERY CHEERFUL
MY HUSBAND TOOK US TO THE AIRPORT.
I HEADED FOR OSAKA WITH MY DAUGHTER FOR 3 NIGHTS.
MY MOTHER WAS REPEATING A FEW DAYS OF HOSPITA-LIZATION AND DISCHARGE. MY SISTER TOOK SOME LEAVE TO DEVOTE HERSELF TO HER CARE.
AH, IT'S NAO.
ONE MORE MONTH.

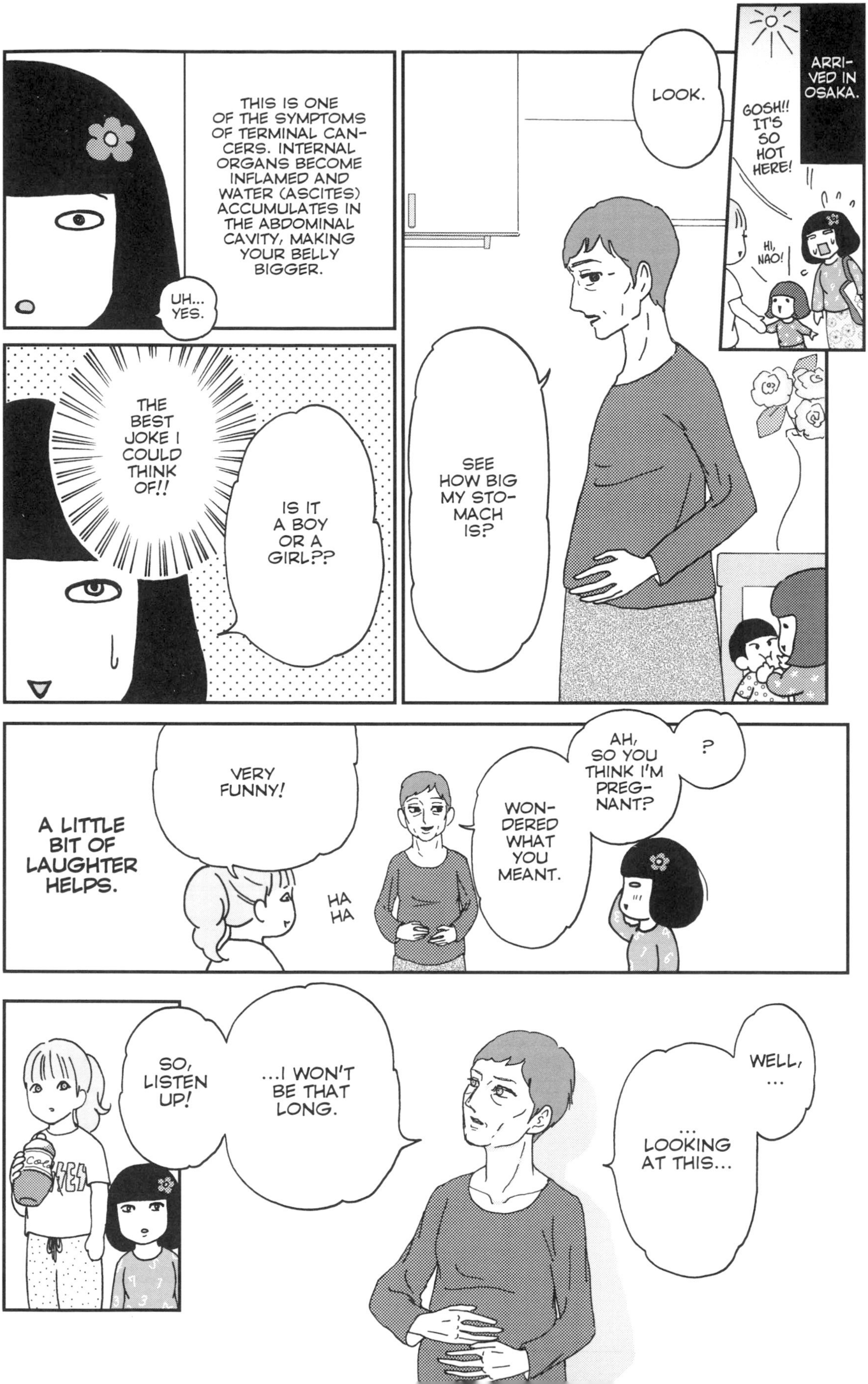
ARRIVED IN OSAKA.
GOSH!! IT'S SO HOT HERE!
HI, NAO!
LOOK.
SEE HOW BIG MY STOMACH IS?
THIS IS ONE OF THE SYMPTOMS OF TERMINAL CANCERS. INTERNAL ORGANS BECOME INFLAMED AND WATER (ASCITES) ACCUMULATES IN THE ABDOMINAL CAVITY, MAKING YOUR BELLY BIGGER.
UH... YES.
THE BEST JOKE I COULD THINK OF!!
IS IT A BOY OR A GIRL??
?
AH, SO YOU THINK I'M PREGNANT?
WONDERED WHAT YOU MEANT.
VERY FUNNY!
HA HA
A LITTLE BIT OF LAUGHTER HELPS.
WELL, ...
... LOOKING AT THIS...
...I WON'T BE THAT LONG.
SO, LISTEN UP!

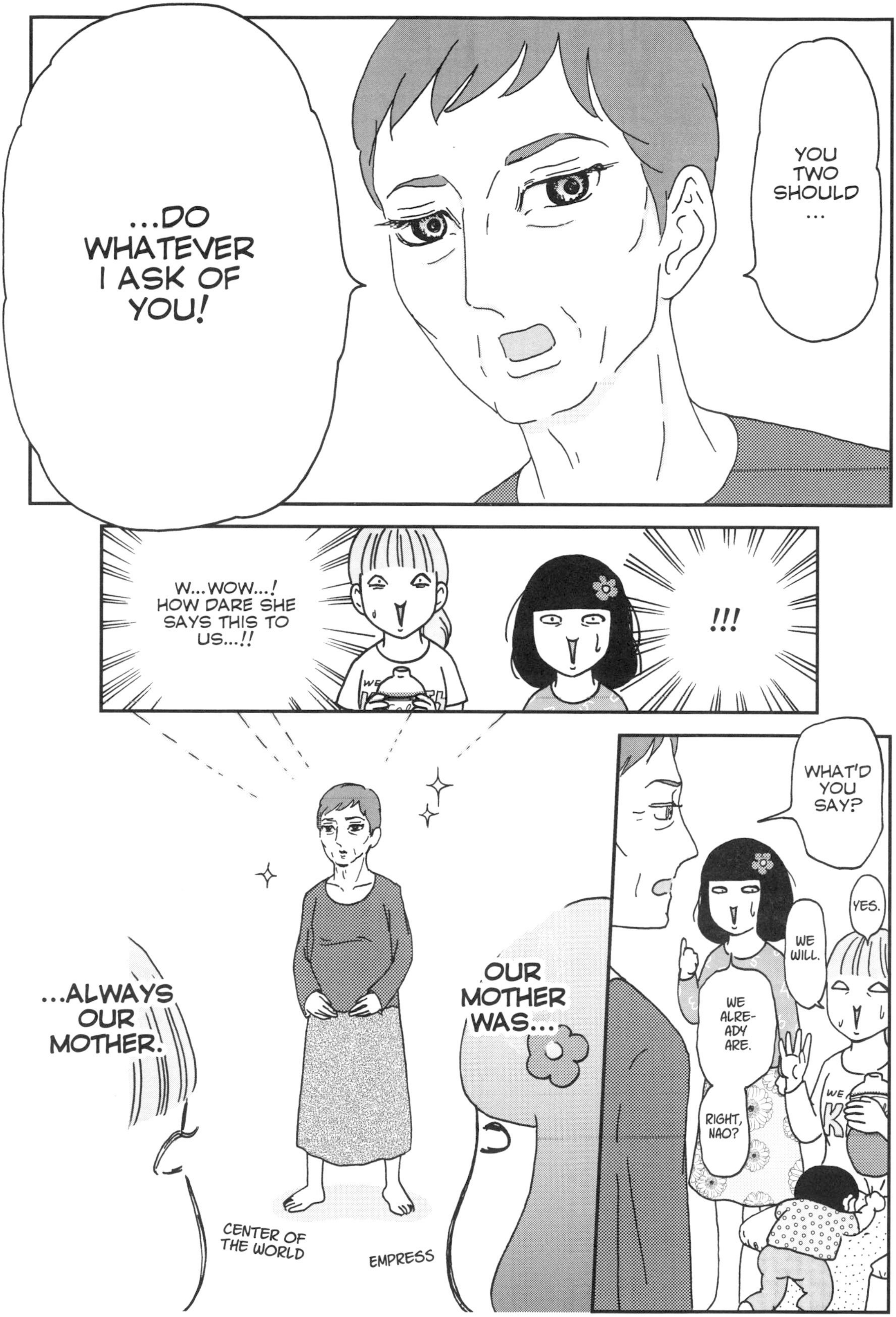
YOU TWO SHOULD ...
...DO WHATEVER I ASK OF YOU!
!!!
W...WOW...! HOW DARE SHE SAYS THIS TO US...!!
WHAT'D YOU SAY?
YES.
WE WILL.
WE ALRE-ADY ARE.
RIGHT, NAO?
OUR MOTHER WAS...
EMPRESS
CENTER OF THE WORLD
...ALWAYS OUR MOTHER.

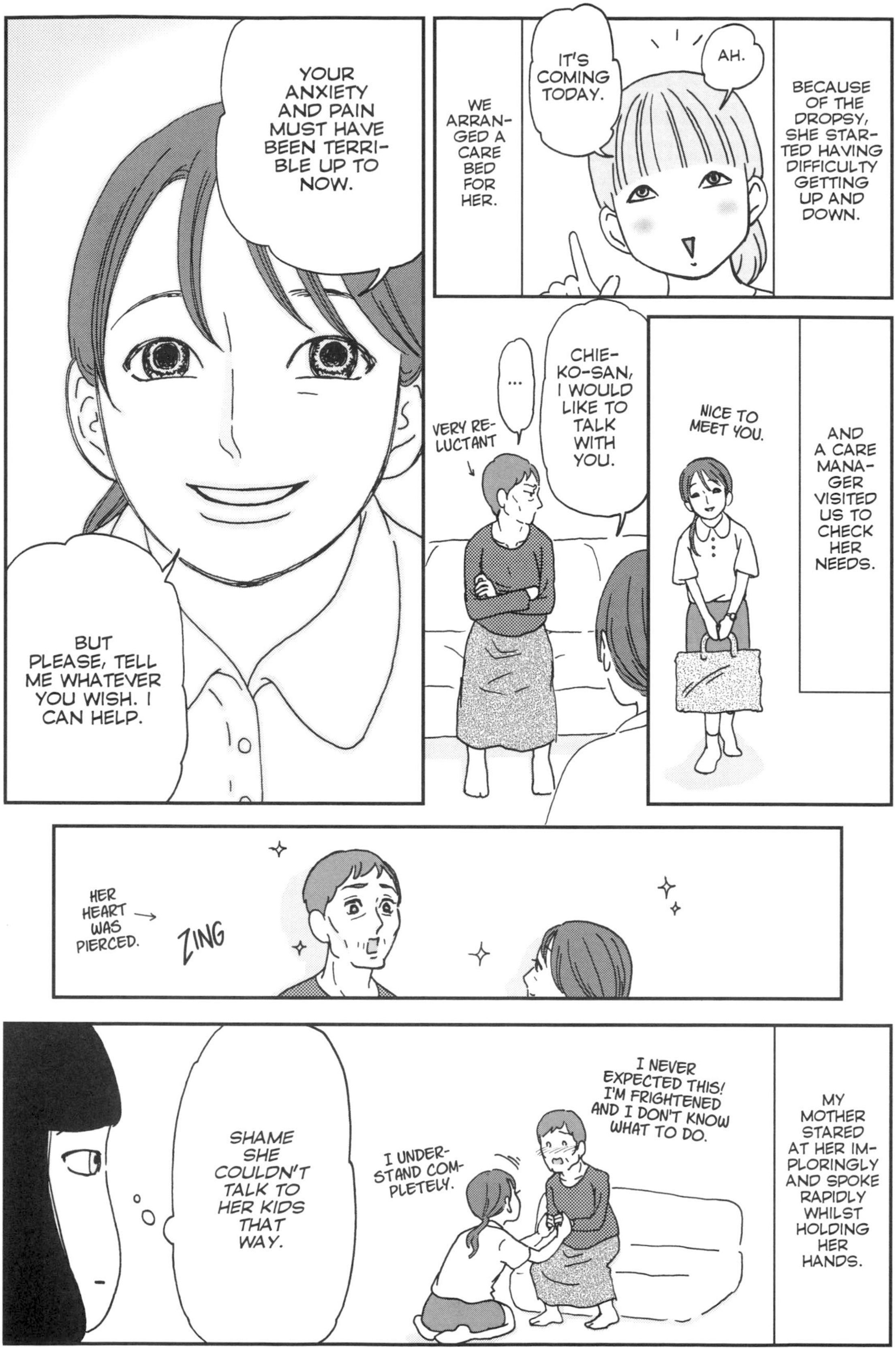

BECAUSE OF THE DROPSY, SHE STARTED HAVING DIFFICULTY GETTING UP AND DOWN.
AH.
IT'S COMING TODAY.
WE ARRANGED A CARE BED FOR HER.
AND A CARE MANAGER VISITED US TO CHECK HER NEEDS.
NICE TO MEET YOU.
CHIEKO-SAN, I WOULD LIKE TO TALK WITH YOU.
...
VERY RELUCTANT
YOUR ANXIETY AND PAIN MUST HAVE BEEN TERRIBLE UP TO NOW.
BUT PLEASE, TELL ME WHATEVER YOU WISH. I CAN HELP.
HER HEART WAS PIERCED.
ZING
MY MOTHER STARED AT HER IMPLORINGLY AND SPOKE RAPIDLY WHILST HOLDING HER HANDS.
I NEVER EXPECTED THIS! I'M FRIGHTENED AND I DON'T KNOW WHAT TO DO.
I UNDERSTAND COMPLETELY.
SHAME SHE COULDN'T TALK TO HER KIDS THAT WAY.

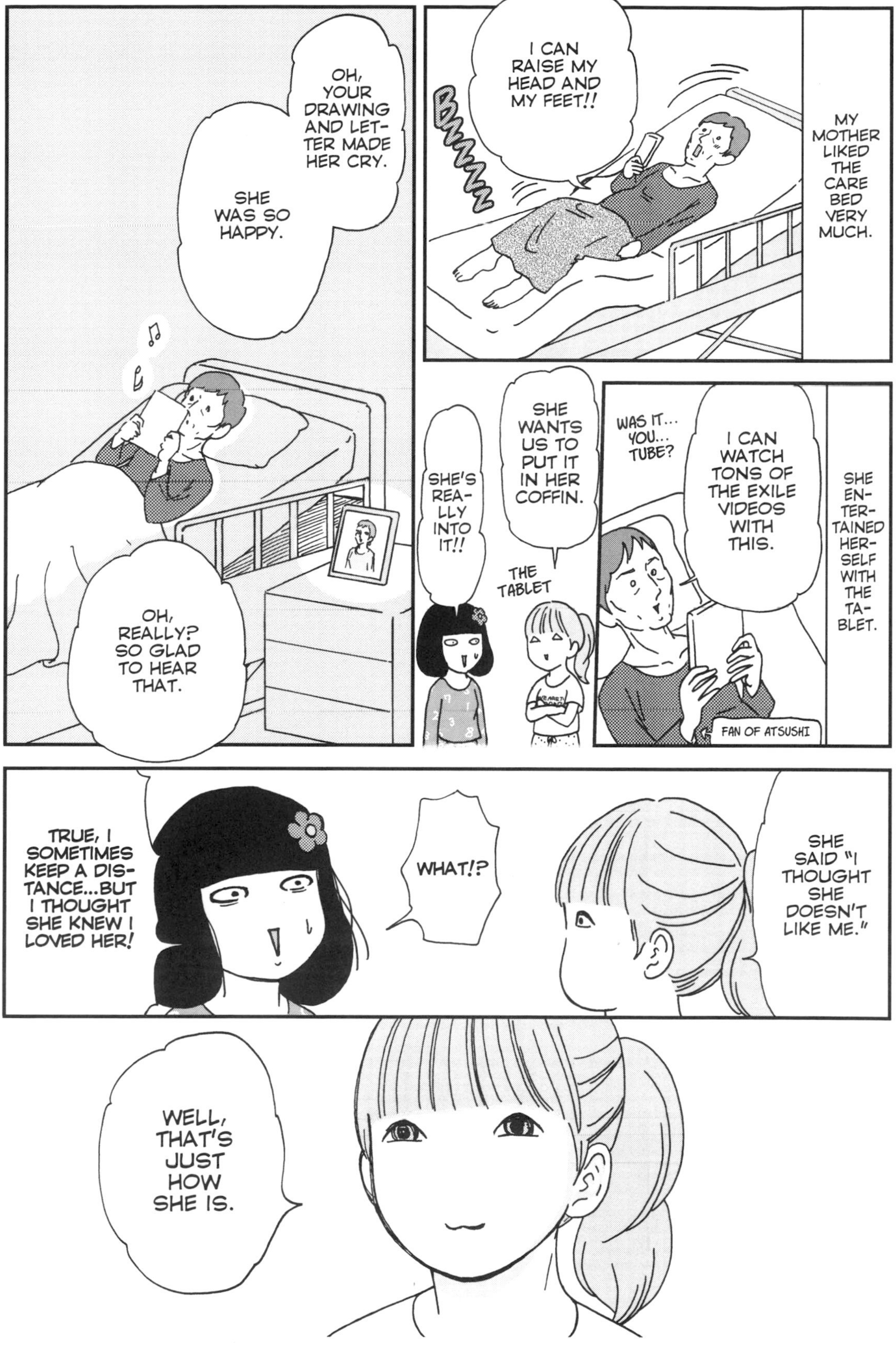

MY MOTHER LIKED THE CARE BED VERY MUCH.
I CAN RAISE MY HEAD AND MY FEET!!
BZZZZ
SHE ENTERTAINED HERSELF WITH THE TABLET.
I CAN WATCH TONS OF THE EXILE VIDEOS WITH THIS.
WAS IT... YOU... TUBE?
FAN OF ATSUSHI
SHE WANTS US TO PUT IT IN HER COFFIN.
THE TABLET
SHE'S REALLY INTO IT!!
OH, YOUR DRAWING AND LETTER MADE HER CRY.
SHE WAS SO HAPPY.
OH, REALLY? SO GLAD TO HEAR THAT.
SHE SAID "I THOUGHT SHE DOESN'T LIKE ME."
WHAT!?
TRUE, I SOMETIMES KEEP A DISTANCE...BUT I THOUGHT SHE KNEW I LOVED HER!
WELL, THAT'S JUST HOW SHE IS.

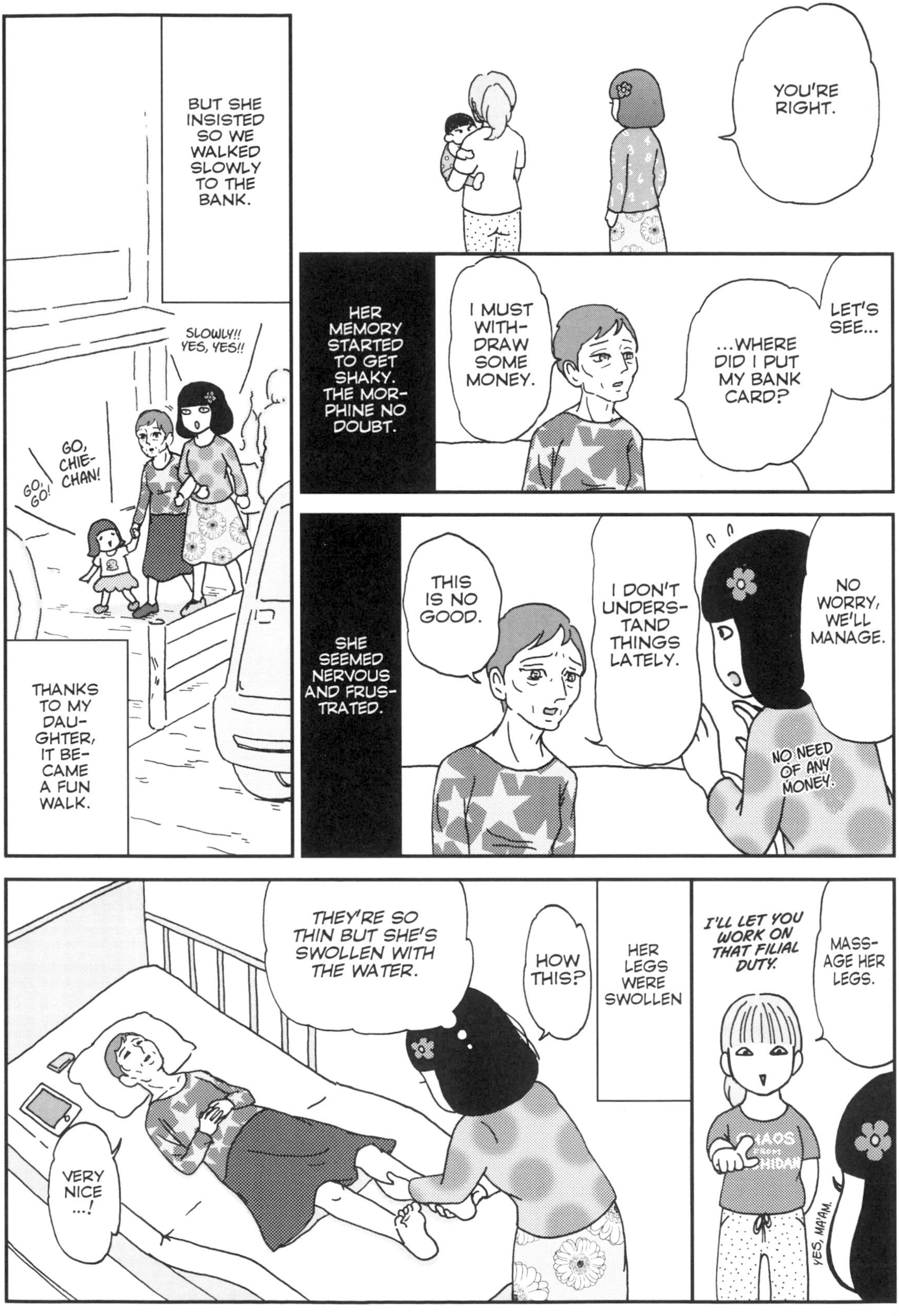

YOU'RE RIGHT.
LET'S SEE...
...WHERE DID I PUT MY BANK CARD?
I MUST WITH-DRAW SOME MONEY.
HER MEMORY STARTED TO GET SHAKY. THE MOR-PHINE NO DOUBT.
NO WORRY, WE'LL MANAGE.
NO NEED OF ANY MONEY.
I DON'T UNDERS-TAND THINGS LATELY.
THIS IS NO GOOD.
SHE SEEMED NERVOUS AND FRUS-TRATED.
BUT SHE INSISTED SO WE WALKED SLOWLY TO THE BANK.
SLOWLY!! YES, YES!!
GO, CHIE-CHAN!
GO, GO!
THANKS TO MY DAU-GHTER, IT BE-CAME A FUN WALK.
MASS-AGE HER LEGS.
I'LL LET YOU WORK ON THAT FILIAL DUTY.
YES, MA'AM.
HER LEGS WERE SWOLLEN
HOW THIS?
THEY'RE SO THIN BUT SHE'S SWOLLEN WITH THE WATER.
VERY NICE ...!

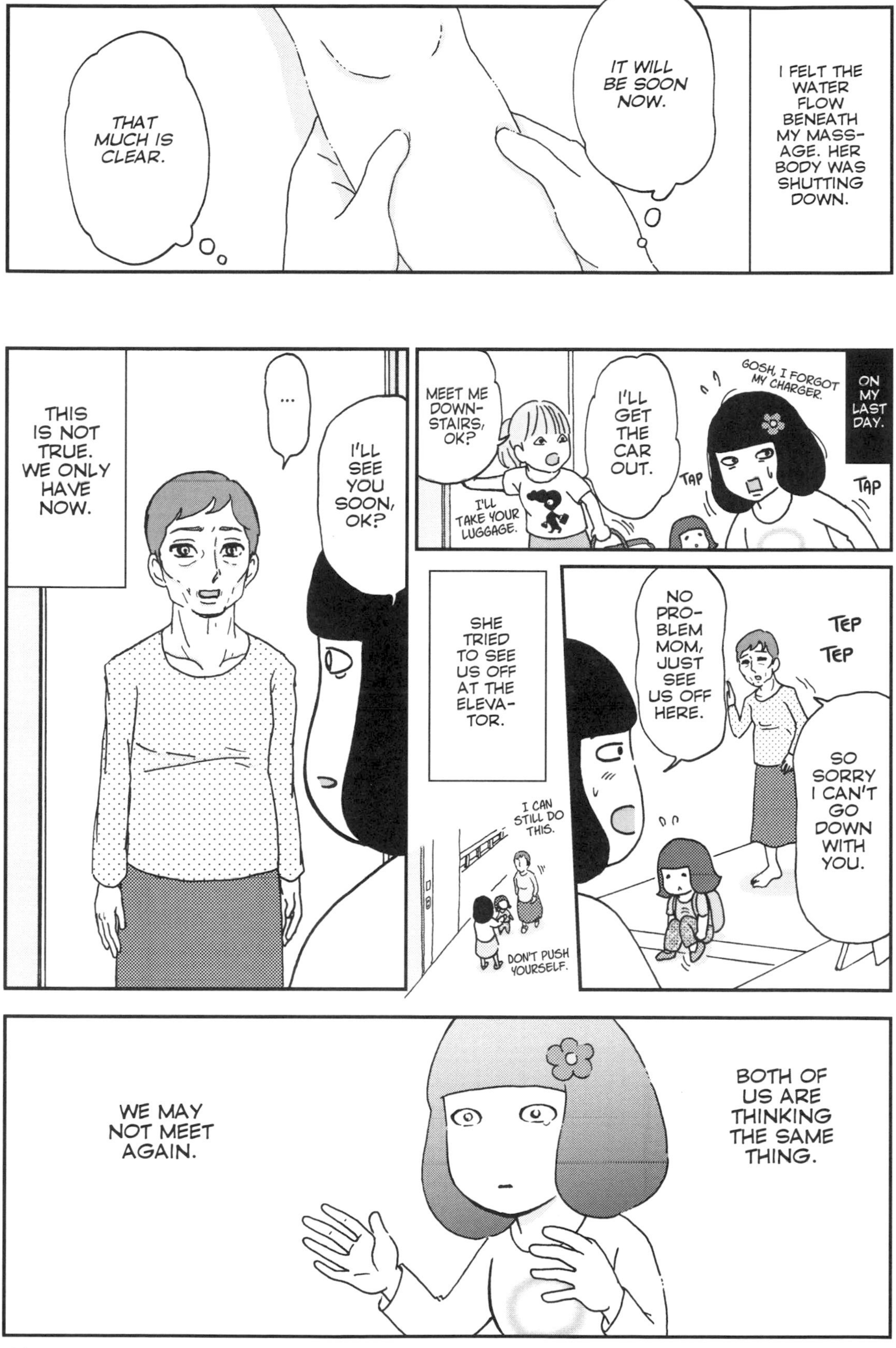
I FELT THE WATER FLOW BENEATH MY MASSAGE. HER BODY WAS SHUTTING DOWN.
IT WILL BE SOON NOW.
THAT MUCH IS CLEAR.
ON MY LAST DAY.
GOSH, I FORGOT MY CHARGER.
TAP
TAP
I'LL GET THE CAR OUT.
MEET ME DOWNSTAIRS, OK?
I'LL TAKE YOUR LUGGAGE.
TEP
TEP
NO PROBLEM MOM, JUST SEE US OFF HERE.
SO SORRY I CAN'T GO DOWN WITH YOU.
SHE TRIED TO SEE US OFF AT THE ELEVATOR.
I CAN STILL DO THIS.
DON'T PUSH YOURSELF.
I'LL SEE YOU SOON, OK?
...
THIS IS NOT TRUE. WE ONLY HAVE NOW.
BOTH OF US ARE THINKING THE SAME THING.
WE MAY NOT MEET AGAIN.

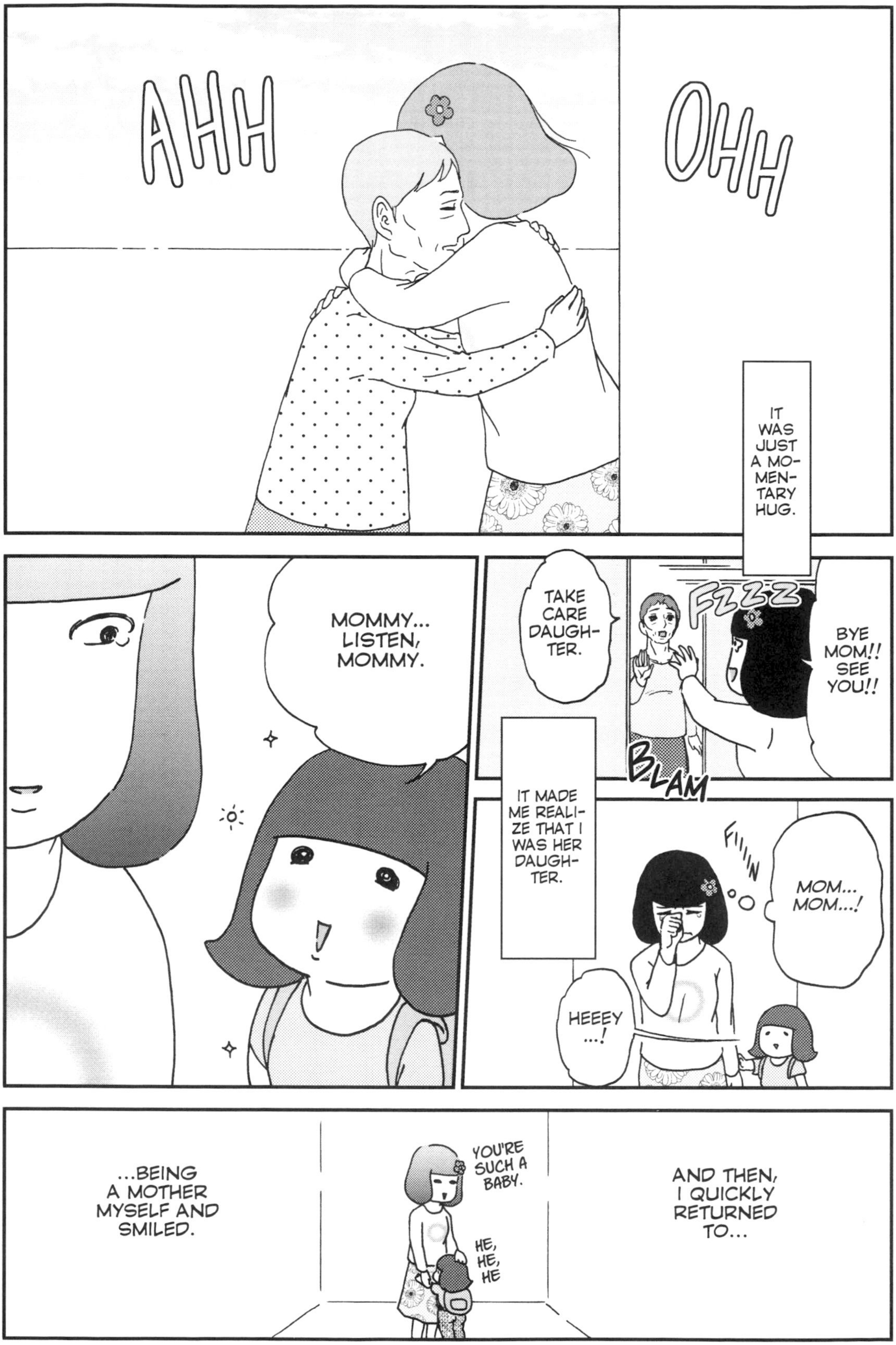
OHH
AHH
IT WAS JUST A MOMENTARY HUG.
FZZZ
BYE MOM!! SEE YOU!!
TAKE CARE DAUGHTER.
BLAM
MOM... MOM...!
FIIIN
IT MADE ME REALIZE THAT I WAS HER DAUGHTER.
HEEEY ...!
MOMMY... LISTEN, MOMMY.
AND THEN, I QUICKLY RETURNED TO...
YOU'RE SUCH A BABY.
HE, HE, HE
...BEING A MOTHER MYSELF AND SMILED.

CHAPTER 12

OUR DAYS ON A TIGHTROPE

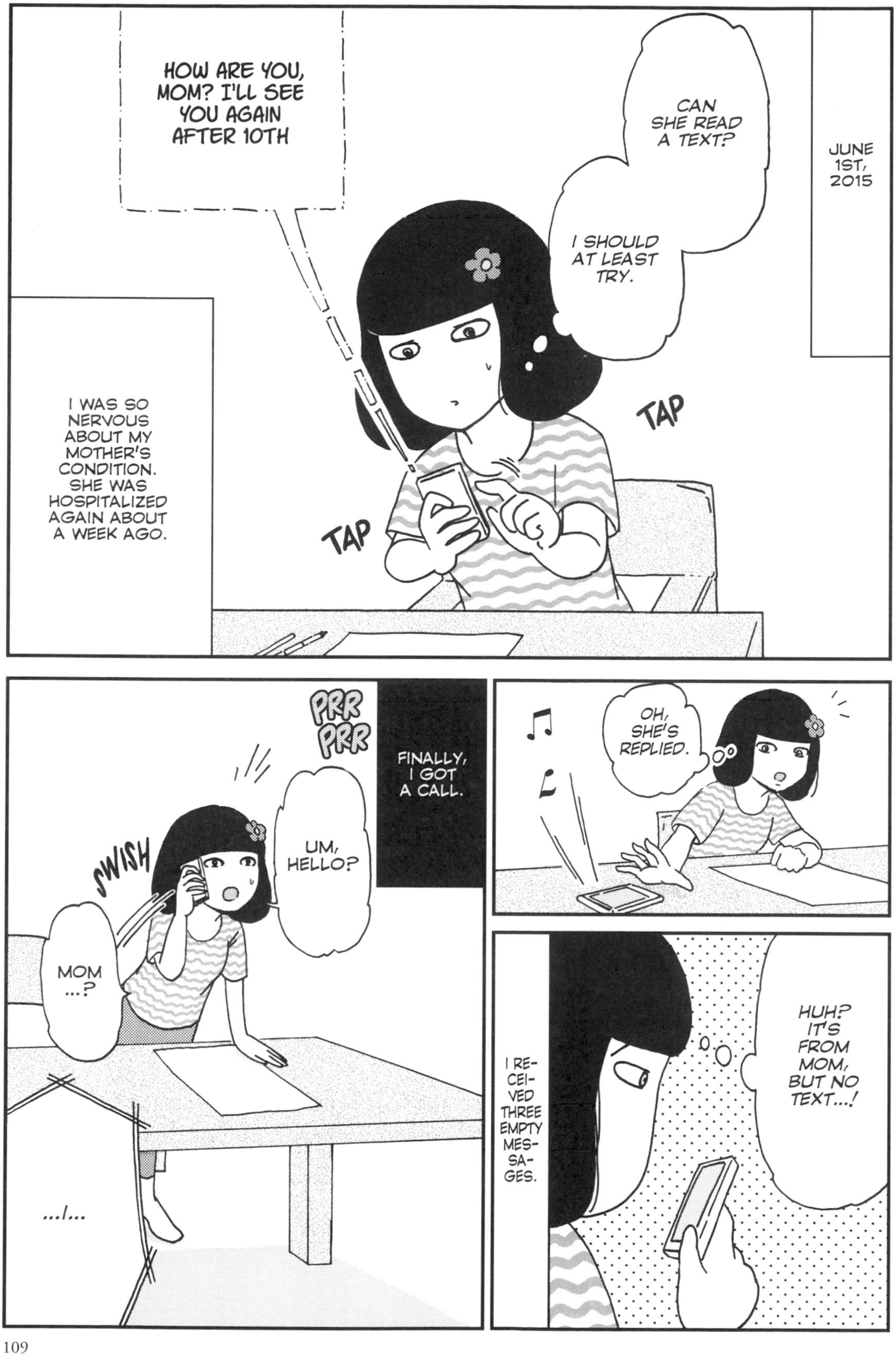
JUNE 1ST, 2015
CAN SHE READ A TEXT?
I SHOULD AT LEAST TRY.
HOW ARE YOU, MOM? I'LL SEE YOU AGAIN AFTER 10TH
TAP
I WAS SO NERVOUS ABOUT MY MOTHER'S CONDITION. SHE WAS HOSPITALIZED AGAIN ABOUT A WEEK AGO.
TAP
OH, SHE'S REPLIED.
HUH? IT'S FROM MOM, BUT NO TEXT...!
I RE-CEI-VED THREE EMPTY MES-SA-GES.
FINALLY, I GOT A CALL.
PRR PRR
UM, HELLO?
SWISH
MOM ...?
...I...

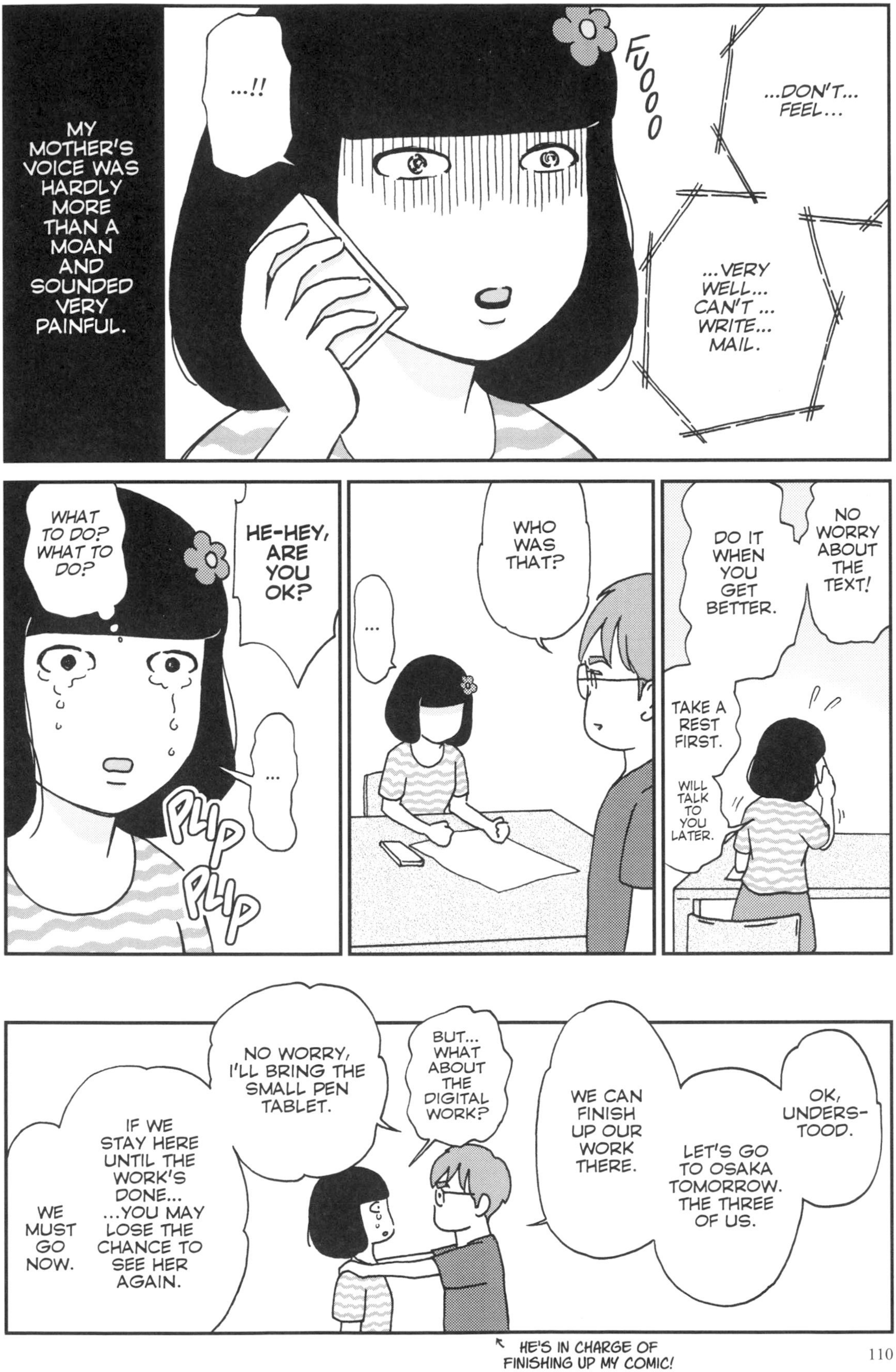
...DON'T... FEEL...
FUOOO
...!!
...VERY WELL... CAN'T ... WRITE... MAIL.
MY MOTHER'S VOICE WAS HARDLY MORE THAN A MOAN AND SOUNDED VERY PAINFUL.
NO WORRY ABOUT THE TEXT!
DO IT WHEN YOU GET BETTER.
TAKE A REST FIRST.
WILL TALK TO YOU LATER.
WHO WAS THAT?
...
HE-HEY, ARE YOU OK?
WHAT TO DO? WHAT TO DO?
...
PLIP PLIP
OK, UNDERS-TOOD.
LET'S GO TO OSAKA TOMORROW. THE THREE OF US.
WE CAN FINISH UP OUR WORK THERE.
BUT... WHAT ABOUT THE DIGITAL WORK?
NO WORRY, I'LL BRING THE SMALL PEN TABLET.
IF WE STAY HERE UNTIL THE WORK'S DONE... ...YOU MAY LOSE THE CHANCE TO SEE HER AGAIN.
WE MUST GO NOW.

↖ HE'S IN CHARGE OF FINISHING UP MY COMIC!

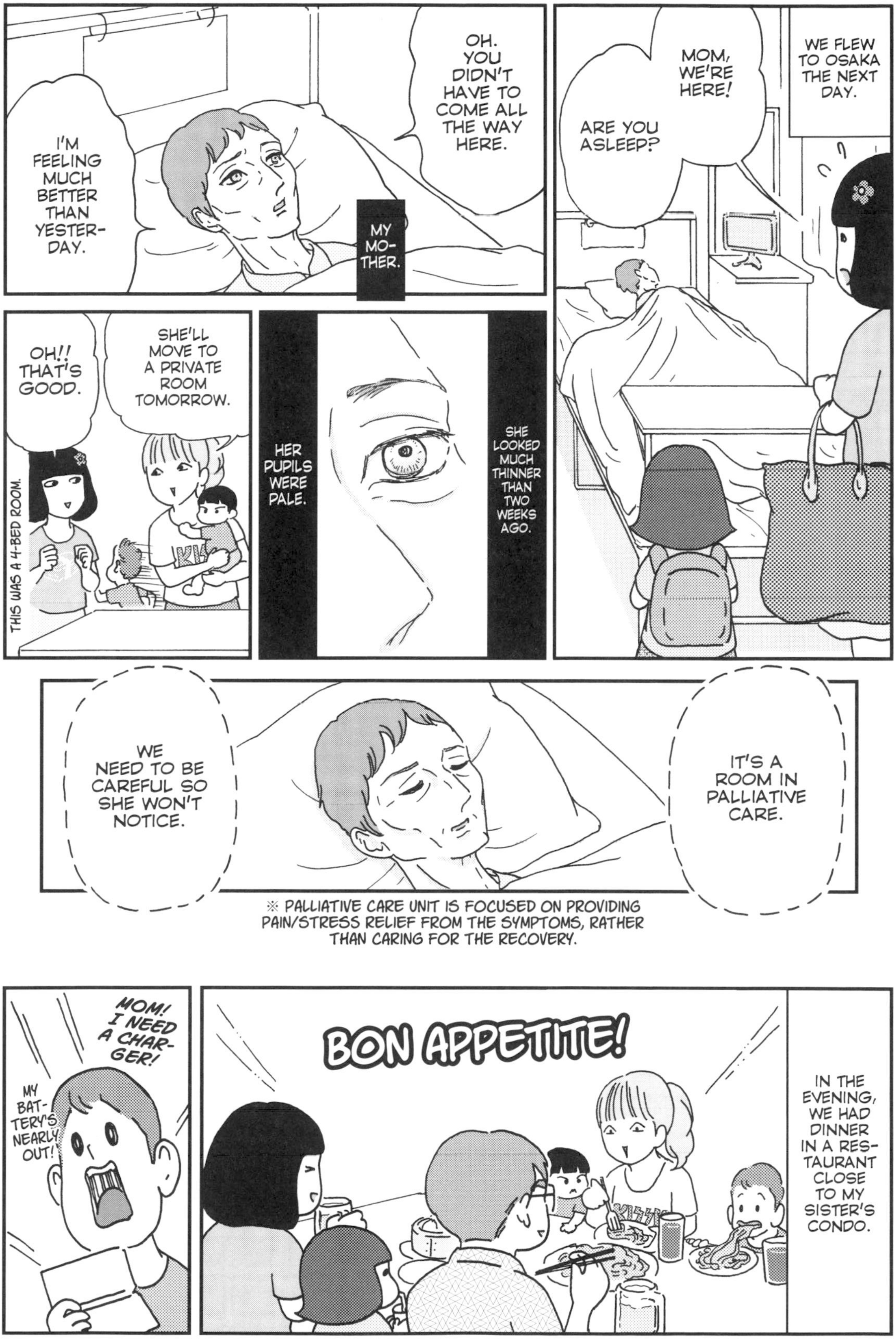
WE FLEW TO OSAKA THE NEXT DAY.
MOM, WE'RE HERE!
ARE YOU ASLEEP?
OH. YOU DIDN'T HAVE TO COME ALL THE WAY HERE.
MY MOTHER.
I'M FEELING MUCH BETTER THAN YESTERDAY.
SHE LOOKED MUCH THINNER THAN TWO WEEKS AGO.
HER PUPILS WERE PALE.
SHE'LL MOVE TO A PRIVATE ROOM TOMORROW.
OH!! THAT'S GOOD.
THIS WAS A 4-BED ROOM.
IT'S A ROOM IN PALLIATIVE CARE.
WE NEED TO BE CAREFUL SO SHE WON'T NOTICE.
※ PALLIATIVE CARE UNIT IS FOCUSED ON PROVIDING PAIN/STRESS RELIEF FROM THE SYMPTOMS, RATHER THAN CARING FOR THE RECOVERY.
IN THE EVENING, WE HAD DINNER IN A RESTAURANT CLOSE TO MY SISTER'S CONDO.
BON APPETITE!
MOM! I NEED A CHARGER!
MY BATTERY'S NEARLY OUT!

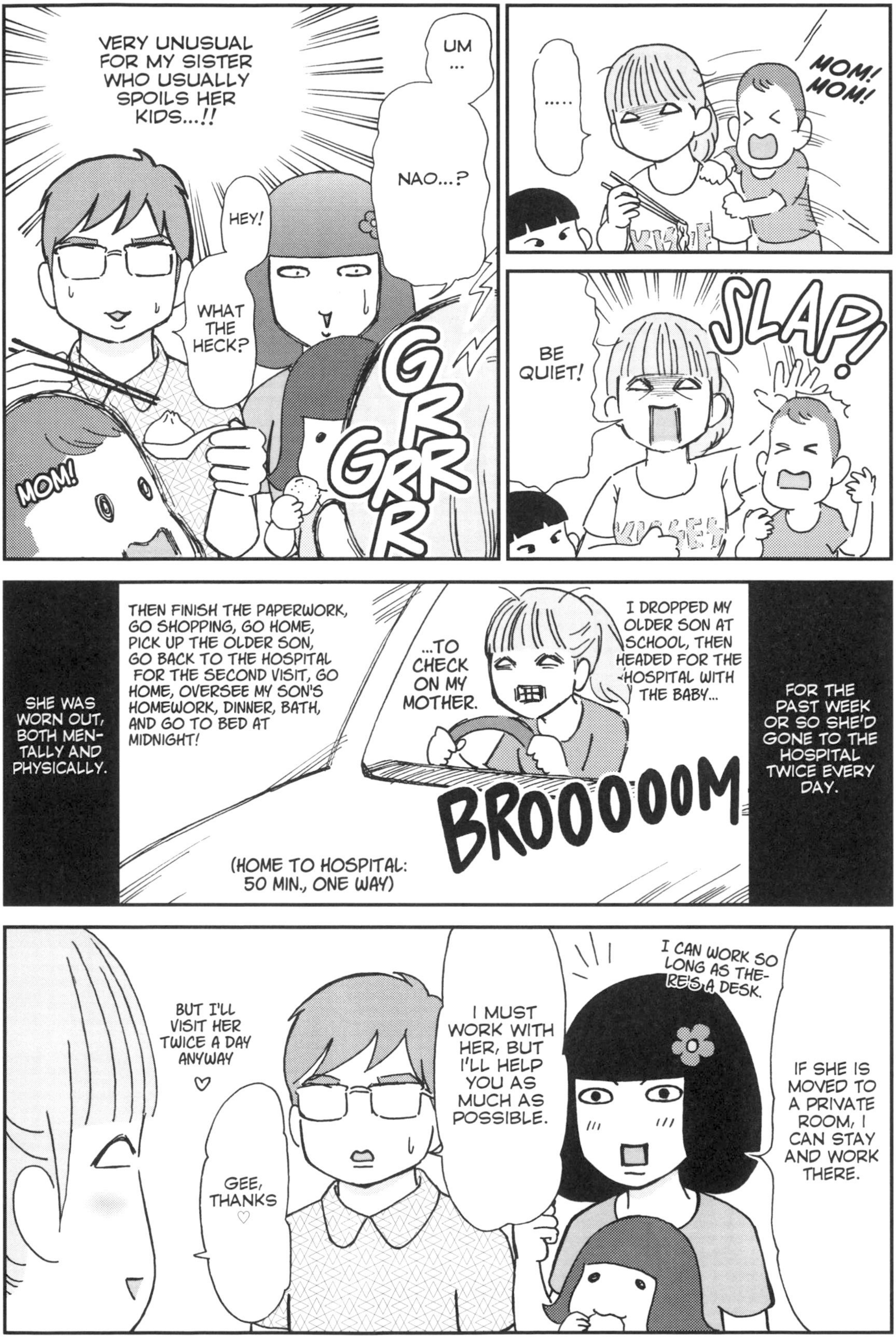
MOM! MOM!
.....
SLAP!
BE QUIET!
UM ...
NAO...?
VERY UNUSUAL FOR MY SISTER WHO USUALLY SPOILS HER KIDS...!!
HEY!
WHAT THE HECK?
GRGRRR
MOM!
FOR THE PAST WEEK OR SO SHE'D GONE TO THE HOSPITAL TWICE EVERY DAY.
I DROPPED MY OLDER SON AT SCHOOL, THEN HEADED FOR THE HOSPITAL WITH THE BABY...
...TO CHECK ON MY MOTHER.
THEN FINISH THE PAPERWORK, GO SHOPPING, GO HOME, PICK UP THE OLDER SON, GO BACK TO THE HOSPITAL FOR THE SECOND VISIT, GO HOME, OVERSEE MY SON'S HOMEWORK, DINNER, BATH, AND GO TO BED AT MIDNIGHT!
BROOOOOM
(HOME TO HOSPITAL: 50 MIN., ONE WAY)
SHE WAS WORN OUT, BOTH MEN-TALLY AND PHYSICALLY.
IF SHE IS MOVED TO A PRIVATE ROOM, I CAN STAY AND WORK THERE.
I CAN WORK SO LONG AS THE-RE'S A DESK.
I MUST WORK WITH HER, BUT I'LL HELP YOU AS MUCH AS POSSIBLE.
BUT I'LL VISIT HER TWICE A DAY ANYWAY ♡
GEE, THANKS ♡

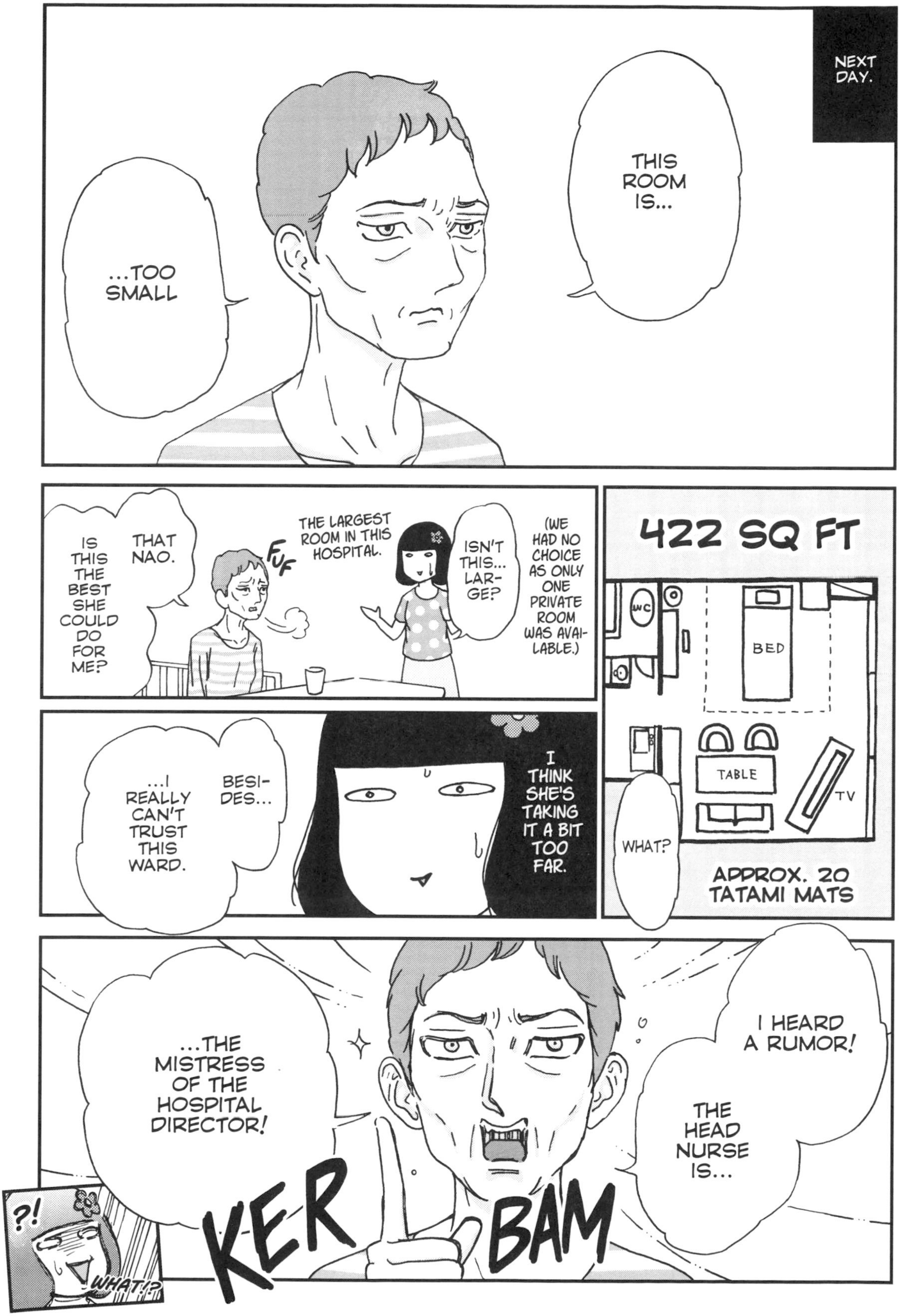
NEXT DAY.
THIS ROOM IS...
...TOO SMALL
422 SQ FT
WC
BED
TABLE
TV
WHAT?
APPROX. 20 TATAMI MATS
(WE HAD NO CHOICE AS ONLY ONE PRIVATE ROOM WAS AVAILABLE.)
ISN'T THIS... LARGE?
THE LARGEST ROOM IN THIS HOSPITAL.
FUF
THAT NAO.
IS THIS THE BEST SHE COULD DO FOR ME?
I THINK SHE'S TAKING IT A BIT TOO FAR.
BESIDES...
...I REALLY CAN'T TRUST THIS WARD.
I HEARD A RUMOR!
THE HEAD NURSE IS...
...THE MISTRESS OF THE HOSPITAL DIRECTOR!
KER BAM
?!
WHAT!?

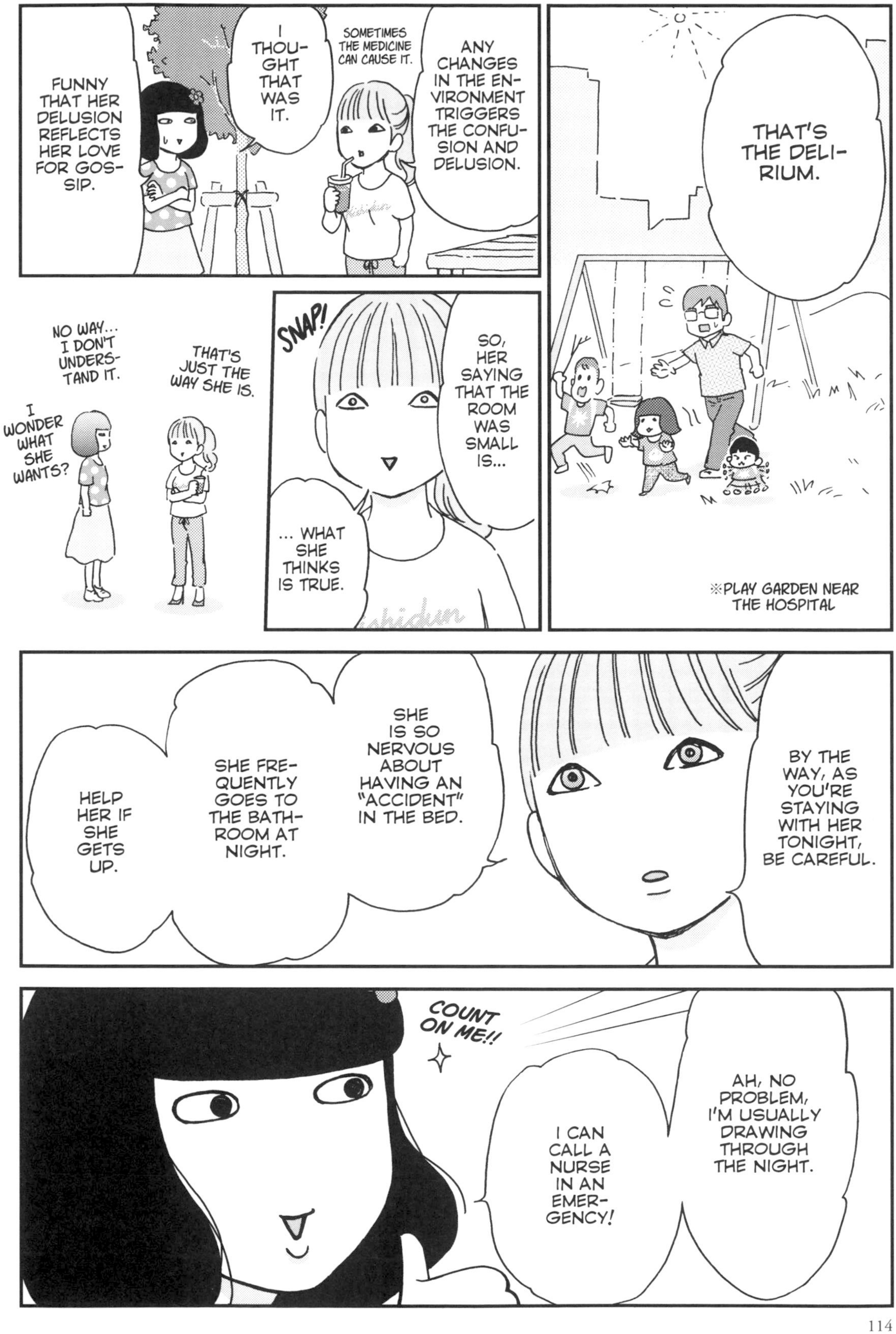
THAT'S THE DELIRIUM.
※PLAY GARDEN NEAR THE HOSPITAL
ANY CHANGES IN THE ENVIRONMENT TRIGGERS THE CONFUSION AND DELUSION.
SOMETIMES THE MEDICINE CAN CAUSE IT.
I THOUGHT THAT WAS IT.
FUNNY THAT HER DELUSION REFLECTS HER LOVE FOR GOSSIP.
SO, HER SAYING THAT THE ROOM WAS SMALL IS...
SNAP!
... WHAT SHE THINKS IS TRUE.
THAT'S JUST THE WAY SHE IS.
NO WAY... I DON'T UNDERSTAND IT.
I WONDER WHAT SHE WANTS?
BY THE WAY, AS YOU'RE STAYING WITH HER TONIGHT, BE CAREFUL.
SHE IS SO NERVOUS ABOUT HAVING AN "ACCIDENT" IN THE BED.
SHE FREQUENTLY GOES TO THE BATHROOM AT NIGHT.
HELP HER IF SHE GETS UP.
AH, NO PROBLEM, I'M USUALLY DRAWING THROUGH THE NIGHT.
I CAN CALL A NURSE IN AN EMERGENCY!
COUNT ON ME!!

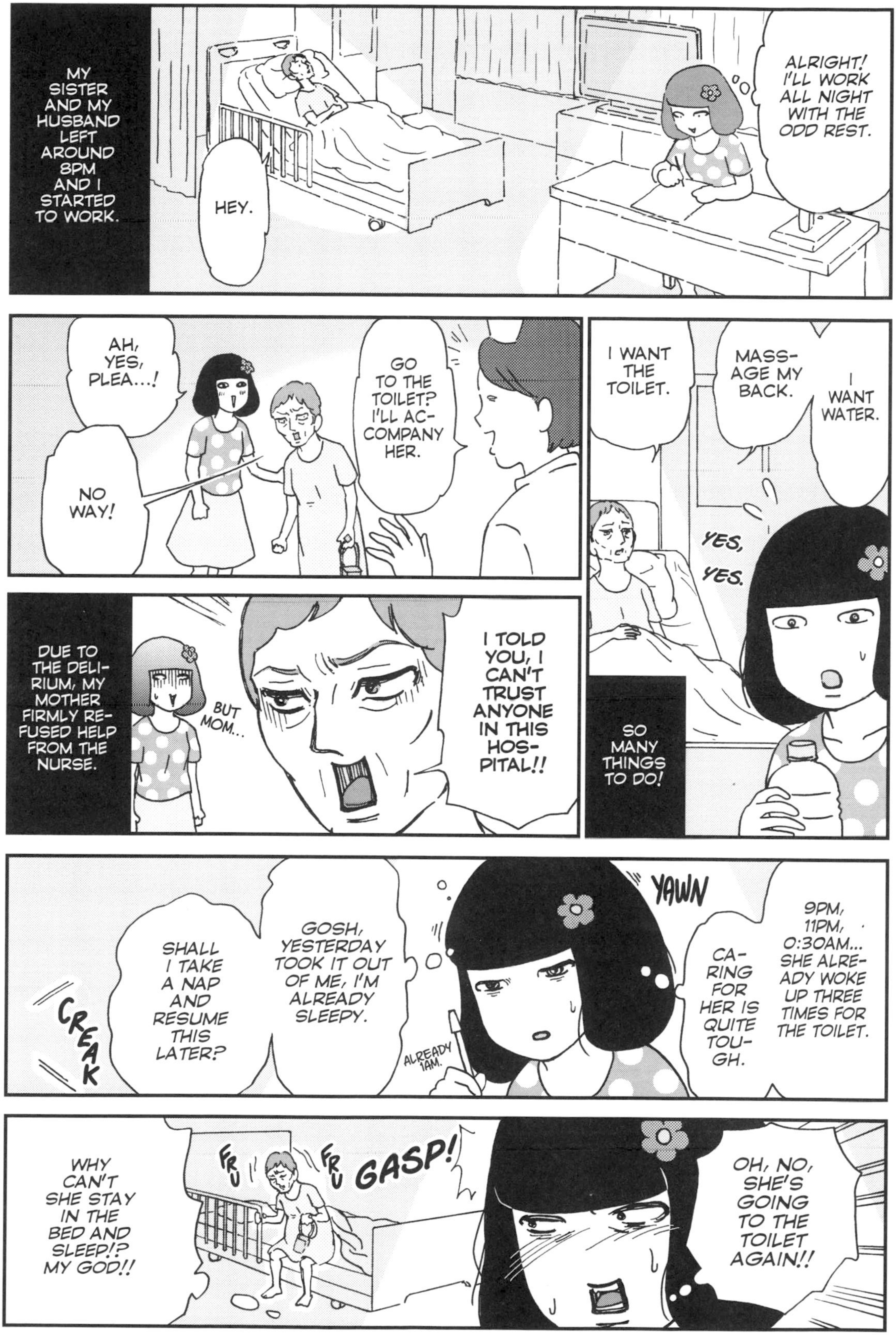
ALRIGHT! I'LL WORK ALL NIGHT WITH THE ODD REST.
HEY.
MY SISTER AND MY HUSBAND LEFT AROUND 8PM AND I STARTED TO WORK.
I WANT WATER.
MASS-AGE MY BACK.
I WANT THE TOILET.
YES, YES.
SO MANY THINGS TO DO!
GO TO THE TOILET? I'LL AC-COMPANY HER.
AH, YES, PLEA...!
NO WAY!
I TOLD YOU, I CAN'T TRUST ANYONE IN THIS HOS-PITAL!!
BUT MOM...
DUE TO THE DELI-RIUM, MY MOTHER FIRMLY RE-FUSED HELP FROM THE NURSE.
9PM, 11PM, 0:30AM... SHE ALRE-ADY WOKE UP THREE TIMES FOR THE TOILET.
CA-RING FOR HER IS QUITE TOU-GH.
YAWN
GOSH, YESTERDAY TOOK IT OUT OF ME, I'M ALREADY SLEEPY.
ALREADY 1AM.
SHALL I TAKE A NAP AND RESUME THIS LATER?
CREAK
OH, NO, SHE'S GOING TO THE TOILET AGAIN!!
GASP!
FRU FRU
WHY CAN'T SHE STAY IN THE BED AND SLEEP!? MY GOD!!

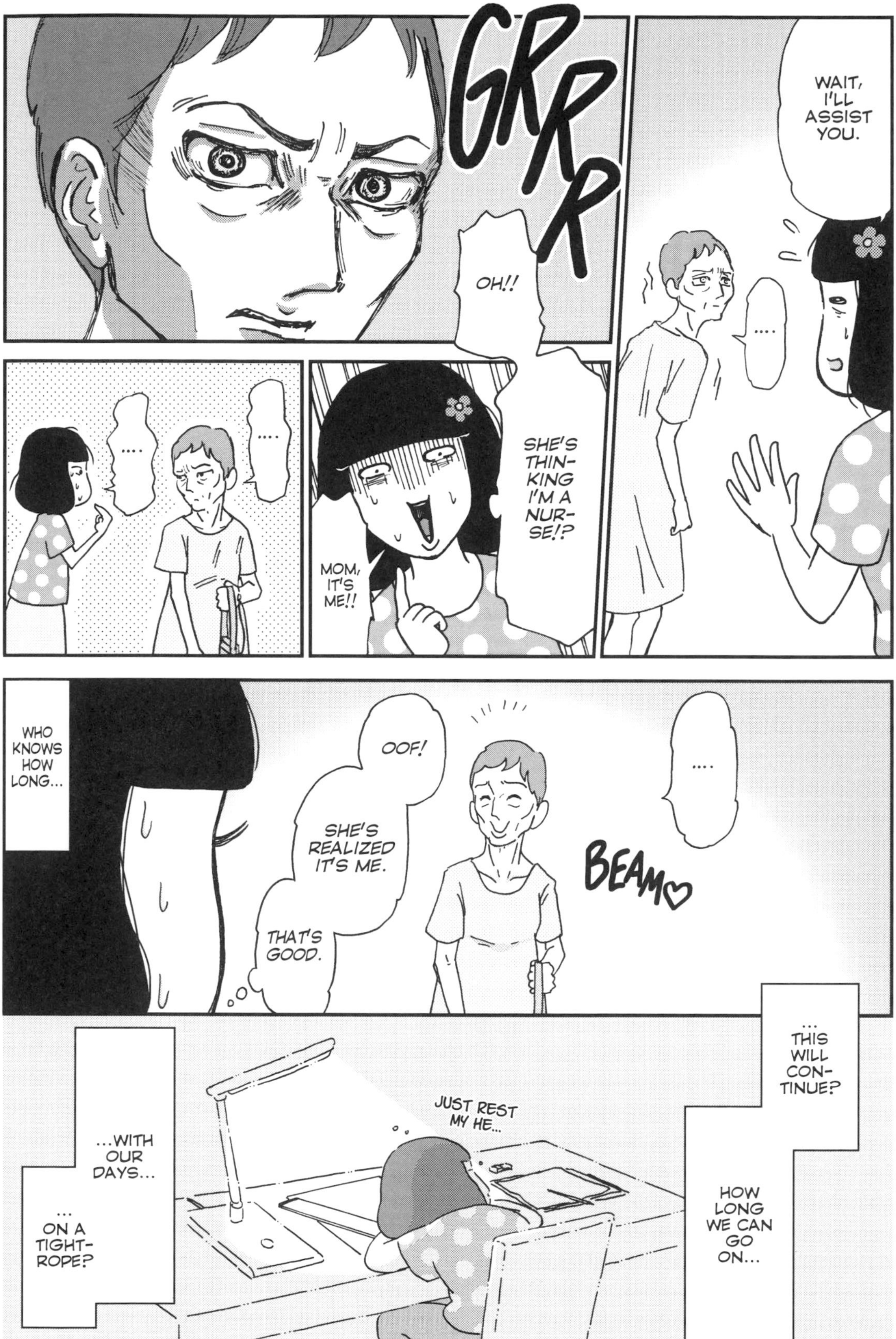

WAIT, I'LL ASSIST YOU.
....
GRRR
OH!!
SHE'S THINKING I'M A NURSE!?
MOM, IT'S ME!!
....
....
....
BEAM♡
OOF!
SHE'S REALIZED IT'S ME.
THAT'S GOOD.
WHO KNOWS HOW LONG...
...THIS WILL CONTINUE?
HOW LONG WE CAN GO ON...
JUST REST MY HE...
...WITH OUR DAYS...
...ON A TIGHT-ROPE?

CHAPTER 13

SMALL THINGS CAN SAVE YOU

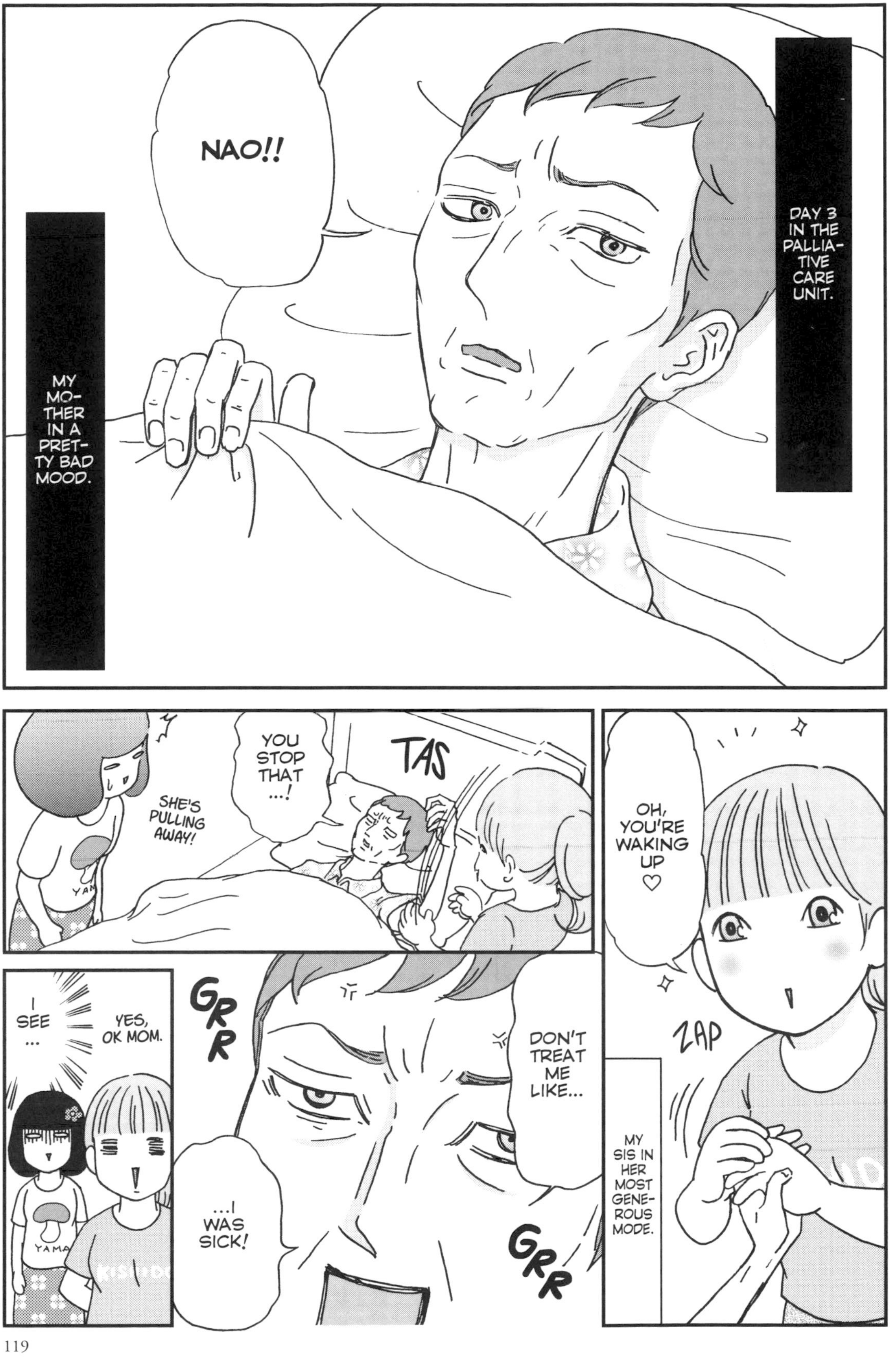
DAY 3 IN THE PALLIATIVE CARE UNIT.
NAO!!
MY MOTHER IN A PRETTY BAD MOOD.
OH, YOU'RE WAKING UP ♡
ZAP
MY SIS IN HER MOST GENEROUS MODE.
TAS
YOU STOP THAT ...!
SHE'S PULLING AWAY!
YAMA
GRR
DON'T TREAT ME LIKE...
...I WAS SICK!
GRR
YES, OK MOM.
I SEE ...
YAMA

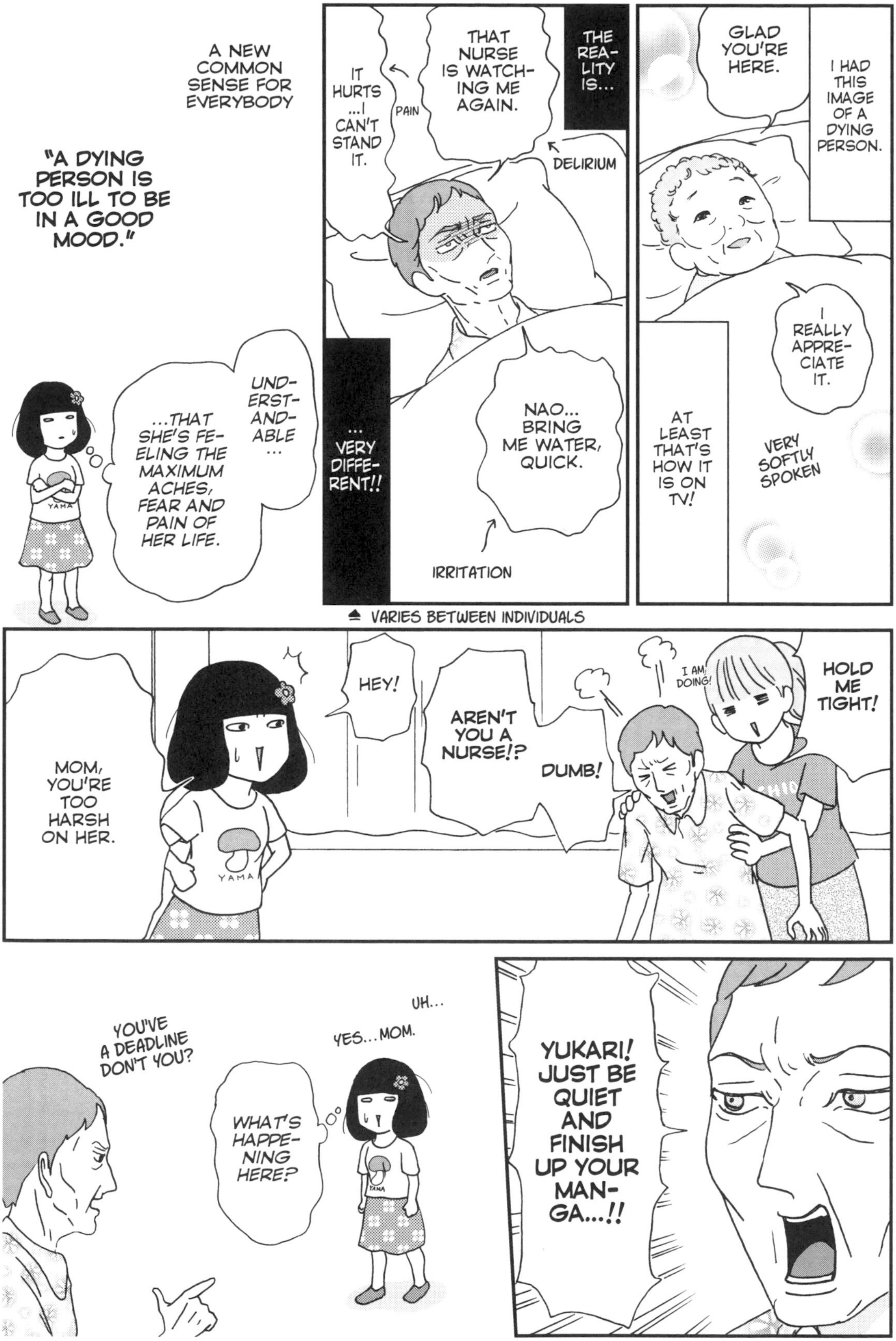
I HAD THIS IMAGE OF A DYING PERSON.
GLAD YOU'RE HERE.
I REALLY APPRECIATE IT.
VERY SOFTLY SPOKEN
AT LEAST THAT'S HOW IT IS ON TV!
THE REALITY IS...
THAT NURSE IS WATCHING ME AGAIN.
DELIRIUM
IT HURTS ...I CAN'T STAND IT.
PAIN
NAO... BRING ME WATER, QUICK.
IRRITATION
... VERY DIFFERENT!!
VARIES BETWEEN INDIVIDUALS
A NEW COMMON SENSE FOR EVERYBODY
"A DYING PERSON IS TOO ILL TO BE IN A GOOD MOOD."
UNDERSTANDABLE ...
...THAT SHE'S FEELING THE MAXIMUM ACHES, FEAR AND PAIN OF HER LIFE.
HOLD ME TIGHT!
I AM DOING!
DUMB!
AREN'T YOU A NURSE!?
HEY!
MOM, YOU'RE TOO HARSH ON HER.
YUKARI! JUST BE QUIET AND FINISH UP YOUR MANGA...!!
UH...
YES... MOM.
YOU'VE A DEADLINE DON'T YOU?
WHAT'S HAPPENING HERE?

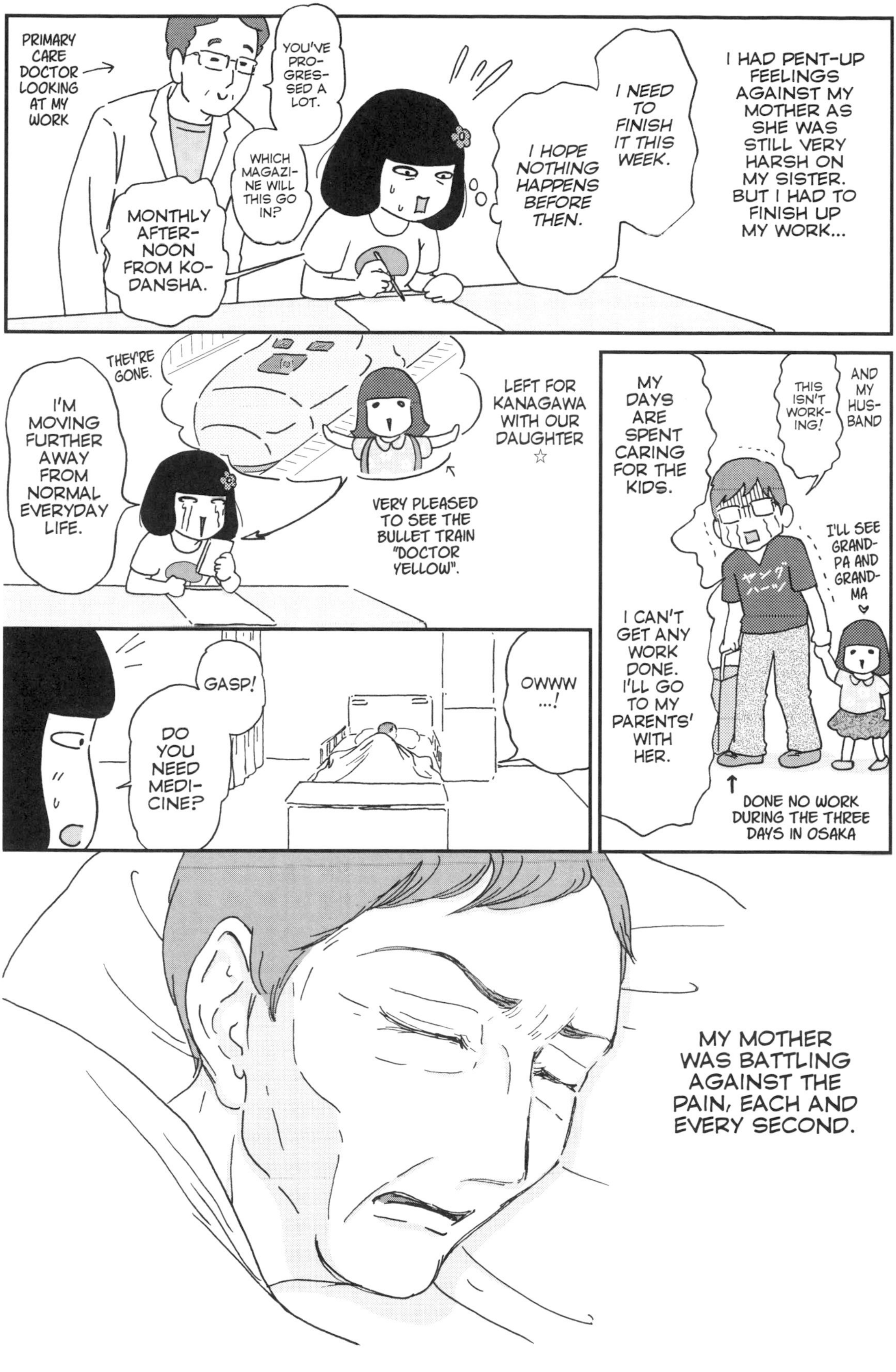
I HAD PENT-UP FEELINGS AGAINST MY MOTHER AS SHE WAS STILL VERY HARSH ON MY SISTER. BUT I HAD TO FINISH UP MY WORK...
I NEED TO FINISH IT THIS WEEK.
I HOPE NOTHING HAPPENS BEFORE THEN.
YOU'VE PROGRESSED A LOT.
PRIMARY CARE DOCTOR LOOKING AT MY WORK
WHICH MAGAZINE WILL THIS GO IN?
MONTHLY AFTERNOON FROM KODANSHA.
AND MY HUSBAND
THIS ISN'T WORKING!
MY DAYS ARE SPENT CARING FOR THE KIDS.
I'LL SEE GRANDPA AND GRANDMA
ヤング ハーツ
I CAN'T GET ANY WORK DONE. I'LL GO TO MY PARENTS' WITH HER.
DONE NO WORK DURING THE THREE DAYS IN OSAKA
LEFT FOR KANAGAWA WITH OUR DAUGHTER ☆
THEY'RE GONE.
VERY PLEASED TO SEE THE BULLET TRAIN "DOCTOR YELLOW".
I'M MOVING FURTHER AWAY FROM NORMAL EVERYDAY LIFE.
OWWW ...!
GASP!
DO YOU NEED MEDICINE?
MY MOTHER WAS BATTLING AGAINST THE PAIN, EACH AND EVERY SECOND.

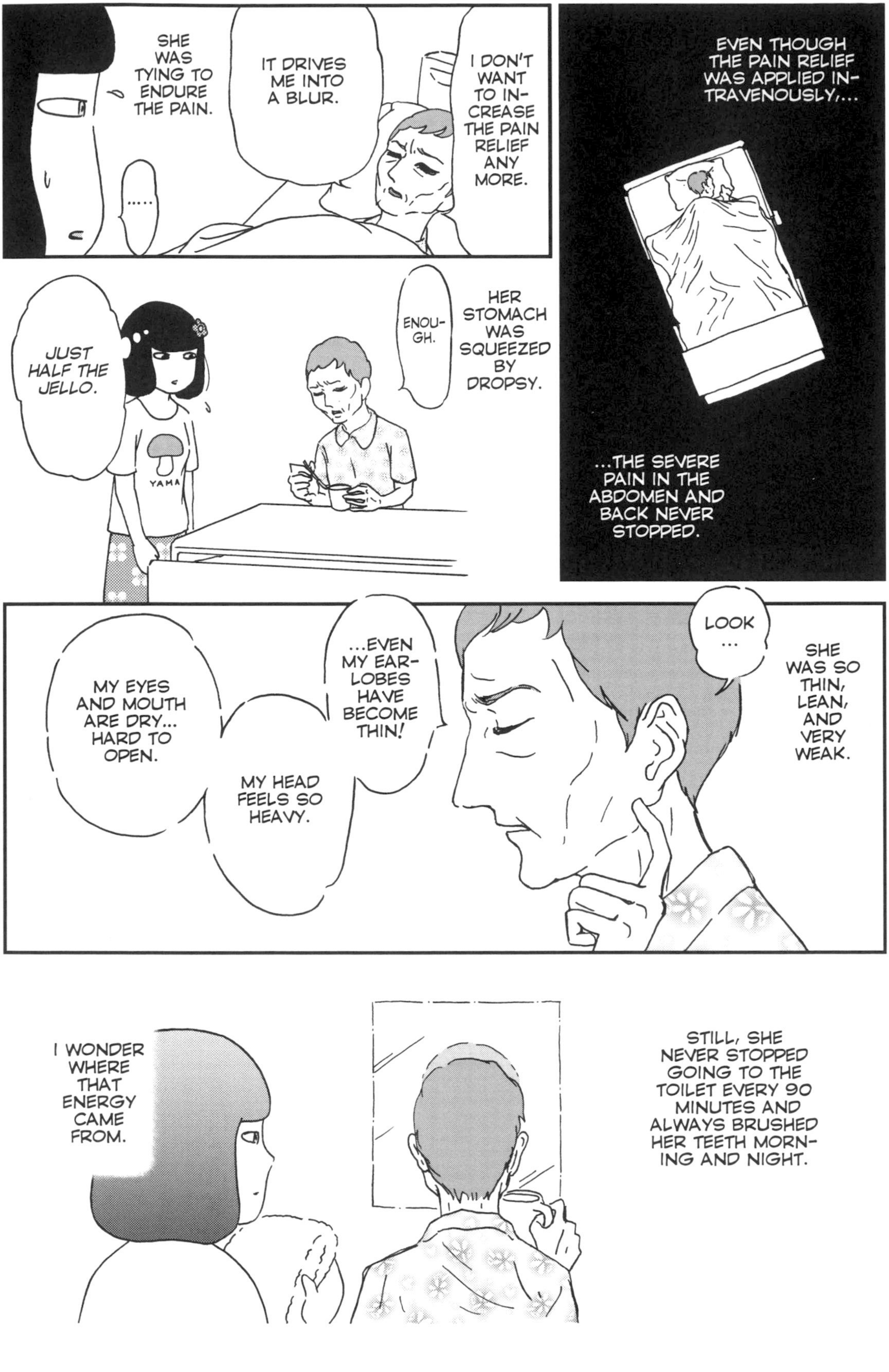
EVEN THOUGH THE PAIN RELIEF WAS APPLIED IN-TRAVENOUSLY,...
...THE SEVERE PAIN IN THE ABDOMEN AND BACK NEVER STOPPED.
I DON'T WANT TO IN-CREASE THE PAIN RELIEF ANY MORE.
IT DRIVES ME INTO A BLUR.
SHE WAS TYING TO ENDURE THE PAIN.
......
HER STOMACH WAS SQUEEZED BY DROPSY.
ENOU-GH.
JUST HALF THE JELLO.
YAMA
SHE WAS SO THIN, LEAN, AND VERY WEAK.
LOOK ...
...EVEN MY EAR-LOBES HAVE BECOME THIN!
MY EYES AND MOUTH ARE DRY... HARD TO OPEN.
MY HEAD FEELS SO HEAVY.
STILL, SHE NEVER STOPPED GOING TO THE TOILET EVERY 90 MINUTES AND ALWAYS BRUSHED HER TEETH MORN-ING AND NIGHT.
I WONDER WHERE THAT ENERGY CAME FROM.

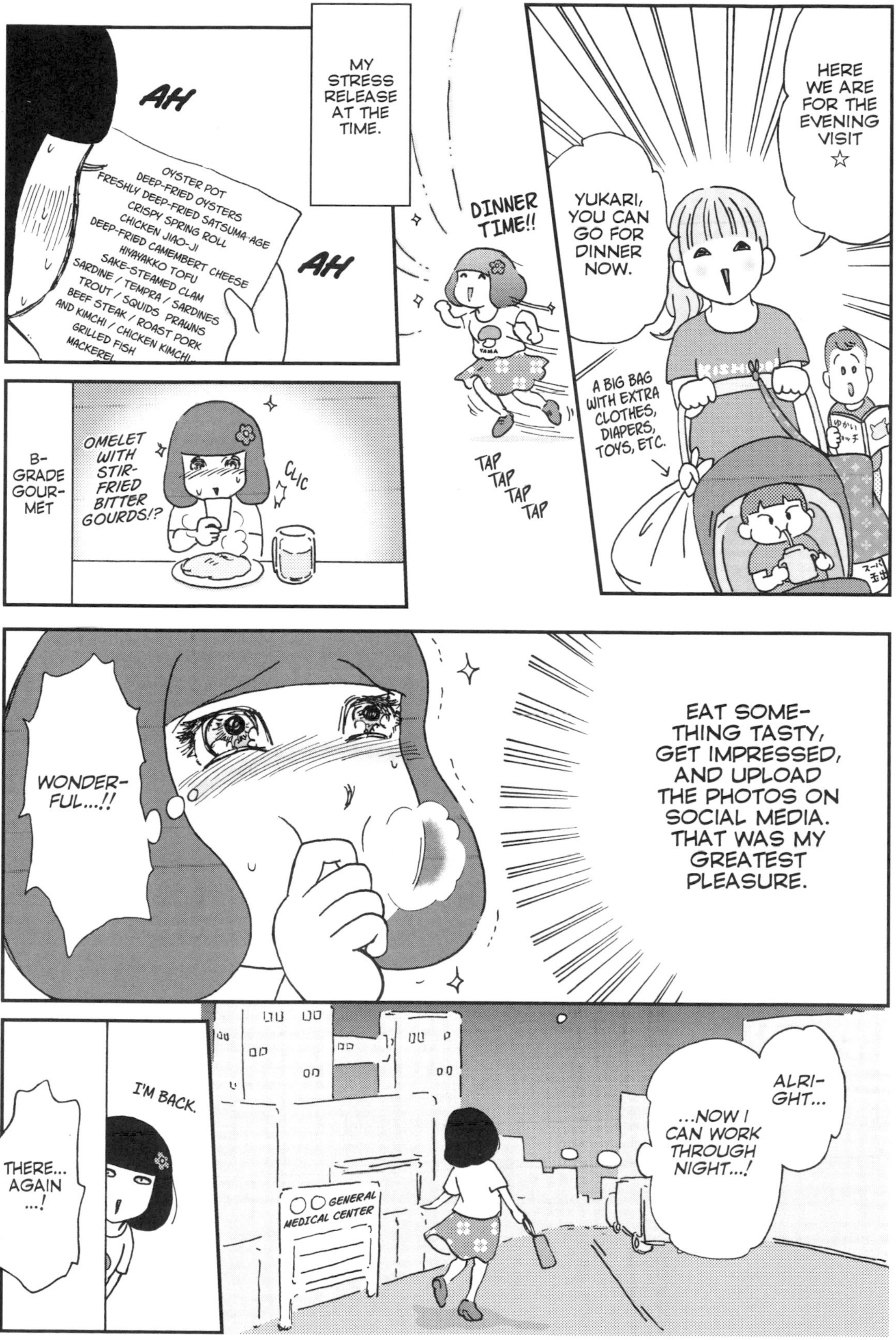
HERE WE ARE FOR THE EVENING VISIT ☆
YUKARI, YOU CAN GO FOR DINNER NOW.
A BIG BAG WITH EXTRA CLOTHES, DIAPERS, TOYS, ETC.
DINNER TIME!!
TAP TAP TAP TAP
MY STRESS RELEASE AT THE TIME.
AH
OYSTER POT
DEEP-FRIED OYSTERS
FRESHLY DEEP-FRIED SATSUMA-AGE
CRISPY SPRING ROLL
CHICKEN JIAO-JI
DEEP-FRIED CAMEMBERT CHEESE
HIYAYAKKO TOFU
SAKE-STEAMED CLAM
SARDINE / TEMPRA / SARDINES
TROUT / SQUIDS PRAWNS
BEEF STEAK / ROAST PORK
AND KIMCHI / CHICKEN KIMCHI
GRILLED FISH
MACKEREL
AH
B-GRADE GOURMET
OMELET WITH STIR-FRIED BITTER GOURDS!?
CLIC
EAT SOMETHING TASTY, GET IMPRESSED, AND UPLOAD THE PHOTOS ON SOCIAL MEDIA. THAT WAS MY GREATEST PLEASURE.
WONDERFUL...!!
ALRIGHT...
...NOW I CAN WORK THROUGH NIGHT...!
○○ GENERAL MEDICAL CENTER
I'M BACK.
THERE... AGAIN ...!

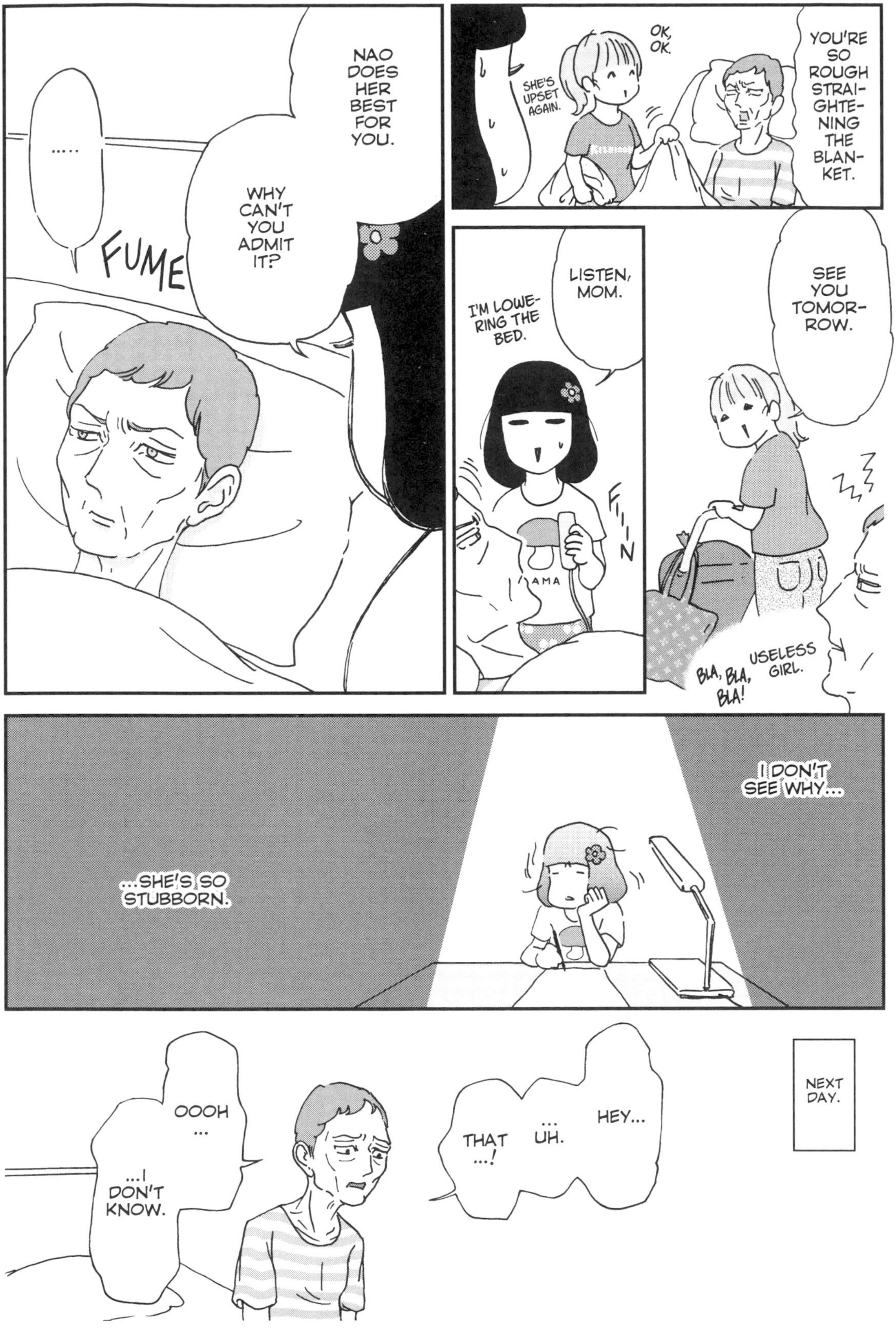
YOU'RE SO ROUGH STRAIGHTENING THE BLANKET.
OK, OK.
SHE'S UPSET AGAIN.
SEE YOU TOMORROW.
USELESS GIRL.
BLA, BLA, BLA!
LISTEN, MOM.
I'M LOWERING THE BED.
FIIIN
NAO DOES HER BEST FOR YOU.
WHY CAN'T YOU ADMIT IT?
FUME
……
I DON'T SEE WHY...
...SHE'S SO STUBBORN.
NEXT DAY.
HEY...
... UH.
THAT ...!
OOOH ...
...I DON'T KNOW.

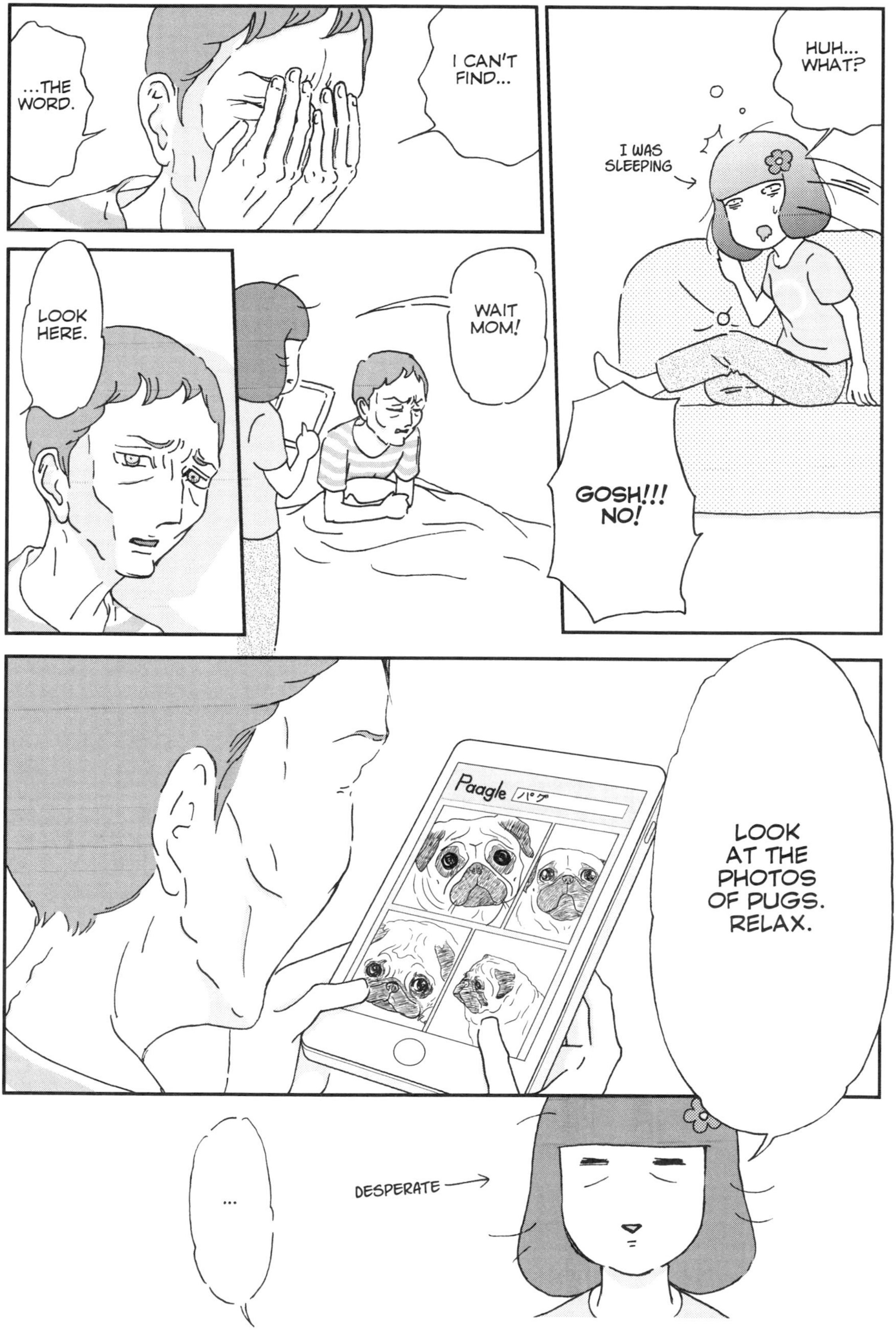
HUH... WHAT?
I WAS SLEEPING
GOSH!!! NO!
I CAN'T FIND...
...THE WORD.
WAIT MOM!
LOOK HERE.
Paagle パグ
LOOK AT THE PHOTOS OF PUGS. RELAX.
DESPERATE
...

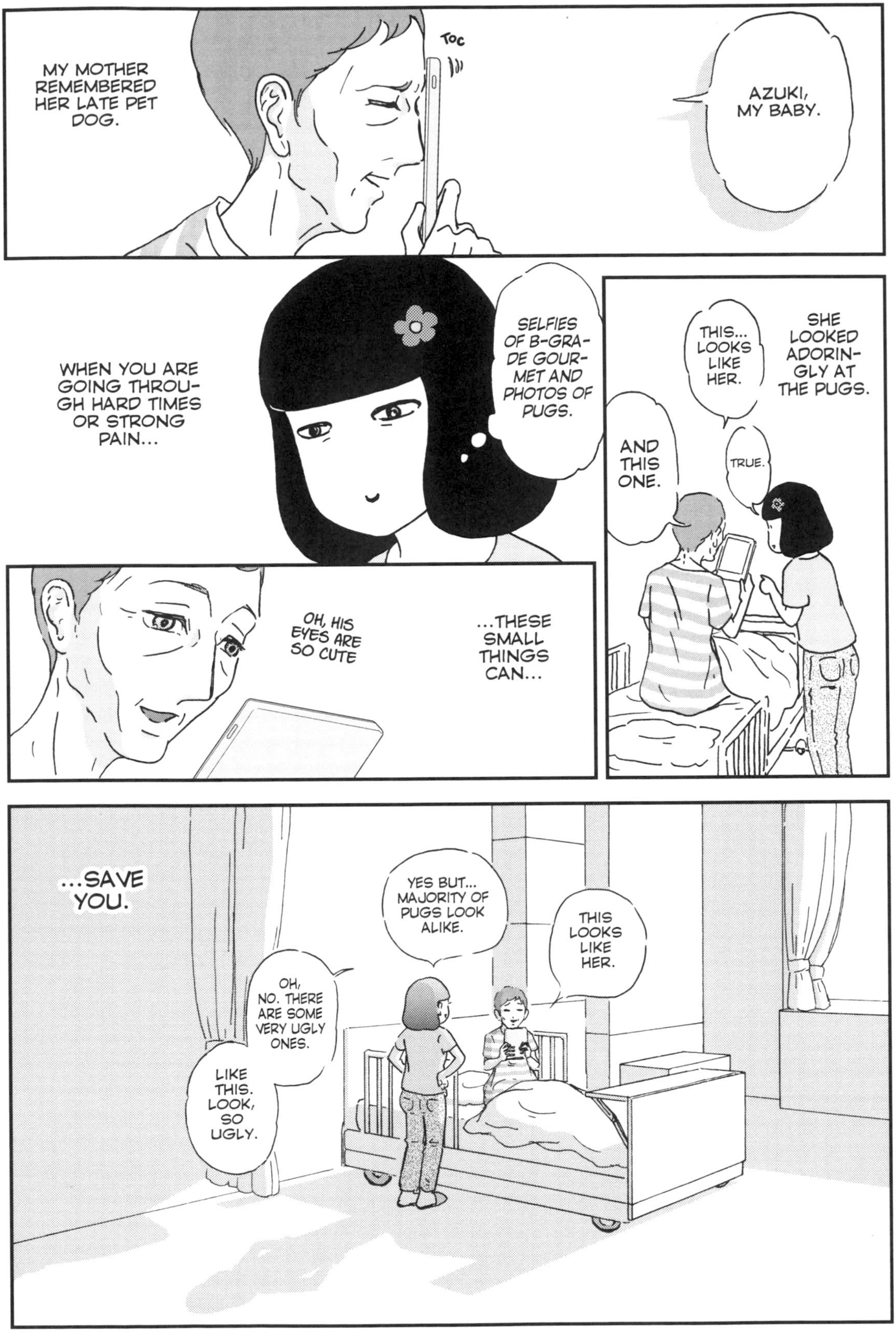
AZUKI, MY BABY.
TOC
MY MOTHER REMEMBERED HER LATE PET DOG.
SHE LOOKED ADORINGLY AT THE PUGS.
THIS... LOOKS LIKE HER.
TRUE.
AND THIS ONE.
SELFIES OF B-GRADE GOURMET AND PHOTOS OF PUGS.
WHEN YOU ARE GOING THROUGH HARD TIMES OR STRONG PAIN...
...THESE SMALL THINGS CAN...
OH, HIS EYES ARE SO CUTE
THIS LOOKS LIKE HER.
YES BUT... MAJORITY OF PUGS LOOK ALIKE.
...SAVE YOU.
OH, NO. THERE ARE SOME VERY UGLY ONES.
LIKE THIS. LOOK, SO UGLY.

CHAPTER 14

WHEN CAN I SAY "THANK YOU"?

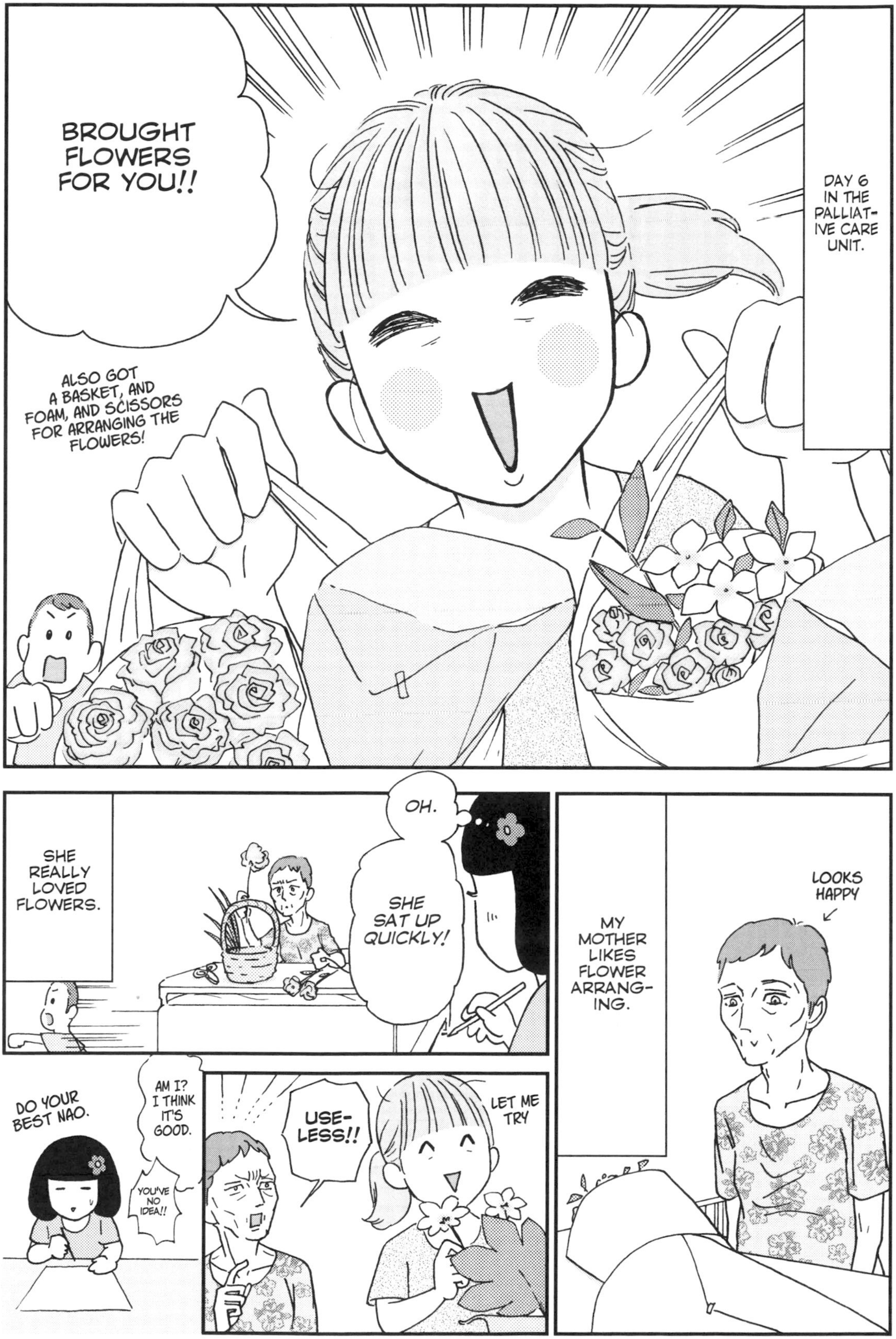
DAY 6 IN THE PALLIAT-IVE CARE UNIT.
BROUGHT FLOWERS FOR YOU!!
ALSO GOT A BASKET, AND FOAM, AND SCISSORS FOR ARRANGING THE FLOWERS!
MY MOTHER LIKES FLOWER ARRANG-ING.
LOOKS HAPPY
OH.
SHE SAT UP QUICKLY!
SHE REALLY LOVED FLOWERS.
LET ME TRY
USE-LESS!!
AM I? I THINK IT'S GOOD.
YOU'VE NO IDEA!!
DO YOUR BEST NAO.

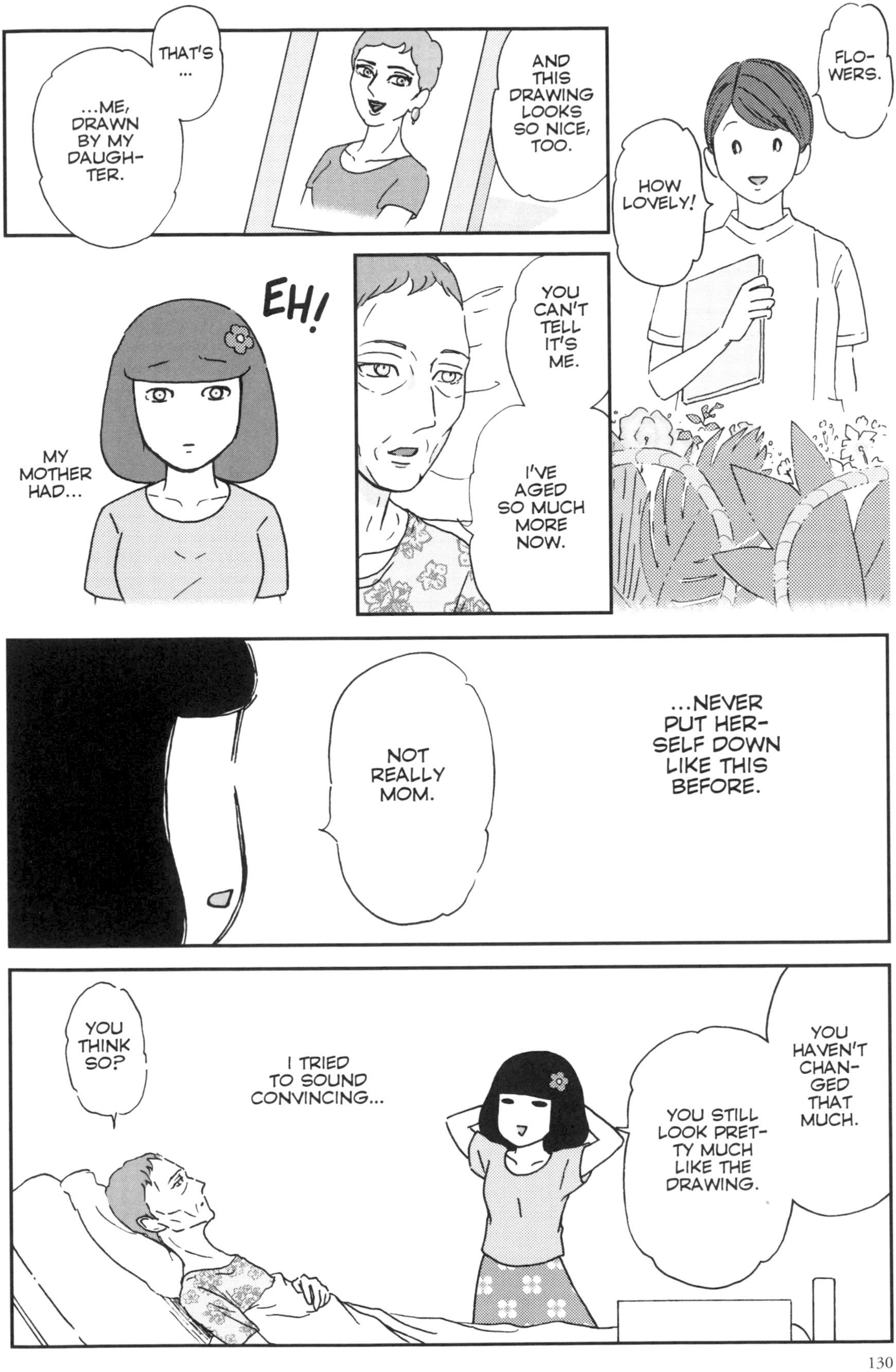
FLOWERS.
HOW LOVELY!
AND THIS DRAWING LOOKS SO NICE, TOO.
THAT'S ...
...ME, DRAWN BY MY DAUGHTER.
YOU CAN'T TELL IT'S ME.
I'VE AGED SO MUCH MORE NOW.
EH!
MY MOTHER HAD...
...NEVER PUT HERSELF DOWN LIKE THIS BEFORE.
NOT REALLY MOM.
YOU HAVEN'T CHANGED THAT MUCH.
YOU STILL LOOK PRETTY MUCH LIKE THE DRAWING.
I TRIED TO SOUND CONVINCING...
YOU THINK SO?

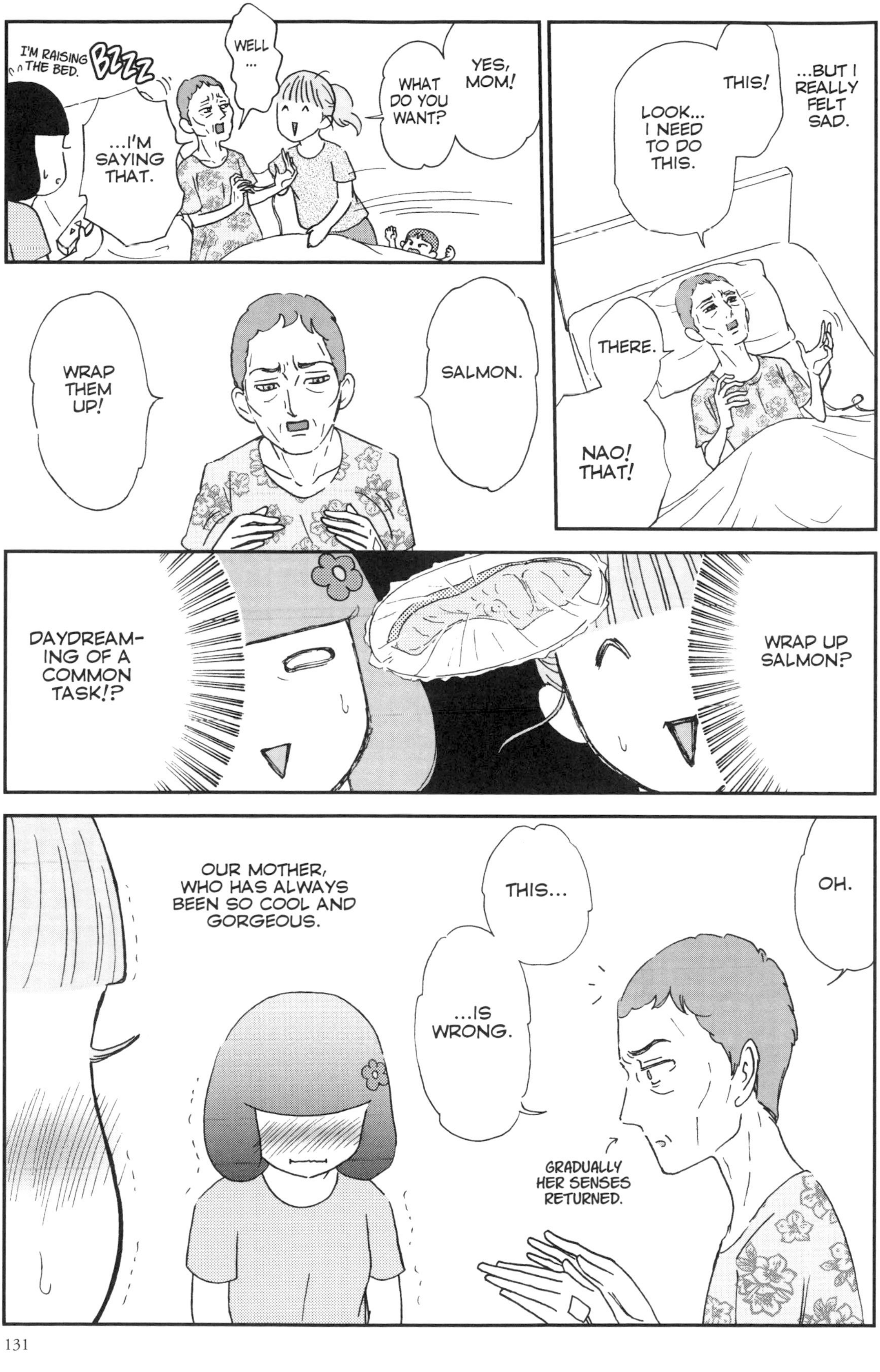
...BUT I REALLY FELT SAD.
THIS!
LOOK... I NEED TO DO THIS.
THERE.
NAO! THAT!
YES, MOM!
WHAT DO YOU WANT?
WELL ...
BZZZ
I'M RAISING THE BED.
...I'M SAYING THAT.
SALMON.
WRAP THEM UP!
WRAP UP SALMON?
DAYDREAM-ING OF A COMMON TASK!?
OH.
THIS...
...IS WRONG.
GRADUALLY HER SENSES RETURNED.
OUR MOTHER, WHO HAS ALWAYS BEEN SO COOL AND GORGEOUS.

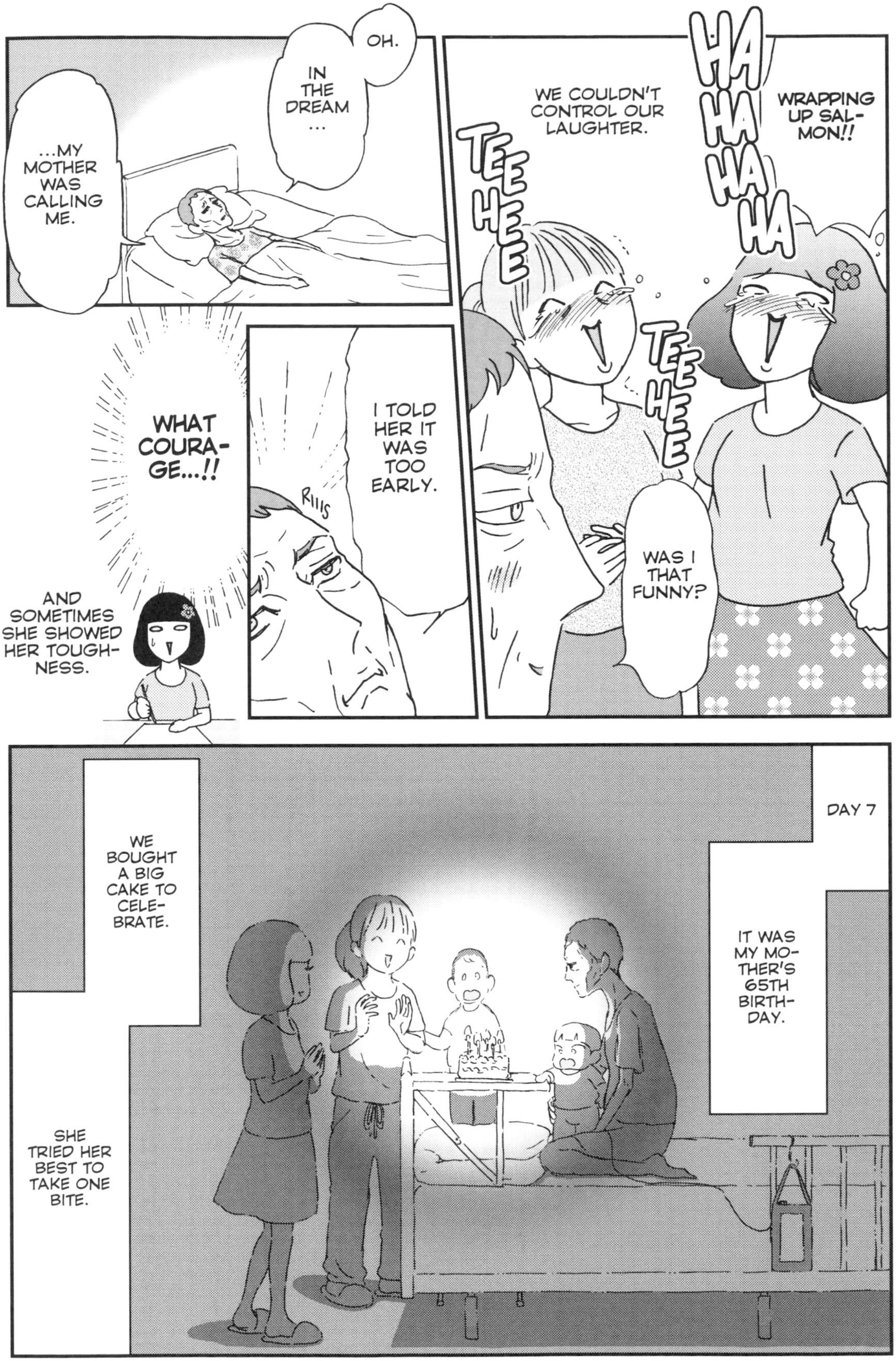
WRAPPING UP SALMON!!
HA HA HA HA HA
WE COULDN'T CONTROL OUR LAUGHTER.
TEE HEE
TEE HEE
WAS I THAT FUNNY?
OH.
IN THE DREAM...
...MY MOTHER WAS CALLING ME.
I TOLD HER IT WAS TOO EARLY.
RIIS
WHAT COURAGE...!!
AND SOMETIMES SHE SHOWED HER TOUGHNESS.
DAY 7
IT WAS MY MOTHER'S 65TH BIRTHDAY.
WE BOUGHT A BIG CAKE TO CELEBRATE.
SHE TRIED HER BEST TO TAKE ONE BITE.

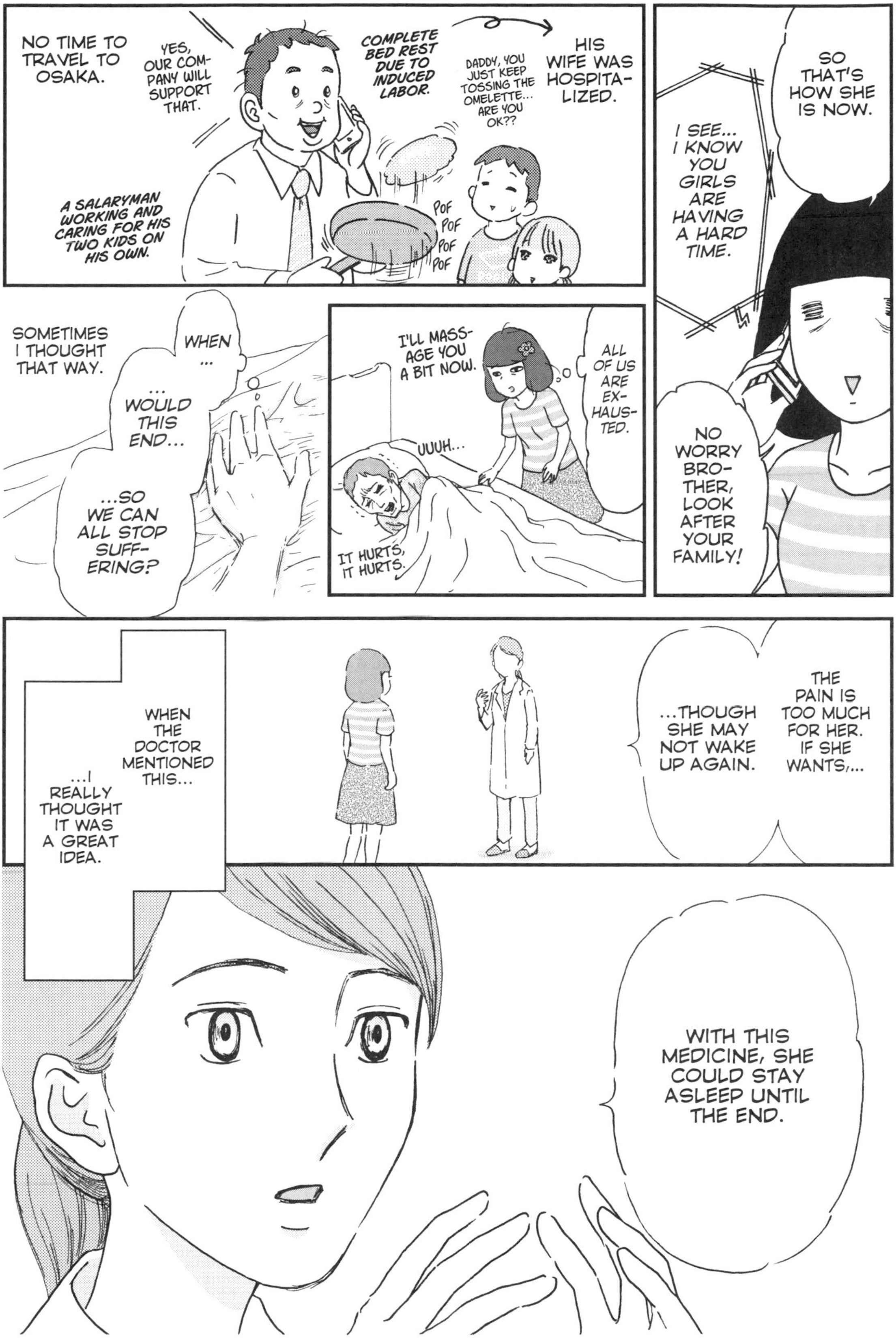
SO THAT'S HOW SHE IS NOW.
I SEE... I KNOW YOU GIRLS ARE HAVING A HARD TIME.
NO WORRY BROTHER, LOOK AFTER YOUR FAMILY!
HIS WIFE WAS HOSPITALIZED.
DADDY, YOU JUST KEEP TOSSING THE OMELETTE... ARE YOU OK??
COMPLETE BED REST DUE TO INDUCED LABOR.
YES, OUR COMPANY WILL SUPPORT THAT.
NO TIME TO TRAVEL TO OSAKA.
A SALARYMAN WORKING AND CARING FOR HIS TWO KIDS ON HIS OWN.
POF POF POF POF
ALL OF US ARE EXHAUSTED.
I'LL MASSAGE YOU A BIT NOW.
UUUH...
IT HURTS, IT HURTS.
WHEN ...
... WOULD THIS END...
...SO WE CAN ALL STOP SUFFERING?
SOMETIMES I THOUGHT THAT WAY.
THE PAIN IS TOO MUCH FOR HER. IF SHE WANTS,...
...THOUGH SHE MAY NOT WAKE UP AGAIN.
WHEN THE DOCTOR MENTIONED THIS...
...I REALLY THOUGHT IT WAS A GREAT IDEA.
WITH THIS MEDICINE, SHE COULD STAY ASLEEP UNTIL THE END.

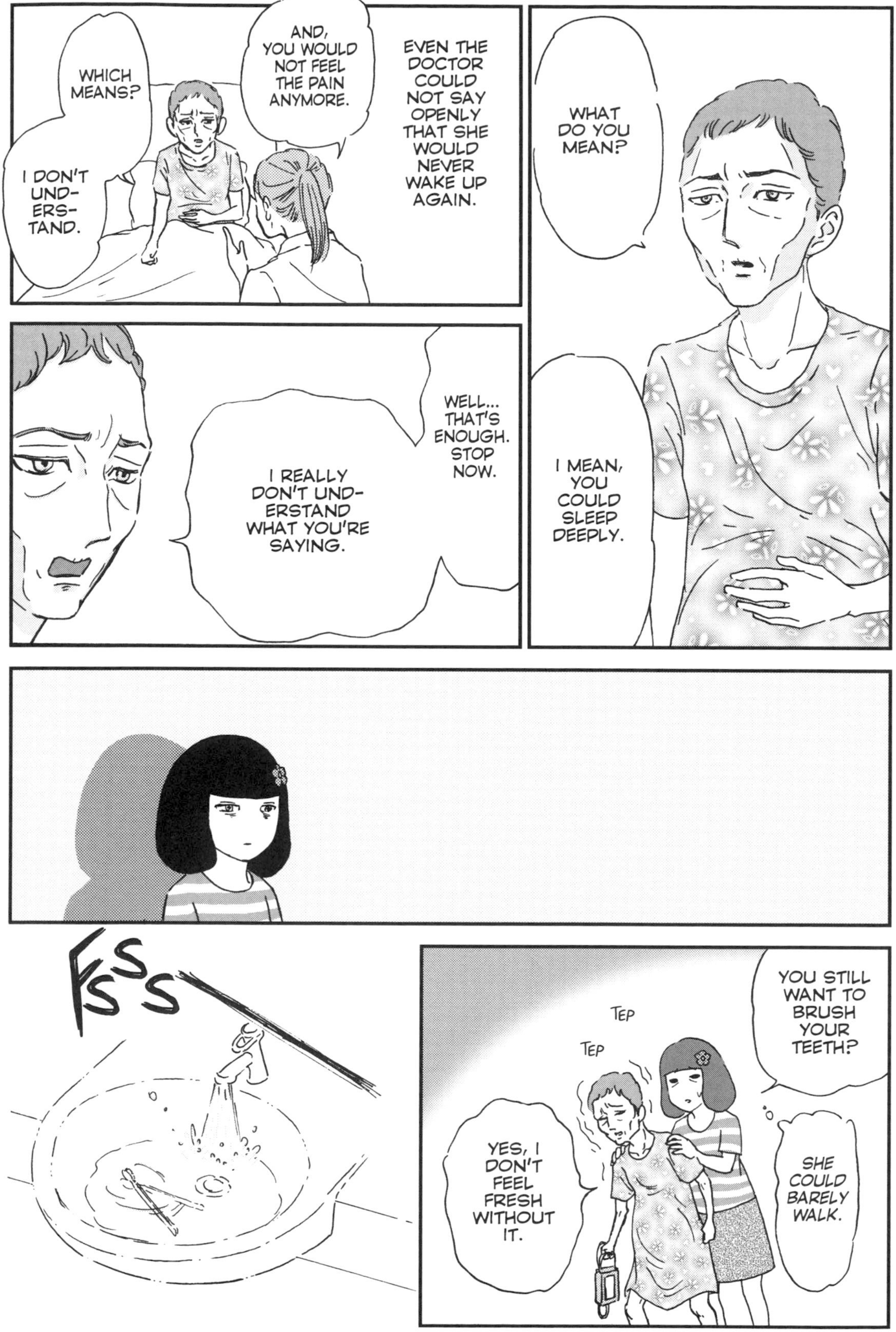
WHAT DO YOU MEAN?
I MEAN, YOU COULD SLEEP DEEPLY.
EVEN THE DOCTOR COULD NOT SAY OPENLY THAT SHE WOULD NEVER WAKE UP AGAIN.
AND, YOU WOULD NOT FEEL THE PAIN ANYMORE.
WHICH MEANS?
I DON'T UNDER-STAND.
WELL... THAT'S ENOUGH. STOP NOW.
I REALLY DON'T UNDER-STAND WHAT YOU'RE SAYING.
YOU STILL WANT TO BRUSH YOUR TEETH?
TEP
TEP
SHE COULD BARELY WALK.
YES, I DON'T FEEL FRESH WITHOUT IT.
FSSS

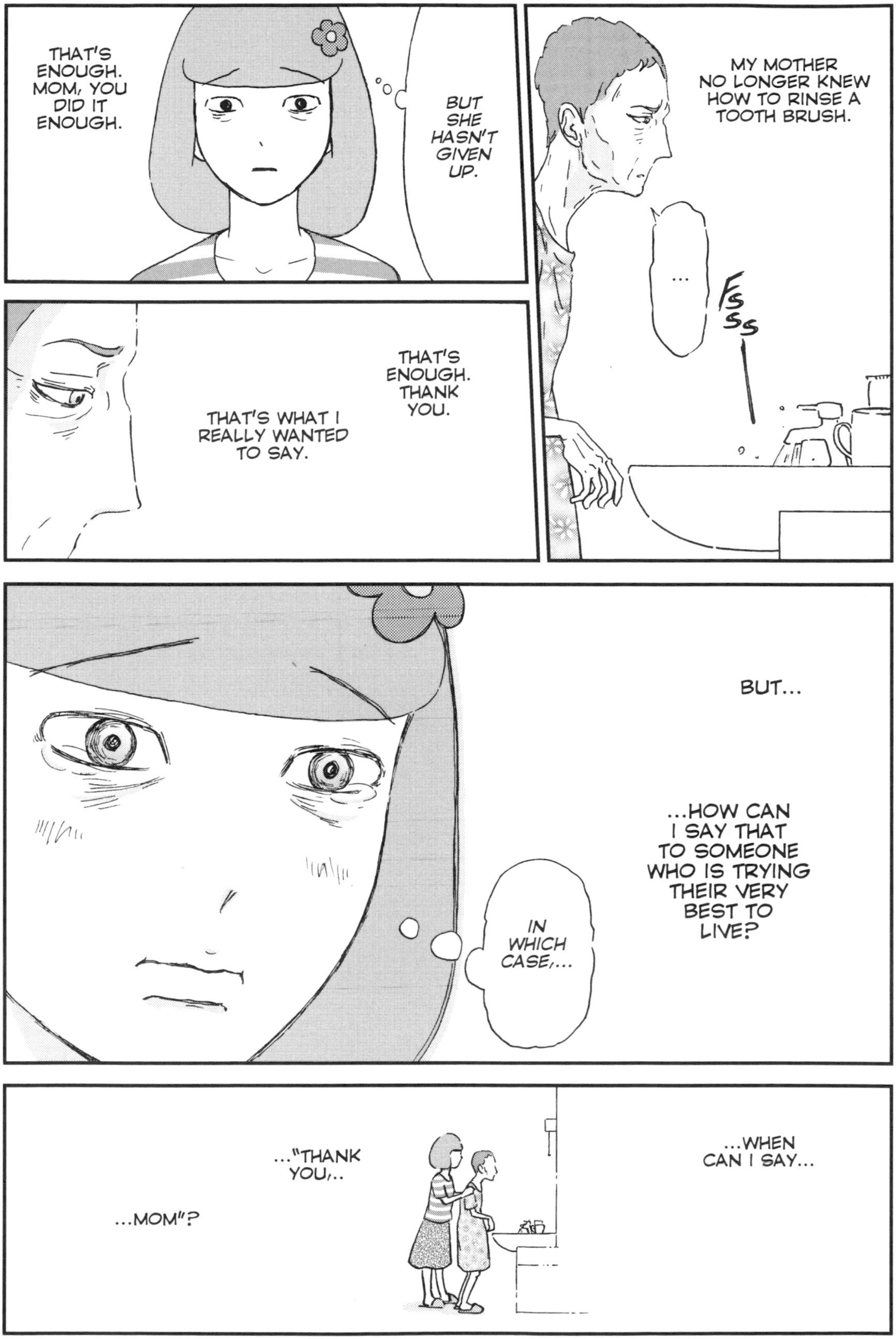
MY MOTHER NO LONGER KNEW HOW TO RINSE A TOOTH BRUSH.
...
FSSS
BUT SHE HASN'T GIVEN UP.
THAT'S ENOUGH. MOM, YOU DID IT ENOUGH.
THAT'S ENOUGH. THANK YOU.
THAT'S WHAT I REALLY WANTED TO SAY.
BUT...
...HOW CAN I SAY THAT TO SOMEONE WHO IS TRYING THEIR VERY BEST TO LIVE?
IN WHICH CASE,...
...WHEN CAN I SAY...
..."THANK YOU,..
...MOM"?

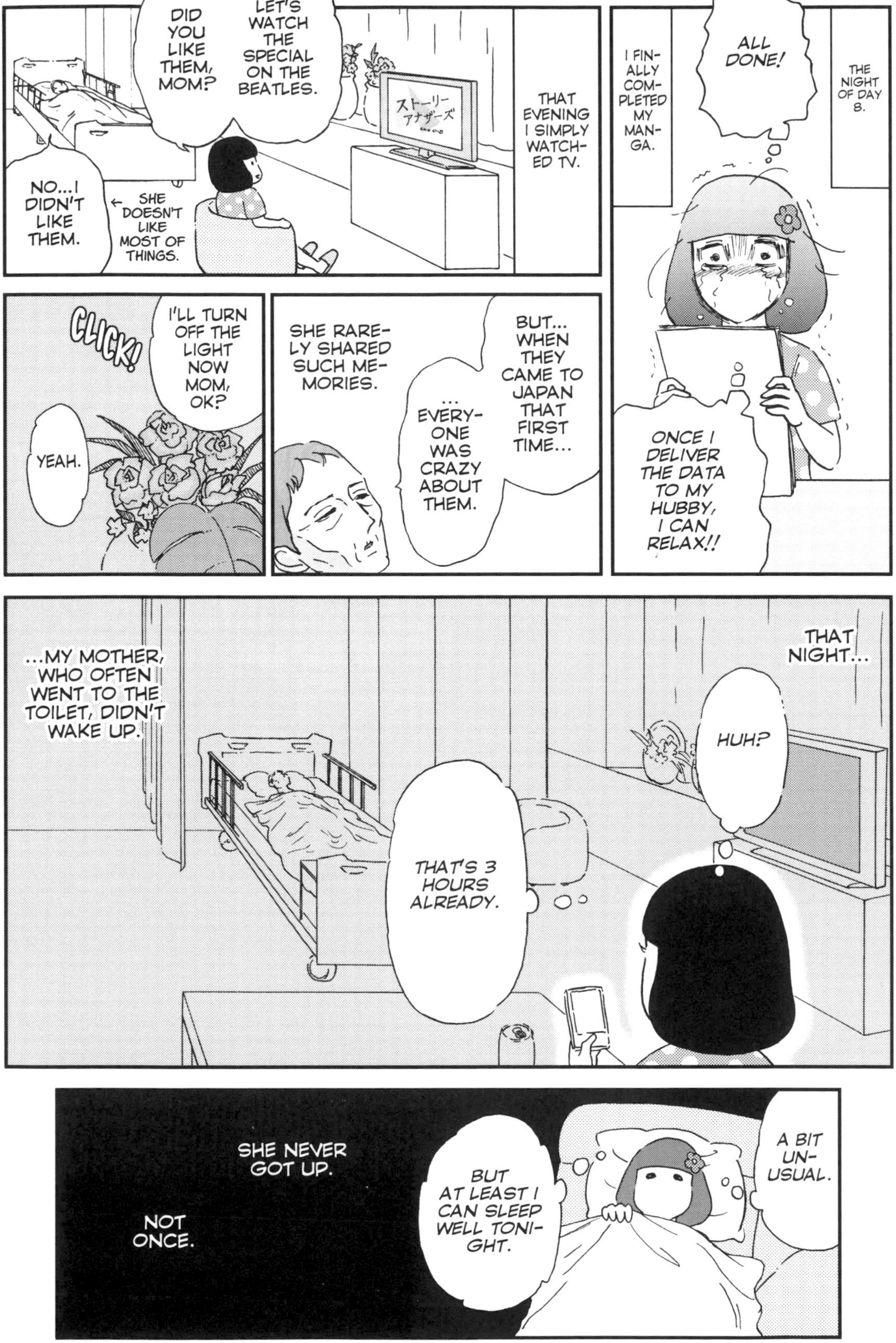
THE NIGHT OF DAY 8.
ALL DONE!
I FINALLY COMPLETED MY MANGA.
ONCE I DELIVER THE DATA TO MY HUBBY, I CAN RELAX!!
THAT EVENING I SIMPLY WATCHED TV.
ストーリーアナザーズ
LET'S WATCH THE SPECIAL ON THE BEATLES.
DID YOU LIKE THEM, MOM?
NO...I DIDN'T LIKE THEM.
← SHE DOESN'T LIKE MOST OF THINGS.
BUT... WHEN THEY CAME TO JAPAN THAT FIRST TIME...
...EVERYONE WAS CRAZY ABOUT THEM.
SHE RARELY SHARED SUCH MEMORIES.
CLICK!
I'LL TURN OFF THE LIGHT NOW MOM, OK?
YEAH.
THAT NIGHT...
HUH?
THAT'S 3 HOURS ALREADY.
...MY MOTHER, WHO OFTEN WENT TO THE TOILET, DIDN'T WAKE UP.
A BIT UNUSUAL.
BUT AT LEAST I CAN SLEEP WELL TONIGHT.
SHE NEVER GOT UP.
NOT ONCE.

CHAPTER 15

THE WORLD SEEMED FOREVER GENTLE AND FULL OF LOVE

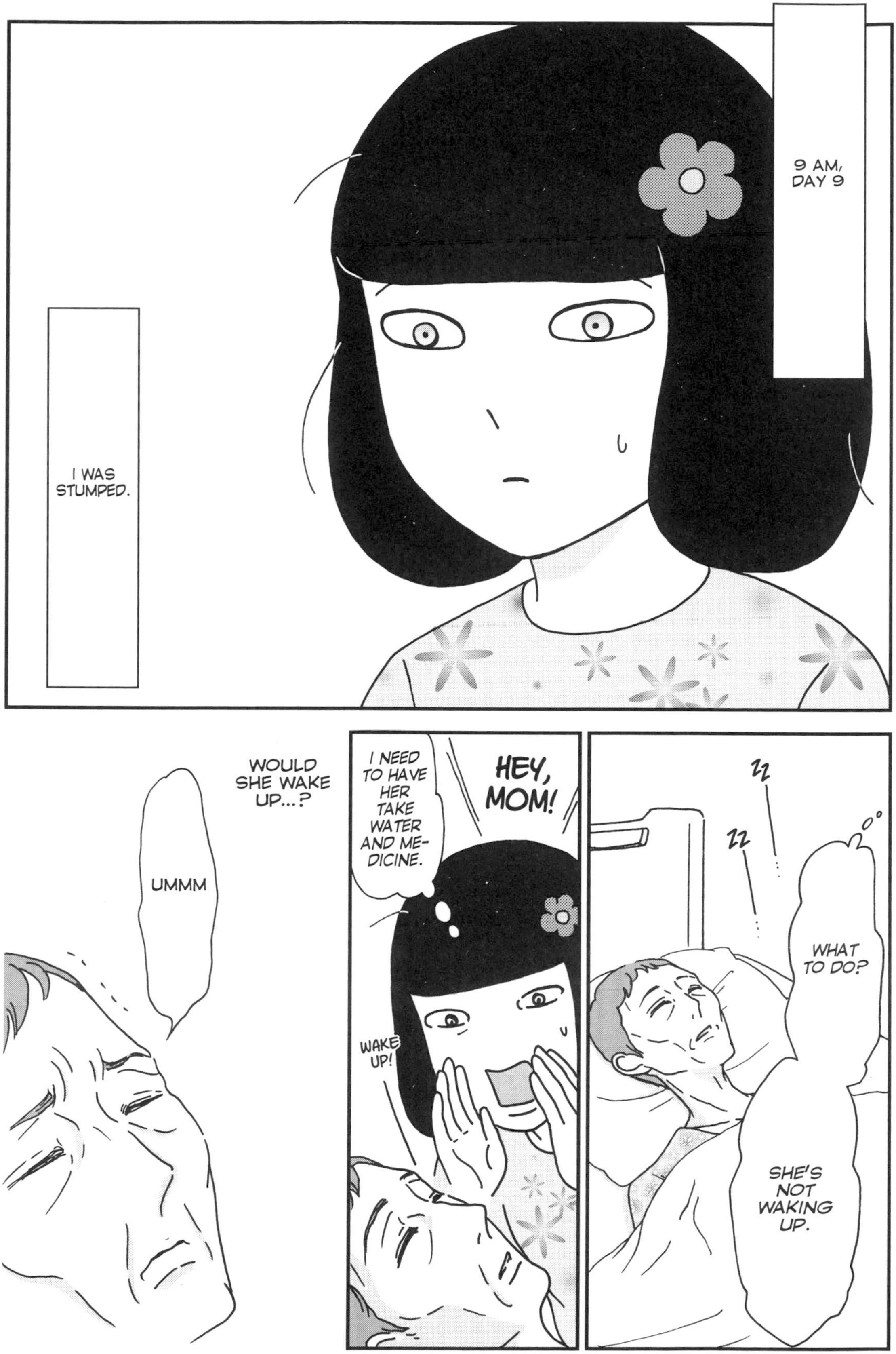
9 AM, DAY 9
I WAS STUMPED.
ZZ
ZZ
WHAT TO DO?
SHE'S NOT WAKING UP.
HEY, MOM!
I NEED TO HAVE HER TAKE WATER AND MEDICINE.
WAKE UP!
WOULD SHE WAKE UP...?
UMMM

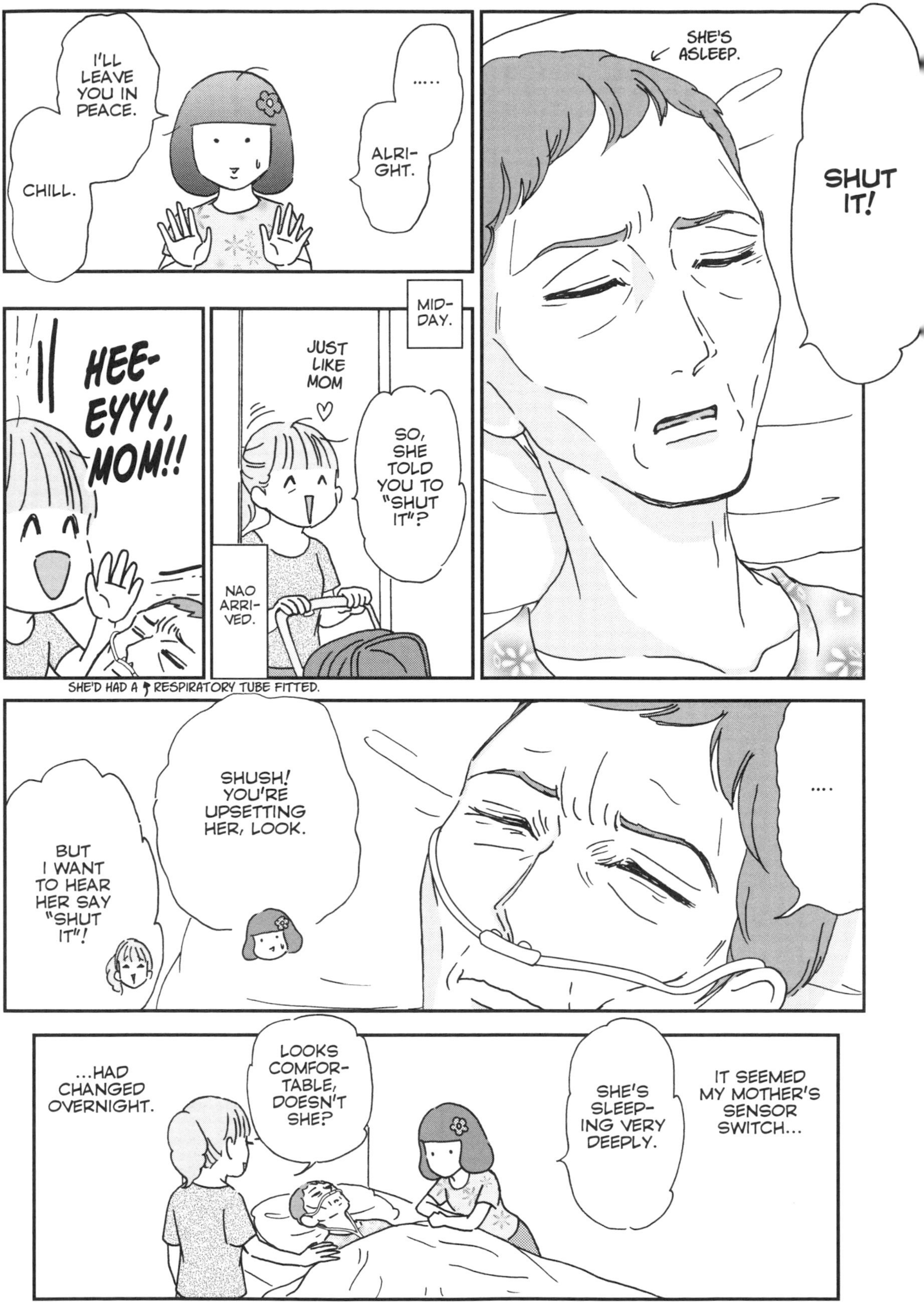
SHUT IT!
SHE'S ASLEEP.
.....
ALRI-GHT.
I'LL LEAVE YOU IN PEACE.
CHILL.
MID-DAY.
NAO ARRI-VED.
JUST LIKE MOM ♡
SO, SHE TOLD YOU TO "SHUT IT"?
HEE-EYYY, MOM!!
SHE'D HAD A RESPIRATORY TUBE FITTED.
....
SHUSH! YOU'RE UPSETTING HER, LOOK.
BUT I WANT TO HEAR HER SAY "SHUT IT"!
IT SEEMED MY MOTHER'S SENSOR SWITCH...
SHE'S SLEEP-ING VERY DEEPLY.
LOOKS COMFOR-TABLE, DOESN'T SHE?
...HAD CHANGED OVERNIGHT.

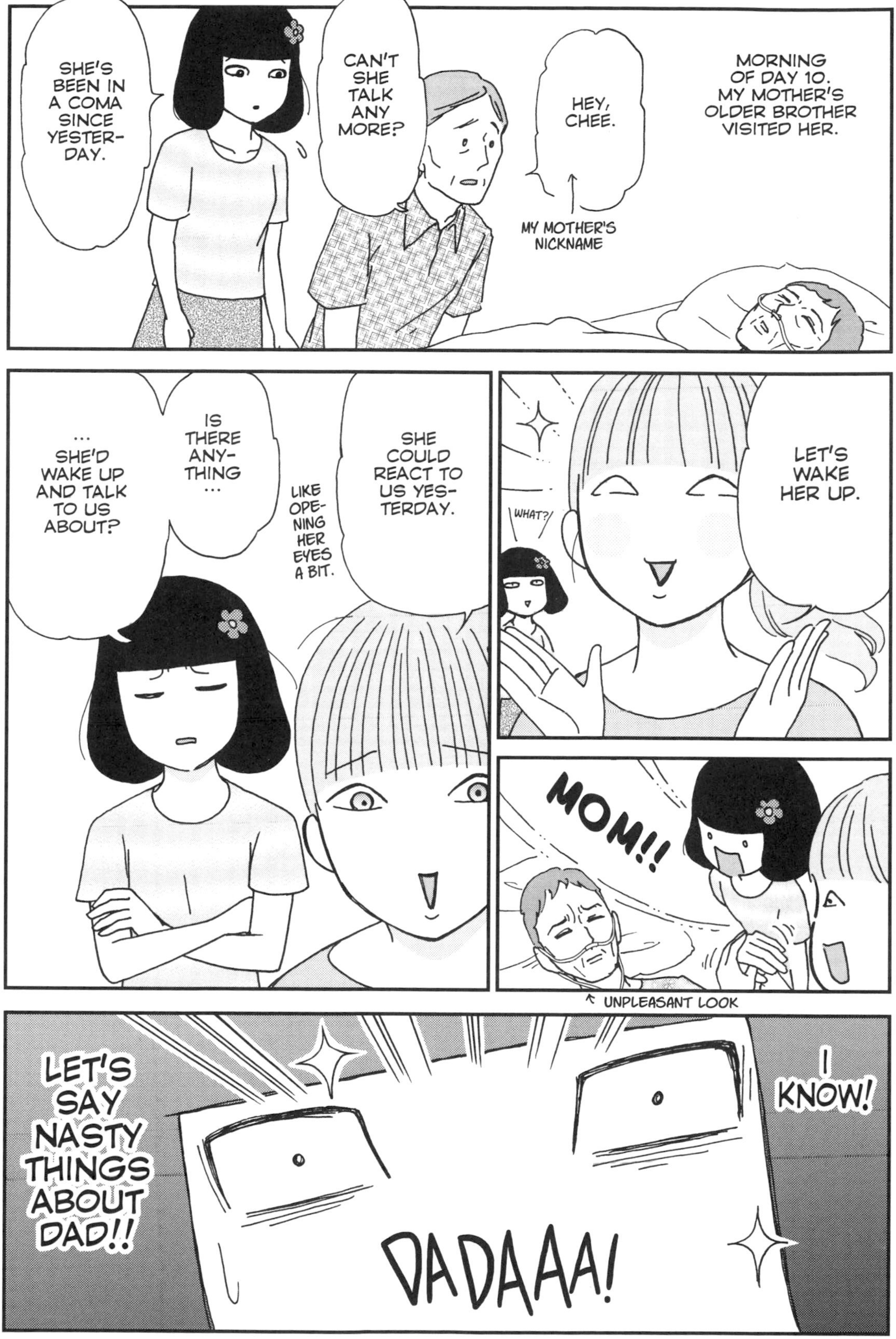
MORNING OF DAY 10. MY MOTHER'S OLDER BROTHER VISITED HER.
HEY, CHEE.
MY MOTHER'S NICKNAME
CAN'T SHE TALK ANY MORE?
SHE'S BEEN IN A COMA SINCE YESTER-DAY.
LET'S WAKE HER UP.
WHAT?
MOM!!
UNPLEASANT LOOK
SHE COULD REACT TO US YES-TERDAY.
LIKE OPE-NING HER EYES A BIT.
IS THERE ANY-THING ...
... SHE'D WAKE UP AND TALK TO US ABOUT?
I KNOW!
DADAAA!
LET'S SAY NASTY THINGS ABOUT DAD!!

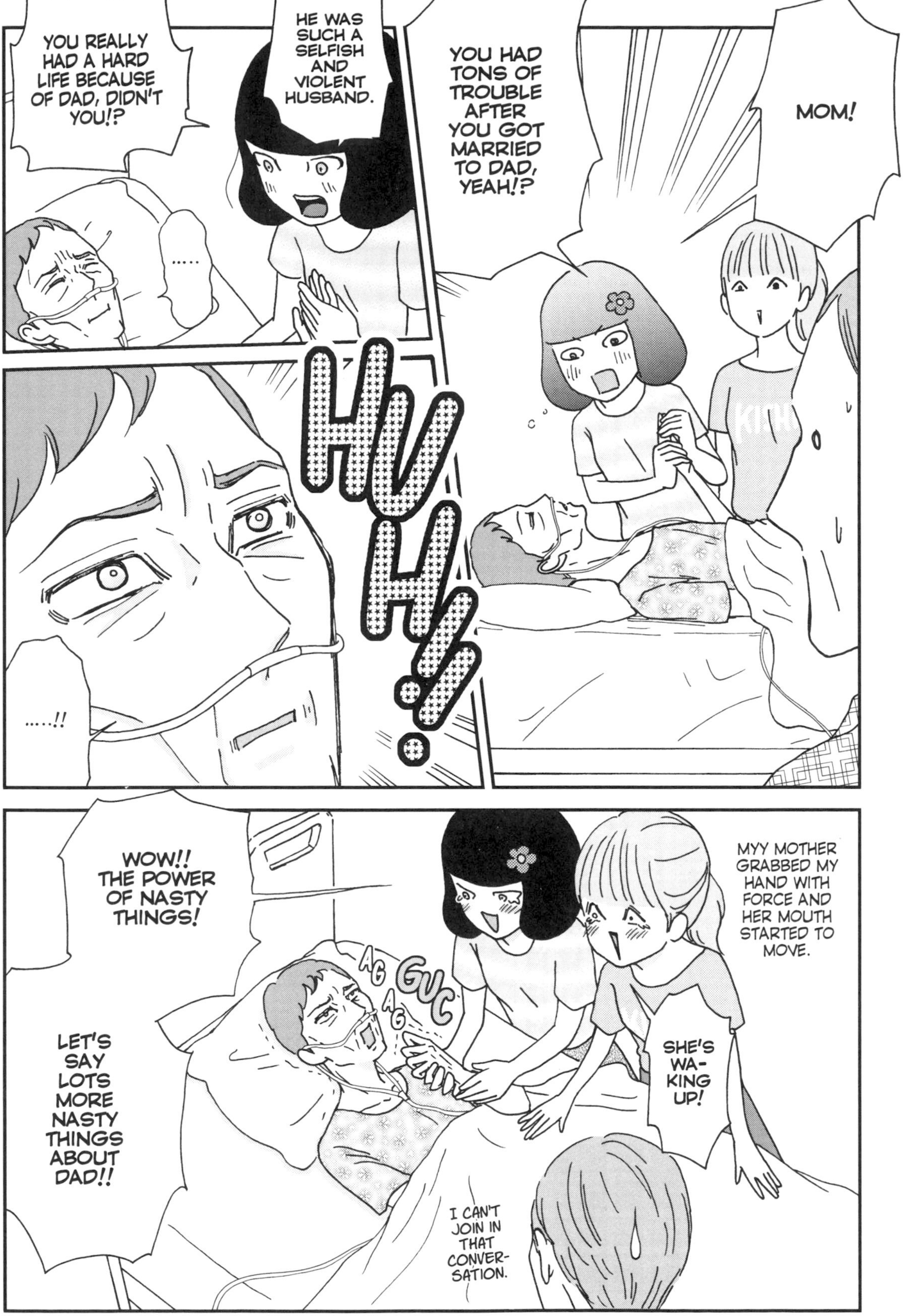
MOM!
YOU HAD TONS OF TROUBLE AFTER YOU GOT MARRIED TO DAD, YEAH!?
HE WAS SUCH A SELFISH AND VIOLENT HUSBAND.
YOU REALLY HAD A HARD LIFE BECAUSE OF DAD, DIDN'T YOU!?
.....
HUH!!
.....!!
MYY MOTHER GRABBED MY HAND WITH FORCE AND HER MOUTH STARTED TO MOVE.
WOW!! THE POWER OF NASTY THINGS!
GUC
AG AG
SHE'S WA-KING UP!
LET'S SAY LOTS MORE NASTY THINGS ABOUT DAD!!
I CAN'T JOIN IN THAT CONVER-SATION.

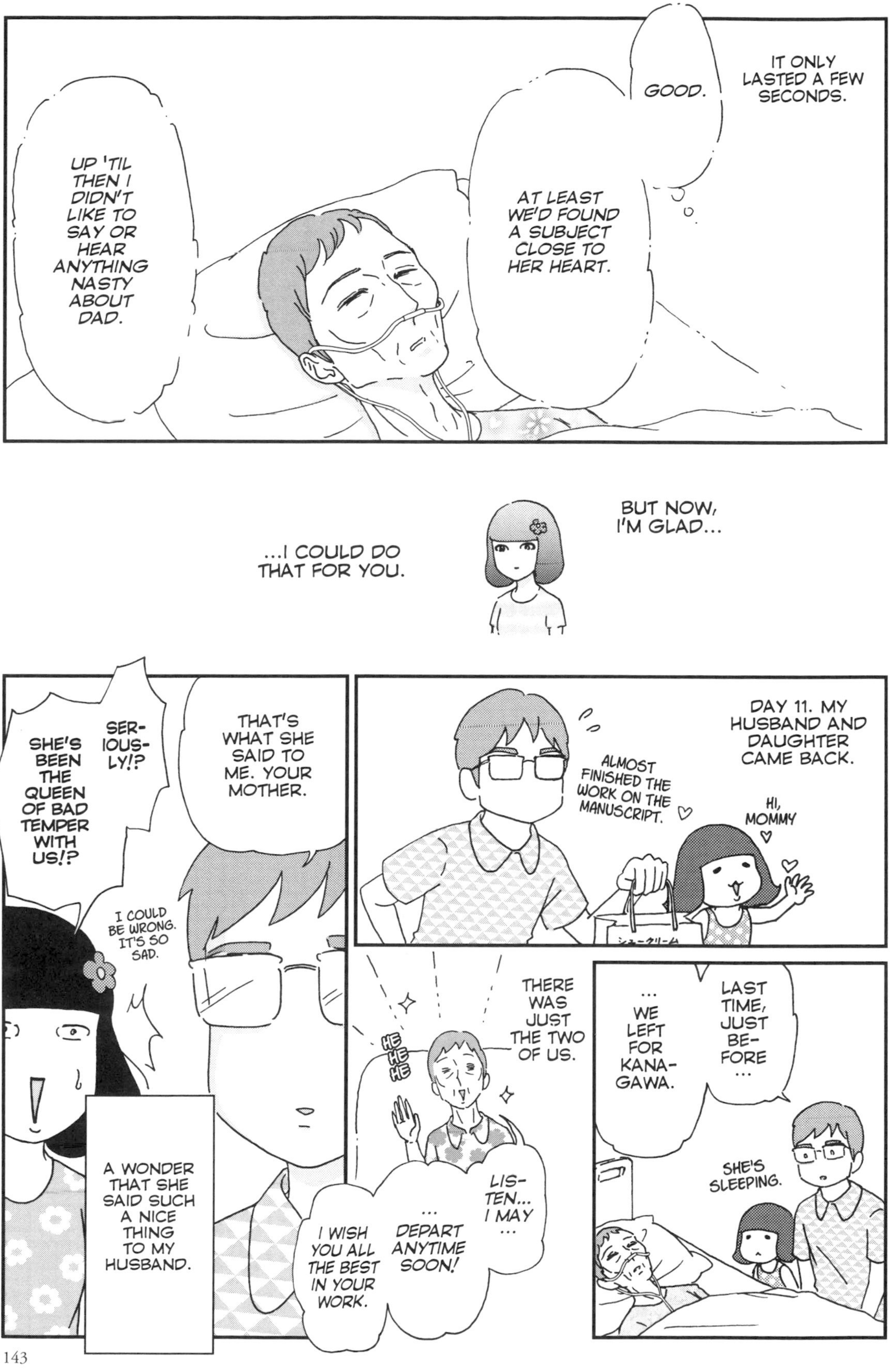
IT ONLY LASTED A FEW SECONDS.
GOOD.
AT LEAST WE'D FOUND A SUBJECT CLOSE TO HER HEART.
UP 'TIL THEN I DIDN'T LIKE TO SAY OR HEAR ANYTHING NASTY ABOUT DAD.
BUT NOW, I'M GLAD...
...I COULD DO THAT FOR YOU.
DAY 11. MY HUSBAND AND DAUGHTER CAME BACK.
ALMOST FINISHED THE WORK ON THE MANUSCRIPT.
HI, MOMMY
LAST TIME, JUST BEFORE...
...WE LEFT FOR KANAGAWA.
SHE'S SLEEPING.
THERE WAS JUST THE TWO OF US.
HE HE HE
LISTEN... I MAY...
...DEPART ANYTIME SOON!
I WISH YOU ALL THE BEST IN YOUR WORK.
THAT'S WHAT SHE SAID TO ME. YOUR MOTHER.
SERIOUSLY!?
SHE'S BEEN THE QUEEN OF BAD TEMPER WITH US!?
I COULD BE WRONG. IT'S SO SAD.
A WONDER THAT SHE SAID SUCH A NICE THING TO MY HUSBAND.

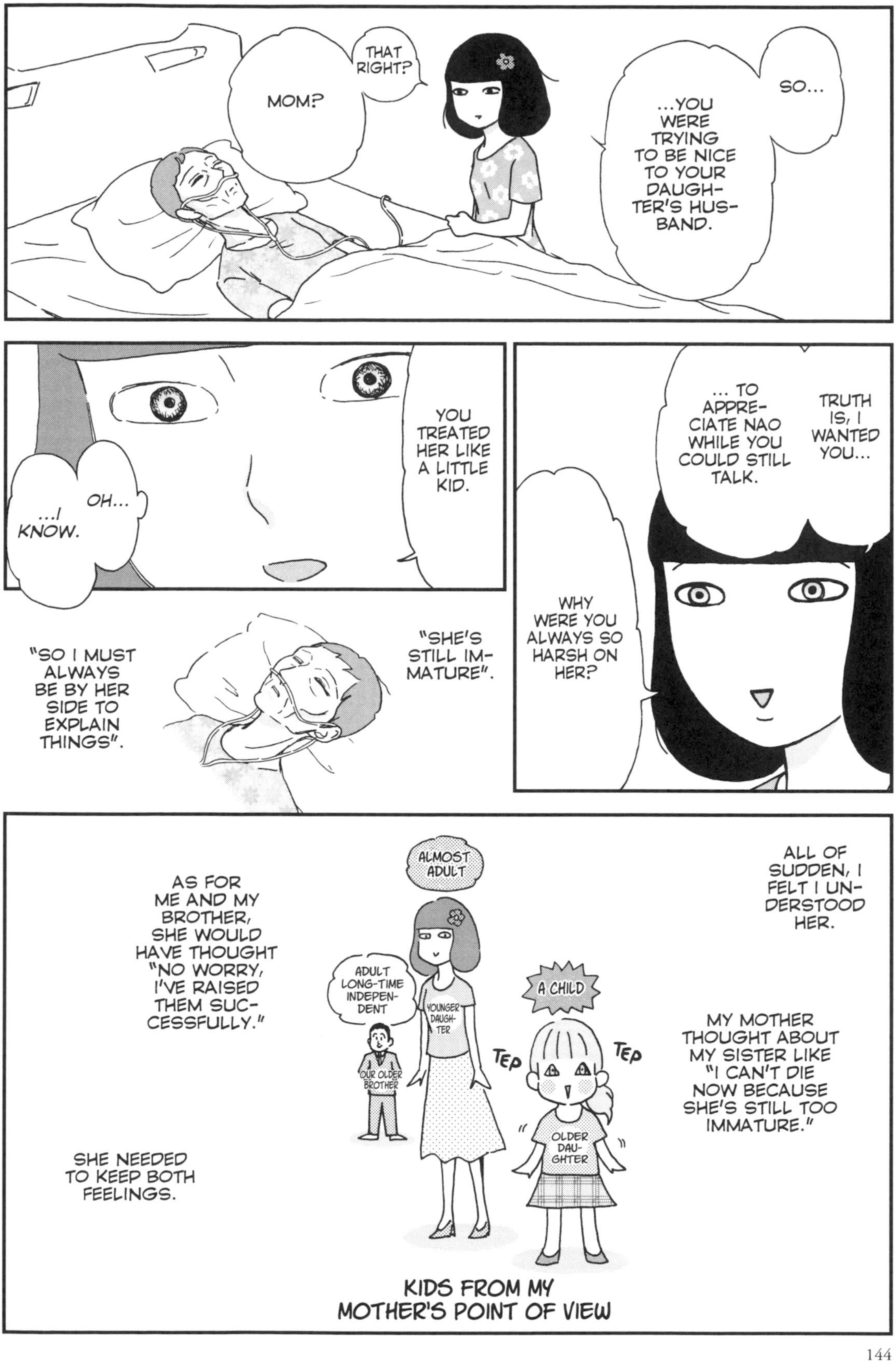
SO...
...YOU WERE TRYING TO BE NICE TO YOUR DAUGHTER'S HUSBAND.
MOM?
THAT RIGHT?
TRUTH IS, I WANTED YOU...
... TO APPRECIATE NAO WHILE YOU COULD STILL TALK.
WHY WERE YOU ALWAYS SO HARSH ON HER?
YOU TREATED HER LIKE A LITTLE KID.
OH...
...I KNOW.
"SHE'S STILL IMMATURE".
"SO I MUST ALWAYS BE BY HER SIDE TO EXPLAIN THINGS".
ALL OF SUDDEN, I FELT I UNDERSTOOD HER.
MY MOTHER THOUGHT ABOUT MY SISTER LIKE "I CAN'T DIE NOW BECAUSE SHE'S STILL TOO IMMATURE."
A CHILD
TEP
TEP
OLDER DAUGHTER
ALMOST ADULT
YOUNGER DAUGHTER
ADULT LONG-TIME INDEPENDENT
OUR OLDER BROTHER
AS FOR ME AND MY BROTHER, SHE WOULD HAVE THOUGHT "NO WORRY, I'VE RAISED THEM SUCCESSFULLY."
SHE NEEDED TO KEEP BOTH FEELINGS.
KIDS FROM MY MOTHER'S POINT OF VIEW

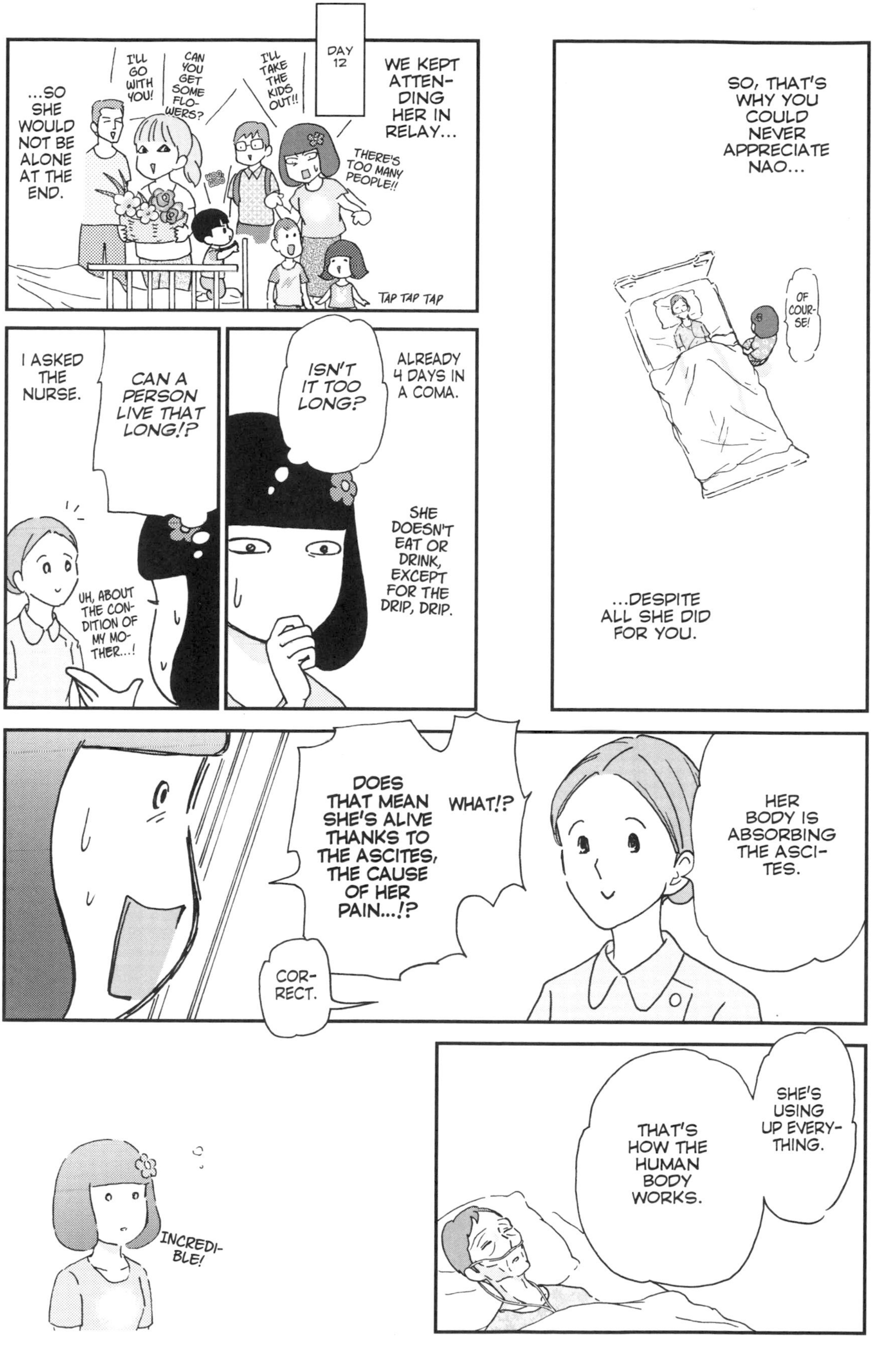
SO, THAT'S WHY YOU COULD NEVER APPRECIATE NAO…
OF COURSE!
…DESPITE ALL SHE DID FOR YOU.
DAY 12
WE KEPT ATTENDING HER IN RELAY…
THERE'S TOO MANY PEOPLE!!
I'LL TAKE THE KIDS OUT!!
CAN YOU GET SOME FLOWERS?
I'LL GO WITH YOU!
…SO SHE WOULD NOT BE ALONE AT THE END.
WOO WOO
TAP TAP TAP
ALREADY 4 DAYS IN A COMA.
ISN'T IT TOO LONG?
SHE DOESN'T EAT OR DRINK, EXCEPT FOR THE DRIP, DRIP.
CAN A PERSON LIVE THAT LONG!?
I ASKED THE NURSE.
UH, ABOUT THE CONDITION OF MY MOTHER…!
HER BODY IS ABSORBING THE ASCITES.
WHAT!?
DOES THAT MEAN SHE'S ALIVE THANKS TO THE ASCITES, THE CAUSE OF HER PAIN…!?
CORRECT.
SHE'S USING UP EVERYTHING.
THAT'S HOW THE HUMAN BODY WORKS.
INCREDIBLE!

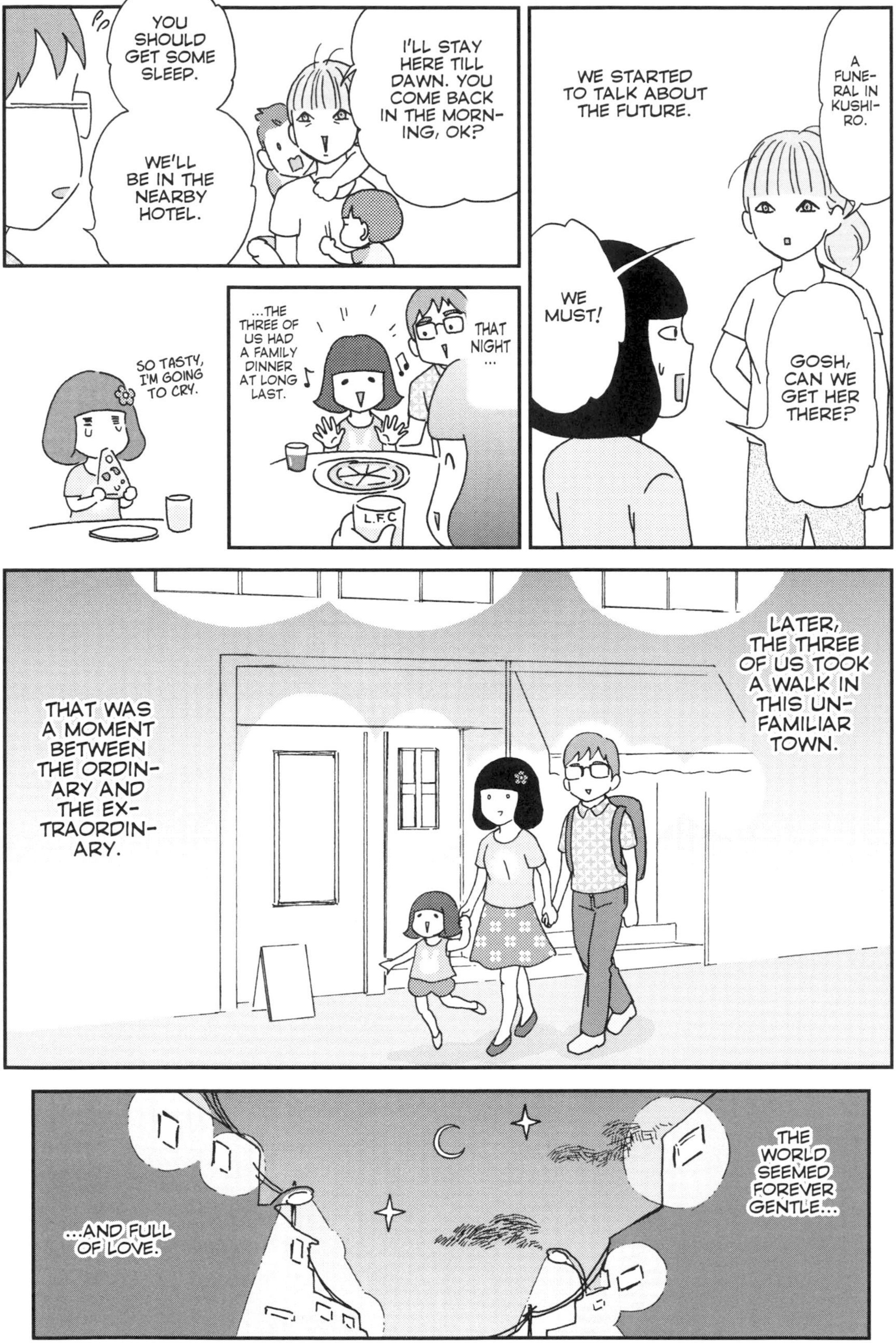
A FUNERAL IN KUSHIRO.
WE STARTED TO TALK ABOUT THE FUTURE.
GOSH, CAN WE GET HER THERE?
WE MUST!
I'LL STAY HERE TILL DAWN. YOU COME BACK IN THE MORNING, OK?
YOU SHOULD GET SOME SLEEP.
WE'LL BE IN THE NEARBY HOTEL.
THAT NIGHT...
...THE THREE OF US HAD A FAMILY DINNER AT LONG LAST.
L.F.C
SO TASTY, I'M GOING TO CRY.
LATER, THE THREE OF US TOOK A WALK IN THIS UNFAMILIAR TOWN.
THAT WAS A MOMENT BETWEEN THE ORDINARY AND THE EXTRAORDINARY.
THE WORLD SEEMED FOREVER GENTLE...
...AND FULL OF LOVE.

CHAPTER 16

MOM, CAN I SAY THIS NOW?

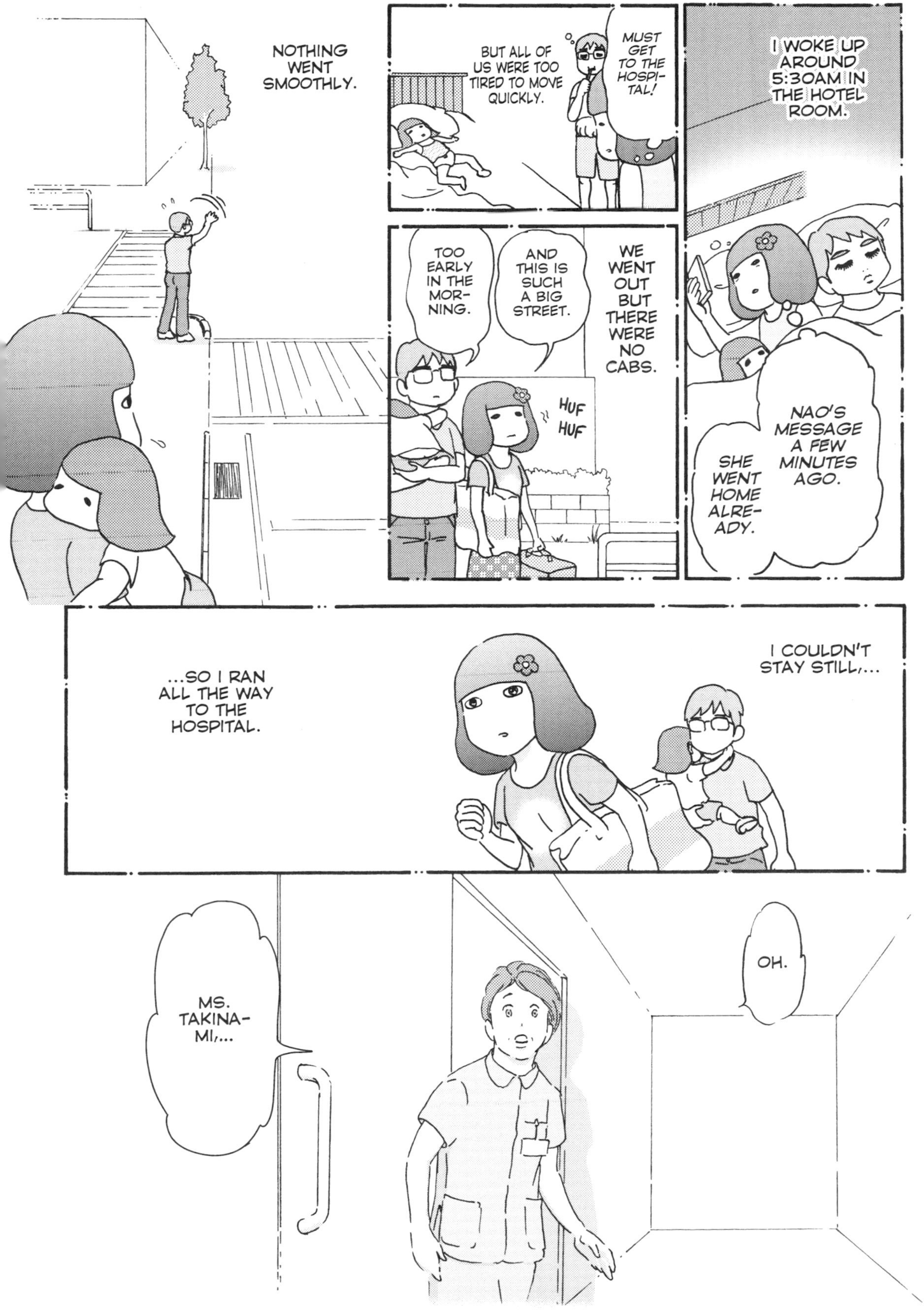
I WOKE UP AROUND 5:30AM IN THE HOTEL ROOM.
NAO'S MESSAGE A FEW MINUTES AGO.
SHE WENT HOME ALREADY.
MUST GET TO THE HOSPITAL!
BUT ALL OF US WERE TOO TIRED TO MOVE QUICKLY.
WE WENT OUT BUT THERE WERE NO CABS.
AND THIS IS SUCH A BIG STREET.
TOO EARLY IN THE MORNING.
HUF HUF
NOTHING WENT SMOOTHLY.
I COULDN'T STAY STILL,...
...SO I RAN ALL THE WAY TO THE HOSPITAL.
OH.
MS. TAKINAMI,...

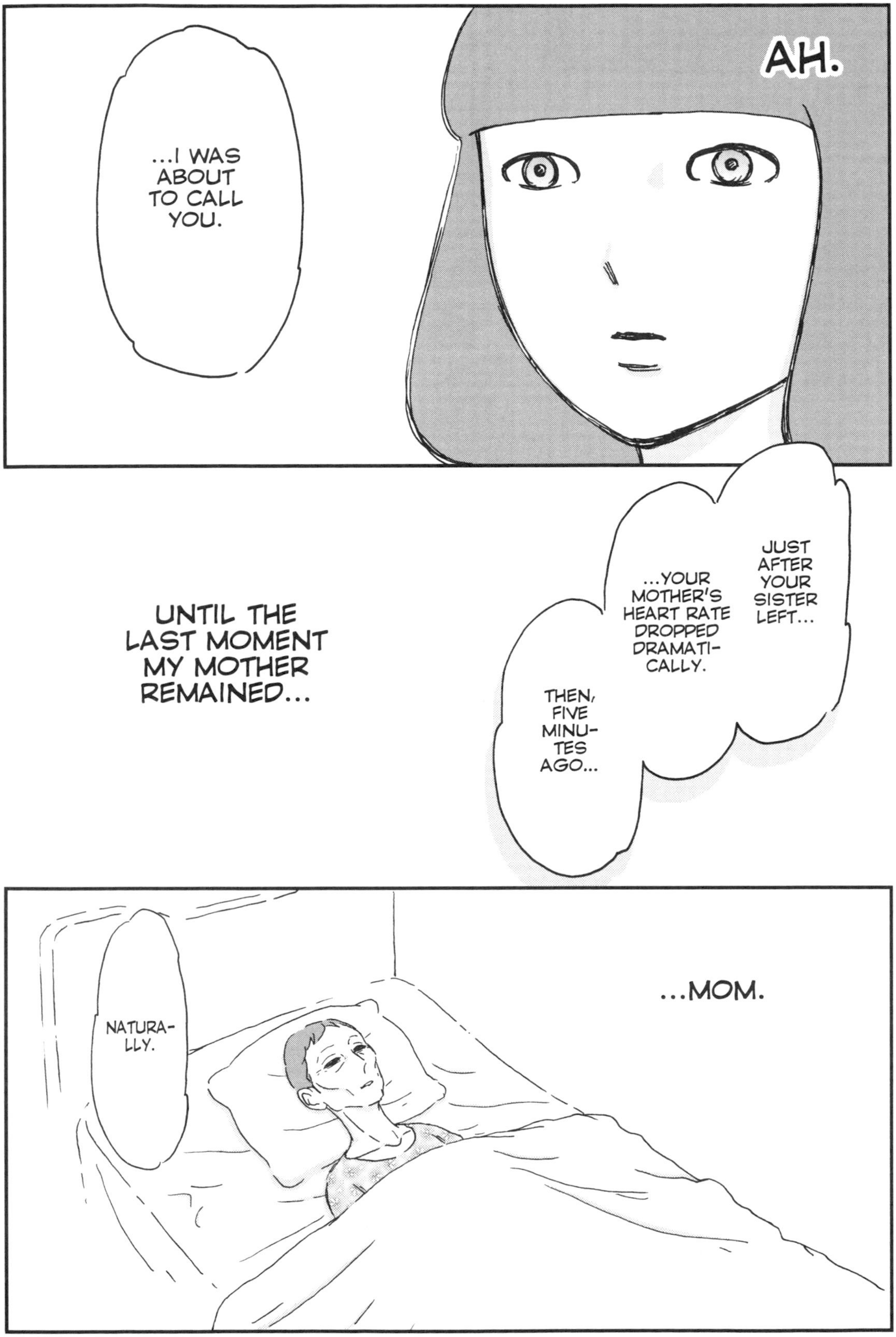
AH.
...I WAS ABOUT TO CALL YOU.
JUST AFTER YOUR SISTER LEFT...
...YOUR MOTHER'S HEART RATE DROPPED DRAMATI-CALLY.
THEN, FIVE MINU-TES AGO...
UNTIL THE LAST MOMENT MY MOTHER REMAINED...
...MOM.
NATURA-LLY.

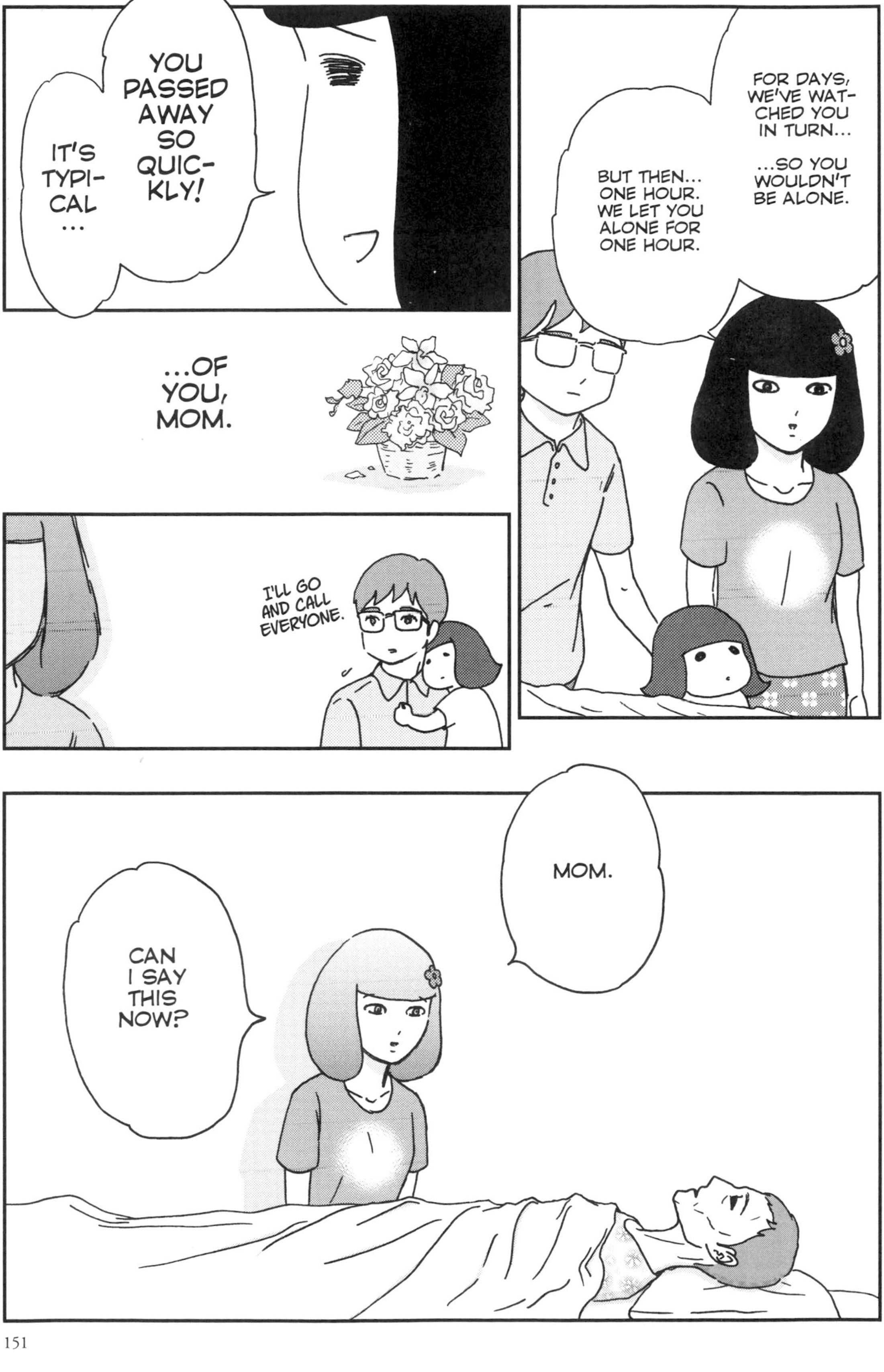
FOR DAYS, WE'VE WAT-CHED YOU IN TURN...
...SO YOU WOULDN'T BE ALONE.
BUT THEN... ONE HOUR. WE LET YOU ALONE FOR ONE HOUR.
YOU PASSED AWAY SO QUIC-KLY!
IT'S TYPI-CAL...
...OF YOU, MOM.
I'LL GO AND CALL EVERYONE.
MOM.
CAN I SAY THIS NOW?

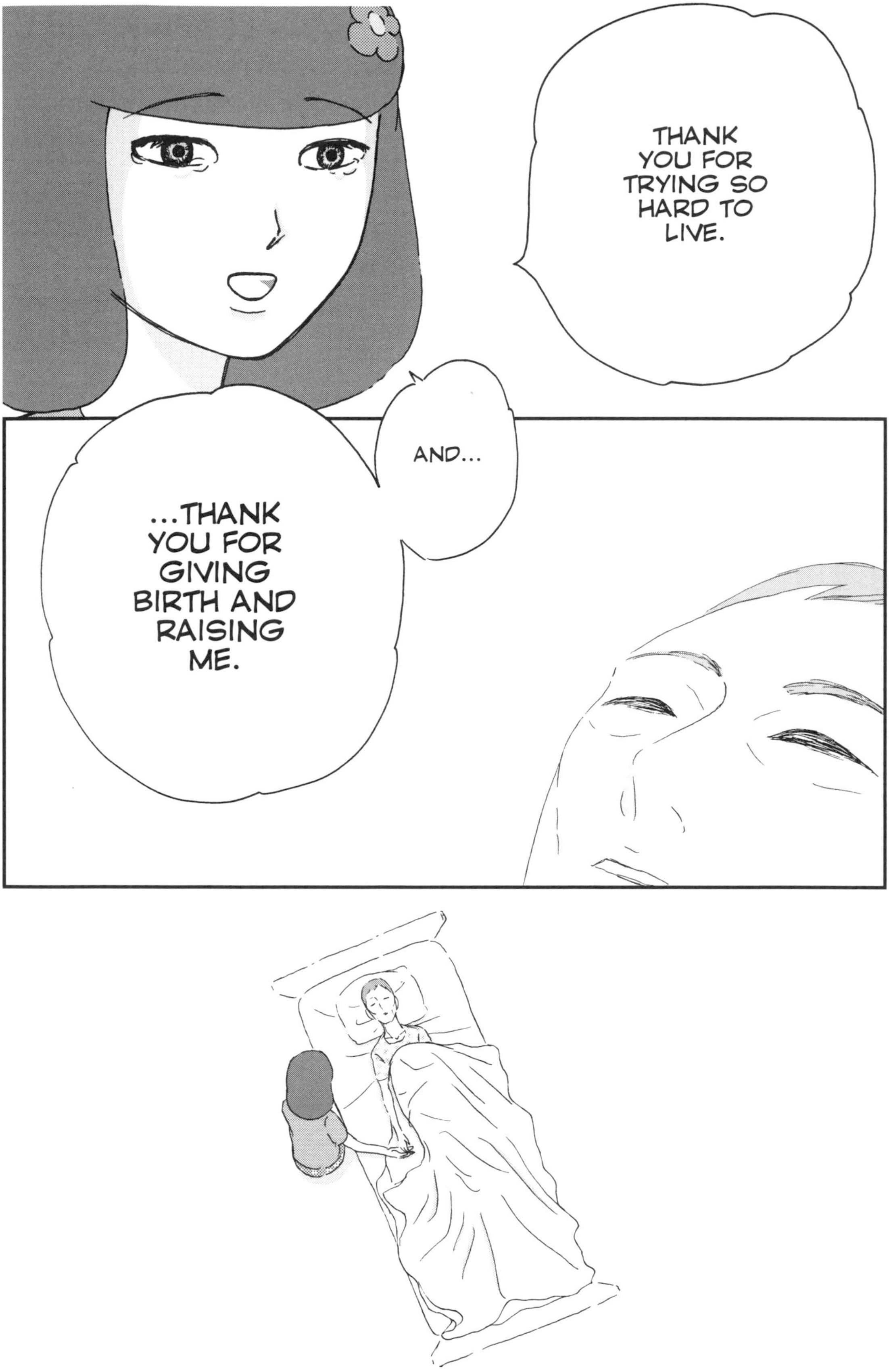
THANK YOU FOR TRYING SO HARD TO LIVE.
AND...
...THANK YOU FOR GIVING BIRTH AND RAISING ME.

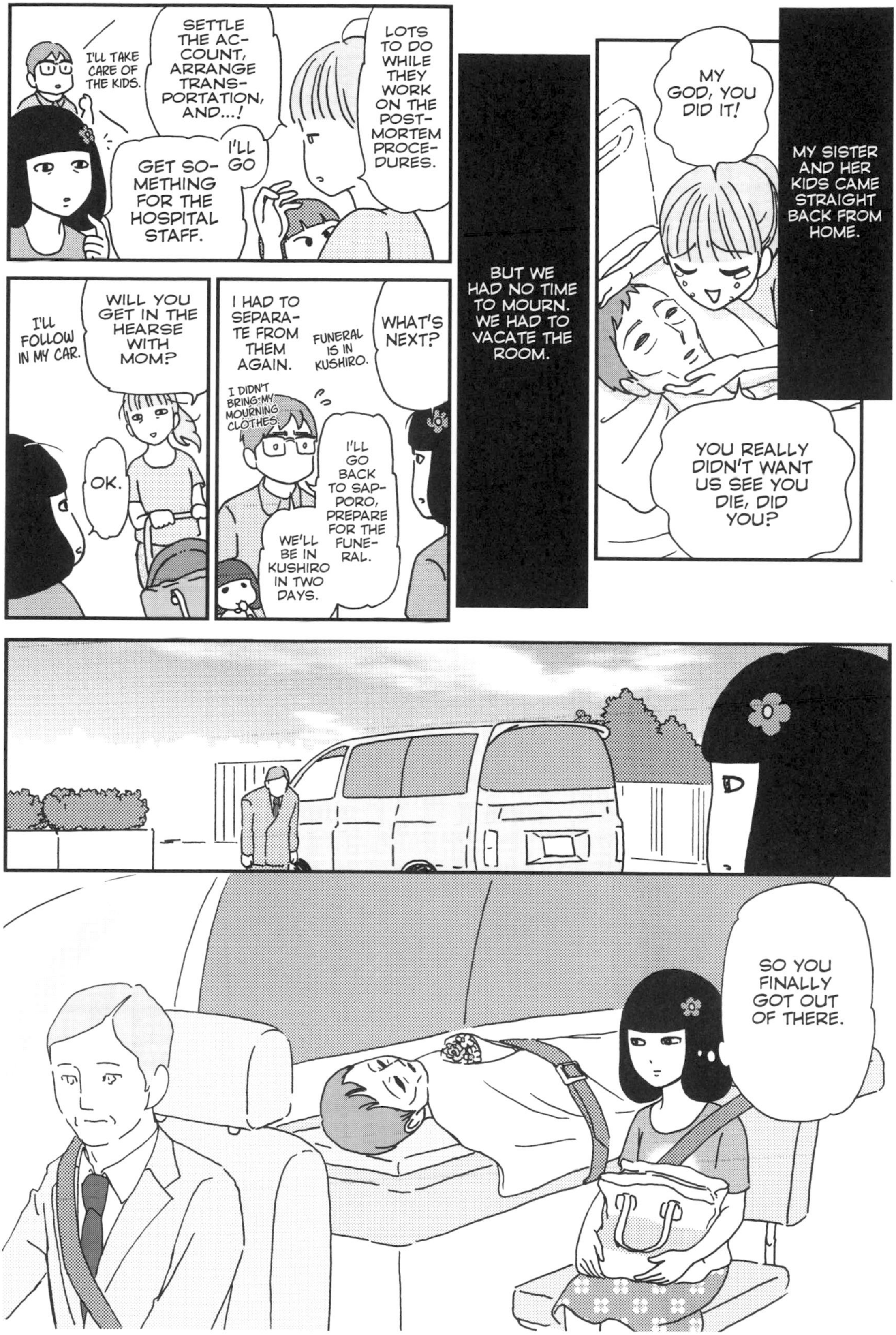
MY SISTER AND HER KIDS CAME STRAIGHT BACK FROM HOME.
MY GOD, YOU DID IT!
YOU REALLY DIDN'T WANT US SEE YOU DIE, DID YOU?
BUT WE HAD NO TIME TO MOURN. WE HAD TO VACATE THE ROOM.
LOTS TO DO WHILE THEY WORK ON THE POST-MORTEM PROCEDURES.
SETTLE THE ACCOUNT, ARRANGE TRANSPORTATION, AND...!
I'LL GO
GET SOMETHING FOR THE HOSPITAL STAFF.
I'LL TAKE CARE OF THE KIDS.
WHAT'S NEXT?
FUNERAL IS IN KUSHIRO.
I HAD TO SEPARATE FROM THEM AGAIN.
I DIDN'T BRING MY MOURNING CLOTHES.
I'LL GO BACK TO SAPPORO, PREPARE FOR THE FUNERAL.
WE'LL BE IN KUSHIRO IN TWO DAYS.
WILL YOU GET IN THE HEARSE WITH MOM?
I'LL FOLLOW IN MY CAR.
OK.
SO YOU FINALLY GOT OUT OF THERE.

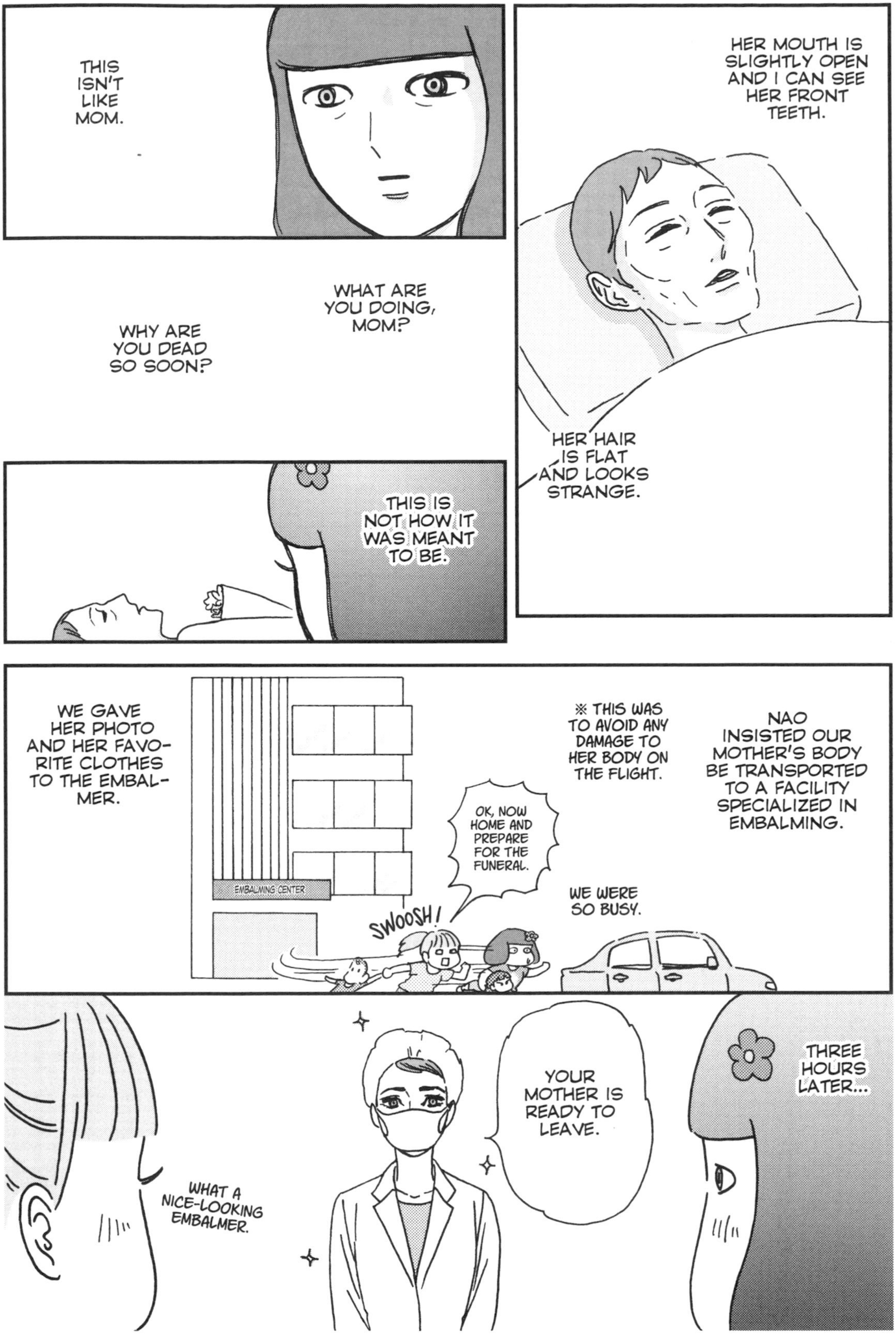
HER MOUTH IS SLIGHTLY OPEN AND I CAN SEE HER FRONT TEETH.
HER HAIR IS FLAT AND LOOKS STRANGE.
THIS ISN'T LIKE MOM.
WHAT ARE YOU DOING, MOM?
WHY ARE YOU DEAD SO SOON?
THIS IS NOT HOW IT WAS MEANT TO BE.
NAO INSISTED OUR MOTHER'S BODY BE TRANSPORTED TO A FACILITY SPECIALIZED IN EMBALMING.
※ THIS WAS TO AVOID ANY DAMAGE TO HER BODY ON THE FLIGHT.
WE GAVE HER PHOTO AND HER FAVORITE CLOTHES TO THE EMBALMER.
OK, NOW HOME AND PREPARE FOR THE FUNERAL.
WE WERE SO BUSY.
SWOOSH!
EMBALMING CENTER
THREE HOURS LATER...
YOUR MOTHER IS READY TO LEAVE.
WHAT A NICE-LOOKING EMBALMER.

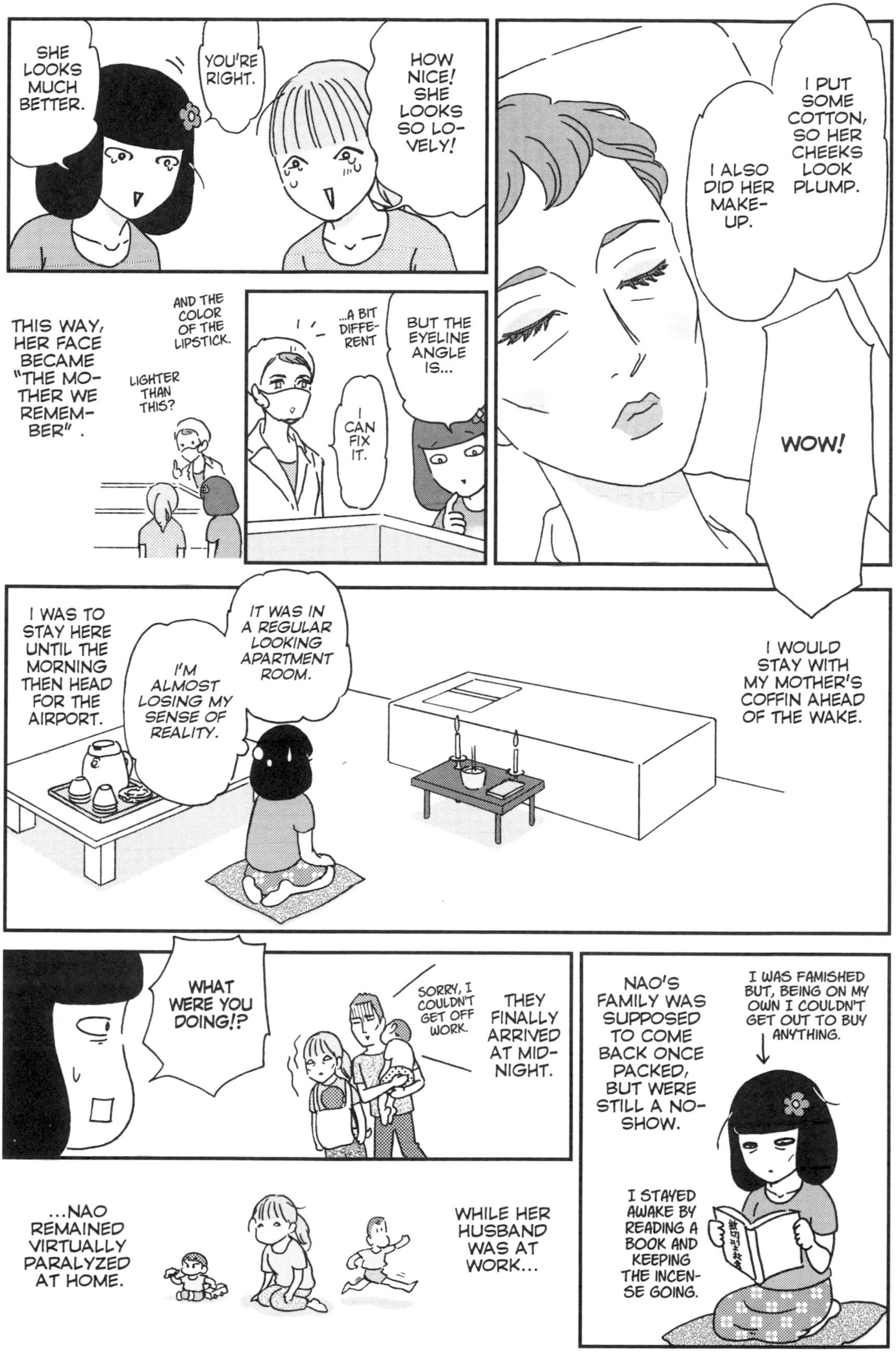

I PUT SOME COTTON, SO HER CHEEKS LOOK PLUMP.
I ALSO DID HER MAKE-UP.
WOW!
HOW NICE! SHE LOOKS SO LO-VELY!
YOU'RE RIGHT.
SHE LOOKS MUCH BETTER.
BUT THE EYELINE ANGLE IS...
...A BIT DIFFE-RENT
I CAN FIX IT.
AND THE COLOR OF THE LIPSTICK.
LIGHTER THAN THIS?
THIS WAY, HER FACE BECAME "THE MO-THER WE REMEM-BER".
I WOULD STAY WITH MY MOTHER'S COFFIN AHEAD OF THE WAKE.
IT WAS IN A REGULAR LOOKING APARTMENT ROOM.
I'M ALMOST LOSING MY SENSE OF REALITY.
I WAS TO STAY HERE UNTIL THE MORNING THEN HEAD FOR THE AIRPORT.
NAO'S FAMILY WAS SUPPOSED TO COME BACK ONCE PACKED, BUT WERE STILL A NO-SHOW.
I WAS FAMISHED BUT, BEING ON MY OWN I COULDN'T GET OUT TO BUY ANYTHING.
I STAYED AWAKE BY READING A BOOK AND KEEPING THE INCEN-SE GOING.
THEY FINALLY ARRIVED AT MID-NIGHT.
SORRY, I COULDN'T GET OFF WORK.
WHAT WERE YOU DOING!?
WHILE HER HUSBAND WAS AT WORK...
...NAO REMAINED VIRTUALLY PARALYZED AT HOME.

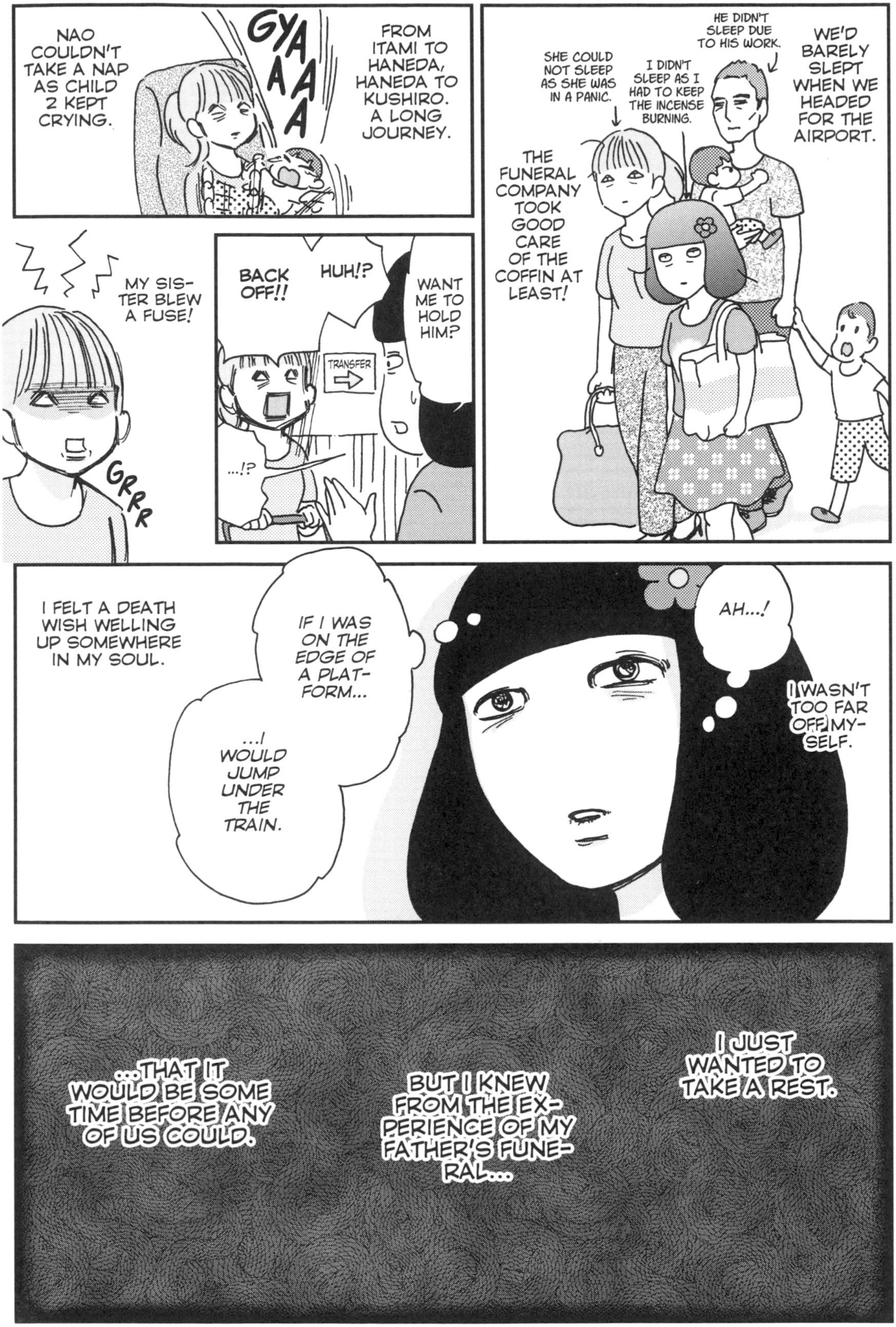
WE'D BARELY SLEPT WHEN WE HEADED FOR THE AIRPORT.
HE DIDN'T SLEEP DUE TO HIS WORK.
I DIDN'T SLEEP AS I HAD TO KEEP THE INCENSE BURNING.
SHE COULD NOT SLEEP AS SHE WAS IN A PANIC.
THE FUNERAL COMPANY TOOK GOOD CARE OF THE COFFIN AT LEAST!
FROM ITAMI TO HANEDA, HANEDA TO KUSHIRO. A LONG JOURNEY.
GYAAAA
NAO COULDN'T TAKE A NAP AS CHILD 2 KEPT CRYING.
WANT ME TO HOLD HIM?
HUH!?
BACK OFF!!
TRANSFER
...!?
MY SISTER BLEW A FUSE!
GRRR
AH...!
I WASN'T TOO FAR OFF MYSELF.
IF I WAS ON THE EDGE OF A PLATFORM...
...I WOULD JUMP UNDER THE TRAIN.
I FELT A DEATH WISH WELLING UP SOMEWHERE IN MY SOUL.
I JUST WANTED TO TAKE A REST.
BUT I KNEW FROM THE EXPERIENCE OF MY FATHER'S FUNERAL...
...THAT IT WOULD BE SOME TIME BEFORE ANY OF US COULD.

CHAPTER 17

FINALLY, WE ARE GOING HOME MOM

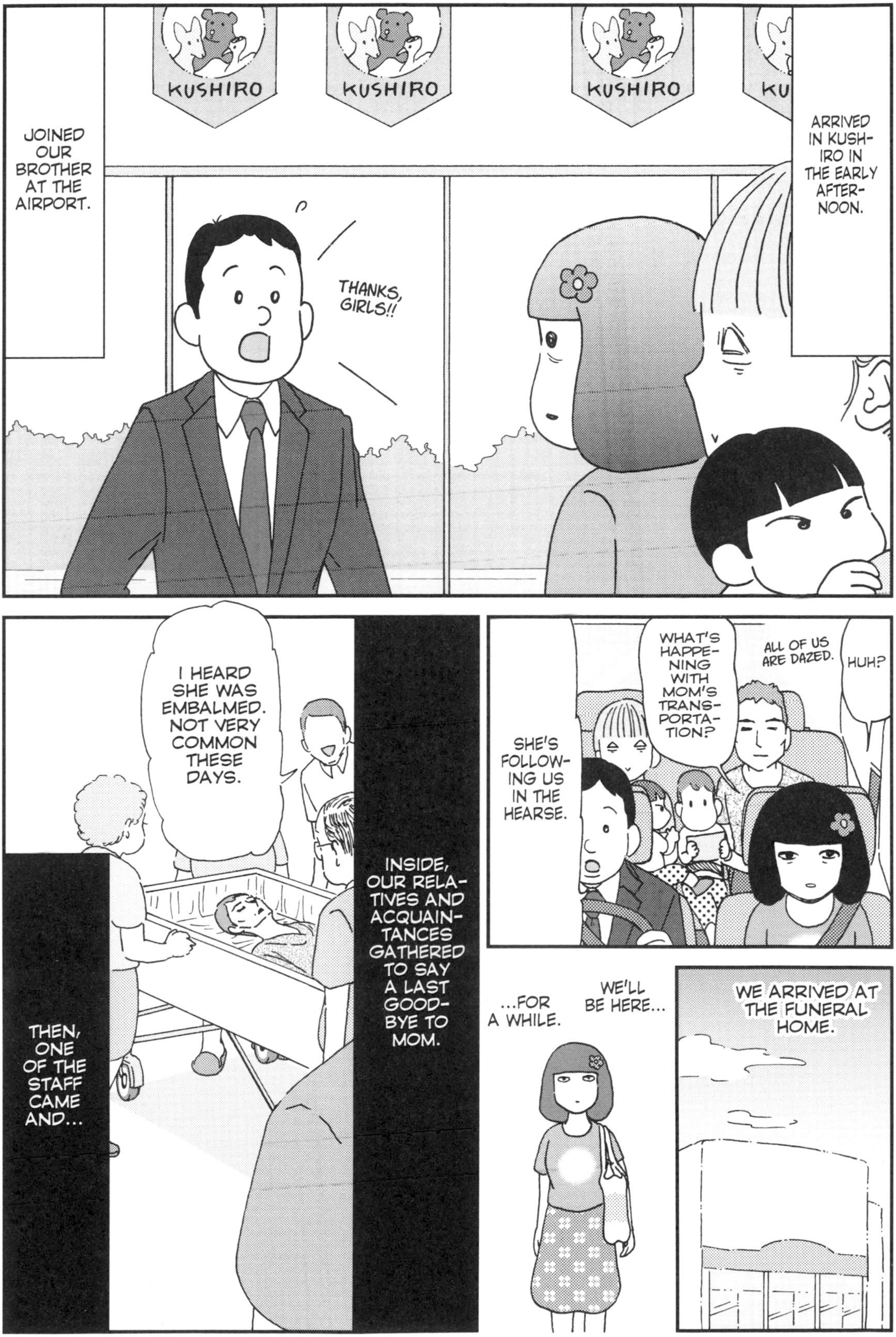
ARRIVED IN KUSHIRO IN THE EARLY AFTERNOON.
KUSHIRO
KUSHIRO
KUSHIRO
THANKS, GIRLS!!
JOINED OUR BROTHER AT THE AIRPORT.
HUH?
ALL OF US ARE DAZED.
WHAT'S HAPPENING WITH MOM'S TRANSPORTATION?
SHE'S FOLLOWING US IN THE HEARSE.
WE ARRIVED AT THE FUNERAL HOME.
WE'LL BE HERE...
...FOR A WHILE.
INSIDE, OUR RELATIVES AND ACQUAINTANCES GATHERED TO SAY A LAST GOODBYE TO MOM.
I HEARD SHE WAS EMBALMED. NOT VERY COMMON THESE DAYS.
THEN, ONE OF THE STAFF CAME AND...

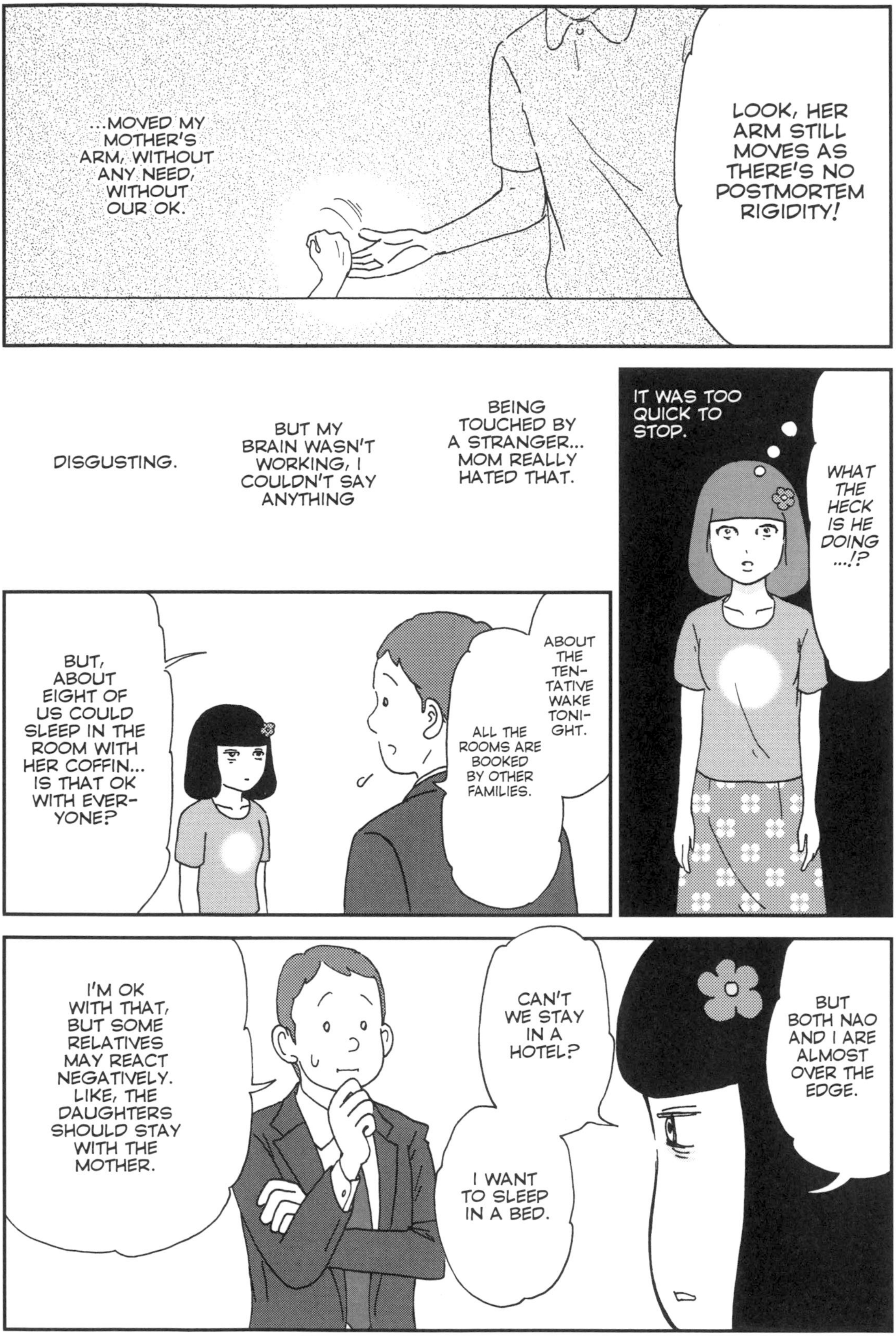
LOOK, HER ARM STILL MOVES AS THERE'S NO POSTMORTEM RIGIDITY!
...MOVED MY MOTHER'S ARM, WITHOUT ANY NEED, WITHOUT OUR OK.
IT WAS TOO QUICK TO STOP.
WHAT THE HECK IS HE DOING ...!?
BEING TOUCHED BY A STRANGER... MOM REALLY HATED THAT.
BUT MY BRAIN WASN'T WORKING, I COULDN'T SAY ANYTHING
DISGUSTING.
ABOUT THE TEN-TATIVE WAKE TONI-GHT.
ALL THE ROOMS ARE BOOKED BY OTHER FAMILIES.
BUT, ABOUT EIGHT OF US COULD SLEEP IN THE ROOM WITH HER COFFIN... IS THAT OK WITH EVER-YONE?
BUT BOTH NAO AND I ARE ALMOST OVER THE EDGE.
CAN'T WE STAY IN A HOTEL?
I WANT TO SLEEP IN A BED.
I'M OK WITH THAT, BUT SOME RELATIVES MAY REACT NEGATIVELY. LIKE, THE DAUGHTERS SHOULD STAY WITH THE MOTHER.

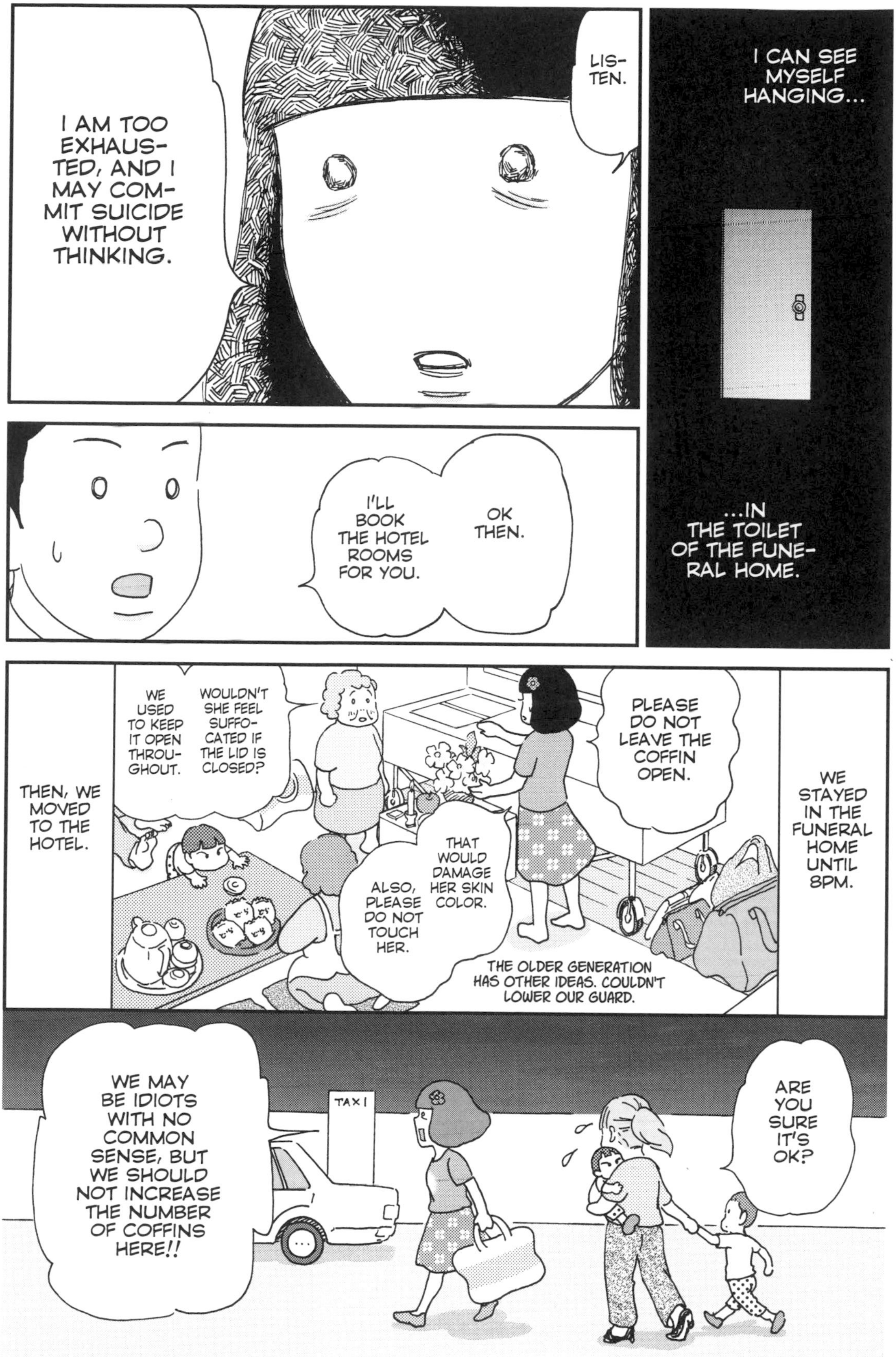
I CAN SEE MYSELF HANGING...
...IN THE TOILET OF THE FUNERAL HOME.
LISTEN.
I AM TOO EXHAUSTED, AND I MAY COMMIT SUICIDE WITHOUT THINKING.
OK THEN.
I'LL BOOK THE HOTEL ROOMS FOR YOU.
WE STAYED IN THE FUNERAL HOME UNTIL 8PM.
PLEASE DO NOT LEAVE THE COFFIN OPEN.
WOULDN'T SHE FEEL SUFFOCATED IF THE LID IS CLOSED?
WE USED TO KEEP IT OPEN THROUGHOUT.
THAT WOULD DAMAGE HER SKIN COLOR.
ALSO, PLEASE DO NOT TOUCH HER.
THE OLDER GENERATION HAS OTHER IDEAS. COULDN'T LOWER OUR GUARD.
THEN, WE MOVED TO THE HOTEL.
ARE YOU SURE IT'S OK?
TAXI
WE MAY BE IDIOTS WITH NO COMMON SENSE, BUT WE SHOULD NOT INCREASE THE NUMBER OF COFFINS HERE!!

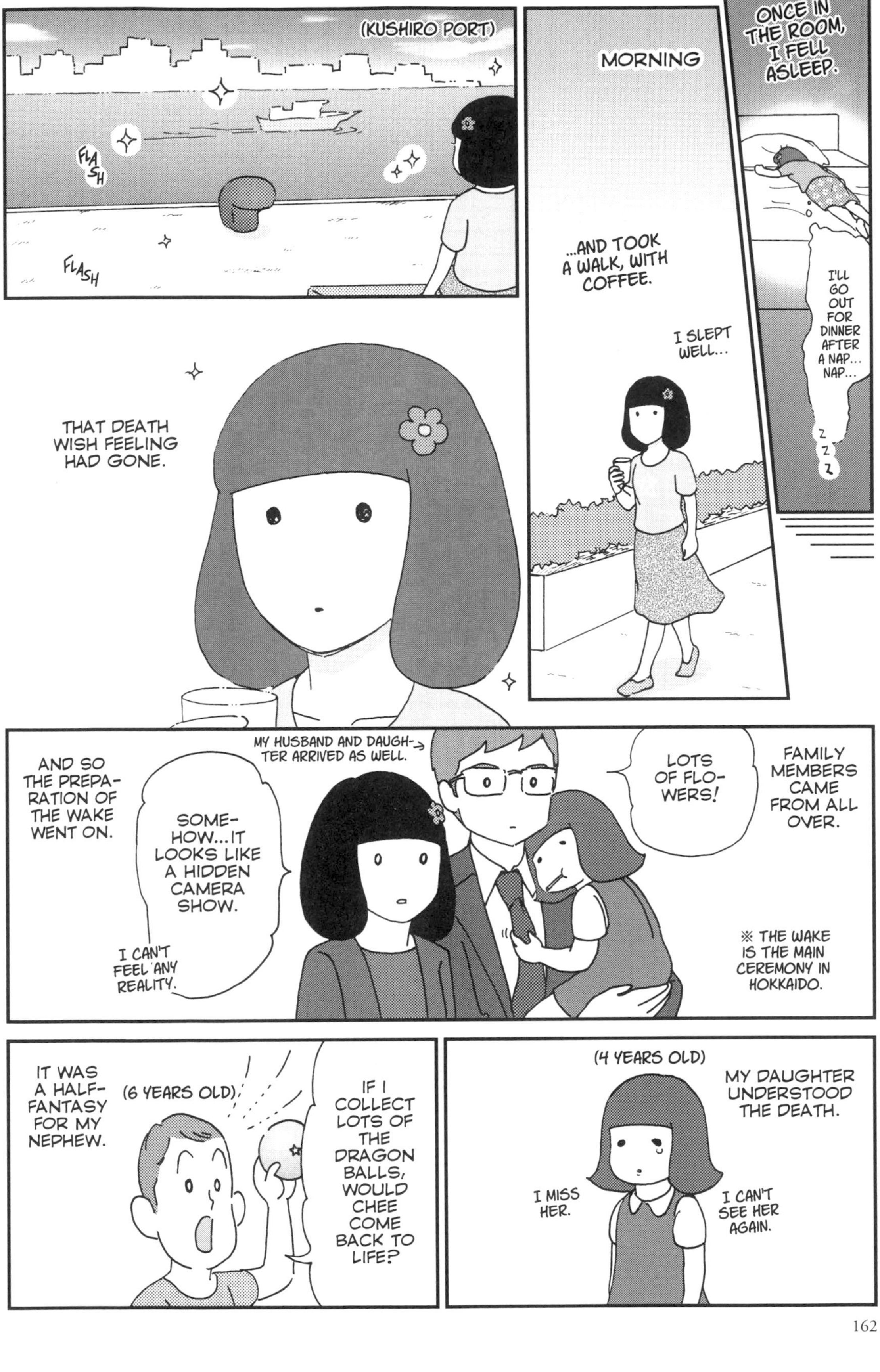
ONCE IN THE ROOM, I FELL ASLEEP.
I'LL GO OUT FOR DINNER AFTER A NAP... NAP...
Z Z Z
MORNING
...AND TOOK A WALK, WITH COFFEE.
I SLEPT WELL...
(KUSHIRO PORT)
FLASH
FLASH
THAT DEATH WISH FEELING HAD GONE.
FAMILY MEMBERS CAME FROM ALL OVER.
LOTS OF FLO-WERS!
※ THE WAKE IS THE MAIN CEREMONY IN HOKKAIDO.
MY HUSBAND AND DAUGH-TER ARRIVED AS WELL.
AND SO THE PREPA-RATION OF THE WAKE WENT ON.
SOME-HOW...IT LOOKS LIKE A HIDDEN CAMERA SHOW.
I CAN'T FEEL ANY REALITY.
(4 YEARS OLD)
MY DAUGHTER UNDERSTOOD THE DEATH.
I CAN'T SEE HER AGAIN.
I MISS HER.
IF I COLLECT LOTS OF THE DRAGON BALLS, WOULD CHEE COME BACK TO LIFE?
(6 YEARS OLD)
IT WAS A HALF-FANTASY FOR MY NEPHEW.

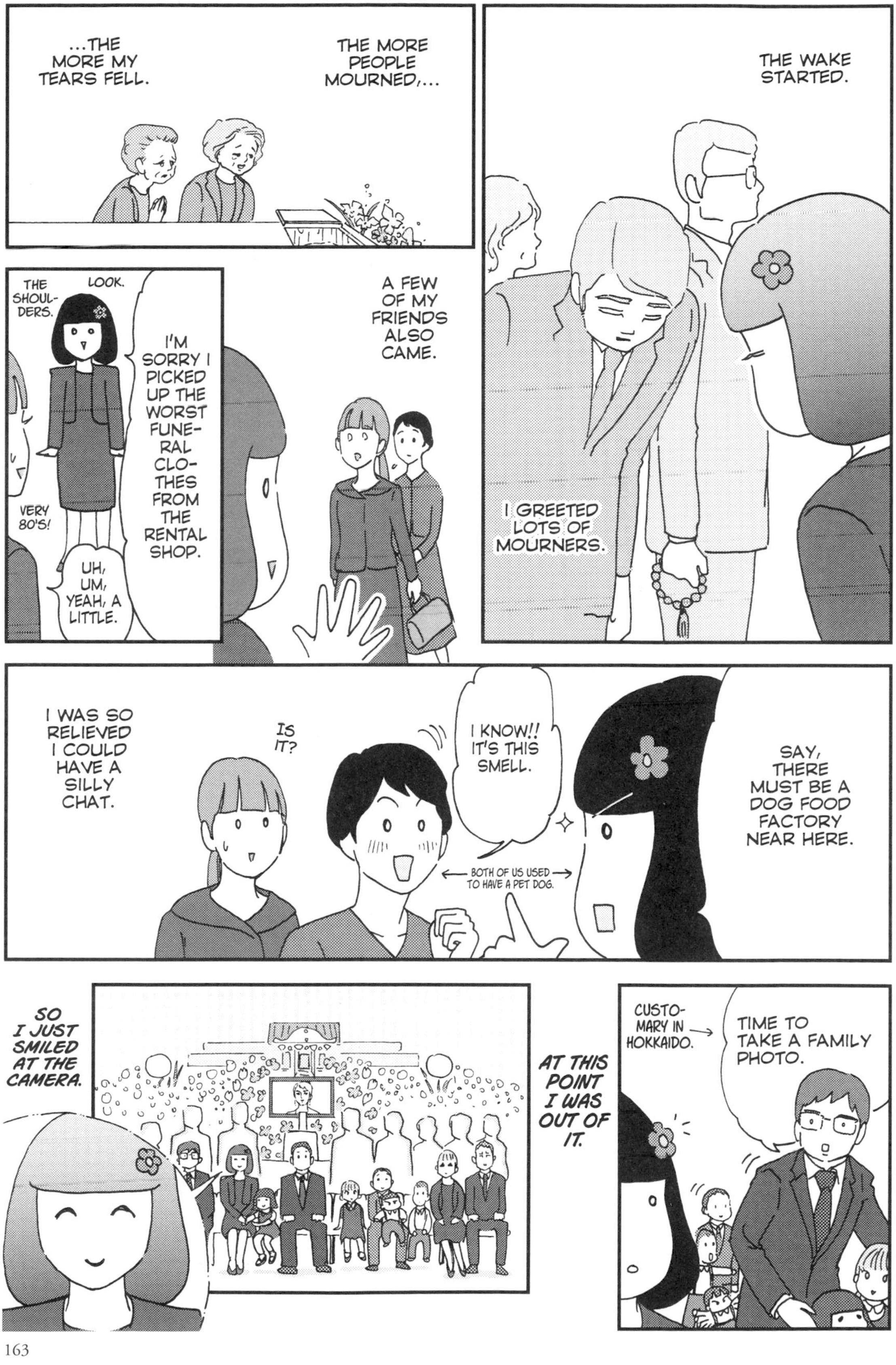

THE WAKE STARTED.
I GREETED LOTS OF MOURNERS.
THE MORE PEOPLE MOURNED,...
...THE MORE MY TEARS FELL.
A FEW OF MY FRIENDS ALSO CAME.
I'M SORRY I PICKED UP THE WORST FUNERAL CLOTHES FROM THE RENTAL SHOP.
LOOK.
THE SHOULDERS.
VERY 80'S!
UH, UM, YEAH, A LITTLE.
SAY, THERE MUST BE A DOG FOOD FACTORY NEAR HERE.
BOTH OF US USED TO HAVE A PET DOG.
I KNOW!! IT'S THIS SMELL.
IS IT?
I WAS SO RELIEVED I COULD HAVE A SILLY CHAT.
TIME TO TAKE A FAMILY PHOTO.
CUSTOMARY IN HOKKAIDO.
AT THIS POINT I WAS OUT OF IT.
SO I JUST SMILED AT THE CAMERA.

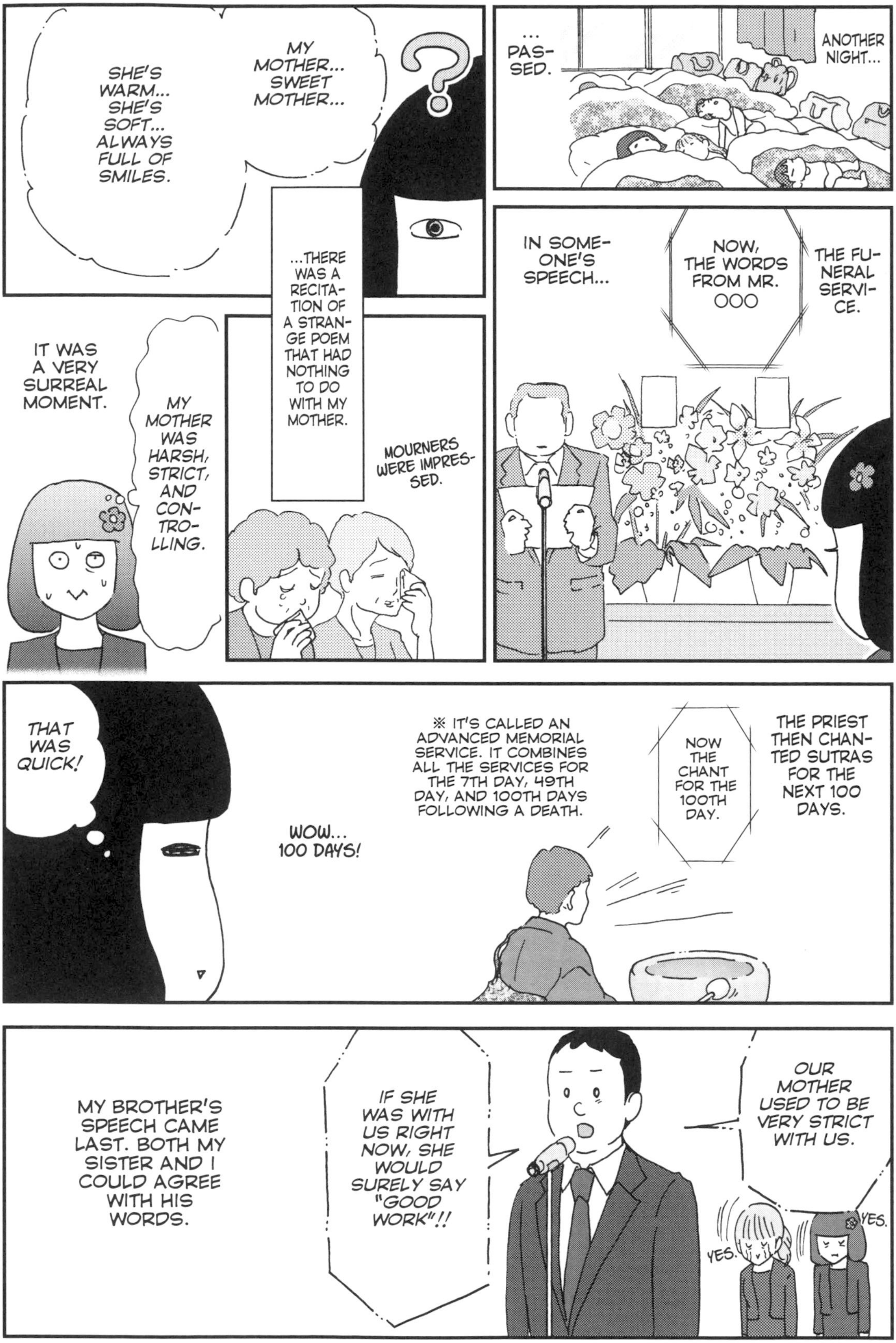
ANOTHER NIGHT...
... PAS-SED.
THE FU-NERAL SERVI-CE.
NOW, THE WORDS FROM MR. OOO
IN SOME-ONE'S SPEECH...
...THERE WAS A RECITA-TION OF A STRAN-GE POEM THAT HAD NOTHING TO DO WITH MY MOTHER.
MY MOTHER... SWEET MOTHER...
SHE'S WARM... SHE'S SOFT... ALWAYS FULL OF SMILES.
MOURNERS WERE IMPRES-SED.
MY MOTHER WAS HARSH, STRICT, AND CON-TRO-LLING.
IT WAS A VERY SURREAL MOMENT.
THE PRIEST THEN CHAN-TED SUTRAS FOR THE NEXT 100 DAYS.
NOW THE CHANT FOR THE 100TH DAY.
※ IT'S CALLED AN ADVANCED MEMORIAL SERVICE. IT COMBINES ALL THE SERVICES FOR THE 7TH DAY, 49TH DAY, AND 100TH DAYS FOLLOWING A DEATH.
WOW... 100 DAYS!
THAT WAS QUICK!
OUR MOTHER USED TO BE VERY STRICT WITH US.
YES.
YES.
IF SHE WAS WITH US RIGHT NOW, SHE WOULD SURELY SAY "GOOD WORK"!!
MY BROTHER'S SPEECH CAME LAST. BOTH MY SISTER AND I COULD AGREE WITH HIS WORDS.

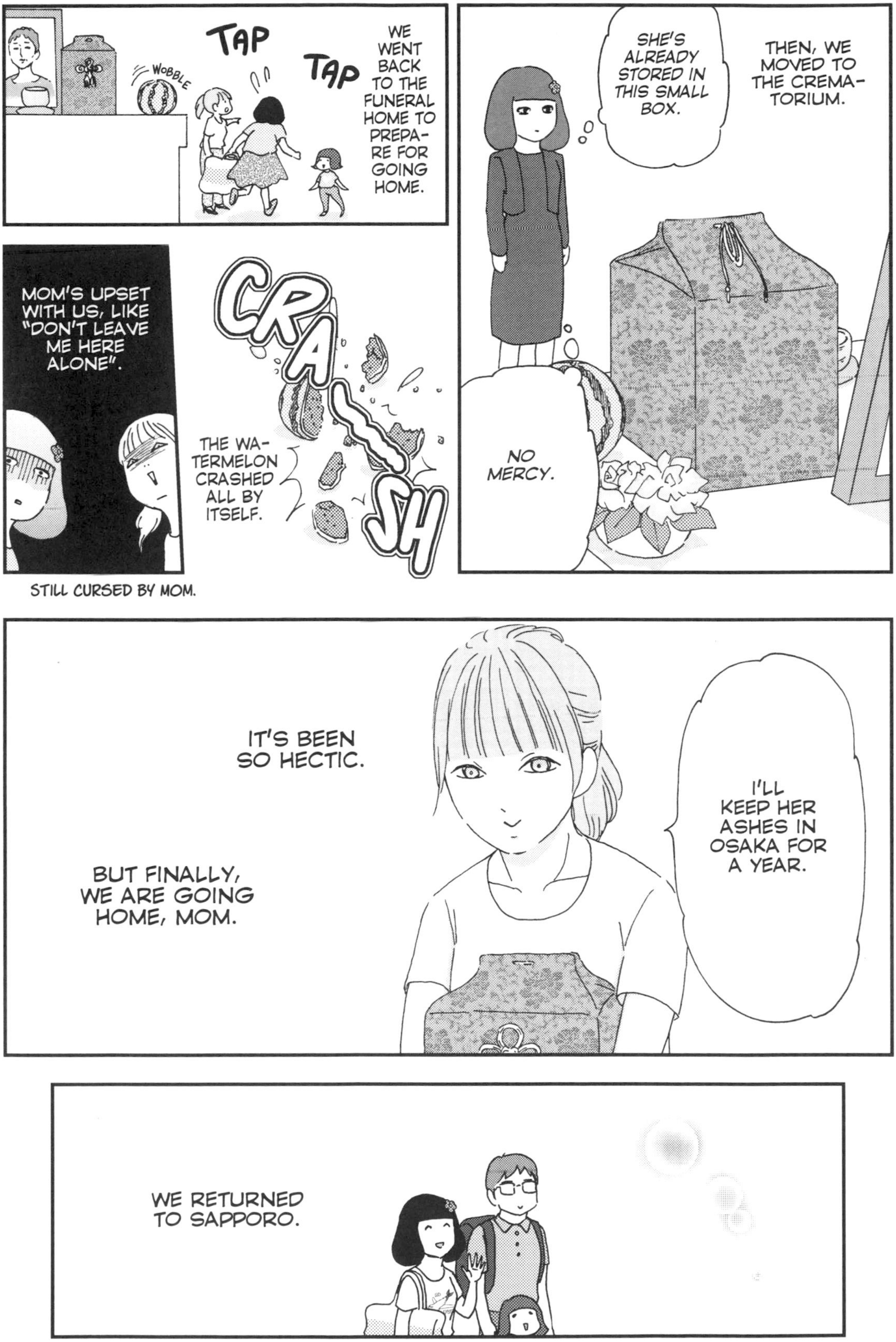
THEN, WE MOVED TO THE CREMATORIUM.
SHE'S ALREADY STORED IN THIS SMALL BOX.
NO MERCY.
WE WENT BACK TO THE FUNERAL HOME TO PREPARE FOR GOING HOME.
TAP
TAP
WOBBLE
CRASH
THE WATERMELON CRASHED ALL BY ITSELF.
MOM'S UPSET WITH US, LIKE "DON'T LEAVE ME HERE ALONE".
STILL CURSED BY MOM.
I'LL KEEP HER ASHES IN OSAKA FOR A YEAR.
IT'S BEEN SO HECTIC.
BUT FINALLY, WE ARE GOING HOME, MOM.
WE RETURNED TO SAPPORO.

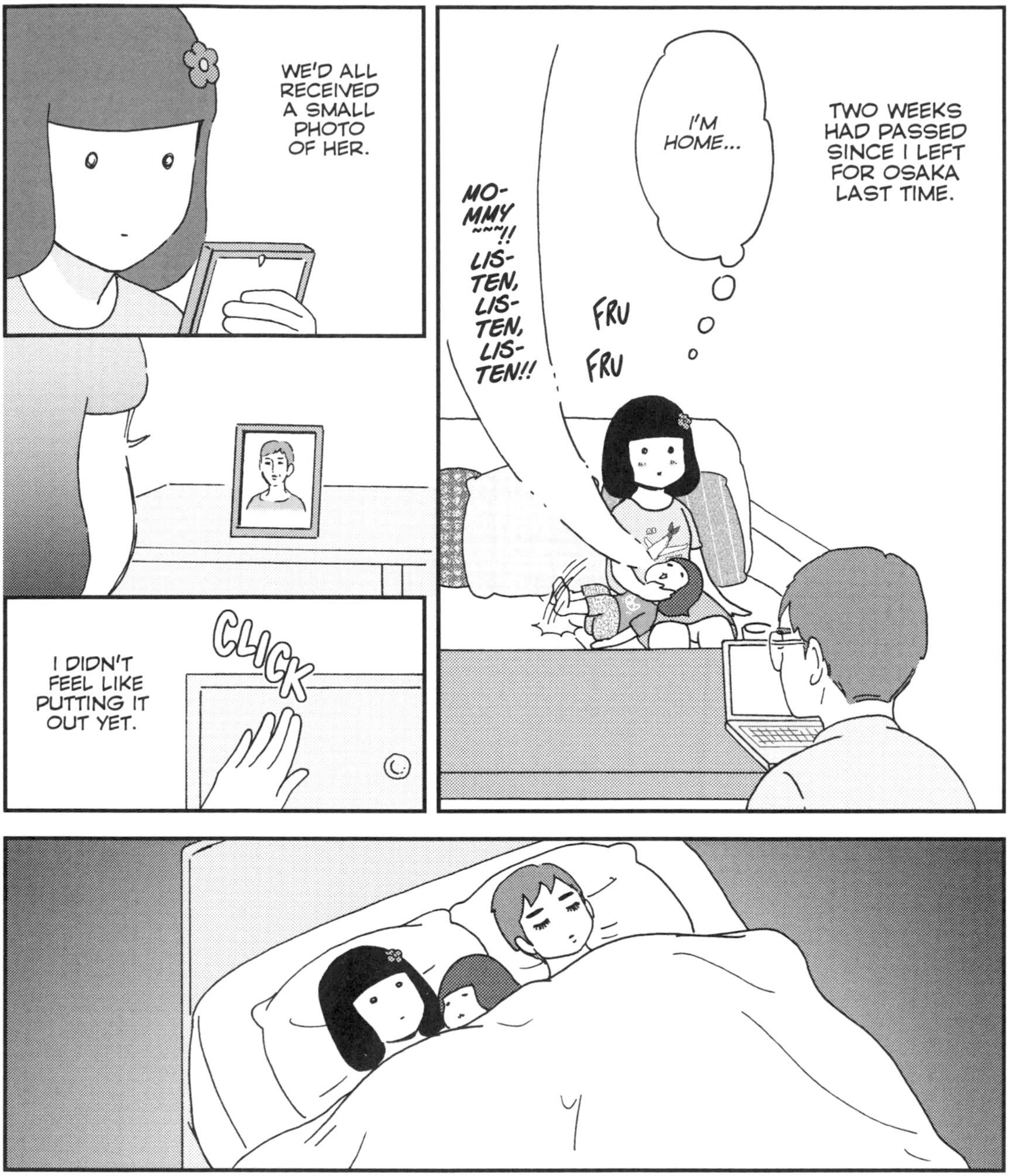
TWO WEEKS HAD PASSED SINCE I LEFT FOR OSAKA LAST TIME.
I'M HOME...
MO-MMY~~~!! LIS-TEN, LIS-TEN, LIS-TEN!!
FRU FRU
WE'D ALL RECEIVED A SMALL PHOTO OF HER.
CLICK
I DIDN'T FEEL LIKE PUTTING IT OUT YET.

"I CAN FINALLY TAKE A REST."

BOTH MENTALLY AND PHYSICALLY,...

...THAT WAS THE ONLY THING I COULD FEEL.

CHAPTER 18

I CARRIED ON WALKING

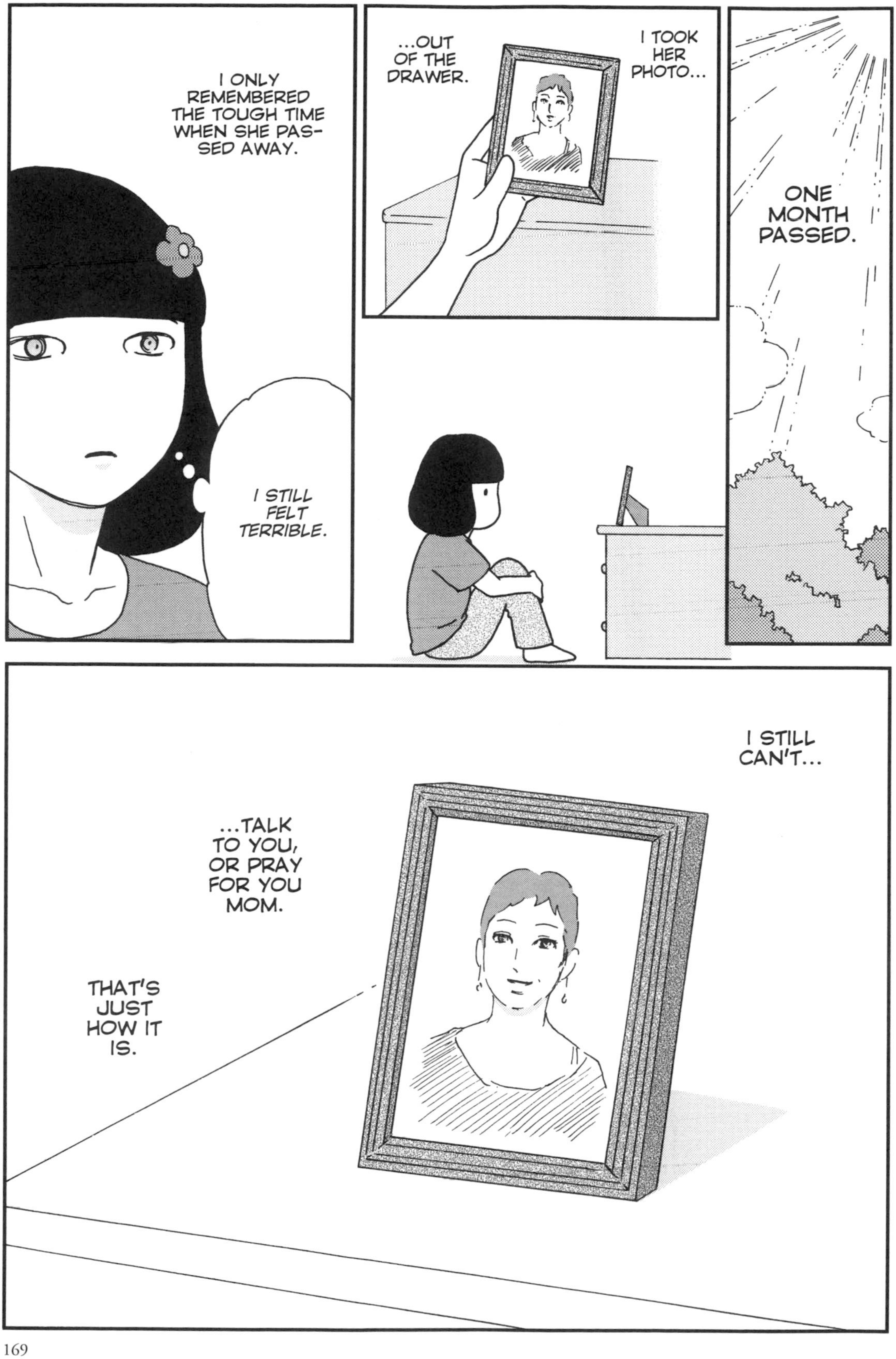
ONE MONTH PASSED.
I TOOK HER PHOTO...
...OUT OF THE DRAWER.
I ONLY REMEMBERED THE TOUGH TIME WHEN SHE PAS-SED AWAY.
I STILL FELT TERRIBLE.
I STILL CAN'T...
...TALK TO YOU, OR PRAY FOR YOU MOM.
THAT'S JUST HOW IT IS.

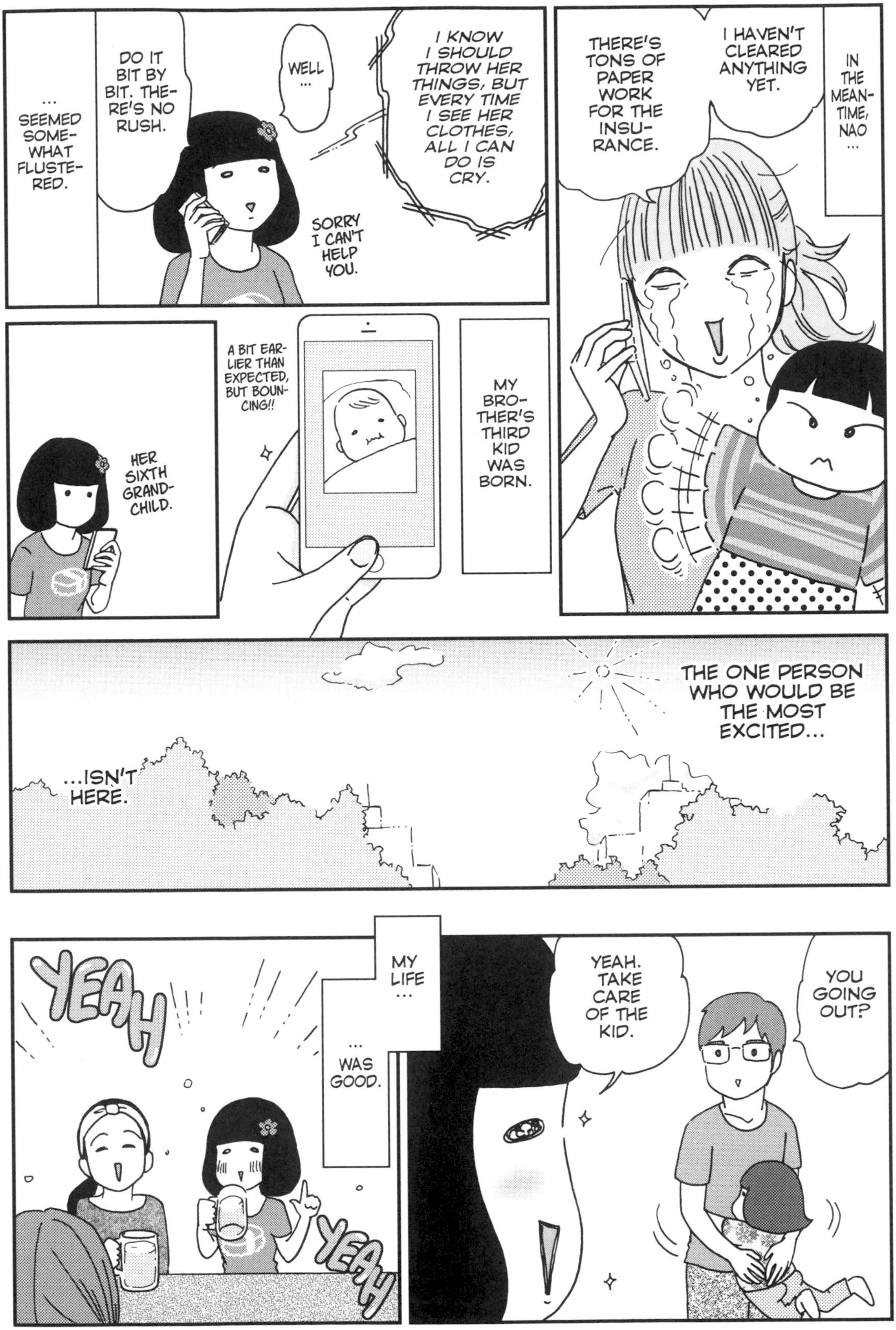
IN THE MEANTIME, NAO...
I HAVEN'T CLEARED ANYTHING YET.
THERE'S TONS OF PAPER WORK FOR THE INSURANCE.
I KNOW I SHOULD THROW HER THINGS, BUT EVERY TIME I SEE HER CLOTHES, ALL I CAN DO IS CRY.
WELL...
SORRY I CAN'T HELP YOU.
DO IT BIT BY BIT. THERE'S NO RUSH.
...SEEMED SOMEWHAT FLUSTERED.
MY BROTHER'S THIRD KID WAS BORN.
A BIT EARLIER THAN EXPECTED, BUT BOUNCING!!
HER SIXTH GRANDCHILD.
THE ONE PERSON WHO WOULD BE THE MOST EXCITED...
...ISN'T HERE.
YOU GOING OUT?
YEAH. TAKE CARE OF THE KID.
MY LIFE...
...WAS GOOD.
YEAH
YEAH

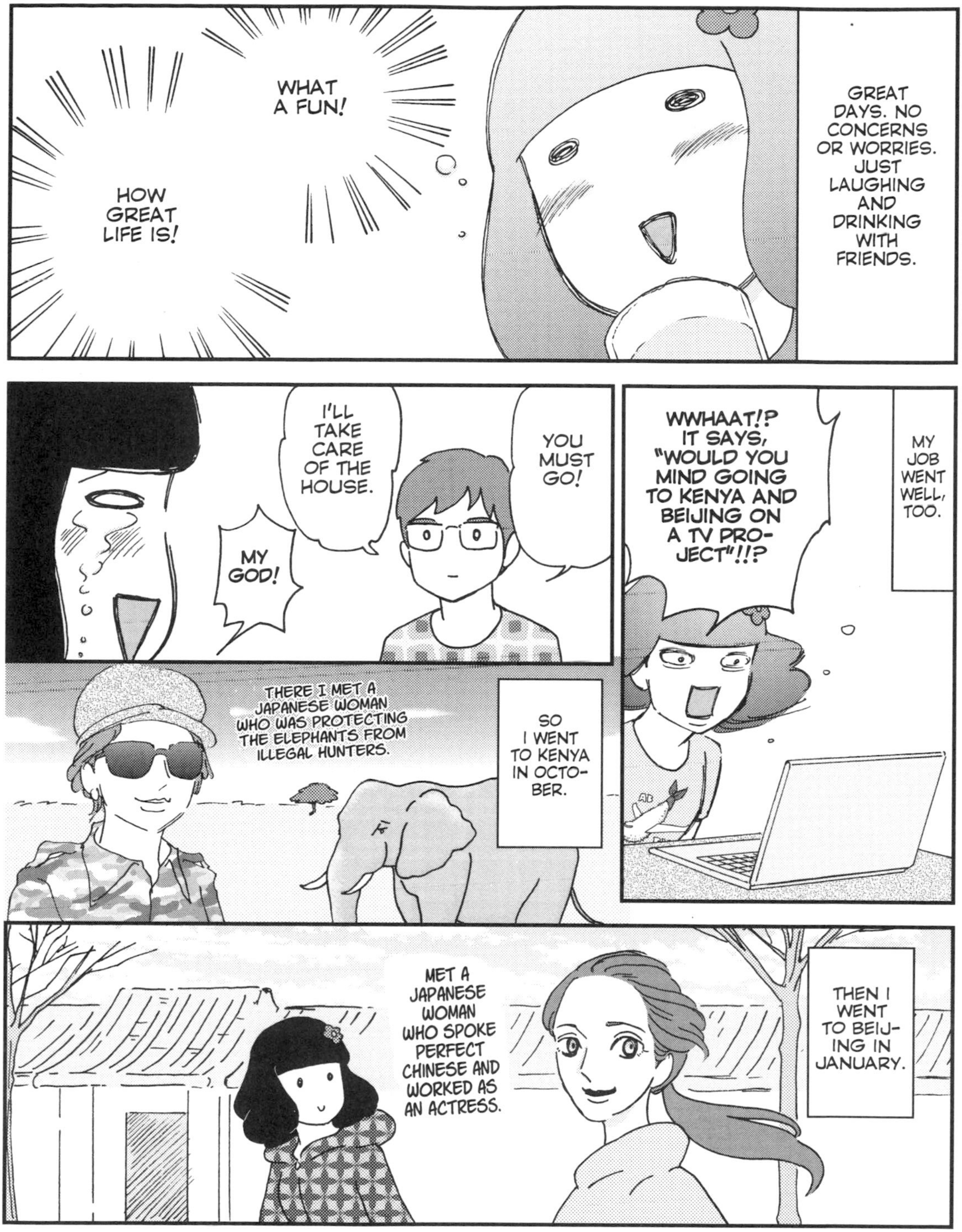
GREAT DAYS. NO CONCERNS OR WORRIES. JUST LAUGHING AND DRINKING WITH FRIENDS.
WHAT A FUN!
HOW GREAT LIFE IS!
MY JOB WENT WELL, TOO.
WWHAAT!? IT SAYS, "WOULD YOU MIND GOING TO KENYA AND BEIJING ON A TV PRO-JECT"!!?
YOU MUST GO!
I'LL TAKE CARE OF THE HOUSE.
MY GOD!
SO I WENT TO KENYA IN OCTO-BER.
THERE I MET A JAPANESE WOMAN WHO WAS PROTECTING THE ELEPHANTS FROM ILLEGAL HUNTERS.
THEN I WENT TO BEIJ-ING IN JANUARY.
MET A JAPANESE WOMAN WHO SPOKE PERFECT CHINESE AND WORKED AS AN ACTRESS.

THESE SIX MONTHS I WAS...

...FAR TOO BUSY TO EVEN THINK ABOUT MY MOTHER.

LIFE JUST KEPT MOVING FORWARD.

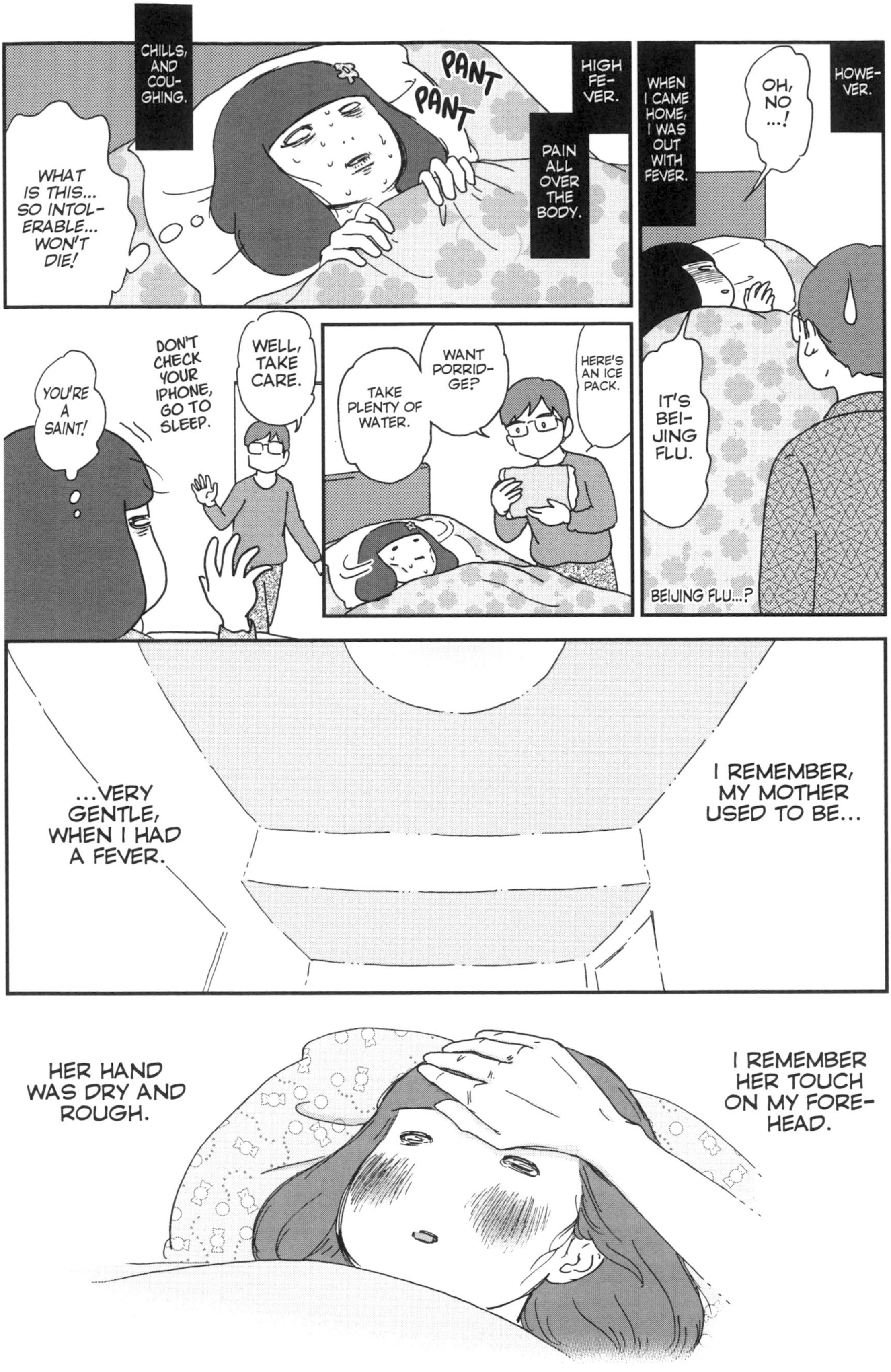

HOWEVER.
OH, NO ...!
WHEN I CAME HOME, I WAS OUT WITH FEVER.
IT'S BEIJING FLU.
BEIJING FLU...?
HIGH FEVER.
PANT PANT
PAIN ALL OVER THE BODY.
CHILLS, AND COUGHING.
WHAT IS THIS... SO INTOLERABLE... WON'T DIE!
HERE'S AN ICE PACK.
WANT PORRIDGE?
TAKE PLENTY OF WATER.
WELL, TAKE CARE.
DON'T CHECK YOUR IPHONE, GO TO SLEEP.
YOU'RE A SAINT!
I REMEMBER, MY MOTHER USED TO BE...
...VERY GENTLE, WHEN I HAD A FEVER.
I REMEMBER HER TOUCH ON MY FOREHEAD.
HER HAND WAS DRY AND ROUGH.

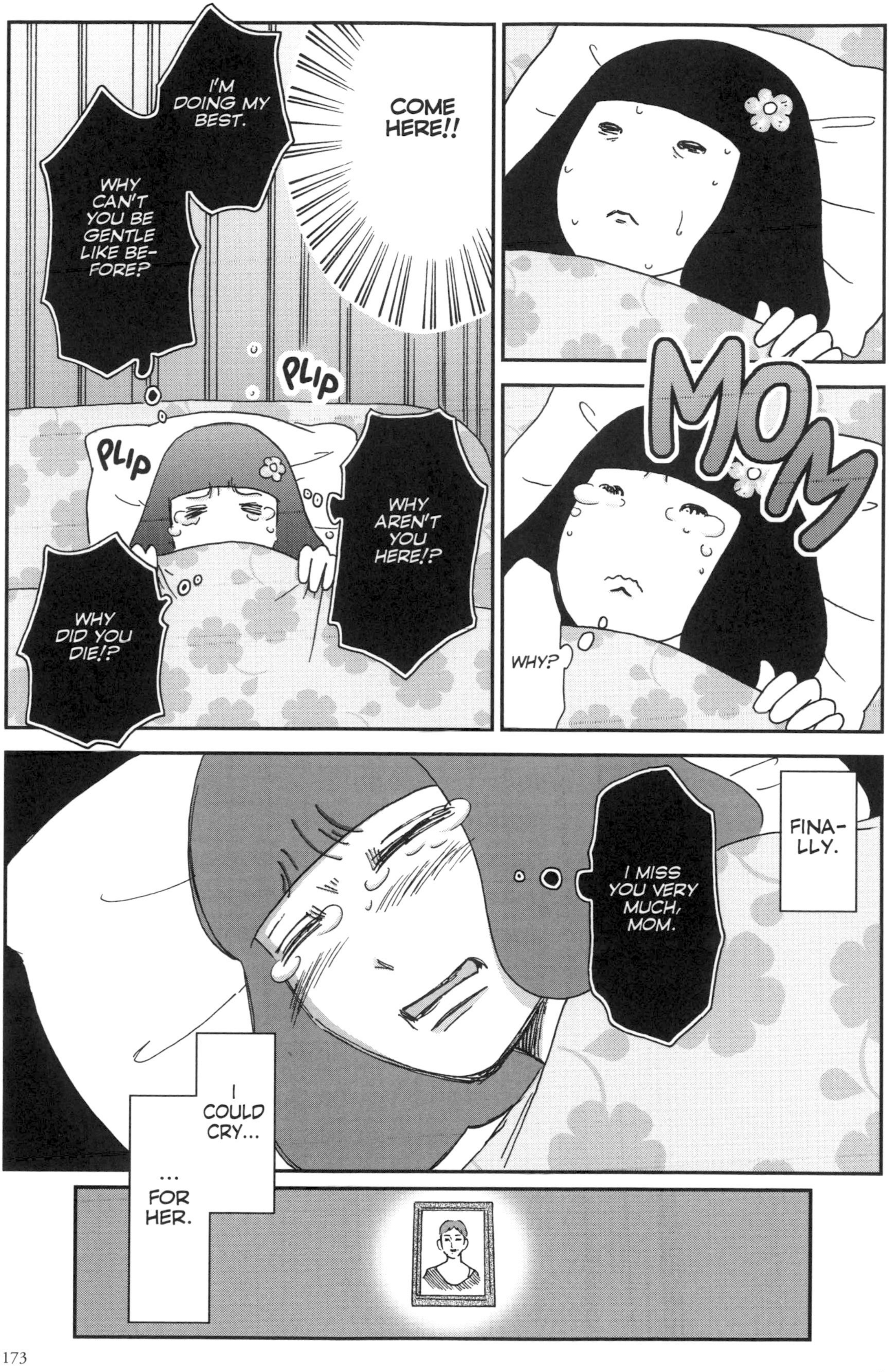
MOM
WHY?
COME HERE!!
I'M DOING MY BEST.
WHY CAN'T YOU BE GENTLE LIKE BE-FORE?
PLIP
PLIP
WHY AREN'T YOU HERE!?
WHY DID YOU DIE!?
FINA-LLY.
I MISS YOU VERY MUCH, MOM.
I COULD CRY...
... FOR HER.

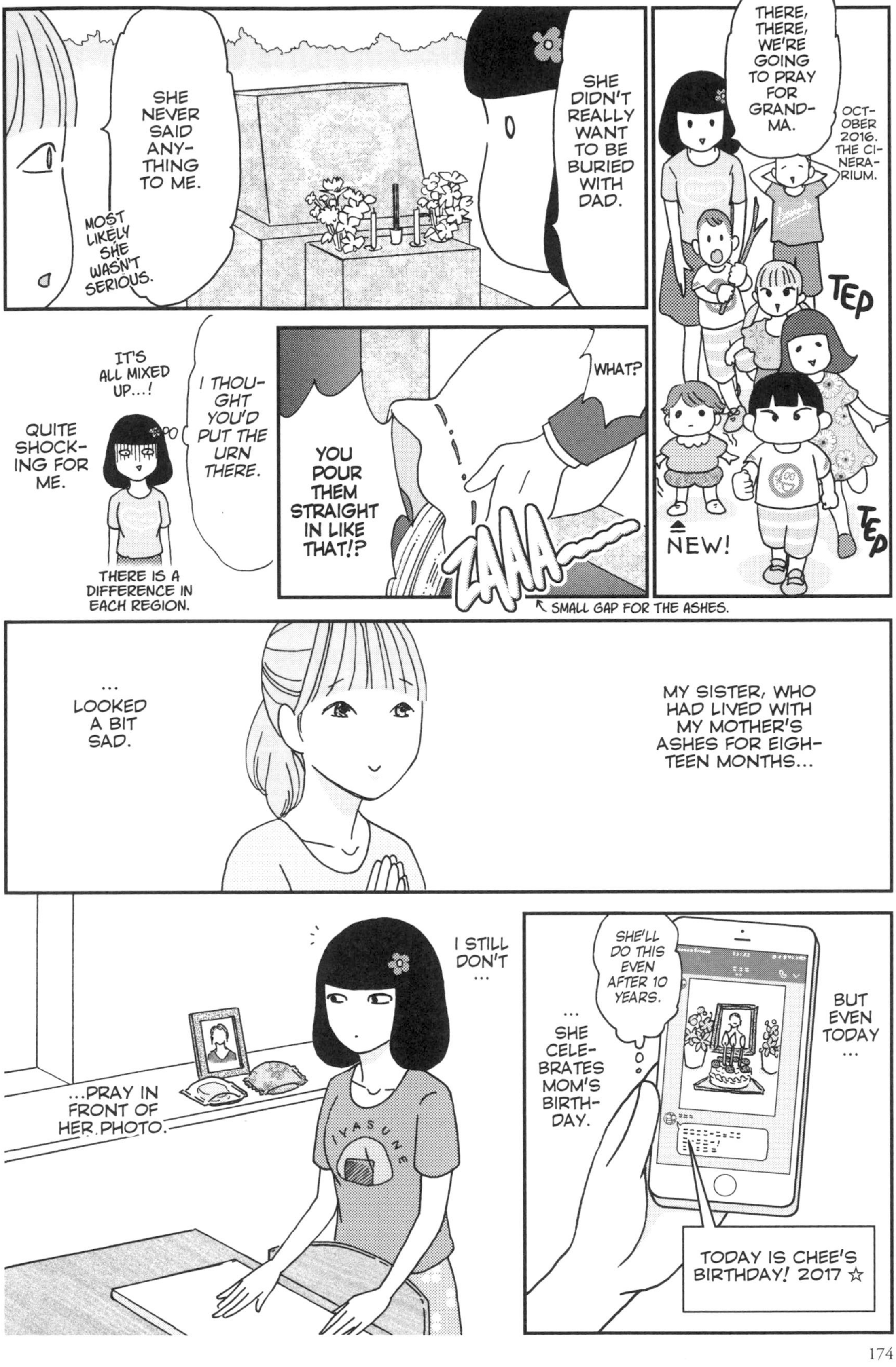
THERE, THERE, WE'RE GOING TO PRAY FOR GRAND-MA.
OCT-OBER 2016. THE CI-NERA-RIUM.
TEP
NEW!
TEP
SHE DIDN'T REALLY WANT TO BE BURIED WITH DAD.
SHE NEVER SAID ANY-THING TO ME.
MOST LIKELY SHE WASN'T SERIOUS.
WHAT?
YOU POUR THEM STRAIGHT IN LIKE THAT!?
ZAAA
SMALL GAP FOR THE ASHES.
I THOU-GHT YOU'D PUT THE URN THERE.
IT'S ALL MIXED UP...!
QUITE SHOCK-ING FOR ME.
THERE IS A DIFFERENCE IN EACH REGION.
MY SISTER, WHO HAD LIVED WITH MY MOTHER'S ASHES FOR EIGH-TEEN MONTHS...
... LOOKED A BIT SAD.
BUT EVEN TODAY ...
SHE'LL DO THIS EVEN AFTER 10 YEARS.
... SHE CELE-BRATES MOM'S BIRTH-DAY.
TODAY IS CHEE'S BIRTHDAY! 2017 ☆
I STILL DON'T ...
...PRAY IN FRONT OF HER PHOTO.

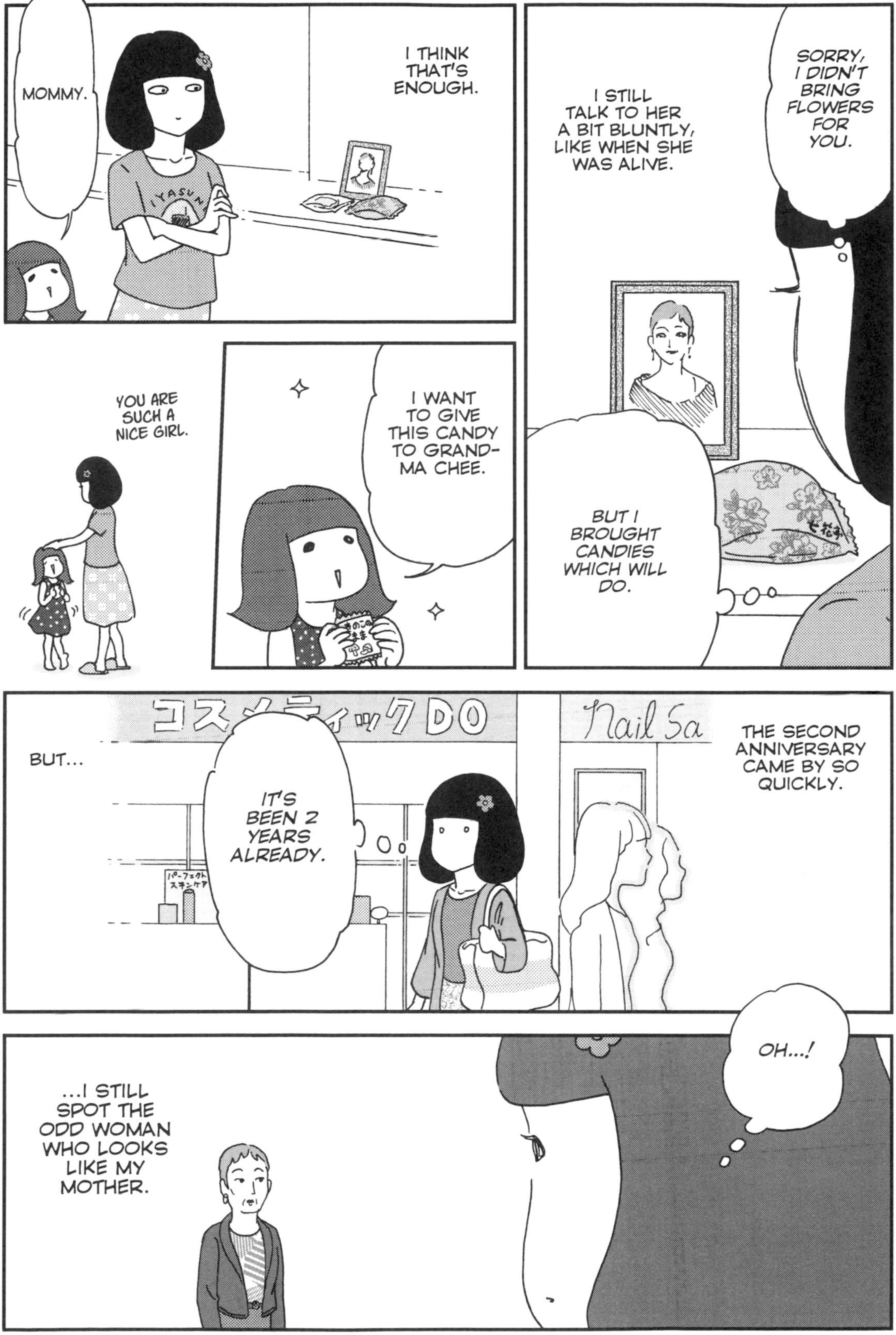
SORRY, I DIDN'T BRING FLOWERS FOR YOU.
I STILL TALK TO HER A BIT BLUNTLY, LIKE WHEN SHE WAS ALIVE.
BUT I BROUGHT CANDIES WHICH WILL DO.
I THINK THAT'S ENOUGH.
MOMMY.
I WANT TO GIVE THIS CANDY TO GRAND-MA CHEE.
YOU ARE SUCH A NICE GIRL.
THE SECOND ANNIVERSARY CAME BY SO QUICKLY.
Nail Sa
コスメティックDO
IT'S BEEN 2 YEARS ALREADY.
BUT...
OH...!
...I STILL SPOT THE ODD WOMAN WHO LOOKS LIKE MY MOTHER.

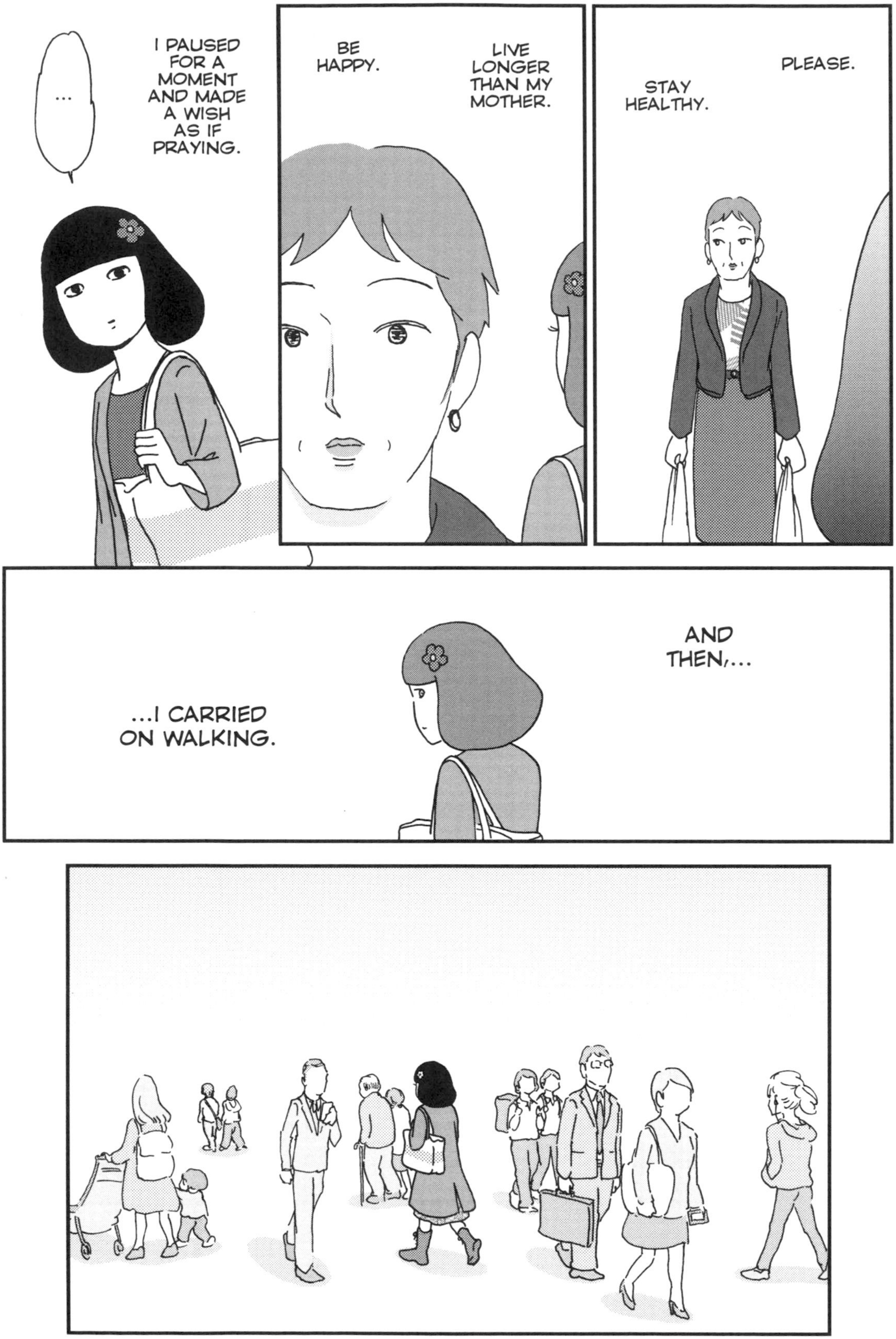
PLEASE.
STAY HEALTHY.
LIVE LONGER THAN MY MOTHER.
BE HAPPY.
I PAUSED FOR A MOMENT AND MADE A WISH AS IF PRAYING.
...
AND THEN,...
...I CARRIED ON WALKING.

EPILOG

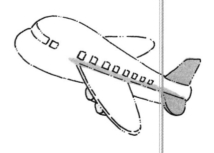

THANK YOU FOR READING MY BOOK RIGHT TO THE END.

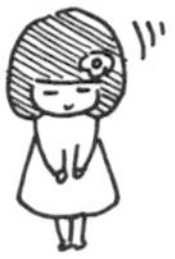

I RECEIVED LOTS OF COMMENTS AND ENCOURAGEMENTS FROM READERS WHILE THE COMIC WAS STILL SERIALIZED IN A MAGAZINE. THANKS TO EVERYONE, IT HELPED ME FINISH THE SERIES AND MEANT IT CAN NOW BE PUBLISHED AS A BOOK.

THE FACT THAT MY MOTHER NO LONGER EXISTS IN THIS WORLD STILL SEEMS UNREAL TO ME, EVEN NOW.

BUT NEXT TIME I VISIT HER GRAVE, I CAN TELL HER THAT "MY COMIC ABOUT YOUR CHALLENGE HAS BEEN PUBLISHED AS A BOOK!!

I CAN SAY NEITHER OF MY PARENTS WERE "ORDINARY" PARENTS.

BUT THEY WERE VERY SYMPATHETIC AND ATTRACTIVE PEOPLE.

NOW I MISS THEM A LOT. AND AS TIME GOES BY, MY FEELING OF THANKS GROWS EVER BIGGER AND BIGGER.

I ALSO WOULD LIKE TO SAY "THANK YOU" AGAIN TO THOSE WHO WERE INVOLVED IN COMPLETING THIS WORK, AND ALSO TO ALL OF YOU WHO ARE READING THIS BOOK RIGHT NOW.

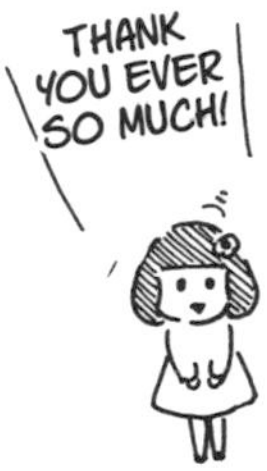
THANK YOU EVER SO MUCH!

HOPE TO SEE YOU AGAIN (^^)

YUKARI TAKINAMI

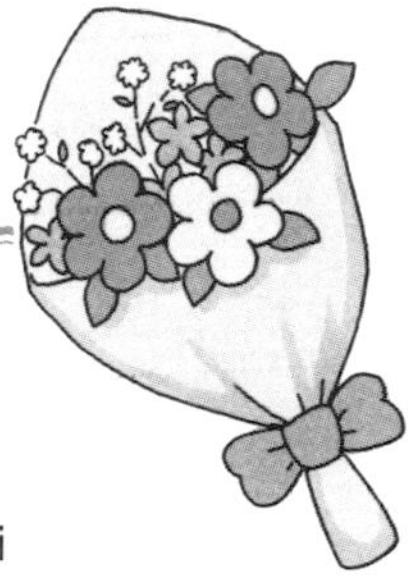

Original Japanese edition published by Bungeishunju Ltd., in 2018.
English translation rights arranged with Bungeishunju Ltd.,
through Bureau des Copyrights Français, Tokyo.

www.ponentmon.com

Translated by Yukari Takeuchi
Edited by Stephen Albert
Layout by RG e HIJAS S.C.P.
ISBN: 978-1-912097-42-5
A CIP catalogue record for this book is available from the British Library.

Printed and bound in the European Union by Spauda, LT